Counseling
and Learning through
Small-Group
Discussion

by HELEN I. DRIVER, Ph.D.
Consultant in Mental Hygiene
and
THIRTY-SEVEN CONTRIBUTORS

Section I

MULTIPLE COUNSELING

A Small-Group Discussion Method for
Personal Growth — The original, una-
bridged volume by Dr. Helen I. Driver.

Section II — **SYMPOSIUM**

Small-Group Discussion as an Aid in
Counseling, Training, and Treatment —
Thirty-nine articles by professional leaders in the fields of education, religion,
psychiatry and psychology, family life
and mental health.

TEXTBOOK EDITION, 1962

Copyright, 1958, by HELEN IRENE DRIVER
Monona Publications, P. O. Box 3222, Madison 4, Wis.

LIBRARY OF CONGRESS CATALOG NUMBER 58-8694

SECTION I – MULTIPLE COUNSELING

TABLE OF CONTENTS

SECTION II — SYMPOSIUM

TABLE OF CONTENTS

PART ONE

School Children and Youth: Group Projects for
Personal and Social Adjustment

TABLE OF CONTENTS

PART TWO

COLLEGE PROGRAMS: ORIENTATION, COURSES, AND LEADERSHIP TRAINING

PART THREE

PROFESSIONAL TRAINING AND RESEARCH PROGRAMS:
SMALL-GROUP DISCUSSION AS A LEARNING MEDIUM

PART THREE, *cont'd*

TABLE OF CONTENTS

PART FOUR

COMMUNITY MENTAL HEALTH AND PARENT EDUCATION PROGRAMS:
SMALL-GROUP DISCUSSION FOR EDUCATION, COUNSELING AND TRAINING

PART FOUR, *cont'd*

TABLE OF CONTENTS

PART FIVE

GROUP PSYCHOTHERAPY, REHABILITATION, AND COUNSELING PROGRAMS:
THE VALUE OF THE INTIMATE GROUP

— *Courtesy of Dr. Camilla Low and The Wisconsin Cooperative Education Planning Program, State of Wisconsin.*

MULTIPLE COUNSELING...
A SMALL-GROUP DISCUSSION METHOD
FOR PERSONAL GROWTH

by

HELEN IRENE DRIVER, Ph.D.

Consultant in Mental Hygiene and Group Therapy

FOREWORD

by

ANNETTE C. WASHBURNE, M.D.

CONSULTING PSYCHIATRIST

formerly

Director of Psychiatric Services, Department of Student Health
University of Wisconsin

FOREWORD

The author has requested me to write a foreword to this book. I am pleased to do so, although my own experience with group therapy has been a limited one.

However, the benefits of such an approach to various human problems, has been well demonstrated by the author. From 1951 to 1953, the Neuropsychiatric Section of the Department of Student Health at the University of Wisconsin, of which I was at that time the Director, referred twenty-four cases to Dr. Driver for group therapy. In all instances this was carried on in conjunction with individual psychotherapeutic sessions by one of our staff. The results were sufficiently encouraging as to suggest that, not only as a method in itself, but also in combination with private conferences, the period of rehabilitation and recovery may be shortened.

Annette C. Washburne, M.D.
(Formerly Professor of Neuropsychiatry and
Preventive Medicine, University of Wisconsin)

Author —

Helen Irene Driver, Ph. D.

Dr. Driver has a varied background including teaching, social work, recreation administration, and counseling. Prior to World War II she was Director of the Department of Student Health and Physical Education for Women at the University of Buffalo. During the war she served overseas with the American National Red Cross as Program and Club Director in Red Cross Clubs, and then became Civilian War Relief Representative in the work of caring for displaced persons in France and Germany. It was through her Red Cross experience that she first became interested in small-group discussion, which was used in England for social, therapeutic, and rehabilitative purposes.

After the war Dr. Driver obtained her Ph.D. degree in Educational Psychology at the University of Wisconsin in the field of Guidance and Counseling. Her research in small-group discussion as a learning medium was supervised by Professor Clarence E. Ragsdale. Later post-doctoral research in the field of group therapy was sponsored by Dr. Washburne and members of the staff of the Psychiatric Section, Student Health Department, University of Wisconsin.

Other books written by Dr. Driver while active in the field of Physical Education are TENNIS FOR TEACHERS and TENNIS SELF-INSTRUCTOR.

Foreword by —

Annette C. Washburne, M. D.

Dr. Washburne is a consulting psychiatrist and a diplomate of the American Board of Psychiatry and Neurology. From 1937 to 1954 she served as Director of the Neuropsychiatric Section, Department of Student Health at the University of Wisconsin. She was Professor of Neuropsychiatry and Preventive Medicine. During these sixteen years, with an average staff membership of four psychiatrists including Dr. Washburne, treatment was given to over 11,000 patients with a total of over 51,000 psychiatric interviews. In addition to this devotion to her own field, Dr. Washburne always found time to give generously of her interest to related fields concerned with preventive Mental Hygiene. The testing and validating of the multiple-counseling method in the therapy of emotionally disturbed persons was made possible only through the coöperation of Dr. Washburne and her staff.

ACKNOWLEDGMENTS

MANY PERSONS HAVE CONTRIBUTED to the development of the multiple counseling method presented in this book: the one hundred and twenty-one participants in group projects; the counselors and psychiatrists who worked closely with me in the projects; the colleagues and friends whose frankness in evaluating the evolving method aided its sound, practical character. To all these persons, hearty thanks and earnest appreciation are expressed.

I make grateful acknowledgement to the officials through whose coöperation many of the group projects were organized: Miss Margaret Fosse, Guidance Director; Professor Clarence E. Ragsdale, head of the Educational Psychology division of the School of Education, University of Wisconsin; Dr. Annette C. Washburne, former Director of Psychiatric Services, University of Wisconsin; Dr. Edward C. Burns, Director of Clinical Services, State Hospital.

For their suggestions and guidance as experts in learning techniques, human relations, and counseling, recognition and deepest thanks are expressed to Professor Ragsdale, Dr. Washburne, Dr. Edna Fitch, Dr. Thelma Hruza, Dr. Edward Hodgeson, and Dr. William Heywood.

I am indebted to the following for their patient reading and constructive criticism of the manuscript-in-process: Dr. Olive P. Lester, Head, Department of Psychology, University of Buffalo; Dr. Eloise Cason, Director of the Child Study and Guidance Department of the Bloomfield, N. J. public schools; Mr. Glyndon J. Webb, psychiatric social worker at the Mendota State Hospital; Miss Mildred Stickney, former assistant principal, State School for Boys, Waukasha, Wisconsin.

To my friend and fellow author, Mrs. Edna Thomas, goes my deepest gratitude for bringing order out of chaos in the Preface and Conclusion. My only regret is that she did not have time to untangle dangling prepositions and split infinitives throughout the book.

This book is a witness to the value of warm human relationships and coöperative enterprise. Without them it could never have been written.

PREFACE

THE MULTIPLE COUNSELING METHOD presented in this book is not a mass production method: it has positive value of its own as a counseling technique. The advantages accruing from group dynamics, interpersonal relationships, and role-playing are, in the opinion of the writer, too great to omit from a counseling process. Not only does the intimate group membership help a client through support, reassurance and frank discussions, but also he helps others, since mutual aid is characteristic of the group activity. Therefore the term "multiple counseling" implies a sharing of the counseling function among the group members as well as the leader's counseling of individuals within the group.

The successful use of this method with one hundred and twenty-one participants in fifteen group projects has convinced the author of the practical value of the procedures for various types of client-groups. Age levels included teen-agers, college students and adults; mental health status of participants included well-adjusted, neurotic, and psychotic. This book is designed, therefore, to assist the organization and leadership of discussion group projects focussed on human relations and personal growth in preventive mental hygiene programs as well as therapeutic programs.

Teachers who have guidance duties in their schools may use the book as a counseling textbook: group guidance projects which follow the techniques described herein will keep within the framework of true counseling. Students in training courses for psychiatric social work, guidance, clinical and educational psychology, will, it is hoped, find new meaning in subject matter courses through the application of group dynamics for counseling purposes. Internees in these fields should find the information, procedures, and case studies helpful in their practical work. Psychologists and psychiatrists who believe that human relationships can be used in the counseling process may use this book as a guide in initiating and directing group therapy projects.

The author hopes the book will be of service to all readers who are preparing for, or active in, guidance and counseling fields. The procedures and materials have been carefully outlined and recommended for various types of groups. They are adaptable for schools, institutions, and out-patient departments. The wide variety of illustrative materials give a selection for either educational or therapeutic programs. Although this multiple counseling method was not designed for group psychotherapy, it may be so used by de-emphasizing the "educational" and "encouragement" aspects in favor of forcing self-revelations and other psychotherapy and psychodramatic procedures. Such use of the method is reserved for qualified psychologists who are providing individualized treatment concommitant with the group meetings.

"Since learning is something that the pupil has to do himself and for himself, the initiative lies within the learner. The teacher is the guide and director; he steers the boat, but the energy that propels it must come from those who are learning."

— JOHN DEWEY, "How We Think."

PART I

ORGANIZATION AND PROCEDURES IN
PERSONAL GROWTH PROJECTS
USING GROUP DISCUSSION

I

THE NATURE OF MULTIPLE COUNSELING

THE MULTIPLE COUNSELING METHOD described in this book uses a small-group discussion activity as the learning medium for personal growth of participants, cojunctive with individual counseling by the group leader. When psychiatric patients are members of a group, the attendant psychiatrist may continue his psychotherapeutic treatment of the patients while the group leader counsels them only in matters pertinent to their group activity.

A group project can be called "multiple counseling" only if individual counseling accompanies the group activity. A face-to-face relationship between counselor and client in private interviews is implicit in the term "counseling." A leader-participant relationship in group meetings is insufficient to meet the requirements of "counseling." Even though the individual counseling is limited to two interviews during a group project which extends over a three-month period, nevertheless the private conferences form a significant part of the learning process in multiple counseling. This aspect is usually not included in explanations of the term (11-pp 221, 222).

Learning is focussed on healthy growth in capacity for personal and social adjustments. The group gives an opportunity for improvement of attitudes and skills in human relationships. Individual counseling provides help in self-assessment of personal strengths and weaknesses, and in specific problem areas which the participant may not wish to present in group sessions. Prerequisite to the aim of skill in personal and social adjustments are the goals of self-understanding and acceptance, understanding and acceptance of others, practice in communication and interpersonal skills.

Learning takes place in four ways: (1) through the discussion content and group activities (2) through the personal relationships of group members (3) through the interactions of group members with the leader during group sessions (4) through the counseling process in private interviews with the leader.

The term "personal growth" is used rather than "adjustment"

or "growth toward maturity," because it is all-inclusive. Thus the well-adjusted adult may strive to add to his personal growth: his aim may be associated with mental growth, spiritual values, or efficiency in his role as husband, father, citizen. An individual who *wants* to continue his personal growth can do so until death.

In the case of a maladjusted individual, however, the aim of a multiple counseling project may be to rid himself of unhealthy attitudes and habits which hinder personal growth, and to improve his adjustive skills. For him, reconditioning is the first step, after which personal growth can start.

The adolescent or young adult in our society resolves his confusion and conflicts regarding values, parent-child relationships, and life-goals in a multiple counseling project. He needs to identify with new models, especially during the time when he has rejected his parents and his religion in his struggle for independence and adult status. He is torn with conflict between love and rebellious hostility toward his family, beset with guilt feelings, and a sense of inadequacy. Seeking counseling aid, he will find in a multiple counseling activity a group of comrades in confusion. Together they can move forward in their personal growth.

Neurotic and psychotic patients likewise find support and reassurance in an intimate group where they are accepted as worthy human beings and can talk freely of their problems. The common characteristic of mentally ill persons is a regression — a childishness — which makes them especially appreciative of a family-like group with an adult leader whom they may consider a parent substitute.

The author has used the multiple counseling method in fifteen group projects which included one hundred and twenty-one participants. The wide range of age and personal growth levels included teen-agers, college students, and adults; normal, neurotic, and psychotic persons.

The characteristics of the method, described and illustrated in detail throughout the book, are outlined as follows:

1. The chief activity is small-group discussion related to personal and social adjustments, human behavior, and personal relationships.

2. Auxiliary activities for group members consist of any of the following:

20

     a. Role-playing

     b. Personality and occupational inventories

     c. Self-appraisals and sociograms

3. Individual counseling by the leader consists of at least two full length counseling interviews and additional short chats with individual participants seeking such contacts with the leader.

4. Learning of certain facts and principles, expected of all participants, includes:

     a. Individual differences pertaining to personality, sexes, inherited and cultural influences.

     b. Adjustive techniques and defense mechanisms commonly used in personal and social adjustments.

     c. Assessment of personal strengths, weaknesses, values, goals.

     d. Basic drives and emotions as influences on human behavior.

     e. Group identifications, beliefs, loyalties, prejudices.

5. Group projects are limited as to number of participants and number of sessions. All participants are expected to take full responsibility for attendance and participation in all aspects of the project.

6. Groups are organized for (1) a common personal interest and need among group members which motivated them to join the project (2) equal numbers of male and female members (3) heterogeneity in personality type, racial and cultural background.

7. The group leader uses eclectic counseling techniques in the group sessions and private interviews according to the needs of the group and clients. In general, two-thirds of the sessions in a project are structured as leaderless discussions and one-third as seminar-type meetings when the group has voted a preference for frank discussions of their personal problems. On the other hand, groups who prefer to keep the discussions on an impersonal level are given a preponderance of seminar-type meetings.

8. An intimate group climate, characterized by permissiveness and friendliness, is established and maintained by the group leader. Participants are urged to act and say what they feel — whether angry and irritated, or gay and loquacious. Frankness and camaraderie are essential qualities of a project.

This method does not follow psychoanalytic principles and techniques. It does, however, accept the everyday usage of psychoanalytic ideas and terms which have become a part of our culture, according to Margaret Mead (ref 16). Social psychology and psychiatry, rather than psychoanalytic psychology, gives the basic principles for the multiple counseling method. The assumption is followed that human relationships can be used as a learning instrument. Thus the sociological definition of personality is used: the social stimulus value of the person. Everyone needs the approbation of his fellow man to maintain self-respect. Personal growth means growth away from egocentricity toward altruism and a desire to contribute to society: the intimate group in a multiple counseling project provides opportunities for belonging and for sharing. In this way human relationships are put to work in the counseling process.

Experts in the National Association for Mental Health show the value they place upon a human relations approach to personal growth and adjustment in their description of "persons with good mental health." Their list of twenty-four characteristics of such persons is a list of objectives for participants in a multiple counseling project:

1. *They feel comfortable about themselves*
   a. They are not bowled over by their own emotions — by their fears, anger, love, jealousy, guilt or worries.
   b. They can take life's disappointments in their stride.
   c. They have a tolerant, easy-going attitude toward themselves as well as others; they can laugh at themselves.
   d. They neither under-estimate nor over-estimate their abilities.
   e. They can accept their own shortcomings.
   f. They have self-respect.
   g. They feel able to deal with most situations that come their way.
   h. They get satisfaction from the simple, every-day pleasures.

2. *They feel right about other people*
   a. They are able to give love and to consider the interests of others.
   b. They have personal relationships that are satisfying and lasting.
   c. They expect to like and trust others, and take it for granted that others will like and trust them.

d. They respect the many differences they find in people.

e. They do not push people around, nor do they allow themselves to be pushed around.

f. They can feel they are part of a group.

g. They feel a sense of responsibility to their neighbor and fellow-men.

3. *They are able to meet the demands of life*

   a. They do something about their problems as they arise.

   b. They accept their responsibilities.

   c. They shape their environment whenever possible; they adjust to it whenever necessary.

   d. They plan ahead but do not fear the future.

   e. They welcome new experiences and new ideas.

   f. They make use of their natural capacities.

   g. They set realistic goals for themselves.

   h. They are able to think for themselves and make their own decisions.

   i. They put their best effort into what they do, and get satisfaction out of doing it.* (21)

The characteristics of mentally healthy persons listed above describe the mature person as discussed in books by Overstreet (23), Hartwell (9), May (15) and Peale (24). Personal growth toward the twenty-four objectives is not limited to any age or maturity level. Sometimes an individual believes he meets the requirements and then circumstances or illness throw him into emotional inbalance. Thus personality is dynamic — it is a process wherein constant re-adjustments must be made to maintain personal, emotional, and social equilibrium.

Although interpersonal relationships rather than inner conflicts are emphasized in this method, the latter are dealt with, both in group sessions and counseling interviews. Stress is placed on the inner conflict which is characteristic of personal growth — two urges pulling

---

* Material from the pamphlet, "Mental Health is . . . 1, 2, 3," is given through the courtesy of The National Association for Mental Health, 1790 Broadway, New York 19, N. Y. Single copies of the pamphlet are available without cost from their headquarters.

the individual in different directions — the desire to remain self-centered and to gratify selfish aims and conflicts with the desire to gain social acceptance through sharing and belonging. Sometimes one of these inner forces is in control; sometimes the other. In either case feelings of frustration, hostility, guilt, and anxiety can result. The solution does not come by forcing the person into a pretense of altruistic attitudes and actions when his true self is rebellious and resentful of social pressures. Rather, the counseling helps the self-centered person to *want* to change. An important part of a multiple counseling project is the griping, blowing off steam, and verbal dueling in the group. Self-revelations — however shocking they may be — are accepted without detriment to the acceptance of the person in the group. Each group member is considered a worthy person in spite of his misdeeds, expressions of animosity, irritation, and hostility during the project. The group leader encourages frankness, both in personal reactions among group members, and in telling of one's feelings toward parents, teachers, rivals, and friends.

This method is not intended as a psychotherapy activity for seriously ill mental patients, but it has been used successfully as "encouragement" and "supportive" therapy for neurotic and psychotic patients. The group dynamics and social interactions which thrive in the friendly group climate seem to help to dissolve inner conflicts based on egocentricity in favor of motivation toward altruistic behavior. A person who is willing to accept active membership in a group project is in a state of readiness for learning: his drive for social acceptance and participation is reinforced and encouraged by the group experience. He may make his first close friendship in the group; he may give help to a group member who is worse off than he. Through sharing his problem with others as they share theirs with him he gains support and reassurance that he is a worthy person.

The group members in a multiple counseling project have a potential for helping each other which the professional counselor does not possess: they are peers and — above all else, perhaps — a human being seeks the approbation of his peers during the "growing up" process. To what avail if mother and father tell John he is a fine fellow, they love him, and they are sure he will be a success in life — if his classmates at school have rejected him and he is an isolate?

Another advantage of a multiple counseling method is the oppor-

24

tunity to observe client behavior which facilitates counseling. The group leader can learn much about his clients in group sessions because their behavior is often significantly different from interview behavior. Whether a participant sits back, aloof from the group, or if he over-acts the part of a social lion — discussion of his behavior in private interviews may prove the wedge to ventilation and insight. In the experience of the author, discussions of why the client acted and felt the way he did in the group uncovered ego defenses and inner conflicts in a natural, unforced process which helped the client understand and accept himself. Even in cases where no real insight developed, the client could learn to reduce inner tensions, to gain self-confidence, and to improve his social skills.

Philosophical Considerations

All human beings at some time or other need to ventilate feelings of guilt, frustration, resentment and confusion; they need to build a personal philosophy of life based on a desire to grow from childishness to maturity, from selfishness to altruism. Suppose we apply the simile of the three bricklayers who are working on the construction of a cathedral. The first, like a college student who "attends classes," simply "lays bricks" without any recognition of the utility or significance of his action. The second, like a college student who may be "preparing for a vocation," knows that he is "earning a living," but his thoughts do not extend beyond his own profit and his own self. But the third, like a college student who is aware that he will be a part of, and a contributor to, society, realizes that he is helping to erect a temple for the glory of God.

Although this group method is in no sense an "inspirational" activity such as used in Alcoholic Anonymous (33), it does provide opportunities for developing an appreciation for the worthiness of the individual and for action based on Christian and other religious principles. Dr. Karl Menninger, outstanding psychiatrist, writes, "The problem of our times is to increase Love and to diminish Hate." (17) This statement sums up an age-old societal problem which is given a prominent place in a multiple counseling project. Through discussions on emotions, personal philosophies and values, well-balanced living, effective personal and social adjustments, significant teachings can be presented. A tap root of THIS I BELIEVE may be germinated because persons who elect a multiple counseling project are needful and eager for such growth.

Therefore, the human capacity for emotional expansion — for loving (in the broad sense), for sharing, for empathy and sympathy — is put to work in the group activity. It makes little difference whether a participant prides himself on being an atheist, humanist, Methodist, or Jew. In an intimate group Agape (2) manifestations have fertile soil in which to grow. The group — a miniature society — has coöperation and good will as a basis rather than competition and rivalry. It is a laboratory for experiencing the satisfactions that come from sharing with, and helping, others.

Psychiatrists and men of science, too, find the answer to mental health in Agape principles and practices. Dr. James Fisher, retired psychiatrist, ends his autobiography, "A Few Buttons Missing" with The Sermon on the Mount (6). Dr. Ian Stevenson, consulting psychiatrist, writes in *Harpers Magazine*,

"My own conception of a constructive change in personality therefore includes not only the value of increased comfort and pleasure to the individual person, but an increased contribution of that person to others. These two features are not incompatible and, I believe, they actually reinforce each other . . . all human societies which have been studied thus far by anthropologists, with one or two possible exceptions, have developed ethical ideals of service to others and self-sacrifice for the common good which are basically similar. This suggests some innate quality of humans, some planet-wide need of the species to feel love for others, to cherish and grow toward the ideal of helping others. . . . May we not conclude that man is equipped with the tendency toward altruistic behavior and the machinery whereby he may practice it." (30)

George Russell Harrison, distinguished scientist, spoke of "Faith and the Scientist" in a Stearns Lecture. After describing the wonders of scientific progress, he analyzed the attribute which separated men from animals, saying,

"Two thousand years is only a flick of time in which to look for changes in man's intellect, but it is not too short a time to look for changes in his spirit. Take so fundamental a quality as empathy, the ability to put oneself in the other fellow's place. A century ago, even in America, one of the fundamental freedoms was the right to starve to death; a beggar could lie dying in the gutter and people would walk by unconcerned. Today, at least in lands where the standard of living has been raised by science to the point where the scramble to keep alive does not take up most of everyone's effort, empathy has developed to the point that no one is refused food or hospital-

26

ization. Over the ages, man's stimuli change, and gradually these change his thought processes and emotions, and through them his spiritual vigor." (8)

The idealistic purpose of the multiple counseling method is expressed in the simple terms of counseling: to gain better understanding and acceptance of oneself and others; to improve one's skills in human relationships. The warmth and friendliness of an intimate group is the catalyst for putting into action the positive attitudes which are developed. Thus Carla found a job for Eddie and Norbert helped him with his Chemistry (group 5). Hulda accepted a date with Mike (group 8) and Barbara invited Eloise to a concert (group 9). These events do not sound out-of-the-ordinary, but they were very significant actions in the lives of these clients. When persons become emersed in private worlds of depression, self-pity, and anxiety, kindly actions through which they forget themselves are important influences for personal growth. When such experiences include empathy and are heart-warming both to the giver and the recipient, they are potent attitude-changers: the tangle of human conflicts and frustrations start unraveling. This conclusion comes from participants in the group projects. It is the basis and inspiration of this book.

Description of this Multiple Counseling Method

The group structure and discussion content depends upon the needs of the group and the type of leadership. The project may be a human relations or personal development course; it may be group or vocational guidance; it may be group therapy or psychotherapy. The extent and depth of the individual counseling given to group members depends upon the qualification of the leader. Thus a guidance worker or personnel counselor cannot activate a group psychotherapy project, but they can direct group projects concerned with personal growth, human relations, or vocational guidance. In such projects the counseling is limited to vocational, academic, and social areas: leaders who are not qualified psychologists must not try to handle psychological counseling assignments.

When this method is used by psychologists and psychiatrists for group psychotherapy, it differs from psychoanalytic group therapy in several respects. First, group members are not forced into self-revelation. Second, discussion topics cover a wide range of personal and social problems introduced by the leader. Third, enjoyment of the sessions as social gatherings is considered an important factor in learning. Fourth, the group leader does not limit himself to nondirective leadership techniques.

A psychiatrist may immediately question the value of such a method for group psychotherapy. He thinks of this activity as focussing on self-revelation and probing psychic wounds in order to dig out the infection or foreign body which is the cause of the patient's maladjustment. In the description of the multiple counseling method he sees that the group activity and learning may not touch the deep cause of the trouble. However, the results of this method for twenty-seven neurotic and psychotic patients included in group projects reported in the appendix of this book shows that the attendant psychiatrists believed the group activity was influential in the successful treatment of their patients. And the projects were economical: none of them extended over four months and the average number of sessions in a project was sixteen. These encouraging results are by no means unique; many psychiatrists and institutions have turned to short-term, group-centered therapy focussed on social rehabilitation rather than psychic probing (1, 13, 14, 19, 22).

Even though this method is not designed for deep psychotherapy, the chief activity is centered in personal development and adjustment problems so that some participants may gain psychotherapeutic benefits from it. And those participants who cannot bring themselves to discuss painful personal problems in group meetings may do so in private interviews with the group leader. Such clients may receive support and reassurance from group members and the group experience in spite of the lack of self-revelation. Such was the case of the young man in an adult group who had just lost his wife after an agonizing malignancy. None of his fellow participants knew that he was in the throes of shocking grief. He had confided in the group leader during the preliminary interview and his adjustment to this personal matter was important in the counseling process. Likewise psychiatric patients with unsocial compulsions and obsessions are not expected to reveal them to the group. In other words, for some group members, a group project may provide encouragement, educational, or social rehabilitative therapy; for others who are able to discuss their personal problems in the group with complete frankness, it may be psychotherapeutic.

28

At the present time, research findings in the use of analytic psychotherapy for groups show such a lack of economy in terms of time and effort for the results obtained (10, 25) that the group therapy movement in our country appears to be in an impasse. Although more and more psychiatrists believe deep psychotherapy is neither practical nor wise for many of their patients, they have not accepted short-term, educational group therapy methods. In Great Britain, however, great strides have been made in the use of methods based on group dynamics and human relationships. Dr. Maxwell Jones and his associates report on the progress of the social psychiatry movement in THE THERAPEUTIC COMMUNITY (13). Initiated as group therapy in military hospitals during World War II it was found that one psychiatrist could handle twenty cases instead of four in psychoanalytic treatment. But after nine years of experimentation with a group process this group of psychiatrists came to the conclusion that psychoanalytic treatment, either individual or group, was not the answer to the social rehabilitation of neurotic and psychotic patients. Rather, group discussions and social interactions in the hospital were found to be more efficacious. The amazing results of four months treatment of over 100 "unemployables" at the Belmont Hospital were reported as follows:

"Our findings appear to justify the conclusion that it is possible to change social attitudes in relatively desocialized patients with severe character disorders, provided they are treated together in a therapeutic community. Our results show that six months after leaving hospital two-thirds of the patients followed up had made a fair adjustment or better, and one-third were rated poor or very poor adjustments; just over one-half had worked the full time since leaving hospital. We believe (but cannot prove) that the results described could not have been achieved by individual psychotherapy and hospitalization alone." (13 p. 156)

Dr. Jones gives implications not only for the treatment of mentally ill persons but also for our guidance and mental health programs focussed on preventive mental hygiene. He writes,

"We believe that too little use is made of educational methods in psychiatric hospitals. Our use of daily discussion groups with the entire patient population, documentary films, psychodramas, etc., represent an attempt to develop such methods; the main principle involved is that social problems and real life situations are either raised in discussion or acted out in psychodramas. The whole group attempts to arrive at a constructive attitude in relation to the problem raised. The degree of participation by the doctor taking the meetings varies with the situation and the personality of the doctor, but in his summing up he has the opportunity to present an informed, comprehensive point of view. To take the patient population repeatedly through this type of discussion and acting out of real life situations does possibly give them a new perception of such situations and so may alter behavior patterns; this new awareness may prove helpful in dealing with the patient's own problems. The awareness may not amount to actual insight, but the very process of acting out or verbalizing of feelings and attitudes gives definition to them, and in so doing, modifies them. However, in our educational procedure individual responses cannot be separated from the group climate ... patients seem to accept new ideas much more readily when these have behind them the weight of group acceptance." (13 p. 160)

This multiple counseling method uses certain techniques mentioned by Dr. Jones: a short-term plan, attitude changing through group influences, learning materials presented by a group leader, opportunity for clients to make specific applications to their own problems. For instance, a group project with accompanying individual counseling may be limited to fifteen group sessions and four interviews per participant. The responsibility for getting something out of the group experience and counseling interviews is placed squarely upon the client. In the writer's experience, this fact has influenced favorably the participant's readiness and motivation for learning.

A second characteristic of this method is the active learning process. The inductive method is used. Noticeable by their absence are definite aims and objectives, course outlines, reading and study assignments. No principles are stated which must be followed or applied; no neatly laid out units, progressions, or sequences are used by the leader. There are no exams or grades. Informational talks and summing up by the leader depend upon the needs and interests of the group; they serve to stimulate thinking on the part of the participants, not stifle it. Auxiliary activities such as personality inventories, self-appraisals, and role-playing are used to help individual members think and feel — these devices have a place in a multiple counseling project only when they aid learning processes.

The reader may be puzzled at this point, having scanned the list of eight characteristics of this method which include "definite learning." There seems to be a contradiction. Perhaps it would be more accurate to say that participants are given the opportunity to gain definite knowledges from authoritative sources; to hear variant viewpoints on a number of provocative subjects. Whether or not they learn anything of value to themselves is, again, their own responsibility. However, the group leader, just as the doctor in charge of the

Type of Participant	Code No.	Group Membership	Drop Outs	Average Attendance per Session	Group Sessions — Total No.	Frequency	Time (Minutes)	Common Problems (for major)	Group Activities	Learning Experiences and Outcomes (majority of participants)	Individual Counseling By Leader
High School Seniors (maladjusted and normal)	1	10 {3M 7F}	0	9	17	wk	50	Conflict parents	Free discussions chiefly. Personality assessments. Role-playing.	Growth toward maturity aided by free expression of hostility, frank self-revelation, blowing off steam, etc.	Average of 2.5 interviews per member plus chats. (One individual projective test)
	2	10 {5M 5F}	0	8	17	wk	50	Vocational choice	Free discussions chiefly. Personality assessments.	Personality assessment in terms of occupational fitness. Personal goals and life values in terms of planning future.	Average of 2 interviews per member plus chats. (One individual projective test)
College (normal)	3	8 {4M 4F}	0	8	17	2 x wk	60	College adjustment	Free discussions chiefly. Personality inventories and sociograms. Role-playing.	Increased feeling of security, social adequacy from free expression of gripes, discussion of college adjustment problems.	Average of 2 interviews per member plus chats. (One individual projective test)
	4	7 {3M 4F}	1	7	18	2 x wk	60	Vocational choice	Free discussions chiefly. Personality inventories and sociograms. Role-playing.	Reassurance regarding vocational choices on decisions. Personal goals and life values ascertained.	Average of 2 interviews per member plus chats. (One individual projective test)
	5	8 {4M 4F}	1	5	11	wk	90	Neuroses	Free discussions chiefly. Role-playing.	Improved college adjustment, tension reduction.	Two interviews per member. (Weekly or bi-weekly interviews by attending counselor)
College (maladjusted and normal)	6	11 {5M 6F}	0	8	12	wk	90	College adjustment	Free discussions. Self-appraisals and sociograms.	Respect for individual differences. Growth in social consciousness, assessing life-values.	Two interviews per member. (Weekly or bi-weekly interviews for 3 by attending counselor)
	7	8 {3M 5F}	1	5	7	wk	90	Personal adjustment	Free discussions chiefly. Self appraisals and sociograms.	Tension reduction from frank self-revelation. Improved self-concept in terms of being a worthy person. Support and reassurance from intimate group membership.	Four interviews per member plus chats.
	8	6 {3M 3F}	0	6	11	wk	90	Conflict parents personal adjustment	Free discussions chiefly. Self appraisals and sociograms.	Facing own personal problems aided by frank self-revelation. Reassurance that others have similar problems.	Average of 3 interviews per member plus chats. (Weekly to monthly interviews by attending psychiatrists)
College (psychiatric)	9	6 {3M 3F}	0	6	15	wk	90	Conflict parents personal adjustment	Free discussions chiefly. Role-playing.	"Encouragement" therapeutic benefits. Group experience augmented or aided psychotherapy treatment.	Two interviews per member plus chats. (Weekly or bi-weekly interviews by attending psychiatrists)
	10	5 {2M 3F}	1	5	12	wk	90	Neuroses	Free discussions chiefly. Role-playing.	Benefits of intimate group acceptance aided self-esteem. Improvement of verbal expression and social interactions. Aid in facing problems.	Two interviews per member plus short conferences. (Weekly to monthly interviews by attending psychiatrists)
Adults (normal)	11	9 {6M 3F}	0	9	6	2 x wk	60	Teaching problems and personal adjustments	Free discussions chiefly. Personality inventories.	PERSONAL APPLICATION OF EDUCATIONAL PSYCHOLOGY PRINCIPLES: Clarification; integration also. Personal adjustment problems given support and help through comparison of self with others in group. Personality assessment and counseling in private interviews.	One counseling interview per member, including test interpretations. One individual projective test including autobiographical questions. Short conferences regarding academic assignments.
	12	9 {5M 4F}	0	9	6	2 x wk	60	Teaching problems	Free discussions chiefly. Personality inventories.		
	13	8 {8M 0F}	1	7	6	2 x wk	60	Teaching problems	Free discussions chiefly. Personality inventories.		
	14	9 {5M 4F}	0	9	6	2 x wk	60	Teaching problems and personal adjustments	Free discussions chiefly. Personality inventories.		
Adults (psychotic)	15	7 {0M 7F}	0	6	26	3 x wk	75–90	Planning after hospital discharge	Free discussions chiefly. Role-playing.	ENCOURAGEMENT THERAPEUTIC BENEFITS: Enhanced self-esteem; information helpful to planning; personality-assessment; support and reassurance through group membership.	Average of four interviews per member plus chats. (Occasional interviews by psychiatrists and social workers)
TOTAL		121 {59M 62F}	5		187						

meeting of patients at Belmont Hospital, has a responsibility for introductions and "summing up" in which he gives information and interpretations pertinent to the group session.

A third characteristic of this method concerns restrictions of group membership. Not more than ten participants are accepted in a group when it is to be a multiple counseling project. Also, seriously maladjusted persons who might harm themselves or others are not acceptable. The exception to this is the group led by a psychiatrist who may admit seriously ill patients if he wishes to do so. His is the complete responsibility for actions which may result from group membership. When a group therapist works under the direct supervision of a psychiatrist, mentally ill patients in a group project are kept under close surveillance and may be removed from the group at any time. For example, a suicidal patient (group 10) was successful in her group membership, gaining support and reassurance from it. Fellow members were aware of her mental illness because she was confined in the college infirmary during part of the project, but they never asked embarrassing questions. They gave her friendly attention whenever possible, including invitations to social affairs, walking home with her, etc.

The problem of the mentally ill participant undiscovered in the preliminary interview, who proves to be disruptive in a normal group as well as a potential danger to himself or others, must be settled quickly. The leader should hold fast to the conditions under which participants are admitted to the group. A frank conference with the unacceptable participant contains a recommendation that he see a psychiatrist. Often such persons resist psychiatric referral and resent the implication that they are mentally ill. The group leader must be firm and refuse to let the person continue in the project until the psychiatric contact has been made and the attending psychiatrist takes the responsibility for the actions of the patient. Even then, the group leader may decide that the patient cannot fit into that particular group, and exclude him from membership.

Variety of Uses and Adaptations of This Method

The multiple counseling method has been used by the author for adolescents, young adults, and adults, including normals, neurotic, character disorder, and psychotic patients. In terms of active participation and satisfaction of group members, the statistics speak eloquently: 126 participants started projects, 121 finished them. All of these group members attended regularly except for legitimate absences; all met their counseling appointments conscientiously. The benefits gained by participants were well worth the time and effort given to the projects, in the opinion of the group leader and attending psychiatrists or counselors. In the majority of cases the group sessions substituted for some individual counseling interviews, thus lightening the case load of psychiatrists and counselors.

The chart at the end of the chapter describes briefly the fifteen group projects directed by the author.

To illustrate the various interactive influences at work in a multiple counseling project a small segment of one session and a fragment of two private interviews are outlined as follows:

INTERACTIVE AND COUNSELING PROCESS

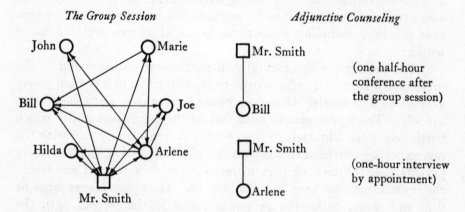

The Group Session   *Adjunctive Counseling*

(one half-hour conference after the group session)

(one-hour interview by appointment)

1. *The leader's interactions*

   Mr. Smith, the leader, interacts with all group members: with

   Hilda — short chat before the others arrive.

   Bill — supports an idea expressed by Bill.

   John — corrects John's sweeping statement and statistics.

   Marie — questions Marie regarding her attitude toward father.

   Joe — answers Joe's question regarding number of patients in state mental hospital.

   Arlene — asks Arlene if Hilda reminds her of older sister.

2. *Interactions among the participants*

Bill seemed to like Joe and to dislike Arlene. He agreed with Joe and asked if he'd like to study for the Zoo exam with him. When Arlene brought in an irrelevant idea Bill tried to get the discussion back on the track.

John supported Arlene when she expressed irritation toward Hilda and he was willing to enlarge on her irrelevant idea.

Marie seemed to dislike Arlene and to be impatient with her monopoly of the discussion. She agreed with Bill that the group should get back to the topic. She tended to disagree with Arlene.

Joe responded to Bill, was unresponsive to Arlene. He was noncommittal in the discussion and did not contribute. He did ask the leader a few questions.

Arlene was the dominant member, interacting with all other participants, expressing her ideas first, challenging the others in a friendly way except for Hilda, whom she seemed to dislike.

Hilda was a listener, making only one contribution to which Arlene responded in a rather insulting manner. After that Hilda withdrew from the discussion. She appeared to be amused rather than hurt by Arlene's aggressive behavior.

3. *Mr. Smith's interviews with Bill and Arlene*

Bill stayed after the session to talk with Mr. Smith. He was unhappy in the group and believed his participation was unsatisfactory. In the half-hour conference Mr. Smith gave him reassurance and suggested that he not force himself to contribute to the discussions until he got over his shyness.

Mr. Smith made an appointment for Arlene to come and talk with him, since she was obviously upset over the antagonisms she had aroused in the group. An hour conference was held in which Mr. Smith analyzed for Arlene the reactions of the others toward her. She admitted that her greatest weakness was talking too much, usually resulting in negative reactions from others. One of the reasons she had elected the group project was to improve her skill in group activity. Mr. Smith asked her to explain the irritation she showed toward Hilda. A discussion followed which revealed Arlene's identifying Hilda with an older sister whom she disliked. Self-revelation showed that Arlene's childhood had held keen rivalry, in which Arlene was the under-dog.

Comment: The above illustration of group dynamics, social interactions, and adjunctive counseling is characteristic of an early session in a multiple counseling project. Later sessions will show more overt feeling-expressions and discussions focussed on personal rather than impersonal approach to the topic. Eventually group members will understand and accept each other better, thus learning about personality differences and the reasons for them. Quite possibly Arlene will learn reasons for her aggressive behavior pattern and, when she gains a feeling of security and freedom from rivalry in the group, she will be able to improve her social skills. Likewise Bill, who thinks he dislikes girls, may find they are human beings after all. Quite possibly he will be attracted to Hilda and get up his courage to date her before the end of the project.

Summary

Definition was given to "multiple counseling" and "personal growth," along with the purposes and characteristics of the method presented in this book.

Eight characteristics of the method were outlined: they set the stage for the later chapters of the book which fully describe and illustrate the method.

The philosophical and psychological reasons for a human relations approach for counseling are given. Examples of successful use of group dynamics in the counseling process are given, based upon changes in psychotherapeutic methods since World War II.

An analysis is made of the ways this method differs from personal development courses and analytic group psychotherapy. It follows a middle course: eclecticism is characteristic of the leadership techniques and "educational" is the term which best describes the method.

The value of this multiple counseling method, not only for preventive mental hygiene and educational purposes among normal populations but also for encouragement or supportive therapy among the mentally ill populations, is attested by the fifteen group projects directed by the author. An outline of these projects is presented. Illustrations throughout the book are taken from actual cases and happenings in these projects.

II

ORGANIZATION OF INDIVIDUALIZED LEARNING METHODS FOR LARGE GROUPS

THE MULTIPLE COUNSELING METHOD described in Chapter I and analyzed at length in Chapters III–XI relates to projects with not more than ten persons in a group. These participants are counselees, or psychiatric patients, all of whom are given close attention by the leader-counselor during the project. All have the opportunity for private conferences with the leader, or counselor, concommitant with the group project. All take active part in group discussions and auxiliary activities of the project.

The reader may well question the practicality of such a method for large groups and wish to know if adaptations of a small-group discussion method for personal growth projects involving large numbers of people is possible. Therefore, mention of such adaptations seems pertinent before proceeding with discussion of this multiple counseling method.

Adaptations for large groups sometimes succeed in keeping the individualized learning and counseling aspects of a small-group discussion project. Types include (1) large meetings which break up into huddle, buzz, or cell groups with professional leaders who can counsel or advise group participants (2) lecture courses with small quiz sections where free discussions and individual counseling by the instructors are used (3) Seminars or study groups with group discussion where the relationship between teacher and students is close, allowing for individual counseling. Examples of successful projects follow:

Example 1.

A college vocational counseling project for fifty students combined assembly meetings of lectures, movies, and panel discussions with small-group discussion by cell-groups of six to eight participants. Leaders of the small groups were qualified counselors who could assist the students with personal as well as vocational problems. Since personal maladjustment often accompanied occupational uncertainty, the counseling was much deeper than so-called vocational guidance.*

---

* Northwestern University, Student Personnel and Counseling Services.

Example 2

    An undergraduate course in applied psychology attracted many college students with personal problems. The demand for individual conferences with the professor was so great that a special graduate assistant, qualified for personal counseling, was appointed for this purpose.†

> NOTE: This course was a lecture-type without opportunity for quiz sections in which the students might have shared their personal problems and engaged in healthy ventilation. However, the application of subject matter by the students for better understanding of themselves and their problems was aided by personal counseling conferences.

Example 3

    A college course in Mental Hygiene applied clinical psychology techniques for solution of personal problems of eighteen students. According to the instructor, the students used the reading assignments to get information pertinent to their own problems. Small-group discussion and role-playing were used in class meetings; critical self-evaluations were encouraged. The method is explained as follows:

> "Educationally, the locus of the knowledge was shifted from the instructor and textbooks to the students and their experiences. Therapeutically, the locus of therapy was shifted from the therapist to the group." (27, p. 95)

Example 4

    The out-patient department of the Boston Dispensary organized a project for more than one hundred over-weight patients which included nine small discussion groups with professional leaders (internist, psychologist, psychiatrist, teacher, minister, and graduate students in psychology). Results were good, since group members were able to progress further toward their objective of weight-reduction through project influence than previously achieved through medical treatment alone (8).

Example 5

    A PTA group discussion project in conjunction with the school child guidance and study department had a child psychologist as leader. The parents wished to understand their children better and six to eight couples met weekly during most of the school year for discussions and psychodrama. Individual problems of the group members were used in the role-playing so that the participants learned fully as much about themselves as their children. Individual counseling was provided for both parents and children. Since the leader was an excellent teacher, this project was a course in applied psychology as well as multiple counseling.

When groups are so large that small-group discussion and individual counseling is not possible, audience participation through which individuals identify emotionally with panel members, role-players, or

---

† University of Wisconsin, 1952–53: Psychology 105 "Psychology of Human Adjustment."

discussants, serves a useful purpose. An active learning process can be activated in which audience members think, feel, and vicariously participate in the actions of others. Most people know the significant experience of attending a problem-play and discussing it until the wee small hours with their friends. One feels frustrated and thwarted when there is no outlet for emotions and ideas stimulated from viewing or hearing a provocative question. The psychological value of the large group with audience participation has been shown by Pratt (22) Moreno (18) Alcoholic Anonymous, Jones (14) and Haas (10). Illustrations of successful use of audience participation through individual identifications follow:

Example 1
A unique adaptation of audience participation coordinated with small-group discussion in a state mental hospital consisted of a panel of patients who review a case, interviewing the patient who seeks hospital discharge. The audience was made up of patients who gave their opinions after the interview and panel discussions were finished. Excellent results in terms of improved insight on the part of audience members as well as the active participants were reported (17).

Example 2
The use of role-playing to present a provocative question was illustrated at a college meeting of the National Convention of The American Personnel and Guidance Association. The group leader first interviewed members of the audience to discover a common problem, viz., the handling of discipline cases on college campuses. A spontaneous psychodrama was then presented in which a Dean of Women disagreed violently with a Counselor regarding the handling of a case. When the discussion was thrown open to the audience, floor debates were even more lively than the role-playing. Attending members were most enthusiastic, declaring this to be the best meeting of the Convention. They felt as though they had taken an active part in the meeting and learned much from it.

Ways to Organize Group Discussion Projects for Educational or Therapeutic Purposes

Many persons welcome an opportunity to join a small-group discussion project focussed on human relations and personal growth. If such an activity meets their needs and interests, persons who lead busy lives such as students and civic-minded individuals are willing to forego other activities in favor of membership in a group project. A PTA father who feels inadequate in understanding and handling his teen-age children; his teen-age children with their feelings of insecurity; an adult student who seeks answers to his personal confusion and inner-conflicts through psychology, and Great Books courses; the wife of an alcoholic as well as the alcoholic himself — all these persons can be helped through intimate group membership, participation in group discussions, and adjunctive personal counseling.

High schools and colleges, adult education centers, and community agencies spearheaded by church organizations, are starting to provide educational groups and courses focussed on personal growth and adjustment. A brief outline of organization for various group projects, follows with some suggestions for recruiting members and planning the first meeting.

1. *High school and college group projects*

Three types of projects may be organized: formal courses in human relations or personal development, special interest clubs, group therapy projects. In all three, the instructor or group leader should attempt to have individual briefing conferences with prospective participants prior to the first meeting. Only through an individual interview can the group leader give to, and receive from the student essential information and rapport-building interactions. Also, careful placement of the student in a congenial group is expedited.

a. *An elective course in human relations or personal development*

This may be offered as a credit or non-credit course in the senior year of high school or in any college year. Credit should be insignificant to insure the sincerity of participants. Discussion groups should contain no more than ten students, preferably five boys and five girls. When a large number of students elect such a course, provision for regular discussions in small groups should be made. If the class cannot be broken down into quiz sections and has to assemble in one room, buzz techniques can be used, but the small groups of six to eight should remain intact during a semester so that students feel an intimate group climate. Rotating student leadership within each small group is recommended.

When quiz sections are included, the professor should try to visit all groups during the semester as well as provide time in the lecture periods for questions and general discussion.

40

When the small-group discussions are integrated with lectures and general assembly discussions, students feel that they are actively participating in the course.

The emphasis of such a course depends upon the department offering it; for instance, it may be a course in "Occupations," "Student Adjustment," "Mental Hygiene," or "Courtship and Marriage." In any case, the purpose of such a course is to help individual students to understand human problems and to gain skill in their own personal and social adjustments. "Working for credit" has no place in it, therefore class preparation and exams are omitted, if possible.

b. Discussion projects in dormitories, clubs, and special interest groups

These groups should be coeducational because high school and college students electing personal development projects often have sex-adjustment problems. They need an exchange of viewpoint — masculine versus feminine — and can gain better understanding and acceptance of members of the opposite sex. Thus growth toward maturity and healthy attitudes regarding sex are stimulated.

A discussion group should have a regular attendance of six to eight members. Since students sometimes cut school and meetings, or take on too many activities at one time, a total membership of ten or twelve to start the project is recommended. Usually several drop out before the project really gets underway.

The project must be group-centered in order to maintain a responsible, interested membership. Unless each member feels a loyalty to the group he may find excuses for missing sessions and finally drops out. A leader-dominated group becomes lackadaisical and unresponsive: members drop out and the project disintegrates after a few meetings. When each participant feels a personal responsibility for attendance and "making the group go," absences, even during exam periods, are kept to a minimum.

c. Orientation and homeroom projects

Group guidance projects in high school homerooms and orientation projects for college freshmen are variations of (b) above. It is recommended that all these projects consist of twelve to fifteen group sessions concentrated in a few months rather than extended beyond one semester. As long as the number of students in a group is kept low enough to insure "an intimate group climate" so that all members can participate actively in the discussions, these projects are successful. For example, at the Eastern Texas State Teachers College, the faculty advisors for entering freshmen keep groups of twelve advisees together for regular discussion sessions during the first semester. The advisor serves as personal counselor for his advisees, providing individual conference opportunities for the students in addition to group meetings.

d. *A "Personology Club" for teen-agers and young adults*

In high schools a group project may be organized as one of the regular activity clubs, meeting at the time set aside for clubs. This allows fifteen to seventeen sessions during a school semester. Membership should be limited to five boys and five girls in a discussion group. Publicity of the club is geared to attract the interest of well-adjusted as well as maladjusted students, i.e., "a club for free discussions on human relations, vocational fitness, personal and social adjustment." (See appendix: groups 1, 2.)

Youth organizations and churches follow the same recruitment techniques for personal growth projects. The YMCA has been a pioneer in small-group discussion methods of this kind, with several protestant church organizations close behind. The churches have had the advantage of coeducational memberships in these discussion groups. It is encouraging to note that YMCA's and YWCA's are coördinating their efforts through mixed groups more frequently of late.

e. *Multiple counseling projects for maladjusted students*

Counselors in high schools and colleges can recruit group members from their own caseload of individual clients, grouping them carefully according to personal problem and need. Six is the optimum number in a group because ventilation and self-revelation is to be encouraged. Regular attendance is expected since the group project is part of the counseling process. Individual interviews can be reduced when the clients are seeing the counselor regularly in the group sessions.

42

This type of project requires longer sessions, with more role-playing and auxiliary activities than educational projects for so-called normal students. It is recommended that sessions last one and one-half hour in a relaxed atmosphere at the end of the school day. In the experience of the author definite time limits for the project were found to be the best plan. Thus the group remains intact until the end, for example, seventeen sessions. However, other leaders prefer to change the membership of the group throughout a school year, dismissing some clients, and adding new members as replacements.

How to Start a Group Project

An example of "selling" a group project to members of a high school home room by the group leader (home room teacher or guidance director) follows:

Leader: We are planning a discussion group for any of you who are interested in learning more about yourselves and getting along with people. The group is limited to eight members — four boys and four girls. It meets during study period on Tuesday and Friday for two months starting next week. You could call it Applied Psychology if you wish, but there won't be any credit, reading assignments, or grades.

Student: Why can't we all join it — why does it have to be limited to eight?

Leader: A group has to be limited to eight so that everyone can talk. But we can organize more than one group, if enough of you are interested. You know that in your classes of 30 or 40 a few students do all the talking. In these groups everyone is expected to say his piece whenever he feels like it.

Student: How do we know what to talk about?

Leader: You will have a chance to vote for a number of subjects which you'd like to have discussed. In fact, I'll pass around sheets which have a large number of topics listed. This will give you an idea of the project. You can look over the sheet, think a bit about it, and if you want to join, check five topics you want discussed, sign the slip and turn it in at the end of the period.

(passes out the topic-check sheets)

Leader: Are there any questions?

Student: Some of these topics are pretty frank stuff. How do we know what we say won't get spread around the school or back to our parents?

Leader: That is up to the group. If you want to decide that everything is to be kept confidential that's the way it will be.

Student: This begins to sound like fun. I have a lot of gripes about this school — I could make a soapbox speech.

Leader: By the way, there is a space at the bottom of the sheets so you can add any topic not listed which you'd like to bring up in the group. These sheets will be kept confidential — no one but me will see them. And if there is anything else you'd like to ask me about, I'll be available for individual conferences after school. We'll let you know who are assigned to groups and when they meet. The first meetings will be next week. We want equal numbers of boys and girls in each group so it will take a little time to get the groups straightened out.

An example of a psychiatrist urging an unsocial client to join a group project follows:

Doctor: You say you'll do anything to help you feel better?

Client: Yes, anything — I've really hit rock bottom. I feel terrible — completely hopeless.

Doctor: Well I have a suggestion. We are forming a group of patients who feel much as you do — meetings will be held weekly and you can talk about anything you want, it's entirely confidential. Some of the others in the group have problems that are different from yours, but they all feel at rock bottom, as you do.

Client: You know how scared I am of people — it would be very hard for me — I'd get nervous and upset. Frankly, the idea of being in a group doesn't appeal to me at all.

Doctor: There is always a nice spirit in such a group. You'd probably make a friend or two there. Even though it sounds hard, you asked me what I recommended and you said you'd do anything — this is what I'm suggesting as part of your treatment.

Client: Will you be there?

Doctor: No. Dr. D is the group leader. She knows much more about group therapy than I do. We are working together on several cases and I think you will fit very well into this particular group.

Client: I was going to say I'd do it if you were there. Now I don't know.

Doctor: Well, I'd like to have you talk with Dr. D. about it. She'll explain things and ask for your ideas on topics you'd like to hear discussed. Can you come back here and see her, say tomorrow at 3:30?

Client: Can I decide whether or not to join after talking with Dr. D.?

Doctor: Yes, in fact I'll make a deal with you. Attend one meeting anyway, and then if you want to drop out, O. K.

Client: All right, as long as I don't have to sign on the dotted line.

NOTE: This patient talked with the group leader and agreed to attend one meeting. He was reassured because of the friendly atmosphere and became an enthusiastic group member. Just as the psychiatrist surmised, his acceptance by a peer group filled a deep need and the practice in social interactions gave him self-confidence which carried over to other groups. Tension reduction resulted from lessened self-consciousness and he became less self-centered. Thus psychotherapy was aided by his participation in the group.

A preliminary interview with the group leader often reassures prospective group members as well as giving the leader a chance to establish rapport. The interviewee participates in project planning by selecting his preferences as to topics, structure and approach. Excerpts from a briefing interview follow: (see Chap. XI for full details).

Leader: Since your counselor didn't tell you much about this group I'll try to explain and answer questions. We're planning to have three fellows and three girls in this group. There is a common problem, since you all have told your counselors that you're not satisfied with your adjustment to college. But there may be different angles to the problem. For example, one person talks too much and is tactless. Another can't talk at all. . . . We are going to try to help each of you with whatever you need. The group meets weekly at 3:30 to 5 on Wednesdays. We take up a number of topics which the group wants to discuss. You are encouraged to say whatever you want — on any subject — and to act the way you feel. No one is forced to talk if he'd rather listen.

Student: What are we supposed to get out of this — what is the aim?

Leader: The aim is for each member to learn to understand himself better and also to get well acquainted with the others — to understand how we differ, one from another. There will be fifteen sessions and by the time you get through you will have learned a lot, I can assure you. The practice in expressing your ideas may help you in other groups, too.

Student: I like the sound of it except that I'd be embarrassed to talk about myself.

Leader: Nobody is forced to do that, except that in the first session each person introduces himself.

Student: Perhaps I should tell you what my difficulty is, or did Mr. M tell you?

Leader: He told me a little but I'd like you to tell me anything which would make me better able to help you. Also if there is any painful subject you want to avoid being asked about in the group, perhaps I could be more tactful if I knew.

Student: My trouble is girls — I am very cynical about them. (He tells of his feelings including a fear that he is not normal. The leader reassures him that the three girls in the group are not gold diggers nor awesome — maybe he will get a different idea of girls from the group experience.)

Other parts of the preliminary interview include a topic-poll and the client's preference of four group structures. (Chap. III).

Preparation for the First Session

It is important for all members to attend the first session which resembles an initiation into a club. Thus the leader should send notices and check with individual members or their counselors as to time and place of the meeting. Self-introductions form the major activity of the first meeting. When they are accomplished en masse, camaraderie and reassurance result. The leader prepares typed outlines which may be followed in the self-introductions. A sample college group outline is given below:

SELF-DESCRIPTION

Group members are asked to introduce themselves so that all may feel better acquainted. Each one has a right to tell as much or as little about himself (herself) as he wants the group to know. The following outline may be used if you wish. It is only to help, in case you don't know how to describe yourself.

1. *Status in college:* year, major and vocational aim; any changes in vocational choice made in high school and college; other colleges attended, etc.

2. *Family background:* hometown, places you have lived. Father's occupation, number of brothers and sisters; any facts about family which have been influential in your aims, attitudes (divorce, deaths, home conditions, etc.). Racial background, religion, and anything else you think is important about yourself.

3. *Work and travel experience:* any work, military service, travel, or other experiences in your life.

4. *What you'd like to be ten years from now:* occupation, marital status, things you think are most important to have (Cadillac? Children? A career before marriage? Service to society?)

The final step in preparing for the opening session consists of arranging the seating plan, with large-lettered name cards on the table in front of each chair. A "round table" grouping is important, and some leaders provide pencils and doodling-paper for motor outlets of nervous participants, especially if they do not smoke. Regarding the seating plan, a hint from research in group dynamics may help: aggressive, talkative participants should be seated *next* to each other rather than facing each other across the table. This prevents two-way monopoly of the discussion. Another suggestion is to place shy members near the leader.

The First Session

The room is prepared well in advance of the first arrival. The leader should know the name or nickname of each participant and address the members informally from the start. The sooner an informal, social atmosphere is achieved, the better. An illustration of the first meeting of a high-school project for five boys and five girls is given below. In this case there were no briefing interviews and the membership list had not been given to the leader in advance:

(*Several of the group knew each other. All ten arrived en masse and the girls sat together, while the boys took the seats that were left*).

Leader: I'll first introduce myself and explain what Personology Club is all about. My name is Miss D. and I am assisting Miss G. in the guidance department one day a week, so I'll be seeing you at this same time each week for the semester.

1st Student: What are we going to talk about?

2nd Student: Can we talk about anything we want — I hope!

Leader: Yes we'll discuss anything you're interested in. As Miss G. told you, the idea is to learn more about your own personalities and ways to get along well with people.

3rd Student: Is this like a Psychology course? I read books on Psychology all the time — I think it's interesting.

Leader: Well, you could call it Human Relations. We'll stick to real life situations and not get off into theory. You won't have anything to prepare or read — it's better just to swap ideas about handling situations and how we feel about different things.

1st Student: Can't we get started?

Leader: Yes, the first thing is to get acquainted. We'll go around the table and you can talk a bit about yourselves. I have typed slips for you that may help — you can follow them or not as you wish. I'll start telling about myself to show you how the outline can be followed.

(Leader gives self-description quite briefly. Others follow in order around the table. Some give full descriptions, others say very little. Ten minutes remain for a discussion).

Leader: Now we have time for a short discussion — what would you like to talk about? Mary, you look as though you have an idea.

Mary: Yes, I'd like to get the kids' opinion on drafting women as well as men. I don't think it's fair that we girls don't get drafted. Anyway, I intend to join the WAAF's after graduation.

    (A lively discussion follows after one boy says that girls are too weak physically to do a soldier's job. The period ends in the midst of a violent argument — girls against boys).

Leader: We'll continue this next week, but for only the first ten minutes. Will you think about discussion topics you'd like. Write down three suggestions on a slip of paper to bring next time — something you want to learn more about as well as anything which has different angles. So the discussions can be lively like this one.

COMMENT: The purpose of the first session is to warm up the group. In the illustration above, six of the ten members got into the discussion but four sat back. Next session the leader will try to draw out the four listeners or at least give them a chance to talk if they wish to.

2. *Organizing projects within an institution*

Group projects for patients, prisoners, or inmates may be organized easily if the institutional policy allows scheduling of group meetings as a regular part of the program. The only obstacle remaining is the scarcity of qualified group leaders. Psychiatrists, psychologists, and psychiatric social workers who might provide excellent leadership are usually over-worked so that group projects cannot be added to their work schedules. At the present time comparatively few hospitals and institutions provide small-group discussion activity, and when such projects are offered, a very small percentage of the total number of patients or inmates are given a chance to participate. Although the value of such projects has been shown during the last decade in certain mental hospitals, prisons and correctional institutions, wide-spread acceptance of such methods has not come as yet. Strangely enough, physical treatment methods such as electric or insulin shock and lobotomies seem to be gaining wider acceptance than group therapy methods even though neuropsychiatrists admit the shortcomings of the physical treatment. The reason back of the lack of interest in group therapy on the part of many hospital and institution administrators is not clear. It is hoped that the encouraging results from projects such as that pioneered by Dr. Maxwell Jones in England will stimulate educational and therapeutic group programs in American institutions.

Illustrations of successful group discussion projects which help patients or inmates to adjust better to their present situations and to plan constructively for life after discharge are found in professional journals published since World War II. Several examples and suggested programs follow.

a. Multiple counseling projects in correctional institutions

The success of group discussion projects depends upon keeping them on the level of intelligence, need and interests of individual participants. Sometimes role-playing is effective, sometimes it does not appeal to the group. Frank discussion of gripes, resentments, and personal adjustment problems is the most suitable activity.

Three types of group project are recommended for reform schools and penal institutions: (1) informal courses in personal development (2) group therapy with emphasis on role-playing (3) group therapy with emphasis on nondirective discussion. Examples of successful projects carried on at the Wisconsin School for Girls follow:

(1) A voluntary course in personal development for twelve to fifteen girls was led by a child psychologist from the University. The group met twice weekly for one school semester. Twelve problem areas were explored, based on a textbook, "Discovering Myself" (19). According to follow-up reports, the girls were helped to adjust better not only to life within the institution but also to develop positive attitudes for better adjustments after discharge (20).

(2) A voluntary psychodrama project was led by a state psychologist over a period of one year. . Weekly meetings were open to all the girls, and membership was fluctuating. Psychological benefits were gained both by the girls who acted out their personal problems and by the audience, according to the psychologist.

(3) A voluntary nondirective discussion group led by the part-time psychiatrist was effective in providing counseling for a much larger number of girls than would have been possible otherwise.

b. Group therapy in psychiatric hospitals

Since the trend is away from giving individual psychotherapy to the majority of patients in mental hospitals, but rather concentrating on educational and rehabilitative activities, group discussion therapy has a definite place in hospital programs (18, 25). The psychiatrist can maintain personal contact with their many patients through short chats on the ward; discussion group therapy, led by psychologists, psychiatric social workers and nurses, can give support, reassurance and catharsis to many of the patients. This type of group therapy may be called "encouragement" therapy because it helps the patient to understand and accept himself and others: it encourages him to plan for life after discharge.

Example

An experimental group project of this type was led by the author who served in the capacity of a group therapist under the supervision of the attending psychiatrist. The group consisted of seven psychotic women patients during their insulin shock treatment series. These patients were able to carry on lucid, meaningful discussions in the early afternoon having had deep or sub-insulin shock treatment in the morning. (See appendix, group 15).

Small-group discussion therapy as a convalescent activity in preparation for hospital discharge has been widely used in British hospitals and much has been written about their social rehabilitation programs and social therapeutic clubs (4). Emphasis on social rehabilitation and a growing awareness of the responsibility of hospitals for continued contact with discharged patients seems to be a realistic, healthy trend.

A suggested program of discussion therapy for the *majority* of patients in a large mental hospital is based on uses made of it in small private sanitoriums, the Belmont Hospital, and a few state and Veteran Administration installations. This is a hypothetical illustration in which the hospital administrators attempt to make full use of group dynamics and close relationships between staff and patients.

A Discussion Therapy Program for a Large Mental Hospital

Three types of group discussion activity are organized for patient groups: orientation, educational or encouragement therapy, psychodrama or psychotherapy.

1. *Orientation*

Upon admission, or as soon after admission as patients are able to participate, orientation groups of 20–25 members hold scheduled meetings to discuss hospital membership, procedures, and programs. Six sessions, one hour in length, twice a week for three weeks may constitute an orientation project. The leaders may be in-service trained social workers, nurses, or other hospital staff members. The group leader represents the hospital, reflecting and interpreting its philosophy, purposes, and treatment methods in helping the patients regain their health. The group structure resembles an open forum, with a speaker who is willing to answer questions and listen to opinions and suggestions from group members. The leader gives information, explanations and advice to the group regarding acceptable conduct in the hospital community. He serves as moderator during free discussions. He assures the group that constructive suggestions they have regarding changes in hospital procedures will be referred to higher officials, although no assurance is given regarding changes being made.

2. *Educational or encouragement therapy*

Patients completing the orientation project are screened by the psychiatrists for admission to small-group discussion projects. These groups consist of 10–15 patients, led by a group therapist (or hospital staff member who has received training in group leadership). Regularly scheduled sessions should include a total of 15–20 meetings to constitute a project. If possible the sessions should be one hour and a half in length and provide an intimate, social atmosphere.

The group structure is a seminar-type and the patients may think of the project as a class with the leader in the role of a teacher. Subject matter and discussions are maintained on a general level; self-revelations and personal references are not allowed to proceed to the extent of upsetting the individual or the group. Informational talks on behavior causes, personal and social adjustment problems, human relationships, and healthy personality growth are used as springboards to free discussions. Rather strict moderation and control of discussions by the leader may be necessary.

3. *Group psychotherapy*

Patients screened by the psychiatrists following participation in educational group therapy are placed in small groups of six members for nondirective psychotherapy or psychodrama. The leaders are psychiatrists or psychologists trained in group techniques. The type of psychotherapeutic treatment depends upon the background of the leader. Probably the majority of qualified psychotherapists would use a psychoanalytic frame of reference. In such cases, the projects are multiple-psychiatry and problems discussed in the group sessions resemble those ventilated "on the couch." Private interviews with group members are cojunctive with the group project. However, according to some reports group sessions can substitute for private interviews, allowing a psychiatrist to carry twenty cases instead of four (14). Nondirective psychoanalytic group projects have been fully described in books by Hinckley (13), Powdermaker (21) and Slavson (24).

HYPOTHETICAL SITUATION

Let us assume that this hospital is a state psychiatric institution with 1000 beds. Perhaps 80% of the admissions could benefit from participating in orientation groups. Of this number 50% are then admitted to educational group therapy. Finally, 10% of the patients finishing these projects might profit from psychotherapy (or can be given treatment). In this way, at least 800 patients receive some kind of social-interaction treatment involving communicative, learning activity. The following histogram shows the program as outlined above: (SEE NEXT PAGE)

Discussion Group Therapy Program in Large Mental Hospital

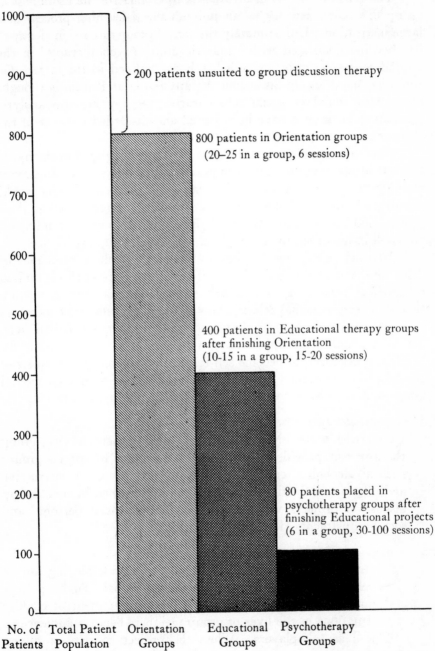

200 patients unsuited to group discussion therapy

800 patients in Orientation groups
(20–25 in a group, 6 sessions)

400 patients in Educational therapy groups
after finishing Orientation
(10-15 in a group, 15-20 sessions)

80 patients placed in
psychotherapy groups after
finishing Educational projects
(6 in a group, 30-100 sessions)

No. of   Total Patient   Orientation   Educational   Psychotherapy
Patients   Population   Groups   Groups   Groups

The purpose of this illustration is to emphasize the usefulness of group discussion activity as an individualized learning process in a large institution. Unfortunately the term "group discussion therapy" has become associated with "analytic group psychotherapy" in the United States, because research has been confined to the latter. On the other hand, group discussion therapy in Great Britain is thought of as educational or social rehabilitative therapy because analytic techniques for groups have been tested and discarded in favor of the more practical group method.

Orientation and educational group therapy suggested in the hypothetical illustration are neither impractical nor dangerous. In-service training of hospital personnel for leadership of such projects would put to work many of the principles and subject matter courses in their professional background. Group leaders would gain understanding of, and skill in handling, their charges through the group experience.

Although many mental hospitals claim to follow principles of "the therapeutic community," too often their concept of this is limited to medical treatment, work projects, occupational and recreation therapy. Interpersonal relationships between hospital staff members and patients continue to be characterized by authority-discipline tele. There is a dearth of opportunity for patients to learn reasons for hospital procedures, to become self-respecting, responsible members of the hospital community, to gain understanding of their own mental illnesses, and to work constructively toward social rehabilitation.

3. *Groups with specialized problems*

Either within the institution or as an out-patient service, group therapy can provide support and satisfaction to special groups such as alcoholics, cripples, chronically ill persons. Constructive attitudes and adjustive techniques may be learned in small-group discussion projects which will result in improved personal and social adjustments (1, 8, 15, 16, 22, 26).

  a. Alcoholics

A small-group discussion project using role-playing can be helpful when alcoholics tend to be non-verbal. Such a project may include 15–20 members. The re-enactment of conflict situations in the lives of group members benefits audience as well as role-players. When the project consists of fifteen sessions, a variety of psychodramas lead into frank discussions and self-revelations. Identification with another participant or empathy with a role-player helps a member to recognize and face the reasons for compulsive drinking. Support and reassurance from fellow participants and the group leader can encourage more positive attitudes reinforced by the group process.

Problems to be acted out come from members of the group. Usually situations such as the following are of common interest:

Employer vs. prospective employee: interview situation.

Foreman vs. worker: problem of absenteeism and drinking.

Cop vs. drunk: right and wrong ways to argue with the law.

Father and child: father's attempt to change gangster ideal.

Husband vs. wife: working out a compromise of drinking problem.

AA Member vs. drunk: arguments pro and con.

Minister and drunk: what has religion to do with drinking?

Short chats or interviews with group members at their request are an important function of leadership. When the project is organized in an institution where 30-day sentences for alcoholics prevail, meetings are scheduled as part of the daily program, five days a week for three weeks. Then the final week is left open for individual conferences with group leader, psychiatrist, chaplain, or AA representative.

b. Diabetics, neurotics, over-weight persons, amputees, paraplegics

Intimate groups of similarly handicapped persons can be therapeutic as well as social. Many examples of such groups, meeting regularly for discussions, and mutual aid, are found in professional literature, magazines, and newspapers: the therapeutic social clubs in England, Recovery, Inc. in Chicago, The On-Leave Society in Iowa, Alcoholic Anonymous are examples. As long ago as 1905 Dr. Joseph Pratt organized groups of diabetic and tubercular patients at the Boston Dispensary for discussion meetings (22). This hospital recently reported successful results for nine discussion groups of overweight persons (8). Husbands of mentally ill wives formed a discussion project which could be called multiple counseling for "a special group." Dr. Gene Gordon, psychiatrist of the San Francisco Langley Porter Clinic, organized this project to help the men verbalize feelings of guilt and problems concerned with their wives' illnesses (26). An organization of wives of Alcoholics has been formed in Madison, Wisconsin, through which group discussions can give to the members support, reassurance and help with a mutual problem.

4. *Community special-interest groups*

In our country there has been healthy growth of small-group discussion as an educational activity for special-interest groups. Sponsored by such organizations as The National Conference for Christians and Jews, the YMCA and YWCA, League of Women Voters, Catholic and Protestant church groups, congenial discussion groups focussed on significant social problems, are available for persons of all ages.

Not so common are opportunities for membership in discussion groups focussed on personal adjustment problems. However, the National Association for Mental Health has started to sponsor such groups. With the growth of county and urban chapters of this organization we can expect to see an increase in the number of discussion groups for persons with psychological problems. Often, of course, such problems are concerned with family living, job maladjustments, etc. In our culture we assume that persons who live with their spouses, do their jobs and stay out of jail are well-adjusted individuals: thus they would have nothing to talk about in a personal adjustment discussion group. This assumption is false and the sooner our preventive mental hygiene programs get underway, the better. Preventive mental hygiene is accepted in theory by all experts in Personality, but these experts are kept so busy treating mentally ill patients that they have no time to help people avoid mental illness. Community groups which concentrate on discussions of personal and social adjustments can be effective as preventive mental hygiene activities.

The interest of the general public in mental health and personality is attested by the increasing number of newspaper columns, magazine articles, and radio programs which present personal problems and give psychological advice. Lectures on mental health draw large audiences. For example, a series of professional lectures on this subject in Milwaukee, Wisconsin, started with an attendance of 100 which increased to 1000 at the final lecture. Assuming that many of the audience wanted and needed to gain better understanding of themselves and others, how much more benefit there would be for these individuals in small-group discussion projects where they could participate in an active learning process. Leadership for such projects could be recruited and trained from the ranks of teachers, physicians, guidance and social workers, ministers and priests. Psychiatrists and psychologists could serve as consultants and supervise the training of group leaders. Thus coördination among medical, psychiatric, educational and social welfare personnel could produce a truly effective program of preventive mental hygiene.

HYPOTHETICAL SITUATION

Let us visualize the mechanics of activating a mental hygiene discussion-group project for a hypothetical community of 25,000 inhabitants. There are two practicing psychiatrists, one of whom is on the hospital staff; ten physicians of whom seven are general practitioners, three are specialists; a Red Cross chapter, Family Service agency, and other welfare agencies with a total of five social workers. There are a total of fifteen professional church personnel. The schools have fifteen administrators, guidance workers, and teachers who are potential group leaders. The chairman of the National Association for Mental Health chapter is a business man who is highly skilled as a coördinator of civic projects. This organization serves as the spearhead and coördinator of the project, in which the other agencies, the schools, hospital and churches take an active part. The project may consist of various lecture series by a psychiatrist, geared for youth, adults, and special-interest groups with small discussion groups an integral part of each lecture series.

Group leaders would be trained by a committee of psychiatrists, physicians and psychologists through an initial course of six sessions, followed by monthly or bi-weekly meetings during the progress of the project. This supervisory committee would be available as informational sources, advisors, and counselors for the group leaders whenever needed. The group leadership course would teach the prospective leaders some of the nondirective techniques useful in a small group, springboards to discussion, reliable information sources, recognition of mentally ill persons and their referal to medical or psychiatric agencies. The discussion projects might include groups interested in human relations and discrimination, personal development, family relationships, courtship and marriage, current problems. The kind of discussion topics, informational talks, and role-playing which can be handled safely by lay leaders are analyzed in the various chapters of this book. A supervisory committee of physicians, psychiatrists, and psychologists would insure proper boundaries for leaders who are not psychologists.

Certainly discussion groups focussed on personal and social problems should be healthier for participants than many of the books, radio and television programs, newspaper and magazine articles which hold the attention of the general public at the present time. The small seminar or democratically-based group process is one of the most effective teaching-learning methods ever devised. Through verbalizing one's worries, fears, and frustrations real growth toward maturity and satisfactory human relations can be stimulated; listening, looking, and reading often are passive activities without meaningful learning. The interpersonal relationships, stimuli and responses that come from frank expression of feelings and opinions — these form the learning medium for personal growth in an intimate discussion group.

6. *Personal assessment projects in professional training courses*

Small-group discussion projects for personal growth of students in social work, teaching, guidance and counseling, medicine and nursing, serve two purposes: (1) facing facts concerning personality qualifications (strengths and weaknesses) for the profession; (2) practice and skill-learning in group dynamics and human relationships.

It is sometimes said that psychologists, social and guidance workers select these fields because of their own basic insecurity: helping others is compensation for the need of being helped oneself.

Even though the professional student is well-adjusted and sure of his vocational choice he has personal weaknesses which, in the shape of biases and ego-defenses, can have a detrimental effect on his professional work. Certainly a person whose life is to be devoted to working with, and helping others, needs to be a mature, unbiased person. However, a professional student becomes so immersed in the task of gaining technical skills and acceptable academic grades that there is little time for self-evaluation or soul-searching. Sometimes it takes a year or two on the job, with personal weaknesses bringing failures in human relationships, to prove the unfitness of the person in the profession.

Professional training courses would do well to emulate the curriculum of counselor training for Veteran Administration hospitals by including a required course in human relations or personal assessment. This course is actually a small-group discussion project focussed on group dynamics and personal counseling of the participants, *viz.*, multiple counseling.*

The fact is, professional students would welcome an opportunity for self-assessment and help with personal growth as a part of their training course. When discussion group projects were organized by the author for counselees at a University counseling center, professional students in medicine, nursing, education, psychology and social work requested group membership. These students were not characteristically maladjusted. They had a sincere desire to evaluate themselves in terms of personal growth and to learn more about group dynamics and interpersonal skills. It is hoped that professional departments and schools will eventually fill the need of their students in this area through small-group discussion projects in the early years of training; such projects can reassure well-fitted students that they are heading in the right direction and can show misfits why they are more suited to some other field. Small-group discussion projects led by advisors or qualified faculty members can help fulfill an educational responsibility for aiding the personal growth, as well as the mental growth, of the students.

Not only for their own personal growth but also for better under-

---

* Two examples are the University of Buffalo, VA clinical counseling training course, and the University of Kansas where the Human Relations Department collaborates with the clinical psychology division to provide training in group discussion therapy methods.

standing of future patients, medical students, nurses, and psychiatric social work trainees need a course in practical psychiatry. When the students themselves form the group on which and for which the materials of the course are demonstrated, the learning includes better understanding of themselves as well as others. Thus the structure resembles discussion group therapy which uses case conference role-playing, and nondirective techniques as well as informational talks by the psychiatrist-leader. Since the shortage of psychiatric nurses and social workers as well as medical students who select psychiatry as a specialty, is acute, interest in such specialties might be aroused through a group therapy experience.

SUMMARY

Examples of adaptation of a group discussion method which individualizes the learning process in large groups were given. While individual counseling is not feasible for members of large group projects, personal application of subject matter can be made in small-group discussions. Likewise identification of audience members with speakers or role-players facilitates an active learning process.

Illustrations of ways to organize discussion groups for personal development study and for multiple counseling purposes in high schools and colleges were given. Suggestions for getting such projects started included sample preliminary interviews, preparation for the first session, and excerpts from an initial session.

Organization of small-group discussion projects for orientation, educational and therapeutic purposes in correctional institutions and mental hospitals was illustrated by established programs in such installations. An example of wide use of discussion group methods within a large mental hospital was shown in a hypothetical situation and program.

Examples of projects for individuals with special problems or handicaps, and for special interests groups were given. A suggested plan was outlined for a preventive mental hygiene program which coördinates various agencies and civic groups in a medium sized city under the leadership of a chapter of the National Association for Mental Health. Leadership recruitment and training for discussion groups was touched on.

Finally a strong recommendation for multiple counseling projects in the curricula of professional training courses was made, not only because students want and need help in personal growth areas, but because the training department should assume responsibility for the personal growth and adjustments of students whose life work is to be closely associated with skill in dealing with people.

III

PROCEDURES IN A
MULTIPLE COUNSELING PROJECT

THE SUCCESS OF A GROUP PROJECT depends upon the leader's ability to adapt group activities and individual counseling to the needs of the individuals in the group so they will learn what they want and need to learn.

The mechanics of a multiple counseling project include:

1. Selection of group members
2. Preliminary organization before the first meeting
3. Group structure and approach
4. Discussion topics
5. Auxiliary activities and counseling devices
6. The leader's role
7. Observations and records
8. Evaluation of outcomes

Examples of the flexibility of the method are shown in the summary of group projects (Chapter I, appendix). In one high school project adjustment was made to the fact that group members could not be selected or given preliminary interviews. Often it is impossible to have prospective members vote on discussion topics or preferred group structure before the start of the project. In one college project the subject of emotional maturity was discussed for fifteen sessions; in another project fifteen topics were discussed in twelve sessions. In one group a teacher-pupil relationship continued throughout the project; in another, the leader was an observer-participant in most of the sessions. The adaptability of the leader is similar to that of a skilled elementary school teacher using the project method. Rigid course planning has no place in this type of small-group discussion activity.

Based on try-out experiments in a large number of different group situations, the following recommendations are made:

1. *Selection of group members*

   a. Six to ten participants can be grouped together. Six is the optimum number for a free discussion which allows all participants to be active. Four or five members tend to be active in a ten-member group: leaderless discussions are not effective in so large a group. Also the larger the group the less personal responsibility each member feels for attendance and participation. Leadership from within the group itself is preferable to leader influence in controlling monopolists and drawing out shy members; a six-member group usually provides satisfactory group dynamics for this.

   b. Equal numbers of male and female participants in a group are strongly recommended unless there is a definite reason for a one-sexed grouping.

   c. A common problem applying to all members is the best basis of grouping — for example — a feeling of social inadequacy, rebellion against parents, desire to learn about human behavior, parental problems with fourth graders.

   d. Heterogeneity in family, racial, and cultural background among group members is helpful. Individual differences can lead to growth in understanding and tolerance of one another. An illustration of wide differences in background is a high school project in which parental status included a tavern waitress, farmer, widow on mother's pension, remarried divorcee, welder, salesman, minister, foster parents. (Appendix, group 2).

   e. Heterogeneity in personality type among group members is also desirable. Not more than one overly aggressive member should be included in a six-member group. Preferable grouping consists of one-third talkers, one-third listeners, one-third who tend to agree or disagree with others. However, a balanced grouping is seldom achieved and the leader's responsibility includes participation and control to bring about effective group dynamics.

2. *Preliminary planning*

   The time and place of meetings, length of sessions, and number of sessions in the project are determined in advance of the individual interviews with prospective group members. Thus a clear descrip-

63

tion of the project can be given to each participant so that he knows exactly what is expected of him in terms of attendance and time expenditure.

3. *Group structure and approach*

The prospective group members assist in the planning by voting for the kind of discussion group and topics they prefer. This is done in the individual briefing interview whenever possible. A sample check-sheet used for young adults follows:

Choice of Method Used in the Group Discussions

(Please check the procedure which you would enjoy most; or which you believe to be most beneficial to yourself as a participant in the group).

( ) 1. *Completely structured discussion sessions:* topic is known in advance so that participants can think about it; leader keeps discussions focussed on the topic; conclusions are sought; summary at end of session; plan for next session is formulated.

( ) 2. *Modified structure:* topic is known in advance, but if group wishes to change discussion focus during the session, it may do so; leader serves only as moderator, letting discussion go in any direction; leader summarizes discussion content but conclusions are not definitely sought; plan for next session is made.

( ) 3. *Slightly structured:* topic is known in advance by the group, but the approach to it is not planned; no attempt to focus discussion or draw conclusions; leader does not moderate except in instances where monopoly of time by one participant is unfair to others. Group votes on topic for next session.

( ) 4. *Unstructured:* no topic is assigned. Participants talk about anything they wish. No leader or moderator. (Leader becomes participant-observer and gives information when asked). Time allotments for individuals having the floor are not controlled except by group itself. No decisions regarding discussion topic for next session.

What is the reason for your choice? _____

Vote on Type of Individual Participation

Which do you prefer: impersonal group discussions in which you don't have to talk about your feelings and personal problems — or — confidential presentations of problems of individual members?

( ) Impersonal   ( ) Personal

Structure 3 and 4 and "the personal approach" usually receive the most votes. Sometimes the group finds that a different structure is needed after a few meetings, especially when a monopolist emerges who prevents the discussions from giving satisfaction to others in the group. Actually a good leader can provide a democratic, group-centered discussion activity in structure 1, as any student knows who has enjoyed membership in a small class with a good teacher.

4. *Selection of discussion topics*

A check-list of interesting topics can be made up according to the age-level and interests of group members. There are many books, especially for adolescents, which give excellent suggestions for discussion subjects. Likewise a practical outline of pertinent topics for special groups such as industrial, housewives, parents, geriatric groups can be constructed from perusing modern books dealing with the problems of such groups. The opinions of prospective group members regarding interesting subjects is one of the best ways to develop a meaningful project. The check-list which follows grew out of interests and needs of college students counseled by the author:

Discussion Topic Poll

(Please check five of the topics which you would like to have discussed in the group project. Star the one you are most interested in. Use the space at the bottom of the sheet to add other topics of greater interest to you, and include them in the five you wish to check).

1. What is personality? Is one's personality determined by heredity or environment? Is personality modify-able?
2. What makes us differ one from another in adjusting to life situations?
3. What is a feeling of security? How do we get it, keep it, lose it?
4. Why is the U.S. the most disliked nation, according to experts. Why do we feel hostile toward certain people or groups?
5. Should an American soldier marry a Korean girl? Do mixed marriages work?
6. Are there fundamental sex differences other than physical differences?
7. What are the common defense mechanisms which we all use. Is there such a thing as *good use* of them?

8. What causes alcoholism, homosexuality, be-bopism and other behavior of which society disapproves? How rigidly should a person conform to conventions?

9. What are the relative values of the three parts of intelligence: abstract, motor and social? If you could have only one, which do you think would be most useful in your life?

10. What is a well-balanced life? Can a person make successful adjustments without certain segments: work, recreation, love, worship?

11. What is "maturity"? Why do some experts say that very few people gain complete maturity during a lifetime?

12. Which do you consider the most important basic drive: to live, to love, to belong, to gain recognition? What values form the basis of your lifetime goal?

13. Is it possible for a person to be honest in our American culture? Do you think of yourself as "a person of integrity"? How do we define this term?

14. Are success and happiness within the reach of everyone, or do heredity, environment, circumstances and luck have a lot to do with it?

15. When should parental control cease? Is there a certain age or point in one's life when independence from father or mother is attained?

16. Is there a duty to love one's mother, father, brothers and sisters because of blood ties? Is there something wrong with a person who really dislikes a member of his family?

ADDITIONAL TOPICS

. . . .

. . . .

. . . .

. . . .

. . . .

Often a participant will add a topic at the bottom of the sheet concerned with sex or religion because these subjects are a source of conflict and confusion to many who seek counseling help.

Inclusion of topics to form a well-rounded survey of personal growth and adjustment factors is the leader's responsibility. This may be done even when one subject, for example, "maturity," is discussed for twelve sessions or a whole project: the skilled leader will steer discussions into related areas which give breadth and depth of learning. The following outline was often used as a framework for discussion coverage by the writer:

Basic drives and emotions
The maturity concept
Individual differences
Sex differences, mores, education
A well-balanced life: personal philosophy, values, goals
Adjustive techniques: defense mechanisms, mental health and illness
Pet gripes: feelings of hostility, prejudices, etc.

5. *Auxiliary activities and counseling devices*

Selection of auxiliary activities include personality inventories and self-appraisals; sociograms; role-playing. Since free discussion is the primary activity, any of the above are subordinated to it. However, any device which meets the interest-needs of the group without being too expensive or time consuming is a counseling aid. With the exception of role-playing the auxiliary activities should be used as outside assignments and results of inventories or sociograms are seldom, if ever, discussed in group meetings.

In general, adolescents enjoy self-evaluation through objective inventories. On the other hand, psychiatric patients and adults prefer discussion of their personal adjustment problems. Thus role-playing is a more suitable activity in these groups.

Auxiliary activities cannot be planned far in advance. Within the same age-grouping wide differences in interests and needs of participants will emerge in two group projects. Thus the leader must be prepared for anything — he should have tests, self-appraisal devices, sociograms and role-playing ideas in readiness when the group project requires them.

6. *The leader's role*

The leader must be versatile: as a counselor and discussion leader he must be able to shift from nondirective to directive techniques as the situation demands. Often an intimate group resembles a family group and participants identify the leader with a parent. Sometimes a participant compares the leader with a teacher, or an adult whom he dislikes. If the leader maintains an objective, impartial, friendly-to-all role in group meetings the reactions of group members toward him will stabilize in time: rapport with each member will strengthen through the group experience together. The leader does not try to disguise what he really is — a teacher, social worker, guidance director, probation officer — but his *counselor* role is predominant at all times during the group project. It is impossible in this method for the leader to assume the neutral, anonymous role of group therapist as described by Slavson, Hinckley, Gorlow and others.

7. *Observations and records*

Since the behavior of individuals in group sessions may have significance in the counseling process, detailed observations are important. An anecdotal report of each session includes individual contributions to discussions as well as behavior descriptions of the participants. The leader can train himself as an observer without taking any notes during a session so that he remembers the discussion and behavior of individual members long enough to jot down full notes immediately after the session. From these notes he can reconstruct the session in a detailed anecdotal form at his leisure. An example of the report sent to the attending psychiatrists describes the twentieth session for six mental patients (appendix, group 15):

Date:

Present: H, G, A, Lu, Lo, D

Topic: Self-understanding: "Do you feel ready to go back home: if not, why not?"

Structure: Exchange of viewpoints, description of attitudes and feelings; case conference questioning of *Lo* and *H.*

Content:

1. *How do you feel? A, Lo, D* gave detailed accounts.
2. Review of research study on Happiness by *HD* (leader). Q to group: What do you think you have learned from this discussion group? All thought they understood themselves better, especially mental illness, and the differences among group members.
3. *Lo* gave account of problems facing her: planning with help of social worker and Judge; decision not to go home for week-ends; attempts to contact lawyer re divorce. The group supported her especially in her resolve to cut all contacts with the tavern crowd and her husband.
4. *A* took the floor and discussed her plans. She must decide whether to move in with her father or try to maintain her children in their home. She expressed strong feeling "to get on my own, not to have to take money from the State." She was discouraged and not ready to cope with her problems. She was worried about relationships with her father and her opposing the social worker in planning — she disliked the social worker heartily.

68

5. *H* was questioned by *HD* and the group — did she want to go home, did she feel ready? She said her dad had visited her last Sunday and thought she seemed fine. She felt preoccupied with worry about her children; was very unhappy and wanted to go home. Yet she hesitated in saying she felt well enough to face the problems there. The group urged her to make an appointment with her psychiatrist to talk things over. She didn't seem to want to do this, appeared to be afraid. *HD* encouraged her and asked her to report on the interview next meeting.

Behavior descriptions:

Lo: Very serious as contrasted with her usual jolly manner. Attempted to reason out problems, plan actions. Anticipated a fight with her family, was worried about it.

D: Physically sick, very depressed. Said she was not sure she could keep down her lunch. At end of meeting she said she felt better.

A: Said she felt very tense, depressed. However, her speech and reactions seemed faster than in previous meetings. Her logic and interactions were good although she did not participate as actively as in many sessions. She complained of an eye twitch which came on when she had inner tensions.

Lu: Very quiet. Listened intently throughout the session but did not contribute. *HD* walked to her building with her. She seemed happy, fed squirrels, enjoyed the fine weather.

G: In good spirits as usual. Expects to leave soon. Many friendly interactions and support of others. Showed good empathy.

H: Had difficulty answering questions: seemed to block, looking intently at questioner without responding. She was quick to defend her husband for not coming to visit her — said he was too busy. She emphasized her one desire — to get back to her children as soon as possible.

The anecdotal report may contain valuable facts related to the condition or progress of a patient which are not known by the psychiatrist. Through the descriptive reports of sessions held two or three times a week he can plan interviews or chats with the patients with greater efficacy.

When the leader is the only counselor for group members, a logbook of session descriptions which notes discussion procedures on the left page and behavior descriptions with verbal contributions on the right page is the most practical record. A selection of verbal content from individual participants must be made; when case histories are well known to the leader he can judge the significance of a participant's contributions. It is a good idea to keep the same order of participants for successive write-ups so that the pages can be flicked through to collect data for each individual quickly at any time during the project. Counseling interviews are aided by a rapid review of the participant's performance in group sessions just prior to the conference. An example of pages from the writer's logbook for a college project follows:

Log Book: Left-hand page
6TH SESSION

Topic: Defense Mechanisms
Present: Six — Do, Dd, Da, Ma, Jo, El
Structure: Free discussion with *HD* as observer-participant.
Materials: Chart with illustrations of defensive behavior — 7 copies.
Content: Discussion points:

1. GP q'd whether *Dms* always imply unawareness.
2. Be-boppers etc., occur only in large cities, based on desire for recognition and belonging.
3. Racial discrimination is based on cultural fear of Negro domination in the South.
4. Identification with a group implies group loyalties, thus group prejudices.
5. Aim of society is to make people identify with world community rather than nationalistic or racial groups.
6. Sometimes the most devout church groups are the most bigoted.
7. Perhaps one's individualistic religious concepts are preferable to a group identification.
8. Wars result from fear and need for living space (survival urge).
9. Individual gets satisfaction for urge to be outstanding, superior to others, or desire for power, through various activities.
10. Women want to be dominated by men. They want to feel the man is more powerful.

The group was asked what topic they wanted for final session, since they had covered all topics receiving four and five votes. They decided on "Religion and its place in a well-adjusted life pattern."

HD gave out typed sheets, "Criteria of College Success" and suggested the group evaluate themselves in terms of progress toward the implied goals.

Leader comment: Excellent interactions and dynamics, with all participants active.

Although *HD* took role of observer-participant, the group continued teacher-pupil relationship.

Log Book: Right-hand page

6TH SESSION — BEHAVIOR DESCRIPTIONS

Activity Rank

Jo 1 (*Very aggressive, logical, provocative. Took over leadership*).
Believes women want men to dominate them.
Is sure *Dms* can be conscious, knows when she is about to use them.
Criticized Catholics. Very prejudiced. Says her brother is a good atheist.
Enthusiastic for a debate: Humanism *vs.* Religion.
Asked about identification of girl with mother, competing for father's love.
Believes society must build for identif. of indiv. with world community.
Does not believe in Negro-white marriages, but would dance with and kiss a Negro.

Do 4 (*Unable to express his ideas clearly. Tended to get off on vague plane which others could not understand. Looked pale, strained, tense, unhappy*).
Believes all so-called instincts are learned.
Repeated belief in the instinct for destruction. Again emphasized importance of Religion.
Couldn't think of any way he would like to get a feeling of power, then said he did enjoy having people come to him for advice.
Agreed with *HD* that perhaps creative dance group would be enjoyable — he would like to do "Frustration," could do an outstanding job of it.
Does not think we have "classes" in our Society. (Jo told him he was crazy).

Da 2 (*Self-assured, ready to speak up in agreement, disagreement, add new ideas*).
He is against Religion, gave example of Irish Catholics on his street not letting Italian Catholics buy houses in that section: bigotry, etc.
Argued for instinctive behavior as basic motivation, insisted that fighting and wars are inevitable.
Anxious to have a debate on "Humanism *vs.* Religion."
Admits he gets much satisfaction from successful competition in exams, and in verbal duels. Wants to be a lawyer.

Ma 3 (*Supportive as well as argumentative, but continues to be impersonal*).
Believes tolerance comes easier to one who does not belong to a church.
Described be-boppers in her city, analyzed their behavior in terms of desire for recognition and belonging.
She gets satisfaction from making people laugh, turning a phrase, verbal dueling.
She hopes to be a writer and to get recognition and superior feeling from it.

El 5 (*Silent during all discussion on Religion, yet her father is a minister. She was willing to vote for discussion on Religion next time, however*).
All her contributions were references to Anthro and Sociology courses which she has had or is taking. Gave good examples of identification, behavior causes, reasons for racial prejudices, etc.

71

Dd 6 (*Very much upset because of receiving notice of physical exam date for AF*).
Related family conflict which also upsets him: mother is doing too much, getting overtired. Father doesn't help her enough, etc.
Couldn't think of way he'd like to get feeling of power, except to have his sister do what he tells her to do.
Agreed that Religion is essential to well-balanced life. Feels strongly in favor of religious affiliation, blames ills of world on lack of Religion.
Told of his fear of being drafted. He can't stand explosions, even fire-crackers.

Note: The reader cannot know the significance of the performances of these participants in this session without the record of the previous sessions, the case histories, and concommitant counseling. The discussion content may sound like "intellectualization" but this session was a useful part of the counseling process for five of the six members. For example, *Do* was rapidly approaching a breakdown which was to necessitate his dropping out of college. He had resisted a psychiatric referral, but the group experience showed him the contrast between himself and the others, thus facilitating the shift to psychiatric treatment.

In addition to the log-book the leader keeps a careful record of all individual talks and interviews with participants. Likewise pertinent data from background, scholastic, and health information is recorded in the case folder. Sometimes a test score can give the clue which aids the counseling process. For example, E was a college sophomore with high scholastic aptitude and failing grades. Although he did what he could to improve his academic performance (a course in Reading and Study skills, psychiatric counseling, group therapy) he was unsuccessful and flunked out of college. A series of deviate profiles on the Minnesota Multiphasic Personality Inventory hinted at the need of this student for extensive psychiatric treatment before he could direct his energies into effective academic work. Thus sometimes counseling emphasis must be the preparation of a person for meeting failure in his chosen goal and planning for constructive alternative actions.

A summary of each case can be capsulated in the form of a psychograph. An example of such a record, devised by the author in multiple counseling projects for high school and college students, is given in chart form.

Leader-counselors who are not trained in psychometrics and interpretation of psychological tests should not attempt to use these devices in multiple counseling projects. Often, however, the coöperation of school, college, or institution psychologists can be secured in cases where psychological tests are indicated. In this event, the psychologist does the testing and test interpretations. These private records remain in his files and are not included in the psychographs or counseling program of the lay-leader. The psychologist should discuss the test results with the leader and advise him concerning handling of the case. When a test interpretation interview with a participant is desirable, the psychologist makes an appointment with the testee for this interview. If psychological counseling is needed, the psychologist becomes a cojunctive counselor in the group project; the leader limits his counseling to performance and personal relationships within the group, discussion content, vocational guidance or social skill training.

Facts, test and sociogram results, observations, etc., are confidential information to be kept in locked files. As a counselor the group leader does not divulge anything to a group member concerning himself or another group member without good reason. For example, a maladjusted, insecure member who rated lowest on all scales of a sociogram (leadership, brain power, sense of humor, attractiveness, desirability as a friend) need not be subjected to a painful analysis of the sociogram outcome. Confidential information given to a participant is reserved for a counseling interview and is never mentioned in a group meeting. When sociogram results are good and a participant needs ego-bolstering, the counselor is glad to discuss his ratings with him.

A good policy in giving out information from the participant's case folder is to use it to substantiate the client's self-concept or opinion of his ratings and behavior in the group project. Thus in a summary interview the participant says, "I felt happy in the group. I think they liked and respected me." The leader may be able to substantiate this fact from his observation notes, comments made by other participants, and sociogram ratings. Likewise, when a participant is dissatisfied with his performance and relationships in the group, counseling may bring out reasons for his behavior and help him to change unpleasant mannerisms, etc. (Chap. XI).

8. *Evaluation of outcomes*
   Three measures of the learning gained through a multiple counseling project are used:
      a. The participant's own idea of what he has learned: ways in which his self-concept, attitudes and behavior patterns have changed (see Chapters VIII, XII).

b. The leader's observations and interpretations of behavior changes which show evidence of group project influence.

c. Factual data which substantiates (a) and (b). This includes reports from attending counselors, psychiatrists, teachers, parents, friends, etc. A follow-up interview, questionnaire, or communication should be used whenever possible to test the permanency of the learning.

Suggestions are often given by group members regarding improvements in project design. This is helpful to the leader in understanding and counseling the participant. Often the suggestions are pertinent and well-thought-out so they can be used to avoid errors in structuring future projects. For instance, when the majority of a group think the leader talked too much in discussion sessions, or that there was too much role-playing, the criticism is no doubt justified. Although another group might react differently to the same amount of leader-talk or role-playing, the leader must learn to be sensitive to group reactions while they are taking place: a majority criticism of a project is a valid evaluation of leadership skill, or lack of it.

SUMMARY

This chapter has outlined procedures in carrying out a multiple counseling project. Included were selection of group members; arrangements for meetings; planning group structure, approach, and topics; preparation of auxiliary activities; the leader's role as counselor; examples of records and evaluations. Enlargement and illustrations of these procedures appear in later chapters. Emphasis on flexibility and adaptability of procedures to fit group needs is continued throughout the book.

PSYCHOGRAPH H.S. SENIOR PROJECT (group 1)

	Status at Beginning of Project	[Status at End] of Project
Aim of Student	Interested in discussion. Likes to talk and argue.	
Appearance Impression Manner, Etc.	Rather fat, sissified, poorly groomed. Self-assured, poised, outgoing.	impression re…
Group Reaction to Him	Accepted as leader in the discussions.	…the part of the …decreasing.
His Role in Group	Assumed leadership. Spoke with assurance on all points discussed.	…ominate group …the group's re…
Participation Quantity Quality	An active, eager participant. Made forceful contributions, using personal references with great frankness. Spoke with ease and fluency.	…opularity. …s opinions.
Biographical Background Family, School, Etc.	Unhappy childhood, filled with conflicts in the home. Claims to hate father, whom mother has divorced. Says father is "crazy hypochondriac." Has worked at many jobs, says "I have always had to work as far back as I can remember." Scholastic aptitude tests and grades show college caliber.	…rced parents. …a girl. Said
Occupation Aim Strong I.I.	Plans to attend University and train for math teaching. Strong I.I. Shows "A" in R. E. Salesman, Sales Mgr.; "B+" in Purchasing Agent, Pharmacist, Business, Life Insurance, Advertising.	…led to see the …at math and …ning shoes to
MMPI Self-Ratings	MMP I shows deviate profiles: HS 70, PT 80; MF 89; PA 70; D 82; PD 70; SC 88. MMP I shows discrepancies with self-ratings. MMP I shows higher PT, D,PD. MMP I shows lower MA, SI.	…im when she …pleased when
Temperament Introv., Extrov. Maps Test	Appears outgoing, talks a great deal. Opinions and ideas seem to have background in introspection. Maps score within normal limits. Themes: Personal, family, fiction. Mood: Depressed.	…ter trying to …op: Showed …r feeling for …contributions
Personal Strengths Weaknesses	STRENGTHS: Above average intelligence, ability and desire to "talk out" his problems — to be social, popular, have friends. WEAKNESSES: Anxiety, conflicts, fears associated with father; dislikes all relatives except mother. Depression in childhood remembrances.	…opolized the …to express.

Evaluation Statements of Student at End of Project

Self-Understanding

Knowledge:
(Insight): "I understand my weaknesses… when I see some others do some things I do… It looks corny… Then you figure yourself out that way and change."
(Tests): "Help you get a better view of the situation… Analysis showed different problems that had never occurred to you before."
"I'm puzzled about myself, can't see why I react way I do… Got to understand myself to understand others… must have self to compare others with… only practical standard is self."

Attitudes:
"Blowing off steam helps… I enjoyed arguments too… I'm pretty good at arguing, always have been."
(Sociodrama): "I don't think it is any good. Don't see how kids can act roles convincingly… they're the same kinds."
(Discussion topics): "I liked 'Why we liked or dislike a person.' I got nothing from discussion of defense mechanisms… understand them but am not interested. It was all said before in a different way."

Skill (Behavior):
"I can control my temper more."

Understanding of Others

Knowledge:
"Getting other people's point of view is helpful."
"Most helpful meetings were those on racial and religious prejudice."

Attitudes:
"I think there will be a carry-over in tolerance on religious problems."
"I now have a different way of looking at people… It should help tolerance."
"At present I am more intolerant, I pick up more faults in people in analyzing them… see why they act… makes me intolerant."

Skill (Behavior):
"I understand and like the teachers better… Sit and think why they act as they do… I don't blow off right away like I used to."
"I understand and like some of the group members better. The two I couldn't figure out I dislike more."
"I should watch what I say when I'm talking to other people."

Student's Statements in Follow-Up Interview

Answered YES to 5 of 6 statements regarding awareness of own strengths and weaknesses through the Project experience.
(Believed he had improved one weakness… he was trying hard not to talk so much.)

Answered YES to 5 of 7 statements regarding improved attitudes, enjoyment of discussion project, desire to improve interpersonal skills.
"I think there should be a year course in this — in the sophomore year so you'd have time to improve. As it is, it's too late. After the course is over you could step back and see, think over what was discussed and learned. Senior year is too late to start finding out about personality weaknesses." "I want to improve. My biggest worry is what people think of me."

Answered YES to 3 of 6 statements concerned with improvement of weaknesses, broadened viewpoints.
Answered YES to 4 of 5 statements regarding own efforts to improve interpersonal skills.
"I don't talk so much. That way you can see better what others think of you."
"In speech class they think I am more rational… I haven't talked so much… Try to say more in fewer words."

Answered YES to 5 of 6 statements regarding better understanding of behavior causes among group members, friends, family.
"I don't think I understand others better… I was and am too busy trying to understand myself."

Rejected statements concerned with improved attitudes and other evidence of understanding others. ("Had good understanding before the Project.")
"I don't think I have changed any… Have always understood why kids can't be trusted. For instance, look at the party I gave. Kids have never learned how to behave… Parents never trusted them."

Rejected statements concerned with improvement as to racial, religious, political prejudices. (Said they didn't apply since he did not have prejudices.)
"Much improved with friends. I always thought the teachers were trying to help… I get invited to lots of parties now… It's hard to come to a new high school in your senior year… That's why I gave the parties, to break into gangs I wanted to go with… It worked too. Now kids speak to me in the halls — never did before."
"Thought I wanted to be a teacher… help people. Now maybe sales work is right thing for me."

Counselor's Summary of Observations and Interviews

OBSERVATIONS: First impression was of a fat, sissified, poorly groomed boy who was very talkative. He assumed leadership in discussion despite the fact that the seven girl members made fun of him.

During the nine weeks he continued to monopolize the discussion time. He gave wordy speeches that didn't make sense to the others or brought disagreement with his viewpoint. He tried to flirt and show off but seemed unaware of his growing unpopularity.

Final impression was the same. He maintained a dominant place in the discussions due to his facile expression and eagerness to give his ideas. He failed to gain respect from the group. He did not improve in logic or ability to express himself concisely.

FIRST INTERVIEW: (At end of Project): He was very enthusiastic about the Project and believed he had gained in self-understanding. He failed to see any improvement of his understanding of others because "he was so busy thinking about himself." There were contradictions throughout his evaluation.

He maintained that his attitude toward members of his family remained the same — he didn't understand them and never would.

He was totally unaware of his unpopularity in the group. Had believed he was the best participant.

Test and observation results were given him in so far as they might aid his understanding of personality weaknesses which he was eager to overcome: (1) Depressed outlook and habit of daydreaming; (2) Extreme self-consciousness; (3) Lack of sensitivity in interpersonal relations. Researcher tried to suggest ways he might work on personality development.

FOLLOW-UP INTERVIEW (3 months later): He reported progress in efforts to overcome his weaknesses. He had been able to control his "talk-too-much" impulses. He had been complimented in speech class for more effective expression. The researcher reinforced this by telling him of the favorable comments of a member of the discussion group who sits next to him in home room.

He still believed he was super-selfconscious but was now able to "step back and observe other people and their reactions to me."

He hopes to go to the University next year and to be deferred indefinitely from military service by ranking in the upper half of his class. The researcher doubted his chances of doing this at the University but agreed he could probably get in one year of college. He thinks that sales or store work will be his ultimate goal, rather than teaching.

The researcher asked him if he would like to re-take the MMPI to see if favorable changes in his personality development would show. He agreed and a tentative date was set for the test.

FINAL INTERVIEW (3 weeks later): The researcher was glad to report to him that the MMPI scores indicated marked improvement in his self and social adjustments. He gave instances of behavior changes to substantiate this.

He has decided to get away from home next year, go to Milwaukee and work his way through Teacher's College there. The researcher complimented him on his decision, based on his view that he would be able to study harder if he was on his own, since his home is overcrowded. (His seeking separation from his mother seemed laudable but this was not discussed.)

EVALUATION OF PROJECT INFLUENCES: It would seem that the project experience at an important time in this student's life, was helpful in his personality development. Though his stated aims did not include a felt need for help in self and social adjustments, he showed through statements made in discussions and interviews that he had feelings of depression, worry, and insecurity. Though he had not indicated vocational guidance as his need, he appears to have gained constructive help in this area. Behavior change directly influenced by project experience is indicated in the areas of:

1. Better self-understanding, recognition of weaknesses and desire to overcome them.
2. Improved attitude of facing reality and basing vocational goal on sound qualifications in line with work experience, aptitudes, and interests.
3. Improvement in interpersonal skills — sensitivity to others, controlling impulse to show off through verbal expression, better skill in self-expression, getting along better with others.

Although the desire to break close attachment to mother, translated into plan to go away from home and work way through college, cannot show evidence of Project influence, the reinforcement given him by the researcher may help his resolution to carry out his plan.

IV

EFFECTIVE PARTICIPATION IN SMALL-GROUP DISCUSSION AND ROLE-PLAYING

THE BEST PREPARATION FOR LEADING DISCUSSIONS in a personal growth project is first to participate as a group member in one. Just as a golf pro or drama director gains our confidence because of their former experience as a skilled performer in the activity, so the effective discussion leader has skill based on experience as a participant in the activity.

In a country such as ours, free discussions — "speaking one's piece" — in town meetings, school classrooms and PTA's, labor and fraternal organizations, women's clubs and political groups, should be a frequent and popular activity from childhood to old age. Theoretically any American who has gone through the public schools and held membership in community groups has a rich background of discussion group experience. In actuality many of our citizens lack this experience: they have not participated as members of either planning or free-discussion groups. For example, health and welfare agencies such as Red Cross, Scouts, hospital auxiliaries, find that a small percentage of a community population "do all the work": the same civic-minded people are found on the rolls of volunteer workers for many organizations. The majority of citizens do not participate in any community group except for their church memberships and far less than half of these can be called truly active in their churches. In surveying group memberships in school and college organizations the same facts are shown: a small percentage of students are active in many organizations while the majority remain disinterested in anything but spectator participation. For example, among the twenty high school seniors who took part in multiple counseling projects under the direction of the author, less than half had participated in free discussion activity since elementary school days. Only five had served on planning committees or in official capacities in school groups. These five were the only group members who had any concept of "free discussion" techniques.

Even though prospective leaders have had extensive experience in planning-groups, the free discussion activity in a personal growth project may be a new experience. The dynamics of free discussions focussed on exchange of opinions and personal experiences differ greatly from the dynamics of a problem-solving group. The inductive method is used: there are no definite aims and objectives either for the group or the individuals in the group other than *to gain in understanding and acceptance of oneself and others.* Countless types of knowledges, attitudes and skills might be included in this aim, but they vary so greatly from one individual to another that classification is nigh impossible. The participant learns whatever he is ready to learn, if he needs the learning and wants it.

Thus individuals in a personal growth project draw conclusions from the free discussions for themselves as individuals — they are not forced into majority-minority opinions or group conclusions. Understanding of individual differences within the group itself is significant learning. The group climate encourages creative discussion and stimulates new ideas. When a new perspective of oneself is gained, important insights may result. Fresh viewpoints, greater tolerance of others, and improved communicative and social skill are available for those who wish to have them. Personal growth is possible for participants of any age or maturity-level: the experience in the intimate group can stimulate a change to healthier attitudes and relationships in the case of other people and groups. An illustration of this is taken from a high school group where griping and resentment against several teachers was frequently expressed in early sessions. At the beginning of a session the leader said, "Today we'll discuss your idea of a good teacher as well as what you consider makes a bad teacher. You can use examples from this school — everything you say is completely confidential. Several of you are considering teaching as a vocation, so let's start with Harry: 'what's the difference between a good and a poor teacher'?" The discussion lasted forty minutes; all nine group members contributed their ideas and made very frank references to teachers in the school whom they liked or disliked. Without leader influence the group worked themselves around to a much more tolerant attitude toward their teachers. One striking feature of the discussion was the individual differences among group members: some defended teachers who were violently criticized by others. Another example of beneficial discussion activity has been carried on in teacher groups in the school system. A school psychiatrist is the group leader: teachers have the chance to ventilate their feelings about school administrators, policies, and pupils as well as to get help in personal adjustment problems.

In preparing for membership in a personal growth project where responsibility for discussion content and learning is placed entirely upon the group members a participant should try to take the following attitudes:

1. I want help from others and I am ready to learn from others. Their opinions and viewpoints will give a perspective which I alone don't have.

2. I will try to do for others in the group what I want them to do for me. I will guard against self-centered thinking and will try to put myself in the place of others when they are speaking.

3. I will try to be frank and honest — not to put up a front. If I feel bitter or irritated I will say so and explain the reasons. If I am asked for a frank opinion I will give it. Since everyone in the group is trying to understand himself and others better, it is important to relax and be oneself.

4. I will try to be sensitive to the way other group members feel. When support or reassurance is needed by someone I will try to give it in all sincerity.

5. If a discussion or person's actions upsets me I will see the group leader about this. Also I will discuss personal things with him which I can't bring myself to discuss in the group.

The participant can analyze his behavior pattern in discussion groups through the following questions:

1. Do I usually sit back and listen to a discussion, or do I tend to talk too much?

2. Do I usually think my ideas are superior to those of others, and close my mind to an opposite point of view?

3. Do I tend to make snap judgments of people: generalize from a particular instance; use guilt by association?

4. Do I feel a responsibility for filling in silences or for steering the discussion. Does it bother me when the group wanders away from the point of the discussion?

5. What are my personal biases? Can I be objective in political, religious, and other controversial discussions?

6. Are there some topics on which I "clam up" — for instance, sex, family relationships? Why do I have these painful or tender areas — should I ask the group leader for advice concerning my participation in such discussions?

The new participant must try to practice spontaneity in the group sessions. Spontaneity means "full response, adequately given, in the situation" (5). It implies complete concentration on *the moment* and the best possible reaction — one person to another — in that moment. Spontaneity takes into consideration individual differences, so that one person might react by disagreeing with the speaker; another person might give enthusiastic support; a third responder might sit quietly, thinking over what was said. An example follows:

Arlene presented her own case to the group for advice and suggestions. She had left home and supported herself since she was eighteen, working her way through two years of college. She had attempted suicide during her last year of high school because of a deep depression caused by the conflict with her mother. She hated both parents, would not answer their letters or accept money from them. She explained reasons for her feelings and actions and asked the group to give opinions as to whether she had done right.

The majority of the group supported Arlene, saying they would have left home as she had done. Edgar, however, said nothing until the others were finished, then he questioned, "Arlene, do you suppose all the fault was on your parents' side — or is it possible that you were at fault, too?" Arlene looked surprised, hesitated, and then replied, "Yes, I think you have something there, but I've never been willing to really look at myself critically."

In this illustration all the group members showed good spontaneity in their reactions. Arlene was courageous to go through with her self-revelation. She had never told anyone except a psychiatrist about the suicide attempt. The extreme bitterness with which she regarded her parents, especially her mother, was so frankly described as to shock the group. The response of the majority was a natural one — sympathy and support. However, Edgar saw that a distorted view of ogre-like parents had been given; a question of Arlene's own behavior was needed in order to improve her perspective of her parents and self.

Spontaneity is not possible when a participant is inhibited and constricted by his own self-interests. When he is so self-conscious that he habitually reacts in terms of himself, he cannot engage in spontaneous interactions with others. Undivided attention and concentration on the discussion content and the participants will help him. It may take many sessions to free him from old habits of inward thinking, to replace them with empathetic reactions and spontaneous responses to others in the group. Of course the trained personnel worker or counselor has gained this skill in interviewing clients. But when the professional person changes his role to that of a client in a personal growth project he will find that the interviewing skill may not carry over: at first he may be a self-conscious, self-centered, inept participant. New skills must be learned in his new role, but his empathetic capacity should speed the process.

The participant may ask, "What if my spontaneous reactions to a person are negative — I am irritated and feel hostile toward him?" Since one of the purposes of the group is to provide an opportunity for griping, sounding off, and arguing, this participant achieves good spontaneity by doing so. It is healthy to get all feelings of irritation out in the open: to lay the cards on the table (3). The negativistic participant can be assured by the group leader that the situation will be controlled and not allowed to go farther than is good for the group as a whole. An extreme example of "name-calling" is taken from a high school project (group 1):

The group was made up of three boys and seven girls, all of whom might be called maladjusted. The leader was a woman counselor assisted by a male graduate student. The first five sessions consisted of name-calling, arguments, insults and interruptions without much respect for the leaders. However, the air finally cleared of aggressiveness and hostility; the group settled down to excellent discussions. They learned to accept each other and the leaders; to control impulses for interruptions; to develop more tolerant attitudes toward each other, their teachers, and their parents. Thus when the seventeenth session concluded the project, behavior changes had already taken effect, showing improved adjustments both in school and at home.

Especially for the training of prospective leaders an objective method of behavior-analysis in groups aids self-evaluation. By comparing his own performance in a discussion group with the other members a leader-trainee learns much about himself. A group dynamics chart adapted from the Bales Interaction Process Analysis (1) proved to be a practical, effective performance recorder in discussion projects of the learning laboratory for Educational Psychology courses at the University of Wisconsin. An observer can classify and record the interactions of several participants in a group discussion by use of the following chart:

OBSERVATION OF BEHAVIOR IN SMALL GROUP DISCUSSION
(Adapted from Bales Interaction Process Analysis)

ROLES	PARTICIPANTS							
	1	2	3	4	5	6	7	8

Positive Reactions
1. Shows solidarity, raises others' status, gives help....

2. Shows tension release, jokes, laughs, shows satisfaction.

3. Agrees, shows passive acceptance, understands, complies..

Attempted Answers
4. Gives suggestions, directions, implying delegated action..

5. Gives opinion, evaluation, expresses feeling, wish....

6. Gives orientation, information, repeats, confirms, clarifies..

Questions
7. Asks for orientation, information, repetition, confirmation..

8. Asks for opinion, evaluation, analysis, expression of feeling..

9. Asks for suggestion, direction, possible ways of action.

Negative Reactions
10. Disagrees, shows passive rejection, formality, withholds help..

11. Shows tension, asks for help, withdraws............

12. Shows antagonism, deflates others, defends or asserts self..

Summarize the behavior of the participants you observed in the following:
Positive Reactions.................................

Attempted Answers.................................

Questions...

Negative Reactions.................................

Non-participation.................................

Give a qualitative estimate of the behavior of the participants: Leader (L); Aggressive (AG); Submissive (Sub); Non-contributor (NC).................................

Illustrations of verbal responses which are checked in the twelve categories are:

1. *Positive reactions*
   a. "I think you expressed that idea very well. Also it's true of other cultures besides ours, according to two books I've read."
   b. "This coke hits the spot — it's just what I needed. You know, I look forward all week to these meetings — I think they are swell."
   c. "I understand what you mean — I feel the same way."

2. *Attempted answers*
   a. "Let's go back to the question — what is the difference between love and infatuation?"
   b. "I feel lost — won't you enlarge on that, John. Do you mean you believe that different races should never inter-marry?"
   c. "I read an article that said 10% of the population are mentally ill."

3. *Questions*
   a. "Does anyone know exactly what projection means — can you give me an example?"
   b. "Jean, how do you feel about petting — do you believe in it or not?"
   c. "Mr. Smith, what do you think we should talk about today?"

4. *Negative reactions*
   a. "You have a right to your opinion, but I think it's cock-eyed."
   b. "For heaven's sake, let's talk about something we're *all* interested in!"
   c. "I know more about this than you do — I've worked in factories. Let me tell you the facts — not just theories like you're talking."

In addition to the interactive pattern of the participant, the leader's observations and comments of fellow members in critical evaluations of each other at the end of a group project can help a person "to see himself as others see him." In the case of a leader-trainee the insight and resulting struggle to overcome personal weaknesses and to learn interpersonal skills are of paramount importance.

Effective discussion techniques

Participation in discussion sessions of a multiple counseling project can be analyzed as: (1) social interactions, (2) group dynamics, (3) discussion content. Suggestions for the new participant follow:

1. *Social interactions*
   a. Interest in others is shown by casual conversation, offering a cigarette, etc.; walking along with others to and from meetings; offering information and assistance to others.

2. *Group dynamics*
   a. A member should vary his participation in the discussion according to the needs of the group. If several are talkative he may take the role of listener; if no one has anything to say, he may take an active role, attempting to stimulate discussion and draw out the other members.
   b. The participant should be sensitive to the group atmosphere: if a joke or light touch is needed to relieve tension, he may try to supply it; if he senses that the majority of the group are dissatisfied with the facetiousness of the meeting, he may try to inject a more serious note.
   c. When a group member needs support or reassurance, the sensitive participant gives it through agreements, enlarging or clarifying an idea, questioning, or drawing out the shy member in his special interest field. Arguing on the side of a member who is being "pushed around" is good support, of course.
   d. When one member is very monopolistic, the skilled participant may steer the discussion away from that member through evasive or direct tactics.

3. *Discussion content*
   a. A topic for discussion may be introduced by a participant, but if the group is not interested in it, the participant should drop it and ask for suggestions from others.
   b. Provocative questions which can stimulate discussion should be thought up and presented at a time when depth and emphasis are needed. The skilled participant is able to argue on either side of a question, keeping his personal bias hidden if the discussion would be improved without it.

c. When a topic has been assigned and the participant has developed several points he wishes to make, he should try to hold back after contributing one of them. Thus other group members have a chance to contribute and he to react to their ideas instead of sticking rigidly to his preconceived ideas.

d. If the discussion is desultory and superficial in spite of the participant's efforts to "get it going," he can turn to the group leader for suggestions.

note: The above suggestions for participation apply to the group leader when he takes the role of "observer-participant" in a group which needs some steering. In reference to (*d*), the leader changes his role to more active control in this situation, often introducing an entirely new topic.

Role-playing

A participant gains the most from a multiple counseling project if he is willing to take part in extemporaneous or planned role-playing activities. Since role-playing is usually unrehearsed and never has set dialogue, the participant is expected to react naturally to the other players or to the situation in which he is placed. However he acts, his performance will contribute in one way or another to the group discussion which is stimulated by the role-playing episode.

The participant's relationship with the leader

When the leader is also the attending counselor for the participant the relationship between the two is a continuation of the counseling process. If, on the other hand, the leader is a group therapist working under the supervision of the attending counselor, the relationship is of a different nature: it is closer in social levels but more distant in intrapersonal areas. Thus interviews are limited to discussions of the participant's reactions to the project and group members, his behavior in the group, his progress in gaining communicative and social skills. Often, however, the leader serves as liaison between client and counselor, bringing to the attention of the counselor any new behavior manifestations and problem areas appearing in the sessions or interviews.

The participant can be completely frank with the leader and should react spontaneously to him. He may feel hostile, dependent, admiring, or irritated. Through ventilation of these feelings — both toward group members and the leader — he will move toward improved relationships and personal growth as the project progresses.

Summary

Participation in group discussion activity for the sake of learning more about oneself and others is essential background experience for a group leader. Experience in free discussions, either for group planning or for exchange of viewpoints, is lacking in the educational process and adult lives of the majority of our citizens.

Suggestions for effective group membership in personal growth projects were outlined. Especially for the leader-trainee, self-assessment of habits of behavior in a discussion group is important. An observational method which aids self-assessment was presented.

Effective techniques for social interactions, group dynamics, and discussions in group sessions were outlined. These apply to group leaders in observer-participant roles as well.

Role-playing and leader-participant relationships were mentioned only in passing, since these subjects are fully analyzed in later chapters.

PART II

EFFECTIVE LEADERSHIP IN
MULTIPLE COUNSELING PROJECTS

V

THE GROUP LEADER AS A
COUNSELOR

THE GROUP LEADER HAS TWO RESPONSIBILITIES in the group activity: one for meaningful discussions in the group as a whole, the other for aiding individual members to gain significant learning and satisfaction from participation in group sessions. When the group leader is also the attending counselor for the participants he has additional counseling responsibilities to be carried out in private interviews noncommitant with the group project. However, the responsibilities are shared in multiple counseling: participants help each other and the sessions often substitute for individual interviews. While information and guidance provided by the leader in group sessions assist learning processes, the active participation of a group member in discussions, social interactions, and personal relationships, is the vital influence in his personal growth.

To many experienced group leaders the task of leading discussions in a multiple counseling project appears simple compared with leading a problem-solving group. After he introduces the topic of the day he lets the group carry the ball. The less active the leader is, the better. When discussions die, the leader sits quietly by, waiting for a group member to take the responsibility of re-activating it; when group members show hostility toward each other, or a monopolist takes the floor, or the discussion veers off course into a totally different subject — the leader remains inactive. He must say to himself during these trying moments, "This is a group-centered activity. I musn't interfere with the dynamics or take over the responsibility which belongs to the group." He must continually remind himself that learning takes place through an active process — through individual participation and interactions, not through passive listening-to-lecture behavior. He must remember that the emotions have to be involved if real learning is to take place. Thus he forces individual members to feel responsibility for each other and for the group activity by his own passivity. (Cantor describes this process for educational groups in his two books on learning (1, 2)). The experienced group leader, especially if he is a teacher, may find that he, like the old dog, has difficulty learning new tricks — that multiple counseling leadership is not simple at all. However, it can be learned and may even produce new skills for teaching or counseling.

The reader may ask if the above description of leadership implies nondirectiveness in the same sense as nondirective counseling. It is best to think in terms of *degrees* of directivism-nondirectivism. Certainly leadership of multiple counseling contains a higher degree of nondirection than a classroom situation or problem-solving discussions. But a highly skilled discussion leader — just as a leader in a "democratic" project — achieves a group-centered and participant-centered atmosphere. Thus a research project which tested occupational types for effective discussion leadership found that insurance salesmen were the best leaders, and teachers rated lower than dramatic directors. A good salesman lets his clients sell himself; the dramatic coach knows the performance must come from within the heart and mind of his actors. Anyone who has been a teacher knows the tendency to talk too much, to become greatly disturbed when silences occur and when discussions get off the track.

Teachers, social workers, and personnel workers who have formed habits of directive leadership can learn to sit back, to listen and to wait. A technique which is recommended for initial training of multiple counseling leaders consists of the following: first the leader gives an introductory talk, or secures a question of interest from the group. After throwing out a question to start the discussion the leader asks the group to go ahead with a free discussion without a moderator. He then sits back, withdrawing from the group psychologically and physically through busying himself with note-taking or other preoccupations. With inexperienced groups he may need to direct a question or two to members of the group whom he thinks will assume responsibility for leading the discussion. As soon as possible the leader withdraws from the discussion circle, not to return until the end of the time allotted for the session. It is recommended that at least five of a fifteen-session project be given over to leaderless discussions as described above. As the skill of the leader increases he is able to stay in the discussion circle as an observer-participant without undue influence on the group dynamics or interactions among group members.

Whereas counseling functions for academic advisors, personnel counselors, social workers and school guidance directors often have a predominance of "information-dispensing" — according to some sources as high as 90% (4), psychological counseling is just the opposite — the counselor or psychiatrist tends to give the initiative to the client for providing information in the counseling process. A multiple counseling leader fulfills both functions: he provides information in group sessions and in private interviews but he also expects to learn many things from individuals through their participation in discussions and their behavior in the group. Thus multiple counseling uses an eclectic approach: sometimes it is directive — sometimes, nondirective. And both counseling methods are used in a single group project.

An analysis of different degrees of nondirectiveness and directiveness on the part of a counselor is given next. This will serve as a self-appraisal instrument for the leader-counselors who know their own counseling pattern in private interviews but are not sure of their leadership pattern with groups. And for leader-counselors who have not had training in nondirective counseling techniques the analysis may provide enlightenment and possibly reassurance. The following chart gives a basis for comparison of various types of counseling:

(SEE NEXT PAGE)

Eleven Degrees of Nondirective-Directive Responses

(three counseling patterns)

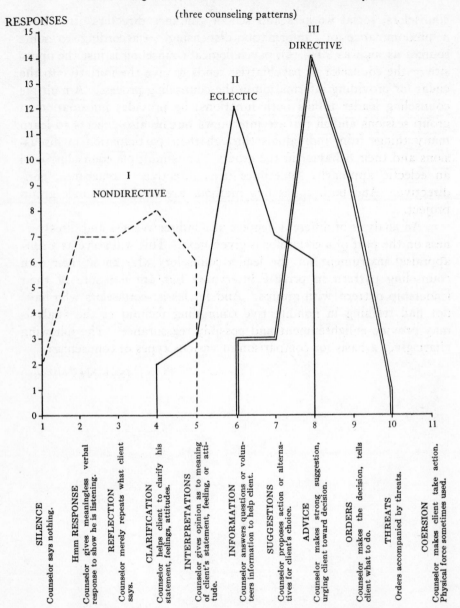

Curve I — Behavior pattern of nondirective counselors and analytic-group therapists.

Curve II — Behavior pattern of eclectic counselors who sometimes use nondirective techniques, sometimes directive, and often a mixture of the two without reaching the extremes.

Curve III — Counseling pattern of physicians, academic advisors, personnel workers whose job analyses show frequent need for directing actions and decisions of clients.

The 30 responses for each type of counselor shown on the preceding chart may be used as a basis for comparison of the leader-counselor's behavior pattern in several counseling interviews and group sessions:

30 RESPONSES OF THE LEADER-COUNSELOR TO CLIENT AND GROUP

	Non-directive	Eclectic	Directive	Self-analysis
1. SILENCE	2			
2. HMM	7			
3. REFLECTION	7			
4. CLARIFICATION	8	2		
5. INTERPRETATION	6	3		
6. INFORMATION		12	3	
7. SUGGESTIONS		7	3	
8. ADVICE		6	14	
9. ORDERS			9	
10. THREATS			1	
11. COERSION				

Recordings of interviews and group sessions provide an accurate, effective means of obtaining the behavior pattern of the counselor or group leader. Much will be learned by the leader-counselor about himself and his counseling habits from play-back and analysis of the recordings.

An illustration of the eleven degrees of nondirective-directive responses which might be made at one point in a counseling interview follows:

The counseling situation: Mrs. G, a widow with one six-year-old boy, has come to a child guidance clinic for help. Johnny is not getting along well in school and his behavior seems abnormal to her both at home and with children in the neighborhood. She has described her worries, continuing as follows:

"Johnny upset me terribly last Tuesday night. We had invited the neighbors over for dinner. He loves that family — all of them — he was delighted they were coming. But the minute they appeared he started insulting them, kicking Mr. S, threatening to spit on Mrs. S. He was so impossible at the dinner table I had to send him to his room. I was so angry with him — if they hadn't been there I think I would have liked to throw him out of the bedroom window. Now I know I shouldn't have felt that way, that I don't understand Johnny, and no mother should feel the way I did. But it seems to me that he is really abnormal — why should he have reacted that way when he loves that family and had looked forward to their coming over? What's wrong with him, and what's wrong with me?"

Response by counselor

1 — Says nothing, cleans and fills his pipe.

2 — Looks out the window, says, "Hmm."

3 — "You say it seems to you that he is really abnormal?"

4 — "Do you think the trouble is more with him or with you, since you both have gone through such a difficult period with the sudden death of your husband?"

5 — "You seem to have a guilty feeling regarding your attitude toward Johnny — getting so angry at him. If this happens frequently perhaps your anger increases Johnny's contrariness."

6 — "There are many possible reasons behind Johnny's acting-up, both at school and at home. Certainly a deep feeling of insecurity is in the picture. Quite possibly, too, he did not feel he was getting as much attention from you and the neighbors as he wanted, so he cut-up to get attention."

7 — "It seems that both you and Johnny are still in an upset condition — the readjustment after your husband's death may take longer than you expected. You can either go along, being as patient as possible with Johnny, letting time heal the wounds and bring the readjustment, or you can start psychotherapy for both you and Johnny now. What do you think?"

8 — "I agree that both you and Johnny need help at this time. We can arrange therapy for you as the mother, and Johnny will be helped through the new child therapy techniques — actually it will seem like play to him."

9 — "There is no doubt about it — this trouble with Johnny has gone on long enough. I want to get you an appointment and one for Johnny too, we'll get this business straightened out as soon as possible. Plan to bring him here once a week for an indefinite length of time — you may have to take him out of school for part of the day. You can start weekly interviews with Dr. J. He will counsel you at the same time that Johnny is having therapy."

10 — "I think the situation is quite serious and that there is definitely something wrong with both you and Johnny. Unless we get this situation straightened out immediately it may affect his whole life — healthy personality growth is most important during the first six years of a child's life. I don't want you to wait one day longer. You fetch Johnny down here and we'll start therapy with both of you today."

11 — "This is very serious — you should have done something about this a year ago. I'm going to see that you and Johnny put your minds on this thing and get squared around immediately. You go get Johnny out of school this minute and come back here with him. And I want you to see me daily from now on as long as it takes to get to the bottom of this conflict situation."

note: In this instance, which was an actual case, the counselor was a non-directivist who used responses 2, 3 and 4. Many eclectic counselors would do likewise in the first interview in order to learn as much as possible about Mrs. G and Johnny from her point of view.

Any counselor of GI's and World War II veterans knows the importance of "letting the client do the talking." Reasons for Rogerian techniques which developed during the last war are apparent: the regimentation of military service — a constant irritant to American youth — makes the GI resent "orders" from anyone. Nondirective counseling is the common sense approach with such a person (3). The same is true of a youth who resents dominating parents. The wise counselor uses nondirective techniques and in so doing, avoids identification with the offending parent in the mind of the client. Such was the case of the rebellious college sophomore (group 6) presented below:

Jerry was referred by the Dean to the counseling center because of academic difficulties. He lived at home and his rebellion against his mother became evident in the first interview. She tried to control his study hours, dates, etc. Although a brilliant student Jerry was flunking out. Weekly conferences and membership in a multiple counseling project gave the client opportunity to ventilate his grievances. There were others in his group who were in similar states of rebellion against their parents. When the home situation worsened the counselor had a conference with Jerry's mother to warn her of his low grades and possibility of being dropped from the college. His rebellion was discussed frankly and she was advised to leave him alone to work out his own personal problems, including his relationship to her.

Jerry received the flunk notice but attended the group session that week. Conferring with the counselor, he decided to appear before the college re-admissions committee to ask for an appeal. The counselor agreed to write a letter stating that an emotional upset had influenced his grades, but she gave him no assurance that he would be re-instated. Jerry spent the time in the interview prior to his hearing rehearsing his speech, but the counselor refused to give suggestions, remaining noncommital regarding his re-entering the college even if the committee granted his request. (Jerry had formerly thought he would like to be drafted, "to get away from it all").

Although none of his group knew he had flunked out, they gave him a lot of attention in the group session the day before he was to appear for the hearing. His performance in the group was outstanding compared with previous sessions: group members considered him very bright and accepted his leadership. This bolstered his self-confidence, and helped his poise at the hearing: he won his case.

During the six-month period of individual and multiple counseling Jerry made good progress in resolving his conflicts with his parents; they were coöperative in changing their handling of him. A more mature relationship was established and the problem of rebellion expressed through unsatisfactory academic work was dissipated.

Comment: It was important for the woman counselor to avoid identification with his mother. Nondirective techniques were essential in order to establish and maintain rapport with this client.

On the other hand, directive techniques are necessary, at least in early interviews, for certain types of clients. Overly dependent and deeply depressed persons often need the support and reassurance of a strong parent-figure at the beginning of the counseling process. Likewise, a group made up of immature, dependent members needs a more directive leader in early sessions of a multiple counseling project. As personal growth starts, accompanied by improved skill in social interactions and in discussions, the group members learn to stand on their own feet, with less support and direction from the leader. Occasionally threats and coercion are necessary in the case of a client who is contemplating harmful action. The most faithful counselor-convert to nondirectivism will take drastic steps to prevent a murder or suicide. An example of a case (group 10) where directive action was essential on the part of both the group leader and the director of psychiatric services, is given below:

Ardith, a deeply depressed college junior, was receiving psychiatric treatment from a nondirective psychiatrist who had assigned her to a discussion therapy group, conjunctive with weekly interviews. Ardith had no friends nor social contacts on the campus until she joined the group. Here she made a close friend of Hulda, who had a similar family background and psychological problems.

One day Hulda conferred with the group leader because of her fear that Ardith planned suicide. Ardith had told her of procuring a rope and way of fastening it from the ceiling of her room. The group leader immediately contacted the director of psychiatric services who asked that Ardith be sent to the office at once. This action was facilitated by the fact that Ardith's group met that afternoon and the leader was able to get Ardith to the director for an interview. When faced with the question, "Is it true that you have a rope in your room," Ardith broke down, admitting her plan, and agreed to confinement in the college infirmary at once.

The subsequent sedation and other medical treatment in conjunction with psychiatric interviews with a different psychiatrist (directive and dominating), produced good results. Continuation in the group project gave her encouragement and support. According to a follow-up a year later Ardith was making good progress in recovery from her mental illness.

Leadership techniques in group sessions

It is recommended that leaders never go beyond point 7, "suggestions," in leading discussion groups in order to avoid any identification with an authoritarian-figure. Occasionally point 8, "advice" may be necessary, but it can usually be given in terms of a suggestion by basing it on something which a group member has said, or done. Examples of steering the group through use of obvious or implied interests within the group are given below:

Situation 1 — In a high school group the discussion on racial discrimination bogged down due to lack of experience with this problem on the part of group members. The leader introduced a new subject by saying, "Since you don't seem to have racial problems in your school, perhaps the question of cliques or snobbishness is something you know about. Can anyone give an opinion on this as it appears in your school activities, elections, etc.?"

Situation 2 — In a college group the discussion was pulled off in a tangent by a monopolistic member. The others became irritated but were unable to squelch the aggressive participant. After ten minutes of unsuccessful attempts by the group to bring the discussion back to the topic (which they were very interested in) the leader said, "We seem to be getting away from the idea which Jim presented some time ago. Since you all seemed to want to discuss it, let's have some opinions from the group. Mal — you give the others a chance to talk now." The leader took control of the discussion, recognizing different members and not allowing Mal to talk until everyone else had had a chance.

This type of control by the leader is not authoritarian; it is action representative of the interests and wishes of the group. It is "directive" in nature, and illustrates the need for an eclectic approach in group leadership.

When the leader serves either as a moderator or observer-participant in discussions, he uses counseling techniques adapted to the group; these techniques include support, reflection, clarification, interpretation, questioning, information-dispensing, and summing up. It is quite possible for a leader to use all seven techniques in a single session. The use of any one of them and its frequency of use depends upon the group dynamics, discussion content, and needs of individual participants. The skilled leader varies his performance from almost complete inactivity in some sessions to energetic support of group members and lively participation in other sessions. In the experience of the author with both teen-age and adult groups, a leader is needed as a source of reliable information and he should be willing to search out the information asked for, reporting it to the group in the form of book references or quotations, etc. Permissiveness in the group includes a participant's right to ask direct questions of the leader and to get satisfactory answers. And when leaderless discussions are used over too long a period even adult groups become dissatisfied: they expect guidance, expert opinion, and facts from the leader. The inductive method proceeds from the particular to the generalization: participants need synthesis and interpretations by the leader — internal leadership by a group member cannot provide this.

Brief descriptions of the seven leadership techniques are given below in the form of leader-actions while serving in the role of moderator-participant:

1. SUPPORT (*giving attention or help to a participant through words of commendation, appreciation, focussing of attention on him, etc.*).

    a. "Lola, your hair looks lovely — are you doing it a new way?"

    b. "I think Jim has given us a very meaty idea which shows he has thought deeply about it."

    c. "It was nice of you to arrange the chairs, Tom. Very thoughtful of you — I didn't know I was going to be late."

2. REFLECTION (*repeating the verbal contribution of a participant to focus attention on the idea or feeling behind it. The purpose may be to encourage further exploration or explanation of the idea or feeling*).

    a. "You say you think people dislike you?"

    b. "Did you say you never want to see your parents again?"

    c. "Did I understand you correctly — 'all girls are gold diggers'?"

3. CLARIFICATION (*enlarging upon, or giving an illustration of the idea, attitude, or feeling expressed by a participant or the group in order to emphasize or clarify its meaning*).

    a. "A good example of what Jim means is the old fable about the fox who couldn't reach the grapes, so he said they were sour anyway."

100

b. "I had a similar case of a GI overseas — he wouldn't leave his barracks, just stayed in his bunk all his free time. We tried to work on him and some others — to get them into activities."

c. "Mary, do you mean by that that you feel something like an adopted child — as though you didn't really belong to your parents?"

4. INTERPRETATION (*explaining the significance or meaning of an idea, attitude, feeling, or action in order to give a definite impression of it for the group to discuss*).

a. "Does it seem to the group that in this case study I've presented Mrs. S feels more emotional over Johnny's behavior than you as parents — or your parents when you were little — would have felt?"

b. "The fact that Lloyd has the longest list of gripes and wants to continue the subject next time makes it look as though he had a lot more to tell us — is that right, Lloyd?"

5. QUESTIONING (*a useful technique for many purposes*).

a. To start a discussion the question should be provocative or present different viewpoints:
"Since statistics show girls get higher grades in school than boys, does that mean girls are smarter than boys?"

b. To redirect the discussion, emphasize a point, bring new-thinking to bear on the topic:
"You have discussed this question of 'one love forever' quite fully, but what do you think about divorce — that subject hasn't been mentioned."

c. To support a participant: encourage him in self-revelation, ask for facts and relationships to help his self-understanding:
"Alice, you have been a good sport to tell us frankly about your ignorance of sex in high school. Do you want to go on and tell us how you got engaged?"
"Jim, you feel so strongly about girls being mercenary, how does this relate to the way you feel about your sisters and mother — do you think they are that way?"

101

6. GIVING INFORMATION (*providing answers to questions as well as giving pertinent information pertaining to the topic under discussion; the leader must be a "resource person" because the group are not expected to study or prepare for discussions*).

Ways of giving essential information are:

   a. Report on research findings, authoritative books in fields of psychology, sociology and education.

   b. Quote directly from experts and case studies.

   c. Prepare typed copies of essential information which can be read over by the group prior to a free discussion.

   d. Answer questions objectively, avoiding a personal opinion. If the answer is not known, the leader is frank to admit it, and promises to find the answer before the next meeting.

7. LEADER SUMMARIES (*summaries may be only a report of points made in the discussion or may include interpretations and implications as the leader sees them*).

Ways of giving summaries:

   a. Plan the last ten minutes of the session for the summary and decision of the group regarding the topic for next time.

   b. Let the discussion continue to the end of the session in case it is a lively one; summarize at the beginning of the next session prior to continuation of the discussion.

   c. Occasionally ask a group member to give the summary or his interpretation of what has been learned in the session. Allow ten minutes for this because other group members may wish to add to, or disagree with the summary.

Methods of Moderating Discussions

Various types of moderation are used according to the size of the group membership, characteristics, and kind of discussions. Analysis of leadership in fifteen group projects totalling 187 sessions showed that nine types were useful. They are listed with brief explanations below:

1. *Around-the-table recitation or opinion*

   This is used in the first session for self-introductions, and occasionally in other meetings when definite statements, reports, or opinions are needed from all members.

· 2. *Two-sided debate*

   Two teams debate a question, occupying seats on opposite sides of the table. This is a free-for-all, with opponents responding to one another as they get a chance for the floor. The leader is outside the fracas, but sets time limits and summarizes the points made by the discussants at the end.

3. *Huddles reporting back to the whole group*

   A group of ten is broken down into two cell-groups, or into couples, for a short period in order to decide on ratings, votes, listings, etc. Results are reported to the whole group and a discussion of them follows in which cell-groups defend their opinions.

4. *Volunteer listings from group members*

   The question requires listing of ideas, traits, etc. The leader takes notes as group members volunteer items to be listed (the leader, or an assigned member, may write items on the blackboard if it is available). A discussion of the items usually results in addition, subtraction, or changes for more correct or inclusive classifications.

5. *Leader calls on members for their opinions, suggestions, ideas*

   This is a formal structure, similar to an academic class. It should be used sparingly and never for the major portion of a discussion period.

6. *Participants raise hands to be recognized by the leader*

   This is rather formal structure during early sessions necessary in groups which are inexperienced in free discussion.

7. *Participants raise hands for recognition by person speaking*

   The leader does not moderate in this structure: it is similar to a leaderless panel discussion on the radio. As the speaker finishes, he recognizes a member who has his hand raised.

8. *Free-for-all*

The leader does not moderate. The discussion is thrown open to the group, with anyone jumping into it who gets the floor and attention of the group. Any leadership of the discussion is done by members of the group itself: a member will suggest control methods when interruptions or monopoly of discussion bring a chaotic situation. Often a discussion will proceed in a leisurely fashion with some pauses while members think through a point that has been made.

9. *Member-leadership*

The leader assigns extemporaneous leadership duties to one of the group, allowing that person to handle the discussion in any way he wishes. In the case of a leader-trainee group all members are given the opportunity to lead discussions and their performances are criticized by the group and the leader.

When the leader follows a skeletal plan of topics to be covered, experiences and skill-practices to be included, for example in a sixteen-session project which has one and one-half hour meetings, many of the moderating techniques listed above will be used. There will be several leaderless discussion sessions (nondirective), several role-playing sessions in which huddles or couples work out spontaneous dramatizations, a gripe session or two, a debate or lively discussion on a controversial issue, several case conference meetings wherein the personal problem of a member is voluntarily presented by that member in order to get suggestions and advice from the group. Every session should contain a free discussion. Even when auxiliary activities take up the major portion of the time, no session can be considered to be fulfilled without the opportunity for all members to express opinions on a subject of common interest.

SUMMARY

The responsibilities of the leader to provide meaningful discussions and to assist participants were described with emphasis on the difference of a multiple counseling discussion session from a problem-solving group.

The question of nondirective leadership was analyzed, with the conclusion that the leader must use a variety of techniques in group sessions, ranging from completely nondirective to slightly directive. Autocratic leadership has no place in a multiple counseling project.

Examples of counselor responses varying in degree of directivism-nondirectivism were given. Examples of frequently used techniques of group leaders in multiple counseling projects were illustrated.

Methods of moderating discussions used in 187 group sessions of 15 multiple counseling projects were classified and explained. A suggested framework for a sixteen-session project exemplified the eclectic nature of leadership in a multiple counseling project.

VI

ROLE-PLAYING: A COUNSELING TECHNIQUE

R OLE-PLAYING APPEARS TO BE A NATURAL ACTIVITY in human societies, both primitive and modern. Children everywhere use emulative play without coaching from their elders; taking the role of mother, father, cops and robbers, storybook characters, is as natural for human offspring as stalking its prey for young predatory animals. Thus the seeds for empathy, human interactions, and understanding of others, could be said to be a human heritage. The normal child enjoys emulative play with plenty of action: other characters provide chance for interactions and give a focus to the role-playing.

If a child plays alone, or keeps his imaginary companion too long, the parents worry about him. They know that experience in human relationships is important to normal personality growth. A little boy who hung himself while trying to copy the fate of the villain in a television show would have seemed more normal if he had tried to string up his boyfriend. Role-playing in children's games becomes experiential learning when two or more role-players interact in life-like situations. (Not that lynching episodes are recommended, however).

Adulthood does not end role-playing activity. Witness the uninhibited behavior at masquerades, costume parties, the Mardi Gras. Remember charades and The Game. Imaginative gamesters do not need costumes to project themselves into the character of another person. Through use of that ability possessed only by human animals — empathy — it is quite possible to forget oneself for the moment: to think, feel, and experience life inside the skin of another person.

A person who is unable to lose his self-consciousness through identification with characters in books, plays, or people he knows, is too self-centered for his own good. He shows signs of a preoccupation which augurs ill for his mental health. Cameron and others use tests of role-playing for children to screen the mentally ill (1). Although many adults are not mentally ill because of their lack of empathy, they tend to have constricted, inflexible personalities. They would be better adjusted and happier if they could share with others through

106

empathetic action — losing themselves in the lives of others more frequently. Sometimes a self-centered individual seems to be feeding on himself so that his personality withers rather than growing through nourishment it could receive from human relationships and inter-personal stimuli. Empathetic activity initiated in childhood as natural imitative play should be continued during adulthood in one form or another to keep a person flexible, spontaneous, mentally youth-ful, and spiritually accessible to his fellow men.

An excellent use for role-playing as a learning device is found in training programs for teachers, counselors, and industrial supervisors. Human relationships and interpersonal skills are learned by the trainee in "practice-teaching" situations. A teacher can recall painful role-playing situations where her fellow trainees acted like fourth graders to whom she tried to teach a well prepared lesson. It resulted in chaos because the "children" did not react the way she expected. She learned that behavior is unpredictable and that adaptability to new situations arising in the classroom is the core of teaching skill. The same is true of counseling skill. The counselor-trainee receives grueling criticism from his supervisor for failure to adjust to the actions and needs of the counselee in the practice-interview. Although the trainee may complain that the role-players did not react "the way real people do," the experienced human relationist knows that variations of human behavior are legion. Unpredictable behavior happens, and the teacher or counselor must react quickly and skillfully to it. Role-playing can help to develop skillful interpersonal reactions.

Role-playing as a counseling technique often helps a counselee to gain better perspective of himself and others. It can be used to prac-tice social situations which are difficult for the counselee. It should *not* be used as a psychotherapeutic method unless the counselor is a qualified psychotherapist. When role-playing relates to social situa-tions or immediate problems it is neither painful nor dangerous for the client. He participates voluntarily because he hopes to learn some-thing he needs to know. The role he is asked to play may be a char-acter he knows very well — his father, mother, roommate, fellow worker, or boss. Perhaps he will play himself while the counselor plays the other character. The client is expected to give full expres-sion to his feelings in the role and this may make him feel better. There is a good chance that his self-concept and understanding of others will be improved: he may see himself as others see him by means of the role-playing. Quite possibly he will learn how to handle human relationships more skillfully in some social situations which he fears.

Counselors and group psychotherapists who use role-playing as a counseling technique claim it shortens the counseling process. For example, Dr. J. L. Moreno, pioneer in the psychodrama field, substitutes the psychodramatic stage for the psychoanalytic couch. His patients re-enact many traumatic life experiences during psychodramatic sessions. It would take many individual psychiatric interviews which use nondirective procedures to gain the same amount of talkout and catharsis, according to the exponents of psychodrama (4). Many counselors who are not qualified in psychotherapy use role-playing without the deep psychotherapy of the Moreno technique. An example of effective role-playing in college counseling was reported as follows:

John was referred to the counseling center toward the end of a semester for low grades. Mrs. W, the counselor, knew that John was a brilliant student from his high school record and college entrance tests.

In the first interview John admitted he didn't care if he failed, he had no desire to stay in college. In the second interview John said frankly he was trying to get even with his father who had forced him toward high grades all through school. It was a case of rebellion against a parent — of cutting off one's nose to spite the face.

In the third conference Mrs. W suggested role-playing. Two scenes were enacted: John took the part of a father in two different situations, while Mrs. W played the child. The first consisted of the father and his crippled, mentally handicapped child. In this scene John was sympathetic and loving toward the son. A discussion followed this scene concerning the problem faced by parents with handicapped children. The second situation consisted of a farmer with a husky son who was very lazy. The crops were going to rack and ruin because of the son's neglect of his duties. John, as the father became very angry, reprimanded his son and warned him that if he didn't change his ways he would never be worth anything. In the tirade John said, "I'm saying this for your own good — it's because I love you that I'm telling you!" At that point he stopped short, changed expression and exclaimed, "My gosh — that's just what my father said to me!" The discussion that followed included an analysis by John of the way he felt as the two different fathers. He realized that failing his college subjects to get even with his father was no solution to the problem of the conflict with him. New insight and emotional acceptance of his folly in flunking brought a changed attitude: determination to make up his work resulted in passing grades and the succeeding semester he received an A — average.

Although John continued to see the counselor occasionally regarding other college adjustment problems, the conflict with his father dissolved without further counseling. Mrs. W believed the role-playing was the significant learning factor in the case and that the counseling process was immeasurably shortened by it.

Role-playing may have a simple structure like the example above, or it may be more elaborate to include many character portrayals, changes of role and situation. It may be informally initiated so that the client hardly realizes role-playing is taking place, or it may be a planned dramatization with a larger number of participants. The core of role-playing is empathetic action and play-out of feelings either as oneself or the character being portrayed. As a counseling technique the purpose of role-playing is usually conflict-solution and insight learning.

The terms role-playing, psychodrama, and sociodrama have specific meanings in counseling and group psychotherapy. The writer has adopted Moreno's terminology (3), but uses "role-playing" as an all-inclusive term.

Role-playing — any kind of action in which a person attempts to portray the character, attitudes, feelings or actions of another person.

Psychodrama — the enactment of a life situation which holds emotional meaning and conflict for the central character.

Sociodrama — the enactment of a life situation which holds a conflict, controversy or problem applicable to a number of individuals, group, or groups. Thus the conflict situation deals with a problem which is common to a number of individuals rather than characteristic of one individual alone.

Illustrations of the above terms follow:

Role-playing — a person shows his friends how the drunk acted in the cocktail lounge.

Psychodrama — a psychiatric patient acts out a number of conflict situations in his life: (1) a fight with his brother, (2) running away from home after a beating by his father, (3) being jilted by his girl friend, (4) attempting suicide, (5) soliloquy of his obsessive thoughts and feelings of anxiety.

Sociodrama — in three different scenes concerning the same problem three persons take the parent-role to show how each would handle a situation where his child appears to be guilty of stealing, without direct proof. The difference in playing the parent-role is discussed, leading into the common problem of parent-child relationships.

It is evident that role-playing is basic to psychodrama and sociodrama; that a psychodrama might present an individual problem which is also a common problem; that a sociodrama could involve personal problems as well as a social problem. For these reasons Moreno and others prefer not to differentiate between psychodrama and sociodrama, calling all role-playing "psychodrama." However, the implication is that emotional content is involved in the role-playing. In this book role-playing is the term used for all types of extemporaneous, spontaneous, and planned situational playouts. Many of the illustrations of role-playing used in multiple counseling projects do *not* include emotional involvement: sometimes they are more of a game for learning purposes than anything else. They do, however, have the purpose of empathetic practice for group members. The person who shows his friends how the inebriated character acted in the cocktail lounge is "role-playing," whether his purpose is to illustrate a funny joke, to portray a character in a psychodrama concerned with the problem of a mentally ill patient, or to assist in the presentation of the social problem of alcoholism.

In multiple counseling projects role-playing is an auxiliary activity, subordinated to verbal discussion which is the main activity. The writer did find role-playing to be a beneficial learning technique in a number of the group projects through which this multiple counseling method was developed. Illustrations from actual case studies are given later in the chapter to show its value. In general, role-playing fulfills the following purposes:

1. To teach empathy and interpersonal skills.

2. To encourage outgoing, spontaneous behavior.

3. To assist in attitude-changes.

This multiple counseling method uses role-playing primarily for presenting provocative questions or illustrating problems which are being discussed by the group. It never uses psychodrama as a psycho-therapeutic technique. The differences in emphasis on role-playing in non-directive group psychotherapy, Moreno's group therapy method, and the multiple counseling method devised by the writer are illustrated hypothetically in the chart which follows:

AVERAGE TIME ALLOTMENTS FOR ACTIVITIES IN A 60-MINUTE SESSION

	Role-playing	Free Discussion
Nondirective group psychotherapy....	0	60
Moreno group psychotherapy.........	50	10
Multiple counseling method..........	10	50

(Comparable emphasis might be found in individual counseling methods based on nondirectivism, Moreno techniques, and eclectivism except that many eclectic counselors prefer tests, inventories, and self-appraisal devices to role-playing).

Specific objectives of role-playing, with illustrations

Analysis of role-playing used in the fifteen multiple counseling projects reported in this book show the following uses:

1. To present a provocative question as a topic for discussion.
2. To clarify, emphasize, or apply subject matter under dis-cussion.
3. To teach empathetic and social skills; to aid self-assessment.
4. To help an individual in working on his personal problem.

Sometimes role-playing focussed on one objective gives experience and learning in line with another objective. If the situation is realistic and closely tied to the life experiences of the group members, role-playing can be a forceful learning device.

Illustrations from actual group sessions are given to show how role-playing aids the multiple counseling process:

1. PRESENTATION OF A PROVOCATIVE QUESTION

Situation 1 — The situation consists of a soldier back from Korea in a small town in Wisconsin. Although he has been home several weeks he has failed to look up his high school sweetheart whom his family expect him to marry. Joe appears

111

to be quiet and depressed. The two scenes include conversations with his mother, then his father (sister or brother). The controversial question emerges as he tells his parents he has fallen in love with a Korean girl and wants to bring her to the States as his wife.

Joe, the neutral character in the sociodrama, uses the same opening sentences in both scenes: "I've been working up my courage to tell you something — I fell in love with a Korean girl and went steady with her for a year. I want to marry her and bring her here to live." Joe also includes in the dialogue the fact that his girl was educated in the U.S. and is of the same religious faith as his own family.

> *Scene* 1 — His mother reacts coöperatively — anything to make Joe happy. She will take the girl into their home and try to get acceptance of her by other members of the family and the community.

> *Scene* 2 — His father (sister, brother) reacts negatively and presents arguments why a mixed marriage won't work; why the affair is an infatuation which Joe can get over; why Joe is too young and inexperienced to know his own heart and mind.

The controversial question discussed in the group after the sociodrama varies according to the emotional interests of dominant members. Thus in one college group the discussion revolved around "is one love forever," in another group, "can mixed marriages succeed," and in an adult group, "how can parents guide impulsive sons and daughters."

Situation 2 — A high school group were interested in the question of dating. An argument developed: how and when should a boy ask his girl for a date to a formal dance? The girls complained that boys wait until the last minute before getting their dates. That isn't fair to the girls, especially when they were going more or less steady and didn't want to accept an invitation from any other boy. Luke, defending his sex, said his girl should know he was going to ask her — she shouldn't worry about it. Sally, representing the girls, argued against this and said she resented the cocksure attitude of the boys.

The leader suggested that the situation be acted out: Luke was to phone his girl, Sally, just two days before the big dance. Sally should react exactly the way she felt on getting the phone call. The situation is staged more or less in keeping with phoning habits: Luke sits on the floor at one end of the room, Sally lounges in a chair at the other end.

In this psychodrama several different girls can try the role and a discussion of various reactions to the late invitation is held. Some girls will happily accept the invitation, others might reject it with vituperous comments to Luke. If Sally is the only role-player, when the scene is over the leader asks, "Would you girls have acted the way Sally did," or "What do you boys think about Sally's reactions — would your girl have done the same." Usually a frank, lively discussion based on sex differences comes from this psychodrama. Eventually better understanding and tolerance of the opposite sex is gained.

112

2. Illustration of Subject Matter Under Discussion

Situation 1 — The use of impromptu dramatizations to illustrate a discussion area such as behavior causes (primary drives, defense mechanisms) helps to clarify the meaning and to give application of the material in real life situations. The following psychodrama was used for a high school group discussion centered on basic needs such as recognition, belonging, and love. It illustrated the need for recognition:

The scene took place in the principal's office where Jim had been sent for a serious misdemeanor involving the police. The principal questions Jim for his lack of interest in school, reasons for his clash with the Law. He lectures Jim on the value of a high school education in order to get a decent job. Jim replies that he hates school and intends to be a barkeeper — he works part time in a tavern now. Questioned by the principal he admits to hero worship of Frank Costello: it is smart to get the better of the Law and the end justifies the means. The principal quizzes Jim to see if he has any feelings of right and wrong, love or loyalty toward his parents and friends. Jim shows one vulnerable area: he loves his mother and feels guilty when his behavior makes her feel bad.

This psychodrama was planned in advance, but was unrehearsed by the two characters. However, they were briefed by the leader after studying specific directions:

Principal: You are to act as much like your idea of a good principal as possible. During your conversation with Jim try to get in the following questions:

1. Why does Jim want to steal, skip school, etc.
2. What is his aim in life, what are his values, what adult does he admire.
3. What are his feelings toward his parents.

Jim: You are to act like one of those fellows you know who is in trouble with the Law and dislikes school. In this role you have a part-time job in a tavern and intend to become a barkeeper with a gambling sideline. Try to get in the following points:

1. You hate school and want to go to work.
2. You admire Frank Costello, believe the end justifies the means. Money is the most important thing in life.
3. Life values involve getting power and recognition from making a lot of money.
4. You do love your mother, dislike hurting her, and feel guilty when she feels bad because of the way you act.

A discussion following this psychodrama may concern any one of a number of provocative questions in addition to illustrating the subject matter. One high school group started to criticize government officials and corruption in high places: the group questioned whether a person could remain honest or follow the Golden Rule in our competitive society. When the discussion got out of hand the leader re-directed focus with the question, "What life values mean most to you" and instituted a round-the-table recitation.

Situation 2 — A college group were discussing defense mechanisms. Typed sheets with definitions had been distributed. The session consisted of questions and illustrations to clarify the meaning of the various mechanisms. At the end the leader suggested the six members plan psychodramas illustrating mechanisms for the next session. In order to make a game of it the leader assigned certain mechanisms privately to three couples. They were not to divulge the assignments to the others.

The role-playing session proved to be amusing and instructive. Overlapping of two mechanisms characterized several of the psychodramas showing everyday use of defensive behavior. The participants had drawn on their own experiences with teachers, roommates and friends. Discussion which followed each presentation usually started with a wrong guess. One member said at the end of the session, "I've studied defense mechanisms in three different courses but this is the first time I really have them straightened out."

An example of one of the psychodramas follows:

John: Hi, Bill, guess where I'm going this afternoon.

Bill: I don't know, but not out for our intramural team practice, that's for sure.

John: You know I'm no good at that stuff — listen, I'm going to a tea at the President's. He was a classmate of my dad's, you know. Gosh, I'm all excited!

Bill: You certainly like to make up to the Brass — I can't see it myself. Being with the gang and working for the dorm sports trophy is more my line, I guess.

John: Well, knowing the right people can pay dividends, and I get a big kick out of hobnobbing with the big guns — you really learn your way around.

In this psychodrama the group guessed that identification was shown by John, since he enjoyed being with important people, thinking of himself as one of them. Bill and John said they tried to show two mechanisms in the role-playing. Finally the group saw that compensation was in it: no doubt John was poor in sports and not popular with his peer group.

3. To teach social and empathetic skills; aid self-assessment

Situation 1 — Two members of a high school group started a discussion on applying for jobs. Their commercial teacher had impressed upon them the importance of a job interview — the right and wrong way to act, etc. Since the group was interested in this, the leader suggested acting out two job interviews to show correct and incorrect behavior. Gerry volunteered to show the wrong way and Bea offered to play the employer. A humorous and realistic performance was given. The group analyzed it, listing eleven wrong actions. Then two other girls demonstrated a good interview. Criticism from the group pointed out faults in the employer: he had not asked pertinent questions regarding training, experience, shorthand ability. In fact he had appeared to be ready to hire the stenographer on the spot and take her out to lunch!

The leader turned the discussion into wider application with the question, "What qualifications would you present in an interview for a job in your field, Bob, or yours, Jack?" This session led into several centered on personal fitness and training for various jobs. The Strong Interests Inventory had been taken by the students previously so one meeting was given over to the results accompanied by frank appraisals of each other in terms of personal strengths and weaknesses.

Situation 2 — The members of a college group were griping about grades, courses, and professors. The leader suggested a psychodrama in which role-players would try to get the professor's viewpoint. The situation was called "The professor and the disgruntled student." A student, dissatisfied with his exam grade, comes to the professor's office to discuss it. Each role-player was supposed to react emotionally to the situation, expressing his feeling about the other quite frankly. (The leader encouraged the participants to do this, saying it was their chance to express suppressed feelings about professors). The rules of this role-playing game included reversing roles at anytime in the conversation the leader dictated, *i.e.*, the professor and student exchanged roles.

The stage was set up at one end of the room, representing the professor's office. Dialogue started when the student entered the office, the professor saying, "How do you do, Mr. (Miss) ——, what can I do for you?" From that point on, the dialogue was spontaneous, usually working up an emotional pitch in the midst of which the leader called for reversing roles. The two changed places and continued the dialogue, trying to adjust to the opposite role. A typical dialogue prior to reversing roles follows:

Professor: You wanted to see me about something?

Student: Yes, I was upset by the grade you gave me in the exam — I couldn't see what was wrong.

Professor: Let me see the bluebook. (Peruses it) Well, you didn't give the points asked for. Your grade of C was really generous of me.

Student: I don't see why my ideas aren't worth something — after all, memorizing the textbook isn't real learning — aren't we supposed to learn to use our brains in college?

Professor: Evidently you think your ideas are better than the expert who wrote the book — he only spent twenty years of research, you know.

Student: I didn't mean that — I just think we ought to have a chance to do original thinking — with this college exam business you don't dare to, you get penalized for it.

Professor: I only wish I thought you students had something to think with — I see very little evidence of it, of any real intelligence among most of the fellows in your class. From your work I would suggest that a trade school is what you want. Most of you just think in terms of getting practical courses aimed at a vocation — you don't belong in college.

Student: Well, what are we here for if not to prepare for a vocation. And grades can be important too. An employer looks over your transcript, a C record doesn't help get a job. That's why we sweat out the grades and have to submit to regurgitating just what the textbook or professor said — I think it's a farce, and disgusting, too.

Professor: If you students had the right attitude about a college education we could treat you more like intelligent adults — as it is, we can't.

Student: Why do they make us take such useless courses — what good is English 2a and European History ever going to do me?

Professor: As I said, I think you belong in a trade school — you'd find the courses are practical there — I haven't time to argue about your required courses here. Let's get back to your exam grade. Is there anything else to discuss about it?

Student: No, I guess there's nothing more, except I think this whole grading system stinks.

Professor: Maybe you'd prefer a college where they have just pass and fail grades, then no one would know you are only a C student.

(Three couples played the psychodrama and in the short time that remained, the discussion turned to "what should a student expect to get out of college, anyway." This subject was explored, with ramifications, during the next three sessions).

The individual students gained a fresh viewpoint from taking part in the role-playing. They learned much about individual differences among group members from the way the roles were played; several gained significant insight and self-understanding; all improved in their understanding of professors who are pestered by disgruntled students.

4. To help an individual with his personal problems

Situation 1 — Dick was in trouble with his English teacher in high school and presented his problem to the discussion project group. He was required to apologize to the teacher before being re-admitted to the class; he didn't think he was in the wrong and saw no reason to apologize. The group discussed his case, advising him to stop being obstinate — to go ahead with the apology. The leader suggested that he rehearse the apology. One of the group was assigned to take the role of Miss S, the teacher. The scene was enacted, but the group criticized Dick's performance: he was too sulky. The student taking Miss S's role agreed that if he were the teacher he would be madder than ever at Dick. Next the leader asked Dick to play the role of Miss S while the leader acted like Dick. It became clear to Dick through this role-playing that he must get over his sulkiness and make the apology sound sincere. After another try at it, and encour-

116

agement from the group, Dick was able to face Miss S and apologize in a satisfactory manner. The results were good, since Dick also learned to be more tolerant of Miss S through the influence of the discussion and role-playing.

Situation 2 — One of the members of a discussion therapy group in a mental hospital asked the leader for a discussion on alcoholism. Although she claimed that she was not, and had never been an alcoholic, she was extremely interested in the subject. Not satisfied with the one session in which the leader gave an informational talk followed by free discussion of alcoholism, Lou requested that another session be used for the subject. In this session the leader queried Lou concerning her deep interest in alcoholism and Lou admitted that drinking always got her into trouble. This paved the way for a psychodrama. Lou described a situation wherein she and her friend Belle were in a tavern drinking. She said Belle was being ruined by drink: the more she drank the more depressed she got, and then she carried on with men. The leader volunteered to play the role of Belle and the stage was set up at one end of the room. Sample dialogue follows:

Lou: Belle, you've had enough to drink, you know it only makes you feel worse.

Belle: Aw come on, let's have one more, I couldn't feel worse than I do now. Waiter, bring us another round and make mine a double.

Lou: Listen, kid, you've been doing this every night, and you drink in the day, too — you know why you lost that job.

Belle: If you are my good friend, you'd get looping with me — that's the only way I can forget how bad I feel.

Lou: Listen, Belle, it's because I am your pal that I want to give you some good advice. I'm dead serious — what you need is a treatment to get over wanting to drink. When you don't drink you are a swell gal — you could make a lot of yourself if you'd quit the booze. Now I know just the place for you to go, and I can help you get there. They have a wonderful treatment and after a month you won't want to go near any liquor. How about it?

Belle: Let's have another drink, I feel awful. Just one more.

Lou: You get feeling worse with every one — you know that. How about my proposition — let me help get you in (names the mental hospital), it's the best thing you can do. You'd like it up there, everyone is so nice and they have dances, entertainments — lots of fun.

Belle: Don't be silly, that's a nut factory — I'm not nuts.

Lou: That's not true. Lots of alcoholics and people who aren't nuts go there for all kinds of treatment, it's a swell place.

In the discussion which followed this short psychodrama Lou told more about her friend and the group asked Lou if she had quit drinking — she had sounded like a very good salesman for AA. Lou became very serious, recounting all the times she had got in trouble because of drinking. She said she had almost talked herself into being a teetotaler in the psychodrama. The leader described her reactions to Lou in the psychodrama; she was impressed with the description of the mental hospital. The discussion turned to the hospital and its good features, including treatment for alcoholics.

SUMMARY

The nature of role-playing was discussed, with its uses in training and counseling programs. The purposes for which it has been successfully used in multiple counseling projects were stated as (1) to teach empathy and interpersonal skills, assist in self-assessment; (2) to encourage outgoing, spontaneous behavior, (3) to teach new attitudes. Illustrations of role-playing were given for presenting a provocative question; applying subject matter; teaching empathetic, outgoing behavior; helping an individual with personal problems.

The use of role-playing in multiple counseling projects is limited by the interests of the group and the qualifications of the leader. It was not used as a psychotherapeutic technique in the fifteen projects reported in this book.

VII

LEADERSHIP IN ROLE-PLAYING

THE LEADER OF MULTIPLE COUNSELING PROJECTS may use three kinds of structure in role-playing: (1) informal (2) interview (3) formal or planned. These three types require different approaches and techniques on the part of the leader. The first, informal role-playing, seems to just "happen" during a discussion. It is an extension of the discussion itself and the leader usually plays one of the roles. The second type, interview role-playing, consists of one person acting like a reporter, employer, etc., who asks questions of the interviewee in order to get information, reactions and ideas from him. The third type, formal or planned role-playing, is a skit conceived by the leader (or a group member) which is prepared in advance. That is, the plot is prepared; members of the cast are selected and briefed on their parts. However, dialogue is not learned. Spontaneous interactions during the role-playing episode determine the dialogue, although each character tries to keep within the boundaries of the assigned role. The extemporaneous, spontaneous nature of role-playing gives it an unpredictable quality which fits in well with the free discussions of a multiple counseling activity.

True psychodrama, which might be called client-centered psychotherapy, was not included in the multiple counseling projects reported in this book. Role-playing directed by the author was used as an auxiliary activity in group sessions. True psychodrama is the chief activity of a group session rather than free discussion. The role of the leader (more appropriately called the director) in client-centered psychodrama contrasts with group leader characteristics as described in multiple counseling activity. The psychodrama director *directs* — he gives orders, threats, and sometimes coerces the central character into actions on the stage. The director should be a psychotherapist who can give psychotherapeutic treatment to the client in private interviews conjunctive with psychodramatic performances (1). However adaptations of Moreno techniques without strong emotional content are widely used for sociodramas and nondirectively led role-playing activities in schools, communities, and institutions (5, 8). Examples of a psychodrama and a sociodrama enacted at Moreno Workshops are included to show how Dr. Moreno's method can be applied in immediate-problem situations as well as for deeper psychotherapeutic catharsis.

In multiple counseling projects informal and interview role-playing are most frequently used because they are extensions of the discussion activity. Formal or planned role-playing episodes are effective as substitutes for informational talks or other springboards to discussion.

Illustrations of four role-playing structures

1. INFORMAL

This illustration is taken from a college psychiatric group composed of neurotic and socially maladjusted students. Carol arrived late: she had had a fight with an instructor and was in an agitated mood. When she told the group about it they told her she was at fault since she refused to conform to class regulations. They said a teacher should be impartial and not allow one student special privileges.

The leader suggested that Carol re-enact the argument with the instructor, but Carol should take the part of the teacher while the leader would assume Carol's role. In the scene the leader tried to duplicate Carol's aggressive manner and uncoöperative attitude. Much to the group's surprise Carol played the part of the teacher as a patient, sympathetic person who explained at length why she couldn't discriminate in favor of one student. She asked for the coöperation of the student in making the class project successful.

In the group discussion which followed, the leader asked Carol if she had consciously acted like the instructor and emulated her behavior in the argument. Carol said she had done so, admitting that she as a teacher would not have been so patient with the student. The group repeated their opinions that Carol had been in the wrong; they advised her to change her attitude in the class.

This psychodrama stimulated a discussion on "how much conformity to academic and social customs at college is necessary in order to get along and still keep one's individuality." Since this was a common conflict-area in the group several sessions were spent in its discussion.

Comment: The leader's activity in the informal role-playing consisted of focussing attention of the group on Carol's problem; participating in the role-playing with her; helping Carol to clarify her feelings in the role of teacher; guiding the free discussion in the direction of the common problem of group members.

2. INTERVIEW ROLE-PLAYING

An illustration of interview role-playing is taken from a college group who wanted to discuss religious concepts. Many of the members were confused and insecure

120

because of rejecting the religion of their childhood and finding nothing to take its place. One avowed atheist had frequently made fun of various Christian doctrines as well as rejecting his own Jewish faith.

The sociodrama was called "Fundamental Beliefs." It consisted of an interviewer and three passers-by: a Catholic, Atheist, and Protestant. All members of the cast volunteered for the parts and the leader selected those who seemed most anxious to be in the role-playing.

The leader gave instructions to the interviewer as follows:

"You are a newspaper reporter, similar to the Inquiring Reporter and his column in our newspaper. You are interviewing to get answers to three questions: (1) Do you believe in God (2) Do you believe in immortality (3) What is your idea of Jesus Christ. Your first interviewee is to be a Catholic, the next an Atheist, the last a Protestant. Be sure to introduce yourself the same way in each interview and to ask the three questions the same way. However, if you are not satisfied with the answer because of its evasiveness or lack of clarity, you may ask other questions to help get a clear idea of the person's concept. Each interview should take no longer than three minutes, but don't worry about the time — it's not important."

The leader briefed the three interviewees by saying, "Each of you in turn is to be interviewed and asked three questions about your religious beliefs. Just try to answer the interviewer as sincerely as you can."

The sociodrama was seriously done, and it stimulated the group to the extent of asking that the other members and the leader be included in the interviews. The interviews were continued and there was not time for a free discussion. The leader summed up the session by giving implications: each individual must develop his own philosophy of life and religious conviction according to his own experience. It was important for the group to know that experts in the fields of anthropology, psychology, and sociology are in agreement on the importance of having some kind of faith which gives man an answer to the reason for his existence. A list of references substantiating this idea was given to the group. The leader emphasized the importance of serious study of such books to help group members in their search for a satisfying philosophy of life.

A second illustration of interview role-playing shows how the leader can change his role of interviewer with each interviewee. He composes the questions according to the situation and type of interviewee. In the illustration the questions were impromptu:

A group of senior students training for teaching were discussing the kind of jobs they wanted next year. The leader challenged their ability to teach, since they had previously complained that education courses were too theoretical and not at all satisfactory. Members of the group appeared to be confident that they could handle teaching assignments in spite of the curriculum so the leader suggested they show

how they would act in job interviews. The leader took the role of various school officials interviewing prospective teachers. Each of the six group members was interviewed in turn. Excerpts from interviews follow:

School Official: So you are interested in the position of art supervisor for our elementary schools. What are your qualifications for the position — have you had a lot of experience teaching art in the various grades?

Applicant: Yes, through the field work at the University in conjunction with practice-teaching I taught in grades one through eight. I enjoyed it and my critic teacher gave me a good rating.

School Official: I have always thought the University courses were very theoretical. We have secured our best teachers from the teachers colleges — the courses seem to be more down-to-earth. Now, in this teaching experience you had — what did it consist of?

Applicant: I taught for one semester in the primary grades and the second semester in the upper grades. It was good experience because I did the planning and teaching with very little help from the critic teacher.

School Official: Hmmmm. Well, frankly I don't consider that very much experience and I think an art supervisor should have much more. I'll let you know about this soon. Thank you for coming to see me.

. . . .

Principal: So you are interested in our opening as speech teacher in the high school. What is your idea of speech courses pupils should have?

Applicant: Well, I did a very interesting experiment in my practice teaching, and I am sold on the idea of not forcing Shakespeare and classic English drama on high school students. We modernized the classics and the teen-agers loved it.

Principal: You mean to say you didn't follow the course of study prescribed in the state syllabus? I'm afraid such a thing would be called radically progressive in our school system.

Applicant: I don't see why schools have to be so old-fashioned, nor why there is so much authoritarianism. Why can't you run your school the way you think best for the pupils? What's the use of forcing subject matter that is obsolete and doesn't apply to our atomic age — why can't the schools become realistic. Certainly the kids are facing life as it is today. It's impossible to arouse their interest in the Elizabethan Stage — actually I'm not interested in it either.

Principal: Well I guess you really aren't interested in a job here, then. I'm afraid you wouldn't be happy because we have prescribed courses of study which must be followed. I hope you find the kind of a teaching post you want, but I warn you — not many schools in our state will allow the freedom in planning your courses that you seem to want. Thank you for coming in for the interview.

(The interview role-playing in this session proved to be a stimulus to various discussions on teaching, school administrators, problems of teachers in small communities. Thus the participants were helped in self-assessments and facing facts concerned with their professional careers.)

3. FORMAL OR PLANNED ROLE-PLAYING

The illustration is taken from a normal college group where the subject of racial discrimination had been introduced. Jane showed great intolerance toward Negroes, saying "Why don't they stay down South where they belong?" Malcolm, a sociology major, countered, "Don't you think Negroes have a right to live and work wherever they please?" Jane was not at all sure of this and the group seemed disinterested. The discussion died: casual conversations, wise cracks, and superficial chatter continued the rest of the session. At the end the leader announced that a sociodrama concerned with racial discrimination would be presented at the beginning of the next session.

Preparations for this included large signs to show various locales, typed directions to the role-players. At the next session Jane, with several others, were asked to take part in the sociodrama entitled "Two Negro students come north to college." The directions to members of the cast were as follows:

Jane — You and your brother are well-to-do Negro students from Alabama. Your father is a physician, your mother directs Negro social work in a large city. Your father has arranged for you to transfer to a northern teachers college for a year, in order to become acquainted with the North. Your applications have been accepted; you and your brother arrive in the small town where the college is located. It is registration time in the fall. Personally you are a very attractive girl who could pass for white. You are looking forward to the new college experience.

Bob — You didn't want to come north to school; you feared that the discrimination problem would arise. You are very dark, thus more aware of the problem than your sister. You think it best for Negroes not to mix with whites.

Cafe waitress — When the two Negroes walk in you must tell them that it is against the rules of the Cafe to serve them.

Hotel clerk — When the two people walk in you must tell them there are no rooms available. If they insist that you are hedging you can say that the girl may have a room because she would pass for white, but that Negroes are not allowed in the hotel.

College registrar — You are much embarrassed when the two Negro students present their credentials. The college did not know they were Negroes when the applications were accepted. Negroes are not allowed in your college and you must explain the error. Because the college could not place them in teaching positions, it would be unfair to take such students.

The purpose of this sociodrama was to stimulate serious discussion of racial discrimination and to attempt to change Jane's attitude.

Results were excellent because the realistic playing of the roles aroused strong feelings and empathy among group members. Jane's feeling of resentment at the treatment she received in the role of Negro student continued after the sociodrama was over: she translated it into a totally new attitude and interest in the Negro problem.

The leader's function in this formal role-playing episode was to plan it, select the cast and brief them. Occasionally during the action the leader helped a role-player when he was at a loss for words. After the sociodrama the leader turned the discussion over to the group. They discussed how they felt during the action, both as role-players and audience members: individual reactions and feelings were compared. When a lively argument started concerning ways in which Negroes are treated, the leader sat back and became a passive participant.

4. MORENO WORKSHOP PSYCHO-SOCIODRAMA

A psycho-sociodrama theme concerned a conflict-situation which two women in the audience presented: the difficulties that career women encounter in competing with men. The two resented strongly "discriminatory practices" against women. Two scenes were enacted with these women serving as central characters. The conflict in each scene concerned an experience with a male boss. The sociodrama director encouraged a full expression of resentment on the part of the women, helping them to "tell off" the bosses for the unfair treatment they received.

At the end the performances were analyzed by the central characters and the audience. A general discussion of the problem followed through which both women received support, reassurance, and better understanding of this societal problem. The leader's function in directing action of the two episodes was a forceful one: he tried to suggest, urge, and force the central characters into expressing their feelings against the bosses.

. . . .

A second illustration from a Moreno Workshop describes a true psychodrama, client-centered, with a full emotional playout by the central character. This was psychotherapeutic activity, effectively directed by Dr. Moreno who is both a doctor and a qualified psychiatrist.

A young man from the audience volunteered to present his personal problem in the psychodrama: he admitted he was depressed, confused, and wanted help. After questioning the young man (Len) to bring out biographic information, Dr. Moreno suggested that Len think of a specific episode in his life which was disturbing to him. Len said he could think of one and started to tell of it. Dr. Moreno stopped him, saying it would be better to act it out. Len was asked to name the characters and helped to select members of the audience for the parts: his mother, and step-father whom he called George. Dr. Moreno quizzed Len regarding the time and place of the scene, helping him to set up the stage to indicate the kitchen, door to the bathroom, etc. Then Len was given a few minutes backstage with the two role-players to brief them on their actions. Meanwhile Dr. Moreno explained psychodramatic procedures to the audience of forty people. He said that this scene would probably be one of many in Len's life which held elements of the conflict which made him unhappy and maladjusted at the present time.

This proved to be the case, for six episodes in Len's life were enacted over a period of one and one-half hours. In each episode Len structured the scene and played the central role. The six scenes were:

1. The fight between Len and his step-father prior to attending the church supper.
2. His feeling of panic and bad dreams last night.
3. His meeting with real father.
4. The break-up with his fiancée.
5. His fiancée's flunking out of college.
6. A future assignment as clergyman in a small town.

The Director's activity in this client-centered psychodrama included a variety of highly skilled techniques. During the various scenes the director questioned, exhorted, and forced a full emotional playout by Len. Dr. Moreno succeeded in probing for hidden feelings and motives: Len was able to gain catharsis through re-living the painful episodes. The use of trained assistants was an important feature of the psychodrama.*

Three notes of caution on appropriateness of role-playing

Three suggestions are made regarding the use of role-playing in multiple counseling projects. These concern the appropriateness of the activity as a learning device.

1. Go Slow

In the first place, don't attempt role-playing until the members of the group feel well acquainted with each other and the leader. Some groups develop camaraderie in the early sessions; others warm up more slowly. Usually the smaller the group the faster the warm up.

---

* Dr. Moreno's philosophy and psychodrama techniques are explained in his two books, *Who Shall Survive* and *Psychodrama* (11, 10).

In the second place, start with casual, informal role-playing as part of the discussion in which you, the leader, participate. When the leader shows his willingness to be one of the group and to play a role, the participants accept the new activity with enthusiasm. Role-playing can be demonstrated most effectively in an informal, impromptu performance characterized by spontaneity.

As soon as the leader is certain that group members can and will play assigned roles, a formal sociodrama may be presented. Selection of participants for roles depends upon the leader's knowledge of their personal traits and keenly felt interests. Again, it is a good idea for the leader to play a role himself in the first big production: he can give encouragement and support to other role-players in so doing. Later on a group member may volunteer to produce a sociodrama, assisted by other group members. In some institutions the patients plan and present sociodramas without any assistance from hospital personnel (8). For multiple counseling projects it is recommended that these productions be limited to the first ten minutes of the session and include material which lends itself to free discussion.

2. USE ROLE-PLAYING FOR VARIETY AND A CHANGE OF PACE

In any learning process a variety of techniques may give emphasis, clarification, new perspective, and new interest to the learner. So role-playing can be a new medium for, or incentive to, learning. Sometimes it serves as "spice in the sauce," adding amusement to an activity which has become dully serious and in need of a light touch. In a multiple counseling project of seventeen or more sessions role-playing is welcomed as a change from "just talking." Also informational talks as springboards to free discussion may become a routine procedure which needs to be changed in order to maintain the interest of the group. Role-taking is an excellent substitute for informational talks — in fact, it is much more effective as a stimulus to lively discussions because it is *warm up activity* for discussion. Depending upon the interest of the group in role-playing, this activity can be given a more or less prominent place in the project. As a minimum for a seventeen session project it is recommended that there be several informal role-playing episodes, one interview-type, and two planned sociodramas.

126

3. Use Role-Playing for Encouragement and Social Skills Training

Encouragement therapy is based on the assumption that each person must learn to get along with himself and others in the best way he can, admitting that some of his personal traits are so firmly established that change is improbable. In spite of his weaknesses it is possible for him to learn satisfactory adjustive techniques and human relationships. The intimate group climate helps him because he is accepted as a worthy person by his fellow members. Role-playing can help him, too. He can practice social skills in simulated situations which bother him. If shy, he may learn social interactions through role-playing. Sometimes a group member is so lacking in verbal ability that he is a "listener." He (or she) never contributes an opinion and answers questions in monosyllables. Yet this person needs and wants to contribute to the group activity: role-playing may be the answer. In the writer's experience the nonverbal members of group projects welcomed the opportunity to try their hand at role-playing, and they were successful in it. The satisfaction gained from performing sometimes served as the catalytic agent to start them in the direction of interactive, outgoing behavior in the group. Often these listeners were able to take active part in discussions following their performance in a psychodrama. Thus role-playing was an effective warm up for discussive activity just as calisthenics warm up the athlete before going into the game.

Learning to meet situations feared by persons because their weaknesses are exposed can be aided through role-playing. For instance a person who has been an alcoholic or mental patient must be ready to face embarrassing questions about his illness. Practice through role-playing in a friendly group can fortify this person for difficult situations. This practice of social situations through role-playing is as useful in individual counseling procedures as in group projects. An example from an actual case is given below:

Sonia, a college freshman, had been very deaf since an early age. She tried to hide her handicap from college friends and professors. By concealing the hearing aid cleverly she had succeeded in deception not only with the professors but also with her boy friend. Difficulties arose, however, which she discussed with her counselor. First, she could not hear the lecturer in Biology because he mumbled: her grades were very low in this subject. Second, her boy friend wanted to be affectionate and she was afraid he would discover the battery to her hearing aid. Through counseling Sonia came to see that she could not continue in the deception any longer. In order to face her professor and boy friend with the true facts role-playing was used. She practiced just what she would say to the two and thus prepared herself for the ordeal. This helped her to accept herself and to face others in a sincere way concerning the admission of her handicap. The results in terms of lessened tensions and anxieties were excellent; her personal adjustments were definitely aided.

The value of a sympathetic group is the support gained from a number of persons all of whom are peers; the influence tends to be more effective and pervasive than that of just one counselor. The group members give reassurance to the participant who presents his problem in a group session. And role-playing may serve as an extension of the counseling process in the group. An example of the use of role-playing and social interactions in helping a very constricted, maladjusted college freshman follows:

Eddie came from an orphanage to college. He lived with his father within commuting distance of the school; he did not participate in activities or have any friends. Social interactions in the multiple counseling project were difficult for him because he was exceedingly self-conscious and nonverbal. One day Eddie talked a bit about how he hated his father and wished he could become independent of him. His father was paying the college expenses since he wanted Eddie to have the advantages he himself had lacked. Eddie said he dreaded going home that night because he had flunked a Chemistry exam. The leader asked, "How will your father feel about that?" Eddie replied, "He'll give me H—, especially if he's drunk, there'll be an awful fight." The leader said, "All right, let's hear what the fight will be like. You act like your father and I'll act like you." The role-playing proceeded and an argument ensued. The leader, in the role of Eddie, was very constrained and defensive while Eddie, in the role of his father, expressed righteous indignation: his son wasn't being fair to him or to himself; college was a great privilege, etc. The group encouraged Eddie to work himself into a wrathful state. His performance became outgoing and uninhibited. At the end the group complimented Eddie on his performance and urged him to talk more in the discussions, to "let himself go."

This role-playing had beneficial results: Eddie entered more freely into the discussions; he brought other problems to the group, and members gave him tangible help. Warm human relationships did more for Eddie than any counseling could do.

The value of the sociodrama for blowing-off-steam and expressing feelings which have been suppressed is worth mentioning. To give members of a college teacher training group a taste of realism in their future jobs a sociodrama with "asides" was produced as follows:

The group were in a state of confusion and conflict — how could they reconcile their convictions concerning good teaching with the stodgy conformity of many of the schools where they might get jobs. The leader questioned the group regarding their feelings about conformity in such a position and they all agreed that they would not take jobs in small-narrow communities: they were aiming at large school systems. The leader asked if they could envisage a problem of conformity in a big school; they could not — a big school was most desirable in their opinions. The subject was dropped until the beginning of the next session when the leader announced that she had made up a sociodrama pertaining to a common conflict situation for new teachers in certain large schools in the state. The situation was described and four roles were assigned: the principal, the social studies teacher and their two doubles. The doubles — or alter egos as they are often called — were to do "asides" while the two characters talked in socially acceptable manner. After the role-players were briefed they went into action. Excerpts from the sociodrama follow:

Principal: Mr. Smith, I've called you in because of the poor performance of your class on our standardized city tests. You know we have great pride in our record of achievement in this school.

His Double: I've tried to be decent to the fellow but he is such a visionary, he has crazy progressive ideas — he'll never get along in this school or any other.

Mr. Smith: I'm sorry about the low scores, but the class got interested in that civil rights project and have worked hard on it — I didn't have time to drill them on the subject matter included on the tests. I feel their project is very worthwhile, you see.

His Double: He's such an old fuddy-duddy. All he thinks about is memorizing stuff for tests. He doesn't know anything about a social science class and what it can do for kids. I don't know why I had the bad luck to land in this school.

Principal: It's not a question of the worth of the project. We have to meet the requirements of the school system and standardized tests are important. I thought I had made that clear to you when you took the position.

Double: He certainly is a misfit here. I hope I can get rid of him. I don't like anything about him. He thinks he's so d— much better than the rest of us.

Teacher: I thought the objective of a social science course was to prepare the pupils for good citizenship. I certainly am working at that objective and the students are really learning something in this project — what's more they are *enjoying* it and doing a fine job.

His Double: I can't stand this smug little man. How in H— do such reactionaries get in the high places. He hasn't looked at an Education book since he graduated from the county normal school twenty years ago. Well I'm going to fight this thing through to a finish. I won't resign and I'll go right on giving the kids something really worthwhile in that class.

This sociodrama proceeded from start to finish without any need for help from the leader. The spontaneity with which the four actors played their roles showed that the unrehearsed, uninhibited type of role-playing can be handled well by the participants. Both the audience and players enjoy the verbal dueling and it is a good warm up for free discussion.

When outgoing behavior and emotional expression is encouraged in role-playing there is a chance that neurotic persons will over-react to situations which are not at all disturbing to healthy personalities. Sometimes simple role-playing may result in a strong emotional or panic reaction in a seriously maladjusted group member. Individual counseling or psychiatric treatment must be made available to such persons immediately. Often the emotional upset is connected with shock-learning: a clearer self-understanding or perspective which "is hard to take." Three examples of over-reacting to role-playing participation follow:

Example 1

Manny, a member of a college psychiatric group, agreed to join the group only if he did not have to talk about himself. In the fourth session the sociodrama "G. I. Joe and the Korean girl," was performed, with Manny in the father role. He gave an excellent performance, arguing strongly against the marriage and urging Joe to think the matter over for a few months. He gave many reasons for believing the marriage would not succeed, and pointed out that "it is not fair to the children."

The next day Manny conferred with the group leader: he had decided to drop out of the group and the psychiatric treatment as well. He said he wanted to solve his personal adjustment problems on his own — he had figured out a method for himself.

Comment: In the opinions of the psychiatrist and group leader Manny had been unable to handle the pressures in the group, since all the other members talked frankly about themselves, their family conflicts, etc. The sociodrama theme was very close to Manny's inner conflicts which concerned rejection of his own family. The role-playing had pushed him too far and this, along with pressures of the psychiatric interviews were more than he could tolerate.

Example 2

Jerry, a college psychiatric group member, played the role of interviewee in a psychodrama which presented the discussion question, "Why do some people have a feeling of security and other people lack it?"

The two interviews concerned the extremes. The leader, playing the role of a reporter, first interviewed a London woman who had lost her husband and son in the Blitz. She had been bombed out and was living in a London subway, where the communal group had voted her the cheeriest of them all. This role was taken by Stella, the one non-psychiatric member of the discussion group.

In response to the questions she gave a common-sense, homely philosophy of life: living day by day and doing the best she could; accepting whatever the Lord sent in the way of pain or blessings. She said it was her job to make the best of things until such time as He ended her earthly sojourn.

Jerry, the second interviewee took the role of the college student who recently attempted suicide from the top of an office building. The leader started the interview, "I know that you are a brilliant student, with a family who love you and — it would seem — you have a great deal to live for. We are interested to find reasons why people try suicide. There were over 16,000 in the U. S. last year. My magazine is doing a feature on the subject; of course no names will be used. Would you be willing to analyze your feelings for me, why you wanted to jump off that roof, and how you feel now, here in the University infirmary?"

Jerry responded to the questions as though he had been thinking deeply about the subject. He tried to explain that a person like himself sets his goals too high. With repeated failures mounting and mounting, he becomes so worn out and depressed that he doesn't want to struggle any longer.

After the role-playing ended and the group started discussing the subject of feelings of security and insecurity, Jerry confessed that his being chosen to play that role was strangely coincidental. If he had known what the role consisted of, he would have refused to play it. Then he shamefacedly admitted that a few days before he had found himself in a panic state, obsessed by the desire to throw himself out of the dormitory window. Several of his friends came to his aid and stayed up half the night with him, figuratively holding his hand. He admitted that the psychodrama had done him good, but it had been a shock to play the part and to realize that he might have been in the same position as the other college student, if not seriously injured or dead.

Comment: The fact that Jerry was progressing well in his psychiatric treatment enabled him to discuss the psychodramatic shock and improved insight. Talking frankly after performing in the role-playing was effective catharsis for him. However, the group leader would *not* have asked Jerry to play the role if she had known of his panic episode. (This illustrates the difference between multiple counseling and group psychotherapy: in the latter the group leader might have forced Jerry to re-enact his panic episode in a psychodrama.)

Example 3

Barbara, 27-year-old graduate student, was a member of a college group composed chiefly of older students. Since the members had griped frequently about college, the sociodrama "The professor and the disgruntled student" was presented.

Barbara played the role of professor first, then the student. She was outgoing in both roles, telling the other player exactly what she thought of him in sarcastic, vindictive fashion. Immediately following her performance she rushed from the room. When she returned ten minutes later her eyes showed signs of weeping. The group were tactful, paying no attention to her. The lively discussion continued the rest of the session, with Barbara sitting quietly, not participating.

Shortly after this session Barbara phoned the leader and made an appointment for a counseling interview the next day. Her next appointment with the psychiatrist was a week away, and she felt the need of talking about herself to someone as soon as possible.

In the interview Barbara divulged the fact that the role-playing had shocked her into self-understanding which she had been resisting during psychiatric sessions: she was a spoilt child. The insight had come to her during the playing of the student role — she saw herself as she was really was, and accepted the new self-concept. This had been too much for her and she had left the room tó have a spell of hysterical weeping: facing "the awful truth" was the hardest thing she had ever done.

Barbara finally accepted emotionally the fact about herself which she had intellectualized for years. Successful psychotherapy during the next few months helped her reach a new level of maturity. The role-playing and group membership expedited the personal growth process.

The value of role-playing in leadership training courses has been recognized for many years by instructors and supervisors in educational, social case work, and industrial personnel work (2, 3, 4, 6, 9). An example of role-playing as a teaching-learning process for leadership trainees in a church youth group follows:

The author was asked to hold three sessions for eight new chairmen of youth commissions in the large student organization. These young people felt insecure and inexperienced in their new assignments; they wanted to learn how to handle commission and committee meetings effectively.

Briefed by the religious director, the author found that the learning needed by group members was in democratic (nondirective) leadership. Therefore the three meetings were structured as follows:

Session 1 — A free discussion including around-the-table presentations of individual problems and feelings of inadequacy of the group members in their new offices. At the end the leader summarized, emphasizing the value of this type of discussion in the first meeting of their commissions or committees.

Session 2 — Presentation of a sociodrama, "Wrong and right ways to lead a small-group planning meeting." Assigning roles to the six members who were present, (such as "the listener," "the know-it-all," "the yes-man," "the disagreer"), the leader demonstrated a badly managed committee meeting. She played the role of an autocratic chairman who has decided everything in advance and simply assigns duties to the group members, finishing the meeting in record time. A discussion followed this performance in which errors of leadership were listed and analyzed. Group members were encouraged to describe their feelings in the assigned roles and to give frank appraisals of their own weaknesses of leadership in past experiences as committee chairmen, etc.

Next effective leadership of a planning committee meeting was demonstrated, with the group members continuing in their assigned roles. This performance was limited to five minutes and merely pointed the direction of democratic planning activity in a group.

Session 3 — A discussion was held of imminent meetings to be led by the various group members. Feelings of anxiety and insecurity on the part of the members in handling their commission leadership assignments were fully expressed. Then the leader suggested that practice-leading by individual members be done. Each member in turn described the situation he wished to enact and the group served as the committee members in the meeting.

There was time for three role-playing episodes with discussion of the leader's performance in each. Selection of the three episodes provided a range of problem-situations which satisfied the needs of all eight members.

At the end the leader summarized the content of the three sessions, emphasized effective techniques of leadership, warned against errors which had been demonstrated in the first session. She said she would be available for individual conferences with group members when they wanted further help in their leadership problems.

> *Comment:* Several group members conferred with the leader from time to time during their first months of commission chairmanship activity. Reports from the others in the group showed that the learning had carried over effectively in their new positions. Role-playing both as "committee members" and as "leader" of a group gave these participants new insights into themselves; and it improved their empathy and skill in working with their own committee members.

Analysis of six techniques of role-playing leadership

From analysis of leader activity in the various types of role-playing discussed in the preceding and present chapters, six techniques are found. However, no one of these techniques stands apart from the others: they merge into a smooth sequence of leader-activity during a group session. Often not more than three of the techniques are needed, especially in nondirective sessions. Thus the reader is cautioned *not* to think of the six techniques as a prescribed set of procedures necessary to role-playing in multiple counseling projects. The techniques are:

133

1. Warm up and selection of problem.

2. Preparation or briefing of role-players.

3. Process-coaching. (Making suggestions to players during their performances)

4. Analytic-synthesis quizz. (Questions regarding the feelings and reactions of role-players after they have finished the performance)

5. Audience discussion. (Discussion by the whole group including the role-players)

6. The sum-up. (Group leader gives the significance, interpretations, or implications of the role-playing and discussion)

The Moreno psychodrama, performed on a stage before an audience, is the only example of role-playing where the six techniques are used in a formal sequence (10, 12, 13). The illustrations of role-playing used in the multiple counseling projects reported in this book show most frequent use of 1 (warm up and selection of problem) and 5 (audience discussion). Since role-playing is an auxiliary activity in multiple counseling projects and not more than ten minutes of the session is devoted to it, leader-techniques 2, 3, 4, and 6 are not needed in many of the psychodramas. Rather, group members take initiative, in keeping with the leader's effort to maintain a group-centered, client-centered activity.

Leaders must use their best judgment in deciding the amount of emphasis given to "direction" in role-playing. The admonition repeatedly made throughout this book is to keep multiple counseling a democratic group activity, free from visible controls that hint at authoritarianism. A group-centered project holds the promise of success; a leader-dominated project is handicapped from the start.

Explanations of the six techniques of leadership, with references to role-playing activities in which they were used, are given below:

1. *Warm up and selection of the problem*

This is best effected through the discussions themselves. A casual conversation, a lively argument, evidence of inadequate understanding of the discussion topic, a member's desire to present his problem to the group — any of these provide a warm up and selection of the role-playing theme.

The leader uses the needs or interests of group members as a guide for proper timing of the role-playing. Sometimes one discussion session serves as the warm up for the sociodrama which is presented in the next session, for example, "Two Negro students come north to college." Often impromptu role-playing is introduced at the height of the group interest in the discussion, for example, interview role playing with prospective teacher candidates. In a Moreno psychodramatic session the leader quizzes the audience for a choice of the pertinent problem and he interviews the central character as part of the warm up, for example, Len's psychodrama.

2. *Preparation and briefing*

This technique gives pertinent information to the role-players concerning the characters they are to portray. For example, in the psychodrama, "The principal and the social studies teacher," verbal directions to the teacher were:

"You are a social science teacher in a ninth grade. Your principal is very conservative and favors prescribed study courses and standardized tests. You, on the other hand, are a modern teacher who uses the core curriculum and project methods. Your pupils are enthusiastic and you are proud of their progress. When the principal calls you in to complain of the low grades your class got on the city tests you naturally defend your teaching philosophy."

The briefing may be done through typed direction slips for each role-player, for instance, the directions given in "The principal and Jim who is in trouble with the Law" and "Two Negro students come north to college." An example of a cryptic briefing consisting only of a description of the situation was used in a nondirective discussion therapy course for internees in clinical counseling. Two members of the group were given cards with the following directions:

1. You are an adult, out for a walk in the country with your niece, aged ten. A rooster chases a hen, catches her and performs the sex act. Your niece asks for an explanation of what one chicken was doing to the other.

2. You are a ten-year-old girl who knows little about the sex act. When you and your uncle see one chicken chase another and get on top of it you are disturbed and curious. You ask your uncle what is happening.

135

3. *Process coaching*

Contrary to procedures in real drama, the action in role-playing can be broken at any time. Thus "stopping the action" is done by the director in order to quizz the actors, reverse the roles, make suggestions. Or he can coach while the action continues, exhorting a role-player to greater emotional playout. Sometimes members of the audience cheer the actor on in a fight. For example, in "Eddie's fight with his father," group members helped Eddie to work into the role of his father through suggested comments and answers that an angry father would give to his son who was failing his college studies.

When the central character is not satisfied with the performance of an assisting role-player he can stop the action and show how the part should be played. For example, in the Moreno Workshop psychodrama where Len was the central character, he objected to the way the role of his mother was being played in the first scene. The action was stopped and he demonstrated how his mother had moved around the room, wringing her hands, and speaking in a high, nagging voice. Then action was resumed, with the person in his mother's role emulating the actions he had shown.

In multiple counseling projects process coaching was used only when role-players needed encouragement or were at a loss for words. Unless the leader is trained in Moreno techniques, process coaching may be so awkwardly done that it disrupts the role-playing instead of aiding it. Also, the leader cannot maintain a neutral, nondirective type of leadership, when he uses process coaching. For this reason many nondirectivists prefer not to use it at all.

4. *Analytic-synthesis quizz*

At the end of the performance the group leader questions the role-players and audience regarding their feelings and reactions during the role-playing. The purpose is to bring out individual differences among the group members and to stimulate new viewpoints or ideas on the subject presented in the role-playing. In multiple counseling projects, the discussion was turned over to the whole group without the leader giving his analysis or interpretations of the significance of the psychodrama. These were reserved for the sum-up, if they were included at all. For example, in "G.I. Joe and the Korean girl," at the close of the second scene the role-players resumed their seats in the discussion circle and the leader addressed the group:

"Well, you see there are two points of view. How many of you agree with the mother? How many believe the father is right? All right, it's 5 against 3. Who wants to start the discussion — anything that came to your mind as you watched the sociodrama. All right, Joe, since you were the main character let's hear your reactions first."

The leader moderates the discussion until everyone who wants to give his reactions has had a chance. After a free discussion gets underway the leader may withdraw into a role of observer-participant until the end of the discussion session. Then he may give his analysis and interpretations of the sociodrama and discussion.

5. *The audience discussion*

The purpose of role-playing is to stimulate discussion as well as to give new viewpoints and ideas. In the opinion of the writer the transition from the role-playing to a free discussion should be made as quickly as possible. This is different from the Moreno technique through which the role-players are the center of attention for a considerable amount of time before a free discussion is started. Audience members are often stimulated by the role-playing and want an opportunity to express themselves. For this reason it seems fair to give them the first chance to air their views after the performance. In multiple counseling projects often the author called on members of the audience for comments before the role-players.

6. *The sum-up*

In small groups where a very informal atmosphere is maintained, the leader often omits giving conclusions or interpretations. Because of individual differences which are always respected, group members are expected to learn different things, applicable to their own needs and interests. The leader does not want to interfere with individualistic reactions, nor to force his own opinions or a group conclusion on the members of the group.

SUMMARY

Suggestions to leaders of role-playing were made through an analysis of role-playing structures and the six techniques of leadership. Role-playing structures used in multiple counseling projects were (1) informal (2) interview-type (3) formal or planned. Moreno psychodrama structure, studied by the author at the Moreno Institute was described. Leaders of multiple counseling projects are advised not to use true psychodrama unless they are trained psychotherapists. Three notes of caution regarding the appropriateness of role-playing in small-group discussion projects were cited (1) go slow (2) use role-playing for variety and a change of pace (3) use role-playing for encouragement and social skills training. Illustrations from case studies were given. Finally the six techniques of leadership were explained, with advice regarding omission of formal steps in informal groups.

VIII

THE LEARNING PROCESS AND OUTCOMES
OF MULTIPLE COUNSELING

THE LEARNING SOUGHT IN A MULTIPLE COUNSELING ACTIVITY differs greatly from the objectives in a subject matter course. It also differs from a group problem-solving objective. In multiple counseling, the focus of the learning is the individual himself: his self-concept, his relationship to others, his growth toward maturity (2, 3, 8, 9).

The group climate is favorable to learning because the participants *want* to learn — they joined the group activity for that reason (1). When the activity is structured to provide a wide range of learning possibilities, each individual can choose from it the particular knowledges, attitudes, and skills which suit his needs. Both the group and the leader help him to recognize, to face, and to solve his personal problems. The interactions, discussions, and role-playing provide an action-medium for learning (10). Individual counseling guides the learner when he needs special help (12).

Classification of participants according to interest-needs

Prospective group members elect a personal growth project for different reasons. An analysis of 121 subjects in 15 miscellaneous group projects showed five categories of participants:

1. Apparently well-adjusted persons who enjoy group discussion as an activity.

2. Apparently well-adjusted persons who are curious about Personality and Human Relations and want to increase their knowledge of these fields.

3. Shy persons who are dissatisfied with their communication and social skills. They want to improve their performance in group activities, especially verbal expression and social interactions.

4. Insecure persons who are dissatisfied with, or uncertain of, vocational choices. They feel the need of counseling in terms of vocational guidance.

5. Unhappy persons who are dissatisfied with self and social adjustments. They feel the need of help with personal adjustment
   problems.

Many of the 121 participants, especially the teen-agers, could place
themselves in several categories. Category V included neurotic and
psychotic patients as well as so-called normal individuals who verged
on the neurotic because of inferiority and anxiety complexes. Some
of the "apparently well-adjusted" individuals in Categories I and II
were found to harbor inner conflicts, deep feelings of inadequacy or
insecurity unbeknownst to their most intimate friends or family.
These individuals often keep a facade of self-confidence and self-reliance, but they feel the strain of their hidden conflicts and anxieties.
Similarly some participants who placed themselves in Category IV
did so to give a socially acceptable reason for joining the group, although they were aware of more serious maladjustment problems.

Theoretically, participants in Category V should gain more from
a group project than those in Category I and II. This is not true
because of greater resistance to learning self-understanding and acceptance on the part of maladjusted persons. Conversely, one would
think that participants in Categories I and II lacked the needs and
incentive for learning as compared with unhappy, dissatisfied persons.
This did not prove to be the case. Often these well-adjusted participants gained fully as much in terms of improved self-understanding
and understanding of others. The conclusion, based upon the above
findings, is that this multiple counseling method is an excellent learning
medium for preventive Mental Hygiene and personal growth for all
kinds of people.

Types of learning

The most important type of learning gained through a multiple
counseling group experience, as in any sound educative process, is the
development of positive attitudes. These include healthy attitudes
toward oneself and others, and toward life itself, with the reasons and
purposes of man's existence (7).

Once healthy attitudes are initiated, the skills for living satisfactorily with oneself and with others can develop. Thus objectives in
a multiple counseling project include the learning and practice of
empathy, sharing with, and doing for, others.

140

Reconditioning for healthier, more spontaneous reactive behavior is important learning for many individuals in this group experience. Learning to gripe and to blow off steam, to engage in a violent argument, and to express one's feelings toward a member of the group or persons outside the group — these outgoing behavior activities help recondition the restricted, inhibited person for healthier growth toward maturity.

Learning progresses satisfactorily only when the individual is in a state of readiness for it. Therefore, while sixteen group sessions may be sufficient to bring the desired outcomes for participants in a preventive Mental Hygiene project, many more sessions may be needed to bring significant changes in attitude and behavior of the neurotic or seriously maladjusted participant. However, such persons can learn *something* worthwhile from the group experience; knowledge, attitudes, and social skills in peripheral areas are not to be scorned. It has been found that psychiatric patients placed in a so-called normal group for multiple counseling activity can gain "encouragement" therapeutic benefits which expedite psychotherapy. This was also found to be true for projects where all members were psychotic or seriously maladjusted. In other words, these patients were in a state of readiness for meaningful learning, even though it was limited to peripheral areas. (Social rehabilitative therapy is becoming a highly respected group activity in our culture).

To illustrate the kind of attitude-changes resulting from multiple counseling projects, statements picked at random from counseling interviews and written evaluations of 121 participants are quoted:

STATEMENTS OF ADULT PARTICIPANTS

"It helped to explain why I do some of the things I do — to clarify or reëvaluate my personality traits."

"I got reassurance that others have similar problems and difficulties."

"It increased my skill in expressing views on a subject, gave me more self-confidence in group discussion."

"It improved my ability to adjust to other people."

"Reasons for racial prejudices were made clear."

"Now I realize that first impressions may be quite wrong."

"I understand better the behavior causes in problem children, and can work out better methods in handling them."

141

STATEMENTS OF UNIVERSITY STUDENTS

"It confirmed my hopes (fears) regarding certain personal traits."

"It helped me in my vocational choice."

"Talking out problems and blowing off steam made me feel better."

"It made me want to improve my personal weaknesses."

"Acceptance by the group gave me reassurance and satisfaction."

"I learned much more than in a classroom because my mind had to work all the time — applying the principles learned, etc."

"It increased my skill in organizing my thoughts and expressing views on a subject."

"It helped me to understand and to get along better with [some person or group]."

"Acting in sociodramas gave satisfaction. It made the problem more real — stimulated thinking because it defined the problem to be discussed."

STATEMENTS OF HIGH-SCHOOL STUDENTS

"It is good to know that others have worries and problems like you."

"I see now that in comparison with the others I am too (moody, pessimistic, self-centered, forward, lacking in an aim in life, etc.)."

"I could feel just like the ones in the sociodramas — could see both points of view."

"I'll try harder to like people and act better (in groups, at home, etc.)."

"Arguing and talking was fun."

"Before this I couldn't stand up in English class and give book reports. Now I can, and have given two in succession."

"I have learned not to have such strong prejudices (racial, religious, or political)."

On the other hand, participants who dropped out or rejected opportunities for gaining self-understanding and warm human relationships within the group made the following comments:

STATEMENTS OF ADULT PARTICIPANTS

"This isn't the kind of group I'm interested in."

"It's been an interesting experience, but I didn't learn anything that I didn't know before."

"I'm leaving the group because I think I can solve my problem better by myself."

STATEMENTS OF UNIVERSITY STUDENTS

"I haven't changed. I always was tolerant and understood people, and my self-understanding was good before I started the group."

"I feel the same way about the group members as in the beginning, and the discussions didn't have any effect on me."

"It's a waste of my time to attend the sessions. I don't enjoy it or get anything out of it."

142

STATEMENTS OF HIGH-SCHOOL STUDENTS

"I can't see that the group has done anything for me."

"I didn't enjoy the meetings and I always felt ill at ease."

"I couldn't see much point to most of the discussions and I don't care for any of the kids in the group."

Among dissatisfied participants, five dropped out after the projects were underway and six finished their projects. Diagnosed and suspected personality disorders among these participants included congenital infantilism, character disorder and neurosis. These group members were not real members of their groups: they rejected membership even though the others in their groups tried to include them in the fellowship. They were not in a state of readiness for the kind of learning they needed. This fact was revealed also in psychiatric and counseling interviews through which they were unable to make progress in personal growth.

The varieties of learning coming from the group experience and adjunctive counseling for the great majority of the participants are contained in: (1) understanding and acceptance of self (2) and others (3) behavior changes including improved interpersonal skills. The stimuli to learning consist of information, interpersonal reactions, and social skill practice. Information which is useful to a participant in changing his attitudes comes from source material presented by the leader, exchange of personal opinions and experiences in the group, comparison of his personal traits with others. Interpersonal reactions which serve as catalysts to learning consist of feeling-expressions of hostility, guilt, sympathy, camaraderie, and reassurance. Practice in communication and social skills is an important aid to learning in an intimate discussion group. If the participant enters the group with a firm resolve to participate actively even though he is extremely shy and fearful, the reassurance he receives from the group and leader leads him to improved self-confidence and social participation.

Examples of the three types of learning process follow:

INFORMATIONAL STIMULI

Miss S, a forty-year-old schoolteacher, joined seven other teachers in a discussion group project in conjunction with a course in educational psychology. This was the first time in her life that she had ever had a truly intimate group experience. She was amazed at the self-revelations of group members and at her own performance in divulging secret personal worries and frustrations. Learning that others had similar problems and feelings did much for her. According to her letter to the group leader six months after the project she had gained self-confidence and a new attitude toward other teachers which resulted in happier relationships and adjustments on and off the job.

INTERPERSONAL REACTIONS

Eddie, a college freshman whose mother was hopelessly insane, feared that he was losing his mind. In addition to membership in a group of students with college adjustment difficulties, Eddie had individual counseling from the group leader and treatment at the Health Clinic for a psychosomatic complaint. In the group sessions he learned to express himself more freely, to argue and gripe. His performance in several psychodramas helped him to be more spontaneous in reactions to group members and the leader. The group participation aided his recovery from a serious neurosis, according to the doctor who was also a psychiatrist.

PRACTICE IN COMMUNICATION AND SOCIAL SKILLS

Ella, a twenty-seven-year-old graduate student had failed in college teaching and wanted to enter a religious group work field. Joining an undergraduate discussion project she had no intention of disclosing her past which included a serious family conflict and a hysteria conversion illness. Because of the fellowship and frank confidences within the group of four men and four women students she found it impossible to stay aloof. Thus group influences were able to change her manner and approach to people in a way which helped greatly in preparing her for the new social work field.

Reconditioning

Replacement of old attitudes with new ones, habitual fears associated with interpersonal relationships with positive interactions and self-confidence — this is the reconditioning process promoted by the permissive atmosphere of a multiple counseling group. In the first place it is a totally new experience for most participants. This fact favors the blotting out of negative reactions formed through unpleasant group experiences. In this group there are no pressures and no competition: the participant can relax; can feel free to say what he pleases, or to keep quiet. When he wishes to confide in the group, telling of his feelings of frustration, conflict, or inadequacy, he has a sympathetic audience made up of companions-in-misery and an adult counselor. He receives support and reassurance from them, regardless of how socially unacceptable (as judged by standards of other groups) his self-revelations may be.

Since personal growth depends on replacing bad habits with good ones, the reconditioning starts by getting rid of fears, inhibitions, resistances, and self-recrimination. An important influence for the group member is the discovery that others have similar feelings. The reconditioning process gets underway as the improved attitudes toward himself and others are formed. The positive change in behavior is completed when the participant puts his new attitudes into action, establishing new behavior patterns which give him greater satisfaction than the old ones.

Examples of the reconditioning process are given below:

1. Greta couldn't recite in her high school English class because of excessive fear. However, she had no difficulty expressing herself in the discussion group chiefly because several of her girl friends were in it and she didn't think much of the boys in the group. After four sessions in which she was the most active participant, she reported to the group leader that she was now able to recite in English class.

2. Dick, a college student training for music teaching, was fearful of speaking in any group, including the multiple counseling project. The leader reassured him that it was not necessary for him to talk in the sessions until he really wanted to. In the sixth session Dick started to show signs that he wanted to contribute to the discussion, but the four dominant members didn't give him a chance. This disturbed him and he conferred with the group leader, telling of his dissatisfaction and annoyance with himself for not being more aggressive. The leader again reassured him that he should not force himself, that the time would come when he could participate without fear or self-consciousness. During the next session Dick responded well when called upon for his opinions. But not until the sixteenth session was the reconditioning process completed. In that session Dick became the most dominant participant, almost monopolizing the discussion time. This pleased the group as much as it encouraged Dick. Just prior to this he had reported to the leader that his practice teaching was improving. He attributed the change from self-consciousness and fear to self-confidence as being strongly influenced by the group experience.

3. Gertrude's personal weakness was her suspicious attitude toward others. While being treated by a psychiatrist she was assigned to a discussion therapy project to help her social adjustments. Extremely self-conscious and aware of the fact that she was older than the others, Gertrude was sure no one in the group liked her. Actually all the group members did like her and she became reassured. However, after participating actively and well in one session, she was upset. Conferring with the group leader she said she had felt that the group members and the leader reacted negatively to her ideas and verbal contributions. The leader expressed surprise because she thought Gertrude had made a good impression. Gertrude asked the leader for an explanation of her feelings, saying, "What *is* the matter with me?" The leader was entirely frank in saying the trouble must be inside Gertrude: her use of projection was explained and she was urged to accept the facts, *e.g.*, she had made a good impression on both the leader and the group; her distorted reaction was caused by something within herself. (The attending psychi-

145

atrist was given the full details of the session and conference before Gertrude's next appointment).

Some weeks later Gertrude told the leader that although she had been very angry at her "accusation," she had given deep thought to the matter and had discussed it with her psychiatrist. Subsequent experiences in the dormitory had proved the leader was right. Gertrude finally was able to accept her personal weakness and to work toward overcoming the habit of suspiciousness.

Translating learning into action

New attitudes may be only a form of wishful thinking unless they are translated into immediate action pertaining to improved human relationships. The self-centered individual may believe that he is developing altruistic attitudes, but to be altruistic he must get into action. Most of us cry, "Touché!", as we read the passage in C. S. Lewis's THE SCREWTAPE LETTERS where the chief devil, Screwtape, advises his assistant how to influence the religious convert away from The Enemy:

"He thinks his conversion is something *inside* himself and his attention is therefore chiefly turned at present to the states of his own mind. . . . Encourage this. Keep his mind off the most elementary duties by directing it to the most advanced and spiritual ones. Aggravate that most useful human characteristic, the horror and neglect of the obvious. . . . It is, no doubt, impossible to prevent his praying for his mother, but we have the means of rendering the prayers innocuous. Make sure they are always very "spiritual," that he is always concerned with the state of her soul and never with her rheumatism . . . in time you may get the cleavage so wide that no thought or feeling from his prayers for the imagined mother will ever flow into his treatment of the real one. I have had patients of my own so well in hand that they could be turned at a moment's notice from impassioned prayer for a wife's or son's "soul" to beating or insulting the real wife or son without a qualm." (4, pp. 21, 22).

Obviously a good attitude or new resolution is useless unless it leads to behavior changes. The actual experience of sharing with others in a group project can produce new actions as well as new attitudes. Examples of neurotic and psychotic group members' actions illustrate this:

John and Carol: Carol made friends with John who was an isolate. She found him a job and helped him to find a better room, loaning him blankets and furnishings. This was a new experience for John who didn't believe there was such a thing as unselfish kindliness. Also John claimed to dislike and distrust girls because they are all gold diggers.

146

Mal and Arlene: When Arlene was confined to the infirmary Mal went to see her to cheer her up. This was the first time that Mal recalled that he ever went out of his way to try to do something for another person.

Lou and her group: Lou, a withdrawn psychotic patient, was able to tell her life story to the group. They proved to be a warm, sympathetic audience. Lou had never before talked of her troubles with anyone except the doctor. The support and friendliness of the group proved to be beneficial in her treatment.

John, Mary, Ella, Jack, et al: these individuals had been isolates until finding friendly acceptance in their various groups. The group influence and friendly contacts aided their personal growth and social adjustments immeasurably according to reports of parents, teachers, psychiatrists, and counselors.

Learning to face oneself

A change in self-concept is significant learning emanating from a multiple counseling project. This was characteristic of the majority of maladjusted participants in the fifteen group projects led by the writer. In many cases the change was a gain in self-esteem, or reassurance that the person was a worthy human being.

A change in attitude towards oneself was expressed in various ways by high school and college students, normal adults, and recovered psychotic patients. Examples of comments made in evaluations of the group experience follow:

GAIN IN SELF-ESTEEM

High school pupil: I'm not as bad a person as I thought I was.

College student: I see myself in a better light through comparison with others.

Normal adult: I have increased self-confidence as a result of confirmation of hopes ... am able to express my opinions more freely with less fear of criticism.

Psychotic adult: I don't feel so guilty about what I did. I can see that mental illness is like a physical illness sometimes.

GAIN IN SELF-ACCEPTANCE

High school pupil: I can see I'm too moody for my own good, but I'm trying hard to improve.

College student: It confirms my fears regarding certain personal traits ... made me want to improve my personal weaknesses.

Normal adult: I got reassurance that others have similar problems and difficulties.

Psychotic adult: I know myself so much better now. I won't let myself get into those high and low moods — I'll check up with my psychiatrist regularly.

The reader wonders how the change in self-concept comes about in a group process. Analysis of group influences showed that *comparison of self with others* and *group acceptance of the participant as a worthy person* were chief causal factors. Thus activities concerned with exchange of viewpoints and experiences, self-revelation, and social interactions were most important.

Associated with an improved self-concept was a new attitude and incentive to get along with oneself in spite of personal weaknesses. Expressions of this attitude by psychotic patients soon to be released from a mental hospital come from the notes in the log book of discussion therapy sessions:

"One thing's for sure. I won't go back to the old dives and get into trouble through drinking as I did before."

"I've decided I should live alone. I can't stand quarreling — it used to upset me for three or four days. . . . I agree that one can get emotions pent up and that's part of my trouble. I know I was in a bad habit of thinking too much all by myself. I'll try to be more friendly and I'd like to do volunteer social service work regularly."

"I hope I can get a job in L—, I'll feel much safer and will try to put the whole affair out of my mind (people involved in her delusion). I got along well in the job there before I became ill. I hope it will work out all right this time."

"I'll never keep anything from my husband again. He knows me better than I know myself. . . . I'll certainly go to a psychiatrist at the first sign of those bad feelings, only I pray to God that we can prevent this from happening again."

"I'm afraid it will happen again (mental illness). I have always felt so guilty about it — that it was all my fault somehow. Now I know there was something organic wrong too. . . . I'm going to depend on my eldest daughter, she knows the signs when I'm slipping, which I can't recognize in myself."

"I'm going to try to get my husband to do other things beside go to the tavern. . . . I know that drinking doesn't do me any good, either. . . . No, I don't think I'd divorce my husband even if the gossip is true. For the sake of the children I don't believe in divorce."

Learning new interactive skills

Participants who are gauche, insensitive to others, overtalkative and tactless, can learn discussive and social skills in a multiple counseling project. Their fellow members teach them in no uncertain terms! Frank criticism and detailed analysis of social-conduct errors in discussion sessions come from friendly participants who sincerely wish to help. Often the unskilled discussant confers with the group leader after a session asking, "How did I do today?" When he has a strong incentive to improve his social behavior, he learns very quickly. For instance, Bob (group 6), constantly asked group members and the leader for criticism of his performance in group sessions; he worked hard to overcome his habits of monopolizing the discussion, introducing irrelevant ideas, saying the wrong thing, etc. In six sessions he was able to improve immeasurably and the learning carried over to his other groups.

Similarly participants — far greater in number — who are fearful, inhibited, and self-conscious in groups can learn to forget themselves; to think in terms of the discussion material and to empathize with other group members. When these shy participants find that others feel the same way they do, perhaps to a greater degree, they feel sorry for the other person in place of pitying themselves. Often in the act of helping another person they start a more outgoing behavior pattern. Even though self-conscious, fearful participants do not get sufficient practice in "speaking up" in a group project to feel completely at ease, they are encouraged and usually improve in other interpersonal situations. Reports from such group members to the leader several months after the conclusion of a project showed an increase in self-confidence and social participation.

In an intimate group the braggart and scared rabbit often like each other and help each other to learn. An appreciation of personality differences tends to be accompanied by a respect for differences in a friendly group. Thus Don, the braggart, says of Tim, the listener, "I like him, he doesn't say much but what he says really means something." And Tim's opinion of Don is, "I wish I could be more like him — he says what he thinks and doesn't worry about what people think of him." A third personality type — the polite, ingratiating person — usually becomes more unpopular during a group project. This person often covers up strong feelings of hostility and aggressiveness with his too-polite facade. He has much to learn from the project and the group members attempt to teach him through frank opinions and criticism of his behavior in the group. For example, Hal's group became so irritated with his overly helpful and coöperative manner that several members conferred with the leader. They complained that Hal tried to lead the discussions, ask all the questions, yet he never gave a frank opinion and never disagreed with anybody.

149

The leader advised the members to be completely frank with Hal; to help him to see the negative effect he had on people. (Hal's background was full of similar failures in interpersonal relations). Perhaps the group influence would be beneficial to Hal's personal growth, too. Through the efforts of the group members Hal learned to see himself as others saw him. In defense of himself, he engaged in frank self-revelation concerning his childhood and past life, expressing strong feelings of hostility and inferiority which underlay his social veneer.

Opportunities for blowing off steam, griping, expressing resentment and hostility are plentiful in a multiple counseling project because of the free discussions and confidential atmosphere of the group. The leader encourages outgoing behavior. Use of role-playing is most helpful when a group contains withdrawn or inhibited members. An example of the leader's use of role-playing to break through the social facade of a graduate student follows:

The psychodrama, "The professor and the disgruntled student" was enacted. Robert, who had been a teacher and was now doing his graduate work, failed to use outgoing behavior in either role. He tried, and the group members made suggestions, encouraging him to "unbend," without avail. After the session Robert remained to discuss the role-playing with the leader. He was upset over his inhibited characteristics and confessed that he had consciously built them up during the years. He told of a traumatic experience at the age of twelve which still bothered him: he had almost killed his brother in a fit of rage. Since that day he had been fearful of "letting himself go emotionally." Now he was a psychiatric patient whose troubles were involved with the inhibited behavior pattern; he knew he should try to be more outgoing.

In subsequent sessions Robert was encouraged by group members and the leader to express his feelings and to "be himself." He was able to unbend somewhat, but insisted that he didn't enjoy it because it usually took the form of griping, resentments, bitterness. He argued that one should concentrate on positive, not negative feelings.

Robert's practice of spontaneity was self-limited, but he did learn the elements of spontaneity, and the chances are, he will put them to good use as time goes on. This learning was helpful in psychiatric interviews.

The reader may criticize the inconsistency of a method which, on the one hand, promotes warm, sympathetic human relationships, only to turn about and encourage expressions of hostility, violent arguments, etc. The fact is, the method attempts to be entirely consistent: when a human being has frustrations and conflicts, his interpersonal relations are colored by them. The intimate group is an excellent medium for ventilating these feelings. Once they dissipate in the healthy sunlight of free discussion, it is easier to get at the reasons for feeling frustrated or irritated — or at least to examine the feelings more objectively. Often the intimate group resembles a family situation (although group members seldom are conscious of it). A participant re-lives his competition with a brother or sister; his like or dislike of a parent. Thus Mal (group 8), competed quite openly for the attention of the leader. At the end of a session he would often ask the leader, "How did I do today?" Barbara (group 9), started to make insulting remarks to the leader in the seventh session, becoming openly antagonistic until the eleventh session. As she entered the room she said, "I've decided that I dislike you heartily." In a short conference after this meeting Barbara told the leader she resented the fact that she was dependent upon her; she worried during and after meetings as to the leader's opinion of her. Barbara was receiving psychiatric treatment from a male doctor, but she needed a mother-figure against whom she could express feelings of resentment and child-like rebellion.

Maladjusted group members may run the gamut of childish reactions during a group project. A participant who has been an only child seems to welcome the opportunity to fight with "brothers and sisters" in the group. However, results have shown that at the conclusion of a group project camaraderie is genuine; the relationships one to another, and toward the group leader, resemble the more mature relationships of adults who find that, after all, they *do* like their brothers, sisters and parents.

Learning to express one's opinions frankly even though they are in strong disagreement with another's — *without becoming angry* — is a useful social skill in a Democracy. Such objectivity seems to be more characteristic of the British than of the more volatile American. Perhaps we cannot set the goal so high: we modify it by saying — *getting over one's anger quickly without personal feeling against the antagonist.* Thus the Democrat and Republican are the best of friends except in the midst of a political argument, when they resemble bitter enemies (5).

An improvement in objectivity during discussions was a significant outcome for multiple counseling participants. It was found that the few group members who finished a project with feelings of dislike for fellow participants were the quiet or too-polite ones who refused to enter verbalistic battles; the most vehement protagonists turned out to be the best friends.

Unpredictable learning

Neither the group leader nor the participant can predict learning which may come as a sudden, intense reaction. A flash of insight or sudden change of attitude and incentive may be the result of a series of longterm influences. According to Mowrer and Stephenson sudden religious conversion, or personality change, is the end result of a long process (6, 11). Although psychotherapists use the technique of forced conflicts to influence personality change, a multiple counseling activity limits its influences to *opportunities for meaningful learning.* Sometimes, however, leader-psychologists utilize anxiety feelings and conflicts in individual counseling interviews.

Several examples of unpredictable learning gained by participants in multiple counseling projects follow:

1. *The situation:* Jeff (group 1), a high school junior, had continued daydreams of becoming a psychiatrist since sixth grade. Although of college caliber, his grades were low, and he was a maladjusted isolate. His fellow members in the multiple counseling project made him face facts: he was unpopular, could not express his psychological ideas logically (the group made fun of his attempted erudition). After four meetings he changed, trying to be more coöperative and ceasing his "showoff" behavior. By the end of sixteen sessions Jeff was accepted as a group member in good standing: the others expressed a liking for him on the final sociogram.

   The learning: In the final counseling interview Jeff was eager to admit the error of his ways and the extent of his learning through the group experience. This was the first group he had ever "belonged" to.

   Jeff dropped out of school, his daydreaming at an end. He enlisted in the Navy and on a furlough sought out the group leader. Expressing appreciation for the group influence in making him see himself as he really was, he said the lesson in "getting along with people" was paying dividends in Boot Camp.

2. *The situation:* Vera, a forty-year-old teacher of handicapped children, was a "listener" in the group of eight teachers and principals. While all the others talked freely of their difficulties handling problem children (their impatience and lack of understanding of such children), Vera did not contribute to the discussions. As a teacher of exceptional children she could have been helpful to the group.

   In the final interview with the group leader, Vera admitted a deep inferiority complex dating back to early school days. She analyzed reasons for it, but said she was so shy she could not participate in group discussions: she believed she had failed badly in the group project, saying "I had nothing to contribute to the discussions."

   The learning: Forcing a conflict on Vera, the counselor was able to show her that she had much to contribute to such a group; she had been selfish not to share her knowledge and techniques of problem children. This new idea of herself was reinforced through friendships she made in the group, and she started to gain self-esteem. She told the counselor she was determined to participate actively in the next group or organization in which she took membership. During the following year her resolution was successful; a change of personality came about. Thus in middle life she was able to throw off the inhibiting bonds of a distorted self-concept and to continue her personal growth.

3. *The situation:* Hulda, a member of a college psychiatric group, had broken her engagement a year ago. She continued to feel guilty and isolated, blaming herself for the failure of the engagement. Her depressed state had been aggravated by unhappy family relationships. She attended weekly discussion therapy sessions in addition to weekly interviews with her psychiatrist.

The learning: One of the male members of the group reminded Hulda of her former fiancé. Through acquaintance with this student she was able to analyze causes of the break-up and to see that she was not to blame: the two were not suited to each other. Support from the group regarding the family conflict also made her feel less guilty about that. She engaged in frank self-revelation which proved to be cathartic. The various influences at work in the group experience aided correction of a distorted self-concept and dissolution of her guilt feelings. Eventually she found a boy friend with entirely different characteristics from her former fiancé, and after successful psychiatric treatment, married him.

The three illustrations given above show the unpredictability of learning. A multiple counseling project sometimes resembles an obstacle course with prizes for everyone at the end. If the participant is willing to strive, he can finish the course and receive a reward, the nature of which may be a happy surprise.

SUMMARY

Explanations of learning outcomes of a multiple counseling experience were given, with accompanying illustrations from actual cases. Five categories of participants seeking membership in group projects were discussed. Varieties of learning gained by these participants are based on a change of attitude toward themselves and others. They include: (1) reconditioning (2) translating attitudes into warm human relations and action (3) improving self-concept and self-acceptance (4) improving personal interactions and spontaneity. Unpredictable learning may occur during the group experience which stimulates personal growth.

PART III

MULTIPLE COUNSELING TECHNIQUES
AND MATERIALS

IX

SELF-APPRAISAL DEVICES AND SOCIOGRAMS

Introduction

A MULTIPLE COUNSELING PROJECT usually includes some kind of self-appraisal or sociogram, the results of which are reserved for private conferences where the participant and counselor discuss self-ratings or ratings given the participant by his fellow group members. The type of self-assessment or sociogram depends upon the needs of the majority of the group. In general the dual purpose of self-appraisals is (1) to give the participant practice in healthy self-analysis; (2) to provide helpful information for individual counseling.

Self-appraisal devices include any kind of personal writing, check lists of personal traits, sentence completion tests, as well as standardized personality or occupational interests inventories, and projective devices. Sociograms may be structured to include choices on such qualities as attractive appearance, leadership, desirability as a friend, etc. Or they may be critical evaluations of fellow members written in essay form.

Group leaders will find that teen-agers enjoy self-appraisals, personality, and occupational inventories, while adults are more interested in discussions concerned with problems of personal and social adjustment. In other words, the teen-ager or young adult is in the process of growing-up and wants to improve his personality; the adult considers his personal growth "finished" and wants to make the best life adjustments possible within the limits of his personal strengths and weaknesses.

Materials illustrating the use of self-appraisal and sociogram devices in multiple counseling projects are given in this chapter. Selection of illustrations was influenced by the practicality of the devices: they were helpful in adjunctive counseling, meaningful to the participants, economical in time and cost.

The Autobiography

One of the most useful devices is the autobiography. After experimenting with structured and unstructured forms, the recommendation is made for a structured autobiography which gives leeway to the participant in writing as much or as little as he pleases. The autobiography may prove significant because of emphasis, or omissions. In a multiple counseling project with voluntary membership, the participant usually includes self-revelation in his autobiography which is of value in the counseling process, because the participant knows that it will be discussed in a private counseling interview, and not divulged to the group. Participants are urged to "let themselves go" in their writing, they don't have to worry about correct spelling and grammar, but rather, they concentrate on telling of their feelings: their frustrations, anxieties, hopes, and goals.

The following outline proved helpful in counseling teen-agers, college students and adults. It is an adaptation of the Bullis approach (2) and a form developed by Professor John Rothney of the University of Wisconsin (7).

Outline for Critical Autobiography

Directions: Write about yourself as frankly as you can, trying to give a true picture. Use the following framework, but make your write-up as long or as short as you wish.

THE PRESENT — WHAT KIND OF A PERSON ARE YOU?

A. *Are you emotionally mature?*

> Able to make and keep friends.
> Able to make decisions.
> Able to accept responsibility.
> Able to bring personal problems out in the open and discuss them frankly with someone.
> Able to "win" modestly and "lose" gracefully, without alibis.
> Able to carry on everyday duties even while under strain or when you dislike what you have to do.
>
> (*Please add any other ways you think emotional maturity is measured, and discuss your strengths and weaknesses*)

B. *Is your life well balanced?*
(*Foundations include*):

1. An educational or vocational goal that holds your interest and keeps you working hard at it.

158

2. Worthwhile leisure time activities which are a change from your work.

3. Comrades in your work and play.

4. A religious faith or philosophy of life — something to live up to, and to lean on in time of crisis.

(*Shock absorbers include*):

1. An ability to relax whenever you want and need to.

2. A sense of humor to keep you from taking life and yourself too seriously.

(*Attitudes include*):

1. Facing reality — facing facts; doing the job that's got to be done, not procrastinating or escaping from situations.

2. Being sympathetic to those less fortunate than yourself — not indulging in self-pity.

3. Trying to expand your areas of interest — not staying in a rut.

4. Trying to cultivate a love of beauty — enjoying nature, art, music, etc.

THE PAST — How did you get this way?

What influences in your heredity and environment have molded you? Are your moods, likes and dislikes, habits and behavior similar to mother, father, brothers or sisters? Did your success or failure in school affect the way you feel about "book learning" or about yourself as a person? Do you remember any teachers or adults who did a lot for you when you were in elementary school? Do you have any happy or unhappy experience in your childhood that made a vivid impression on you, that helped to make you the way you are?

THE FUTURE — What do you hope to become?

What are you striving for? What would you like to be ten years from now? Do you think you will be able to achieve your goal? If not, what second best goal can you reach which would be satisfactory? Do you think you will be happy?

Examples of autobiographies written voluntarily by high school and college students in multiple counseling projects are given to show three different ways of following the same outline:

Example 1

Greta is a seventeen-year-old high school Senior, average intelligence, sophisticated and popular with boys. She is in a state of rebellion against her parents, and has told the discussion group frankly that she dislikes both her father and mother. She wants to get away from home and their control as soon as possible. Either nurses' training or marriage would accomplish this end. The autobiography was written prior to her meeting an ex-G.I. who had a good job and was a good marital prospect.

159

The Present

A. emotionally mature: I usually make friends quite easily. The friends I have I have known since I started at — high school and they are usually nice.

decisions. Making decisions usually don't bother me but I usually wait until the last minute to do it.

responsibility. When mom was sick and Dad worked I took the responsibility of doing the cooking and housework. The thing I don't do so good is remembering, I forget or just don't pay attention well enough.

problems (personal) — My problems I usually don't discuss them with anyone and if I do I don't tell the whole thing just part of it.

Yes I think I honestly can say I win modestly & lose gracefully. Cause in football & baseball, etc. There isn't much you can do even if you didn't agree on the score or something.

When I don't like to do something I usually try and get out of it. (doing dishes) but I feel guilty if someone has to do something I was supposed to do and didn't.

My worst weakness is remembering. I can be told to do something & five minutes later I forget. Another weakness is believing a boy I have gone out with many times. Although I have learned not to believe or trust any boy. What I do best is forgiving and forgetting anything that may or should have happened. I also think I talk too much in Personology Club and I become aggervated quite easily with some people. I also laugh a lot, even if some people think its' not funny I usually do unless they are just obnoxious.

B. Life Well Balanced

1. I have always wanted to be a nurse of some kind. I am still thinking of being one. I have tried to take all the sciences etc. to help me but I am still sure I'll never become a nurse. I honestly don't think I'm smart enough & all my bad points wouldn't go well with nursing.

2. In my leisure time I usually daydream. I love to daydream. Also in my leisure time I like to sew. I haven't much leisure time though.

3. I believe in religion very strongly. I think everyone has something in their thoughts on life hear after. If people didn't believe in some kind of religion their would be more stealing, killing & every thing that is against the ten commandments. Of course the law is still against them. I think a great saying is: "Do unto others as you would have them do unto you." Also try & think how life is so short on earth comparing to heaven or where ever you go.

2.

1. I can't relax when I should. If I am going to give a talk or something I am just tied in a knot until its over.

2. As I said before a sense of humor I guess I have. I think it helps a lot if you are feeling blue, if something didn't go the way you expected it to go, if you are sick

it cheers you up & also it can make someone else feel better. Course you can be to silly to. I probably am sometimes.

1. I am a great one for putting things off until the last minute. Facing facts I guess I do alright. But if I want something bad enough I try & overlook the true facts & try believe the way I want too. I also hope things will go a certain way and usually wait & see if it will. In doing a job I try & get it over real fast and am likely to do it a little less neat if I don't like it.

2. When I see someone sick or less fortunate than I, I just feel so awful I could just about give my last cent to make them better if I could have the money to do it. If I was real rich I would fast find everyone poor and give them everything they needed. I don't feel sorry for me ever. Unless I can't go out at night when I would like to & then I'm just mad, I guess.

3. I don't think I stay in a rut very much although I don't like to go places I have never been for fear I might not have a good time or do something foolish. I have many interests, like going skiing, skating, sewing, dancing etc. Most kids do.

4. I love music, I like to listen to waltzes, and slow popular songs also balads, like Old Kentucky Home etc. I love to play the piano & I took about 4 or 5 years.

The Past

My family and friends have molded my life also I have done what I wanted to do. My environment has been kind of a quarreling one so I guess I have an awful temper although I sure have improved since a couple of years ago. I can control it a lot better now. My Mom and dad & two sisters all have tempers. One is a lot more cross than I am and she doesn't like me too much unless she wants something. My younger sister is a lot sweeter. She isn't near as stingy as the other. I think schooling is important even if you have more difficulties than some. My teacher in 9th grade English was one who taught me quite a lot of grammar. I guess even when I was small I wanted to help people who were less fortunate & still do.

The Future

I hope to become a nurse. I would like to be married and be loved. Also a few kids. Yes I think I will someday get married. If I never get married I probably will keep on being a nurse if I am ever one. If I'm not a nurse I would like some job working with little children."

(*This girl failed to qualify for nursing training, but she married an ex-G.I. with a good job shortly after graduating from high school and became a mother within a year. She saw the counselor, displayed the baby with great pride, and seemed blissfully happy in her new role*).

Example 2

Dana is an 18-year-old high school Senior who is rather unsocial, belonging to none of the activity clubs, never attending the dances or dating. He is very uncertain of a vocational choice and appears to be insecure and confused.

161

"Am I emotionally mature? I would say I was and still am. I have few personal friends, for I seem altogether different from the other fellows. My likes and dislikes vary greatly with theirs and to tell the truth I think a lot of the fellows I associate with each day are in their second childhood or else they never got out of their first one. Decisions sometimes are very hard to make, such as at the present. My folks and brother think I should try and get a deferment from the army to go to the university, but I don't think so. I feel that it's a great deal better to get something of that sort out of the way, so you don't always have to be thinking about it, then to just leave it drag along. I try and I believe I accept all or most of the responsibilities that I am capable of handling, I feel that if another person is better fitted to handle something than I myself, and he has got the time he should undertake that task. I wouldn't think of taking my personal problems out from the discussion of my folks and brother, for I feel they are better fitted to help me and more willing to do so than an outsider would be. My personal problems haven't been so difficult that I couldn't get them straightened out by myself or with a little help from my immediate family. Winning or losing in a correct manner, I believe should come under good sportsmanship and the ability to face reality. I feel that if you lose you lose and you might as well make the best of it, for you can't change matters anyway. I can carry out my duties most of the time without grumbling, but when I see that I'm being taken advantage of the task doesn't set so well with me. There are times and I believe this is true with us all, when we are moody and when asked to do something we sort of resent it, don't you think so? One thing that I'm not mature in and that's that I don't have enough confidence in myself, but I suppose that will come in time.

I wouldn't say my life is well balanced, for my interests are too confined. I like hunting, nature and animals. Religion is a grand thing but for me many things are so darn hard to understand. Some of the people I see going to church turn my stomach for I know they aren't real Christians, for an example I'm going to take a song that was quite popular a little while ago, I don't know its name but a line of it goes like this, "I raise cane on Saturday and go to church on Sunday." How can people be like that and still go to church? A lot of people that don't go to church are much better Christians than those that go to church every Sunday and profess to be good Christians. Agriculture holds my interest and I not only intend to own my own farm but I am going to! In my estimation my only true friend is my dog, for it takes a crisis or a pile of trouble to really show person whether he has a true friend or not.

Another thing I do is to take things too seriously, I guess my sense of humor is buried a great part of the time.

My attitude toward most things I believe is better than average. School gives me a pain but instead of doing like some kids I know I try to make the best of it. Actually it isn't the school that gripes me, but certain classes and home-work that I dislike. Some kids flunk their courses and have to take them over, because they don't like school in general. I know this is a foolish attitude to take for they have to go through the same class again and waste a years time whereas if they would have made the most of it they could have had another year of school behind them.

One big influence upon me was brought about by my brother's drinking. He got going with a gang and almost over night they started to drink. When I saw how much misery his drinking caused in our family I made up my mind that I wasn't ever going to start. I'm glad to say my brother got straightened around before it was too late. I believe a child is influenced to a great extent by his mother because the mother is with the child much more than the father, anyway in early childhood.

In grade school I had a teacher by the name of Mrs. Stone. She was a grand person. When I had her we were learning to spell and read and it so happened that I missed several weeks at this time. I was getting low grades in my spelling tests so I started to cheat, after that I got hundreds until one day I got caught. I had to come after school and she talked to me about the happenings in the morning. She even postponed the spelling test to give me a little extra time. I can remember how hard I worked on that spelling lesson and when she gave the test again I got eighty-five. I was really proud of that grade and I made up my mind then and there that I would never cheat in another test. Now when I see someone cheating in an exam I just feel sorry for them. They may benefit at the present time by getting a high grade, but what have they really learned, nothing!"

This student had especially painful growing pains concerned with the common conflict: egocentricity versus desire for social acceptance. By the end of his senior year he regretted his isolationistic behavior during high school. In the follow up interview with the leader-counselor he said, "When I have kids I'm going to see that they don't make the same mistake — they are going out for a lot of activities in school and really have fun, which I never did."

Writing the autobiography coupled with comparison of himself with others in the group helped to give this student important insights and a new incentive to change from a self-centered suspicious individualist to a person "with social stimulus value."

Example 3

Sarah is a college senior in the teacher training course. She hopes to teach English and Speech, but is frank to admit that her fears of racial discrimination are deep seated: will her being a Jew influence her chances of getting a job? She is a well-adjusted student, never having needed or sought counseling. The group project was her elected field work in Educational Psychology.

163

I. Emotional Maturity

THE PRESENT

Since society is made up of individuals, and their ability to work and play together is perhaps one of the most adequate means by which to measure its progress, it is important that one make and keep friends. Fortunately I have little trouble making friends, and I don't often lose friends. There are, of course, a number of friends to whom I feel closer than to others and with whom I would discuss things which I would rather leave unsaid in the presence of some. There are, then, those in whom I confide more than others.

I have noticed, especially this year, however, that I am respected by many girls in the dormitory and members of my classes. This has come to my attention by appointments I have received to positions of varying degrees of importance. Also I have been asked for advice on many occasions, perhaps because I am considerably older than many and a bit more mature. This may sound like a somewhat flattering account, but as soon as I begin to relate the past, my writing will take on an entirely different vein.

As to my ability to make decisions I am not so sure, and hesitate to make any definite statement. Spur-of-the-moment decisions are difficult for me to make, and when I do make them, I often find myself thinking about them afterwards. Someone told me some time ago that I lived in retrospect. There is probably some truth in that statement.

However, when I have some time in which to make my decisions, I can think about them and find myself in a more favorable position later. At any rate I know why I made that particular decision.

I am often very reluctant to accept responsibility, perhaps because I underestimate my ability, but I am gradually overcoming this, and am quite willing and able to undertake responsible jobs. I am thinking particularly of a responsible appointment I had this year, which I seemed to handle quite successfully.

My discussion of personal problems is limited primarily to my immediate family. I have complete confidence in my family and feel most at ease to discuss my personal affairs or problem there. I also feel that my personal problems are of greater interest to members of my family, and their advice is always frank and sincere.

During my high school years I debated and partook in forensic activities. In both of these activities I took honors and was also defeated. This, I think, taught me to win and lose modestly and graciously.

And now to my everyday duties. I usually do my every day work, but I procrastinate as long as I can in activities which I dislike. Hence I do not always do my best work, and this is made quite evident in my school marks. When I am under strain, my work lacks the quality it has when it is accomplished under normal conditions, because I find myself pressed for time. However, I am always very conscious of getting my work done at the specified time.

II. Balance

At the present time I am working toward a teachers certificate in order that I may teach when I graduate from college. Since my main interest lies in the field of speech, it is that phase of my college work in which I place the greatest emphasis. I feel that teaching is one of the most gratifying and lucrative fields for women and certainly always something to fall back on.

I spend my leisure time in various ways. I may sit down and read a book, or I might do some knitting — usually for someone in the family. Then again I may listen to the radio — opera, play, music or other entertaining programs. I have no particular hobby of any sort, except miniature painting from the Metropolitan Museum of Art which I receive monthly. I am of the Jewish faith, but am not a church-goer. (I do frequent the synagogue but not regularly). To me religion is something totally individual, and I do not believe that the synagogue is the only place of worship. I do not belong to the orthodox branch of the Jewish religion, rather I am reformed, as many German Jews are. I do not believe that the Jewish religion is the *only* right one — for me it is right. I am of the opinion that religion is a belief, and every human being, being of a different type, constitution, coming from a different and individual home, is entitled to his individual belief which is consoling and comforting to him.

As regards relaxation, I seem to have little or no difficulty. There was a time when I was completely unable to relax unless all of my work was fully completed. I found however, that I was very nervous as a result, and that my work was considerably poorer. When however I have something pressing on my mind I cannot relax. As a result I am moody and temperamental and try to stay away from my friends so that I do not become obnoxious.

As for my sense of humor — it is there. I am by no means a humorist, but am often told that I am the "serious type." I generally do not appreciate "corny jokes," but am very fond of "good humor." My life is not completely devoid of humor, not full of it, but enough to keep me away from many worries, and get along with people.

I think I am quite a practical person who faces reality. I do what has to be done; I generally don't escape situations, however I do procrastinate. I'm not as bad as Hamlet, who was the greatest procrastinator ever.

I am a sympathetic person — especially sympathetic with the less fortunate, if their misfortune was caused by pressures not controllable by them. I have no sympathy with those who deliberately make themselves miserable. I feel sorry for myself in one place only — in bed. This may sound very strange, but it is there where I can, if the situation calls for it, "weep over my sorrows." I like to be completely alone when I indulge in self-pity which, however, happens rarely. I remember when I was in high school and "broke up with my boy friend." How sorry I did feel for myself then.

My interests are quite varied, and I try to widen them daily. I am by no means a narrow-minded person, especially since I come from a family in which many interests prevail. My appreciation for art, music and many of the finer things in life is apparent by the music I enjoy over the radio, my Metropolitan Art miniatures, by the concerts and plays I attend.

In general I believe that I am quite a balanced individual, my interests ranging from some of the finer things in life to outdoor sports. There is however, great room for improvement. Often I find myself very critical of others and sometimes unduly so.

165

THE PAST

As regards my hereditary and environmental background I can say that my physical constitution was inherited from my parents. No one in the family is heavy. Many of my habits and mannerisms were likewise inherited.

My environmental background seems to show itself in my interests. Coming from a European background I am much interested in classical music. I myself play no musical instrument. I sing for my own enjoyment. I am also interested in art all of which things I have been exposed to in my early childhood. My family is also very reserved which element has undoubtedly had an influence upon me.

And now to my education and its influence on my general outlook on life and learning. As for my failures, they seem to have little or no influences on my book-learning inasmuch as they were mostly in Germany, where I failed one grade completely and got considerably poor marks in all other grades with the exception of first grade which was before my long illness. I think however that my failure in school in Germany, and the attitude taken by one teacher who insisted that I was an abnormal child, may have some bearing on my feeling of inferiority which I display in some situations.

My successes have all been in the American schools, where I was treated like a "normal" child. My first American teacher was particularly patient with me, since I could not understand any English when I first came here in 1939. My successes have definitely had an influence on my choice of career and my willingness to learn.

In my childhood I did a great deal of traveling in Germany and to the Baltic Sea. This was one of my happy experiences which had an influence on my present appreciation for nature.

I think my most unhappy experience in Germany was the element of being persecuted. When I went to school in Berlin, I was forced to go to four different schools within a two-year span, because one by one the Jewish schools were forbidden to operate. When the Nazi situation reached its zenith my father was in the concentration camp for close to 8 weeks. All my other relatives were there also and some of them were in Buchenwalde which was the most vicious concentration camp in Germany.

Because of the fact that I lived under this Nazi regime I was unwilling to acknowledge my faith when I first came to the United States. This I think is understandable. I am still very sensitive to any remarks which have a malicious intent. Whether or not the following has been influenced by my unpleasant experiences in Germany is hard to say: I am inclined to think so, however. During my elementary school years and also most of my high school years, I took on quite a distinct feeling of superiority in an attempt to cover up my inferior feeling. Consequently, I was considered by many to be "stuck-up," "stubborn," "egotistic," "hard to get to know," and the like. I was not particularly liked by my class mates, although I don't think I was ever abhorred. During my last year in high school and my college days, I have bettered myself considerably. I am still a very frank person, and I sometimes catch myself at a sarcastic remark. But I think I am now beginning to use more and more discretion all the time.

The Future

If I were to choose my occupation for ten years from now, I think I would choose that which is the desire of every young girl — that of being a mother.

If, however, I will not become the wife of a "desperate" young man, I would like to be teaching in a high school. But in this wavering world situation, who knows what the future may hold.

. . . .

This is by no means a beautiful treatise of any sort: it is merely an objective account. I am sure I have disobeyed all the rules of journalism.

Sarah was able to share with the group all the content of this autobiography. The ventilating of her feelings of inferiority and apprehension because of being a Jew helped to bring about a new self-concept: the fact that Sarah was the most attractive and popular member of her group was important in this change. Adjunctive counseling, limited to only three interviews, added support, helping to dissolve the inferiority complex and defensiveness which had dominated her life for fifteen years.

Sarah secured a fine teaching position and when last heard from (two years after the group project), she was successful and happy in her position; she was also seriously interested in an eligible bachelor of her own Faith.

The examples of case studies and autobiographies given above show the possibilities for use of autobiographical material in the counseling process. Facts and feelings which the participant can't talk about in a group are given in a confidential writing. However, in many cases the participant was able to talk more freely about himself in the group after writing the autobiography.

When participants were asked to evaluate the experience of writing the autobiography the consensus was: self-understanding was aided immeasurably; a new, more accurate perspective of oneself as a person and of one's relationships with others in the past and present was achieved.

Self-ratings on behavior traits

A simple self-rating sheet of temperament characteristics, devised for use by the counselor in comparing client ratings with scores on the Minnesota Multiphasic Personality Inventory (5) proved to be interesting to participants and helpful in the counseling process. (This was also used in projects where the MMPI was not given). The self-rating device was an outside assignment for participants: rating sheets were given out at the end of one session and returned privately to the leader-counselor. Self-ratings were not discussed in group sessions, but were used in individual counseling interviews. However, general questions about personal traits follow an informational talk by the leader in a group session. Such a discussion gives the leader a chance to explain individual differences in personality. Focus on vocational guidance is recommended. Thus a discussion of the kind of person who is best suited to certain occupations keeps personal trait analysis realistically centered.

A sample of the self-rating sheet follows:

TEMPERAMENT INVENTORY

Directions: Mark yourself on a five-point scale for each question:

Seldom if ever...................................	(1)
Once in awhile..................................	(2)
About half the time.............................	(3)
With a few exceptions...........................	(4)
Habitually......................................	(5)

1. Do you worry about your health and have symptoms which you want to find out about... ( )

2. Are you very active and full of energy so that you want to be doing something all the time during the day and in the evenings........................... ( )

3. Do you have any chronic complaints such as stomach trouble, muscular twitching, headaches, or tendency to dizzy spells, etc. (Any of these — or any other)... ( )

4. If you tend to be a "perfectionist," that is, are dissatisfied with a job because you haven't done it perfectly — does it worry you so you want to do it over again.. ( )

5. Are your favorite activities concerned with music, art, drama, literature.... ( )

6. Are you self-conscious so that you dread criticism from others, or worry about what they think of you...................................... ( )

7. Do you tend to be more pessimistic or depressed than your friends and acquaintances.. ( )

8. Do you dislike having to abide by rules and regulations.................. ( )

9. Do you tend to be very interested in your own thoughts and to day-dream, even when there are people around you or when you are out in a crowd.... ( )

10. Do you prefer to spend your leisure time by yourself — reading, listening to the radio, fishing, etc. — instead of doing things with a crowd (gang)...... ( )

CHECK ANY OF THE FOLLOWING IN WHICH YOU BELIEVE YOU ARE NOT "AVERAGE" (FOR YOUR AGE)

casual conversation

shyness

self-centeredness

social conscience

honesty

egotism

feeling of inferiority

feeling of inadequacy

feeling of inner security

emotional maturity

regard for the opposite sex

fondness for parents

conformity to conventions (of your school, community, etc.)

suspicions regarding motives of others

trust in a Divine Providence

confidence in oneself to work out problems

ability to make friends

A third self-appraisal device concerns personal values, philosophy, strengths, weaknesses. This stimulates discussions on personal goals and philosophy in group sessions; it is an effective basis for frank discussions in counseling interviews. The sample below was filled in by a 21-year-old graduate student who had sought counseling help for feelings of depression and social inadequacy. The outline given to the participants is indicated by the capitalized headings:

VALUES — GOALS — STRENGTHS — WEAKNESSES

THIS I BELIEVE:

"(1) *Social principles:* the right of each person to develop on his own, free from unnecessary interference. The provision in society of equal opportunities for each to realize and fulfill all his potentialities on the economic, social, aesthetic, intellectual, and sexual levels; the right of the individual to refrain from doing what he does not believe in (psychologically).

(2) *Socio-political principles:* beliefs in the primacy of human needs, the sacredness of human life, the necessity for cooperation, and as a result, the need for an equitable distribution of wealth and property; freedom and equality as above; devising a program of action consistent with these principles (democratic socialism).

(3) *Life orientation:* a philosophy of the present, in which the individual is oriented toward getting the most out of even the most routine of *current* activities; as

169

for me, a concentration on friendship, music, and intellectual stimulation as ultimate values which have already been realized, plus an attempt to reach others, notably, love."

FIVE MOST IMPORTANT CHARACTER TRAITS (in my opinion)

1 — impersonality
2 — inhibitions
3 — friendliness   (this student misunderstood the question
4 — over-conscientiousness   and listed his own most *prominent* traits)
5 — excitability
6 — competitiveness

I SHOULD TRY TO:

1 — be selfless and altruistic
2 — develop close and loyal bonds of friendship
3 — contribute to myself and mankind by self-fulfillment (social principles)

MY PERSONAL STRENGTHS ARE:

1 — Awareness of self and others
2 — Capacity for friendship and deep feeling
3 — a well-developed intellect
4 — a strong desire for self-determination and self-development

I SHOULD TRY NOT TO:

1 — concern myself with fame, prestige and recognition
2 — search for the truth but never find it
3 — lean on others too heavily
4 — withdraw into myself

MY PERSONAL WEAKNESSES ARE:

1 — Egocentrism
2 — Inability to realize the potentiality to fullest extent because of neurotic defenses. (This is an understatement)
3 — An inability to harness the intellect as it could be harnessed, and an outsized perspective on it
4 — A lack of devclopment of the skills of self-relianee and self sufficiency

ADDITIONAL SELF-EVALUATION

"My understanding of the situation is that since my high school days I have been gradually advancing in many of these areas where the rift between potentiality and actuality appears so tragically wide. Each step forward has given me great satisfaction, but an advancement in some areas, for example, in awareness of self and others, in intellectual ability, and in the wish for independent growth, has left me painfully aware of what is probably my basic problem, the inability to relate myself meaningfully to others in terms of warmth and love. However, I'm still trying to reduce the conflicts and anxieties in which these inadequacies are rooted though with very mixed success."

170

This student, who intellectualized continually in group sessions, gained insight through the frank criticism of his fellow members: he tried to stop hiding behind a facade of intellectual verbiage. With successful counseling, supplemented by the group experience, he changed from a defensive behavior pattern to a realistic one through which personal growth was stimulated.

A novel type of self-appraisal, which appeals particularly to "date-able" groups, is a questionnaire entitled, "How Lovable Are You?" used in a University course in courtship and marriage.

The following example was filled out by a member of a college multiple counseling project. He had good reason to be upset at this low score because it substantiated other appraisals, including those of several psychiatrists, to the effect that he was seriously maladjusted.

HOW LOVABLE ARE YOU?

Directions: After each of the following questions you will find a set of five scoring figures. Circle the figure which represents your answer to each question on this basis:

    0 ....not at all, never
    1 ....somewhat, sometimes, a little
    2 ....an average amount, about as often as not
    3 ....usually, a good deal, frequently
    4 ....entirely, practically always

1. You maintain a happy disposition and cheerful outlook on life....   0 (1) 2 3 4
2. You are neat, clean, and well-groomed........................   0 1 (2) 3 4
3. You are considerate and unselfish, not taking advantage of her (his) generosity...   0 1 2 (3) 4
4. You have a normal and wholesome attitude toward sex..........   0 1 (2) 3 4
5. You take an active part and constructive part in the affairs of your group, school, church, or community.....................   0 (1) 2 3 4
6. You are responsive...   0 (1) 2 3 4
7. You get along well with your own parents and other relatives.....   (0) 1 2 3 4
8. You are sincere, honest, genuine, and unaffected...............   0 1 (2) 3 4
9. You are tolerant and adjustable, seeing good or finding interest even in things quite different from those to which you are accustomed..   0 1 2 (3) 4
10. You are distinctly feminine (masculine).......................   0 1 (2) 3 4

             Total...   17

Now add up these scores. You cannot expect a perfect score of 40, but if your score is less than 20, you will have to take some energetic measures of self-improvement, if you expect to win the love of a man (woman) and hold it.

Another type of self-evaluation which can be used in conjunction with a group session discussing "personality modifiability" is taken from the inspirational book, "The Art of Real Happiness." (6). The self-rating sheet is called, "What Kind of a Person Are You?" and true-false answers are used. Results are not discussed in the group, but one of the questions often stimulates a discussion — especially No. 8.

WHAT KIND OF A PERSON ARE YOU?

( ) 1. Am I self-centered? (or do I take other people's needs and desires into account)

( ) 2. Am I intolerant of other people and of opinions that differ from mine? (or am I prepared to concede that others have a right to their own habits and beliefs: in short can I live and let live)

( ) 3. Am I constantly irritated by large or small annoyances? (or do I take things as they come with a minimum of friction)

( ) 4. Do I maintain an unrelenting, high pressure pace? (or have I learned the inestimable value of setting aside some time each day for complete mental and physical relaxation)

( ) 5. Do I have real resources within myself? (or am I depending on others to entertain and amuse me)

( ) 6. Am I growing a crop of hatreds and resentments to sour and embitter my life? (or do love and affection dominate my relationships with others)

( ) 7. Does an appeal for help make me close my mind and pocketbook? (or am I generous with my time and money)

( ) 8. Do worry and guilt gnaw at my peace of mind? (or am I content to do my best to solve each problem as it comes, forgetting past failures)

( ) 9. Lastly, do I merely pay lip service to the principles of my religion? (or are they a practical, dynamic part of my daily life)

Discussion topics stimulated through this questionnaire may be:

1. Griping about parents or grandparents.

2. Feelings of anxiety and guilt common to group members at present time.

3. Rationalization concerning school or job pressures which force one into "an unrelenting, high pressure pace."

4. Individual differences among group members regarding causes of irritation.

5. Is a religious conviction necessary?

Sociograms

Group members seem to dislike sociograms: they are embarrassed to rate fellow members and they find total rank orders in which they must include themselves particularly difficult. Although sociograms are usually done at the beginning and again at the end of a group project so that comparison of first and last impressions can be made, the writer found that this gave undue emphasis to "the pecking order." Thus written estimates of fellow members or informal discussion of them in the final counseling interview proved more beneficial. Several types of sociogram were used in multiple counseling projects. Examples follow:

SOCIOMETRIC TEST

(mixed group of 8 or more high school or college students)

Girls' ratings of girls

Rank the girls in your group 1st, 2nd, and 3rd choice in the following categories:

1. Attractive appearance (taste in clothes, hair style, good features, figure, etc.)

    1   2   3

2. Attractive personality (friendliness, sympathetic, good talker or listener — whatever you think is desirable)

    1   2   3

3. Someone you would like as a friend to bring home to meet your family, etc.

    1   2   3

4. Someone you would vote for as a leader in school organization — class officer, representative of school government, etc.

    1   2   3

5. Someone you would select as co-worker in academic assignment when there is a partner-project — research, report, term paper, etc.

    1   2   3

Which girl appeals to you the least? Why? List reasons why you feel the way you do about her.

1.

2.

3.

4.

• •

Male Ratings of Males

(Same as above except in the first two items, which are worded as follows:

1. Attractive appearance (good features and physique, wears clothes well, etc.)
2. Good personality (friendliness, good sport, good talker or listener, etc.)

. . . .

Girls' ratings of fellows
(same as *male ratings of males*)

Male ratings of girls
(same as *girls' ratings of girls*)

The sum of the numbers 1, 2, 3, represents the rank order of popularity or esteem with which the group members are held. Analysis of male ratings of males, of girls, and vice versa may be significant for a discussion of sociometric results in the individual counseling conference at the end of the project. Likewise, the least liked member occasionally has the idea that he is the most popular person in the group! Of course, the counselor should use the results of the sociogram with great caution.

A second type of sociogram is well-suited to students who are failing to make satisfactory college adjustments. It is used in conjunction with group discussions on college adjustment, a well-balanced life, personal goals, etc. Based on nine criteria of success in college given in the book, "Did They Succeed in College" (3), the sociogram is done at the end of the group project. Two sheets are given to each participant: the first containing definitions of the nine criteria (fully discussed in previous group sessions), the second is the sociogram sheet with the names of all group members listed and spaces for rank orders to be assigned on all nine criteria for all participants (including the person doing the ranking). The results of the sociogram are discussed *only* in the final counseling interview, when other information and test scores are given the participant.

Sheet 1

CRITERIA OF COLLEGE SUCCESS

1. *Physical Fitness:* gained through a well-balanced schedule of exercise, sufficient sleep, good food — thus keeping in condition for efficient study and work, and for enjoying life.

174

2. *Intellectual competence:* as evidenced in scholarship, intellectual curiosity and drive that carries you beyond course requirements; use of scientific method in work and thinking; effective study skills and habits.

3. *Cultural development:* as evidenced in the use of leisure time, in the arts, such as music, concerts, writing, dramatics, painting; other student activities such as management, forensics, publications, or social activities; social service and church work; hobbies.

4. *Practical competence:* as evidenced in ability to handle personal and group financial problems; ability to obtain and keep a job, if needed; environmental adjustment in the college and community; effective distribution of time.

5. *Philosophy of life, personal pattern of goals:* as evidenced in vocational planning, reasons for attending college, ethical standards and ideals, religious attitudes, tolerance toward others.

6. *Character traits:* as evidenced in such characteristics as integrity, responsibility and initiative; self-respect in keeping with high moral standards.

7. *Emotional balance:* as evidenced in general factors such as self-control, self-confidence, sense of humor, independence; family relationships on adult rather than child-parent level; mature adjustments with other students; religious outlook.

8. *Social fitness:* as evidenced in ability to keep friends; poise and manners; social accomplishments; taste in dress, grooming.

9. *Sensitivity to social problems:* as evidenced in concern about campus issues; awareness of contemporary social, economic, and political problems; ability to criticize intelligently; willingness to assume responsibility of citizenship and to make personal sacrifices.

Sheet 2 (example of Mal, group 10)

SOCIOGRAM: RATINGS OF EACH OTHER, FIRST TO SIXTH

Directions: Please be as objective and honest with yourself as possible. Rank yourself along with the other group members and be sure to place the number of rank in each square. Start with the first criterion and fill all spaces. It is easier to place the highest and lowest rankings first, then fill in the others as fairly as you can. Do *not* assign the same ranking to 2 persons.

	Gertrude	Judy	Ardith	Elbert	Arthur	Mal
1. Physical Fitness	3 (4)	1 (1)	2 (3)	4 (2)	5 (5)	6 (6)
2. Intellectual competence	1 (1)	5 (6)	4 (2.5)	6 (2.5)	3 (5)	2 (4)
3. Cultural development	4 (2.5)	2 (4)	3 (2.5)	5 (5.5)	6 (5.5)	1 (1)
4. Practical competence	4 (2)	2 (4.5)	5 (3)	1 (1)	3 (4.5)	6 (6)
5. Philosophy of life	5 (1.5)	2 (3)	4 (4)	1 (1.5)	6 (6)	3 (5)
6. Character traits	3 (1)	2 (4)	1 (2.5)	6 (2.5)	5 (6)	4 (5)
7. Emotional balance	6 (3.5)	1 (2)	2 (3.5)	3 (1)	5 (6)	4 (5)
8. Social fitness	5 (3)	1 (4)	4 (2)	2 (1)	3 (5)	6 (6)
9. Sensitivity to social problems	5 (4)	4 (5.5)	3 (3)	2 (1)	6 (5.5)	1 (2)

(*Mal's rankings are given first, the total group rankings are bracketed.*)

175

The above sociogram helps to stimulate better attitudes and motivation toward personal growth: the counselor can use results in the individual counseling interview either for ego-bolstering or for "facing facts." In the case of Mal, the results were helpful as a forced conflict. He admitted that ranking himself along with the other group members was painful self-evaluation, but when he was shown the results of the total group rankings, he felt reassured. The group experience had a great influence on Mal's personal growth — in fact, it was the first hopeful sign in many years of psychiatric treatment, including attendance at a school for emotionally disturbed boys. The fact that the group had accepted and liked Mal, and had ranked him first in "cultural development," second in "sensitivity to social problems" (even though they had ranked him lower than his own self-ranking in several other criteria), gave him the encouragement necessary for new motivation toward "growing up."

Standardized Personality and Occupational Interests Inventories

Multiple counseling projects led or supervised by qualified psychologists may include psychological tests. It is recommended that these tests be considered part of the personal counseling of participants and not part of the group discussion activity. Except for occupational interests, results are reserved for private counseling interviews. Tests and inventories found to be most helpful in over-all counseling of participants in the fifteen group projects led by the author were the MMPI and the Strong. Because of the time and cost involved in testing it is recommended that participants assume the extra expense. Useful personality tests and inventories are discussed and evaluated in "Essentials of Psychological Testing" (4). Usually a leader-counselor has certain test batteries which work well for him in counseling, or uses those adopted by the school or institution in which the group projects are carried on. In the author's experience with multiple counseling, standardized tests and inventories, and projective devices, were not essential factors in the success of the projects.

SUMMARY

Practical self-appraisal devices found to be interesting and helpful to participants in multiple counseling projects include an autobiography, self-rating sheets on personal traits, values and goals, lovability, kind-of-person. Sample sociograms included personality traits (social stimulus value) and criteria of college success. Personality and occupational interests inventories included the Minnesota Multiphasic Personality Inventory and the Strong Vocational Interest Inventory, but other psychological tests may be equally effective and less expensive. Such standardized tests and inventories should be considered part of the individual counseling rather than an activity for group sessions. They are not essential to the success of multiple counseling projects.

X

SPRINGBOARDS TO FREE DISCUSSION

THERE ARE MANY DEVICES through which the leader can start and steer discussions: seven types were used in the group projects directed by the author. The first is the informational talk consisting of essential knowledges, presentation of case studies, book reviews, or quotations from books, magazines and newspapers. A second device, also giving tangible material for discussion, is the check-list or self-appraisal sheet. A third springboard is role-playing which presents a controversial issue or different human reactions to the same situation. A fourth technique is the use of a "bombshell" question to the group without comment by the leader. A fifth springboard consists of a preliminary session, exploratory and thought-provoking in itself, which prepares the group for discussion of a vital subject, for instance, racial discrimination, sex problems, and religion. A "warm-up" session or two is especially necessary with neurotic or psychotic groups because the participants' thought and discussive activity tends to be rigidly set in an egocentric pattern. A sixth device consists of stimulating discussion through enlargement on a subject found in the casual conversation of group members before the formal opening of the meeting. By careful listening the leader can locate a question of interest to the majority of the group at that particular moment which will make a significant discussion. Another device, often used in nondirective sessions, is to let the group discuss anything they wish. Thus no springboard is given by the leader. A simple way to start a non-directed session is for the leader to reflect something one of the group members has said or to ask a member how he feels about a statement made by one of the others.

Examples of seven devices used as springboards to discussion in fifteen group projects are given below:

1. Informational talk, with typed reference sheets (college and adult groups).

Example:
    The topic was "defense mechanisms" and a seminar-type session was used. Typed
    sheets containing definitions of defense mechanisms were passed out and read

178

thoughtfully by participants. As questions came up, the leader clarified the meaning of words and thought. Next the leader reviewed the reference sheet, giving homely illustrations of the mechanisms. Finally the leader asked group members to recall instances of their use of defensive behavior where one of the five common defense mechanisms was operative.

NOTE: This was the first of several sessions concerned with the subject of defense mechanisms and adjustive techniques. Other sessions used role-playing, provocative questions, and self-assessments. Since objectivity in a self-appraisal requires insight into personal use of the defense mechanisms, especially identification and projection, plenty of time should be given to discussions of the subject.

The definition sheet used in college and adult groups is reproduced on the following page:

DEFENSE (BEHAVIOR-ESCAPE) MECHANISMS

General definitions: "Tools of self-deception . . . ways of thinking and behaving which help the individual to avoid facing reality or guilt feelings, or feelings of inferiority or inadequacy . . . behavior patterns which bolster or protect the ego and conscience (super ego) . . . behavior patterns which give socially acceptable expression to elemental impulses."

ALLPORT, FREUD, GATES and others.

Identification — "process by which an individual allies himself emotionally, or feels himself one with another person or group."

Projection — "Process of placing one's own wishes, fears, interests, motives, attitudes, on other persons or groups" . . . "A wish, attitude, or habit-hierarchy which is not compatible with other habits or attitudes of an individual — which that individual attributes to other persons rather than himself (usually the individual does not have insight, or realize that he himself has the trait in question) . . . "Placing blame for one's own mistakes on others"

Rejection — "Dislike or hatred for a person, usually accompanied by lack of insight — unawareness of the reasons for the negative feelings."

Repression — "The unconscious process by which impulses (desires) which would be painful to consciousness, are excluded from consciousness and from direct motor expression" . . . "Every impulse of aggression which we fail to gratify is taken over by the super ego (conscience), increasing its aggressiveness. Or these ungratified impulses result in behavior unpredicted by the person himself, or by others."

Compensation — "Adjustment of the individual to failure or disappointment by taking some other course of action which he is able to engage in."

Sublimation — "A form of substitute behavior which replaces desired behavior which is not socially acceptable" . . . "Primary impulses directed into socially acceptable and personally acceptable channels without contingent suffering."

179

Rationalization — "Justification of one's condition or opinions or actions by fallacious reasoning" . . . "Giving *good* reasons instead of *real* reasons."

> NOTE: Since defense mechanisms imply lack of insight or awareness on the part of the individual using them (he is kidding himself, escaping from facts, etc.) we might conclude that it is impossible for the individual to analyze his own behavior in terms of defense mechanisms. However, it is possible for a person to *look into his past*, viewing himself objectively, and recognizing his own use of the mechanisms — as long as it is not part of his present behavior pattern.

TERMS CONCERNED WITH THE DYNAMICS OF PERSONALITY

Id	Super Ego	Ego
Emotional impulses	The conscience	Self-consciousness
Unconscious emotions storehouse	Socialized awareness	Conscious selfhood

Motive — "Conscious experience or unconscious condition which serves as the stimulus in determining an individual's behavior in a given situation."

Desire — "Anticipatory thinking in conjunction with either localized or non-localized bodily conditions."

Drive — "Any intra-organic activity or condition which supplies the stimulation for a particular type of behavior."

Urge — "A strong tendency to perform a certain act" (based on structure and instincts according to some psychological sources).

2. The use of a check-list or rating sheet is particularly effective as a springboard to discussion in groups where participants feel inadequate and self-conscious in group discussion. The paper and pencil help a nervous or insecure member to feel more at ease. Three examples are given.

Example 1 (from an early session of a high school project):

> *Leader:* Today we are going to compare our high school with one in Indiana where a study was done on personal traits which the students thought most important in "a smooth person." I have slips for you with the eight traits listed, but not in the order of importance, according to the boys and girls in the other high school. Put in the rank you think they deserve and then we'll discuss the results.
>
> *Mary:* Just a minute — how do we know what they mean by "a smooth person?" Maybe they think it is good — I personally don't like smooth people, the way I think of the meaning of it.

Leader: That's a good point, Mary. According to the article telling about the Indiana poll, the term "smooth" was used in a good sense — it meant "attractive," "popular," "a wheel." So let's consider it a complimentary term, as they did.

(*After the poll was made and results tabulated, the discussion concerned differences of opinion regarding important personal traits. A good start was made in learning about sex differences and self-appraisal techniques*).

A sample of the check-list is given below:

HIGH SCHOOL POLL — "What Makes a Smooth Person?"

What boys think of girls	*What girls think of boys*
(rank according to importance starting with 1 as most important)	(rank according to importance starting with 1 as most important)
Friendliness....................	Good manners..................
Good manners.................	Being a good dancer............
Being a good dancer...........	Having other boys like him........
Being a good sport.............	Being a good talker.............
Appropriate clothes.............	Being a good sport.............
A good figure.................	Sense of humor................
A sense of humor...............	Good grooming.................
Good grooming................	Friendliness....................

Example 2 (college groups where vocational guidance is emphasized):

The use of a personal inventory, listing likes and dislikes, past experiences, training and successes helps a student to face himself. Acceptance of personal weaknesses often dissipates vocational day dreams and stimulates constructive planning for goals that can be reached.

Leader: Since you all have the problem of a vocational choice, it is important to appraise yourselves in terms of personal strengths and weaknesses. After that, we can discuss different kinds of jobs and personalities which fit them. I'm handing out this personal inventory sheet for you to fill in at home. Please bring it to the next session. You can take time now to glance it over, and bring up any question about it.

(*The questions usually concern the short-answer sections. The participants are urged to use other paper to enlarge on any of the answers where space is too small, and to write down any confidential information they wish the counselor to have. They are assured that their answers will not be discussed in the group unless they do this themselves*).

181

The personal inventory sheet is reproduced on the following pages:

PERSONAL ASSESSMENT (relating to vocational choice)*

I. *The present state of my occupational choice.*

    A. In order of preference, these four occupations are possible choices in which I would like to earn my living:

        1. .. .. because ....

        2. .... because ....

        3. .... because ....

        4. .... because ....

    B. The following statement best describes the status of my vocational choice:

        1. Very certain......2. Somewhat certain......3. Very uncertain......

    C. I have considered and rejected the following occupations as my goal:

        ...., ..., ..., ...

II. *Analysis of yourself.*

    A. Your skills. (Do not confuse your skills and abilities with "interests").

        1. My best high school grades (subjects)......, ..., ..., ...

        2. My poorest high school grades........, ..., ..., ...

        3. My greatest skill has always been in the following kinds of activities:

            a ....themes, essays, term papers   f ....handcrafts, manual arts

            b ....oral reports   g ....taking tests

            c ....laboratory work   h ....reading

            d ....art projects   i ....other...................

            e ....class discussion

        4. My poorest skills among the above has been........, ..., ...

        5. I feel my strongest actual or potential skills and abilities are:

        ...., ..., ...

        6. I feel my weakest abilities are the following:

        ...., ..., ...

        7. High school extra-curricular activities, hobbies, and work experience show that I have skills well developed (as compared with my fellow students) in the following:

---

* Credit is due Dr. Louis J. Stacker who developed the personal-assessment sheet from which the above inventory was adapted.

a. ....

b. ....

c. ....

d. ....

8. In summary, I think my strongest abilities can be best used, and my weaknesses avoided, in the following kind of life work (brief statement)

B. Personal traits.

1. I enjoy and work best in the following fields (check one):

.... a. Working with people because...............................

.... b. Working with mental problems, because......................

....

.... c. Working with practical things (mechanical, handcraft, etc.) because...

2. I feel that I have the greatest ability to deal with the following kinds of people. (Check as many items as you think apply to your skills).

.... babies

.... elementary school children

.... junior high school pupils

.... high school pupils

.... college age people

.... adults

.... old people

.... sick people

.... professional people

.... laboring people

.... farmers

.... business people

.... women

.... men

.... my inferiors

.... my superiors

.... my equals

.... people in trouble

.... happy people

.... people as individuals

.... people in groups

3. In what way do the wishes of your parents influence your decisions?

4. In what way do friends, teachers, or others, influence your decisions?

III. *Job analysis.*

Answer the following questions about the occupation you listed as first choice:

1. Is the field overcrowded? .... Where did you get your information?.........

2. Is the field growing? ....

183

3. Does the occupation require (1) a general education (2) special training?.....
.... How many years? ...... Information source was?............
4. Is the necessary training available at this college? .... if not, where?........
5. What is the beginning rate of pay? ....
6. What is the average pay after ten years? ....
7. Do you know the day-by-day routine of the job? .... Source of information?
....
8. What personality characteristics are required on the job?..................
....

IV. *Testing your decision.*

Check in the left-hand space if you have tested your vocational choice in any way. On the right side, tell how you have done so:

.... school subject...
.... extracurricular activity.....................................
.... vocational testing and counseling...........................
.... observation of the occupation..............................
.... work experience..

1. What limitations or compromises do you think might be necessary, which may prevent you from reaching your vocational goal?

V. *Request for assistance. After assessing your personal assets and liabilities in relation to your choice of vocational goal, where do you feel you need help?*

Kind of problem	*Help from whom:* counselor, faculty advisor, instructor, books, outside agency, etc.
.... 1. Analyzing my own aptitudes..............	....
.... 2. Analyzing my own interests..............	....
.... 3. Developing certain skills................	....
.... 4. Developing certain personal traits........	....
.... 5. Planning ways to test out my choice.......	....
.... 6. Finding the right occupation for my skills and interests.......................	....
.... 7. Planning my school major and electives in order to reach a certain goal.............	....

184

.... 8. Getting information about certain kinds of work.................................... ....

.... 9. Planning my extracurricular life to help certain goals or help in my decisions.......... ....

....10. Securing work experience which will test my decision, or advance me toward my goal... ....

....11. Making long range plans to achieve my goal. ....

....12. The whole problem of choosing an occupation and deciding on a college major or training............................. ....

....13. Other problems:......................... ....

....

....

Example 3 (groups of teen-age and college participants who are maladjusted, unhappy and rebellious):

Ventilation of feelings of hostility and resentment by all group members is encouraged by listing of gripes. Discussions concern resentments and dislikes of all kinds (group acceptance of unsocial feelings give support and reassurance to individual members).

Leader: Several of you have talked freely of your feelings of resentment against parents, teachers, etc. It seems a good idea to have a real gripe session, a chance to express your ideas and blow off steam. Let's start by listing all the things we resent or dislike. I'll make three columns on the blackboard and contribute three of my gripes.
(Titles of columns are written: people, ideas-values, things-activities. Leader fills in "God-bosses," "profiteering from war," "radio commercials").

Rod: I can't see the point to this — I try to keep my mind on positive things What's the use of getting worked up about gripes — it just makes you feel worse.

Harry: I disagree. This is the kind of activity I really enjoy—a chance to gripe, and get it off my chest. You can't do it around most people. I have so many gripes I could fill the whole board by myself.

Leader: Rod, you don't have to participate if you don't want to. Would you be willing to serve as scribe and write down the things as the group suggest them? We'll get at individual differences in the group through doing this, and I know you are interested in that subject. You'll learn a lot about each other from the different gripes you have.

185

SAMPLE GRIPE LIST (group 9)

People	*Ideas-Values*	*Things-Activities*
God-bosses	profiteering from war	radio-commercials
McCarthy-politicians	religious fanaticism	Chicago Tribune
pedants-officious people	discrimination-prejudice	University of W—
narrow-minded people	Joe-College ism	gossiping
insulting people	Chauvinism	malicious rumors
door-slamming people	snobbery	herd-instinct
censors-self appointed leaders	inconsiderateness	sororities-fraternities
fault-finders	over-possessive love	wrestling
self-righteous people	sentimentality	boxing
do-gooders	provincialism	card games
crude, infantile humor	superficial religion	charades-skits
practical jokers	keeping up with Jones	war
people without sense of humor	plagiarism	
sanctimonious people	treason	
my-way-is-the-only-right-way	sadism	
sick people	masochism-martyrism	
self-pitying people	vandalism	
people who tell me what to do	drunkenness	
hecklers-kibitzers	lack of imagination	
monopolists of conversation		

(The whole session was spent in listing and commenting on the gripes. Typed lists were prepared by the leader before the next session, in which the discussion was continued).

3. Role-playing has been discussed as a springboard to free discussion in chapters 6 and 7. One further example from a teachers' group is given below:

The question of high school students staying up all night after Prom was timely and provocative. An extemporaneous psychodrama was presented to emphasize the student's viewpoint. Joan, the student, was the central character in two scenes. In the first, she talked with her father, arguing for the all night party which had been planned by her gang. She wins over her father. In the second scene with her mother she doesn't fare so well: her mother is adamant, ordering her to cancel the plan and to be in by 2 a.m. on the night of the Prom.

Members of the group allied themselves with father or mother and a lively discussion resulted. In this instance the role of Joan was well done, winning over members of the audience who had previously been unwilling to consider an all night party for students. The role-playing provided an excellent warm-up for the discussion because members of the group could identify themselves closely with the situation or the actors.

4. A provocative question in which the group members are emotionally involved often needs no introduction or springboard. However, the leader may steer the direction of the discussion by the phrasing of a lead-off question.

Example (teen-age and young adult groups):

Leader: You all seem interested in exchanging viewpoints on desirable traits in dates and mates. Let's start off with this question — do you think marriages are more successful when the husband and wife have similar personal traits and share common interests?

Jane: I don't know what you mean — how can a man have the same kind of personality as a woman. Naturally they are different.

Bob: No, I don't think men and women are so different — and I read in a Psych book that most of the differences are just cultural. Kinsey's book on women says that, too.

Leader: Well, go ahead and battle it out. What do the rest of you think?

5. The technique of using one whole session as preparatory to a frank discussion on a touchy, difficult subject is necessary in some cases. For instance, a mixed group of adolescents may be too self-conscious to talk freely of sex problems, even though their minds are obsessed with this subject. The leader can bring important knowledges and a frank structuring of the discussion which helps break down the verbal inhibitions of group members.

Example (from a college psychiatric group):

Mike, who was sex-obsessed, embarrassed the girl members by asking them questions about their sexual behavior and feelings. He brought to the group an outline of the play he was writing. Homosexuality played an important part in it. Although the other group members did not care about having a discussion on sex, the leader decided to clear the air of Mike's unpopular innuendos.

Leader: Since Mike has brought up the subject of homosexuality and is so curious about the feminine angle of sex, I think I'll tell you some facts — at least what some research articles have to say about masculinity-femininity.

(Gives 15-minute talk on the continuum of sex traits in males and females, homosexuality, perversions, and frigidity. By the time the talk is finished there are few questions left to be asked, even by Mike.)

Mike: That sure answers a lot of questions. One thing, I've never worried about being a homo myself.

Leader: Does anyone have a question about the information I've given you?

Alice: I don't see why we have to talk about sex all the time just because Mike wants to.

Elbert: I know you girls don't like to talk about sex, but it's pretty important, and this is the first chance we fellows have had to get a frank feminine viewpoint. We really want to learn how you girls think and feel about sex.

187

Gwen: I agree with you, Elbert, but I've never had any experience and I don't expect to get married, so I don't think about sex much — there's no point in it.

Leader: Well, let's not put the girls out on a limb today — you fellows will have to be patient and not expect answers right now. I'd like to hear what you males think about physical attraction as a basis for marriage. And how would you decide that a strong physical attraction is real love or just a passing fancy, an infatuation?

(Thus the discussion focussed on the difference between love and infatuation, ending in a conclusion that love grows over the years in a successful marriage even though sex activity lessens.)

6. An effective springboard device consists of enlarging upon a subject of interest in casual conversation before the formal opening of the meeting. This may be used to help shy members forget their self-consciousness and really "talk" in the discussion.

Example (taken from group 2):

MacArthur had just been recalled from Korea and the casual conversation concerned this event. The leader notices that two of the listeners in the group, Don and Josie, were active in the conversation.

Leader: There seems to be a difference of opinion about the MacArthur affair — what is your view, Don?

Don: I think its all wrong — we should have gone right up to Manchuria and finished the war.

Del: You're right. That's just what my officer (Naval cadets) says and this is once when the army and navy agree on something.

Leader: Josie, you are shaking your head. What do you think?

Josie: My father and a lot of other people I know think MacArthur is crazy — he talks like he was God. Anyway, it isn't right to go against what the President and Congress think is best.

(The heated discussion which followed was significant for two reasons: many of the boys and girls in the group were thinking of enlisting in the Armed Forces after high school graduation; Don and Josie became active participants in a group discussion for the first time.)

7. The absence of a springboard and a topic makes a truly nondirected discussion session. The leader can sense the need of the group for a completely free talk-fest and should encourage frank expressions of feeling about oneself and toward others in such a session.

Example:

A graduate student group contained one unpopular member and irritation against him had mounted steadily over five sessions. His initial statement before the session opened formally gave an opportunity for a "truth party" type of meeting.

Harry: I'm fed up with this place. That's why I didn't come last time — everything including this group has got me down.

Betty: What have we done. Do you dislike us?

Harry: No, but I just don't like groups. And the fellows at the dorm keep pestering me — they want me to go out drinking with them — I wish they'd leave me alone.

Betty: What's the harm in going out with the fellows. You must be snooty, you don't like them and you don't like us.

Harry: I like to lead my own life. Besides, the fellows are such kids. They bore me.

Rod: You're always talking about how few real friends a person has. How do you expect to make friends if you resent people trying to be friendly with you?

Eloise: Miss D—, what are we going to discuss today?

Leader: Why don't you go ahead and talk frankly about your feelings toward each other — perhaps you can help Harry analyze why he is so unhappy on this campus and how to make a better adjustment. I'm sure you'd like that, wouldn't you, Harry?

Harry: Sure, I always like good advice, although I seldom follow it. But I'd be glad to hear what the group thinks of me.

Eloise: Well, Harry, frankly I think your attitude toward college and toward people is lousy.

Elliot: I agree with Harry about the fellows on campus — they are very immature and superficial.

> (*The leader withdrew from the discussion circle and the session took on the complexion of a case conference with Harry as the case. Although Elliot supported him, the others were frank in criticizing his attitudes and behavior. Actually a psychiatrist, whom Harry had left in disgust, had attempted to bring him to the same insights which the group forced upon him.*)

Conclusion

Seven types of springboard to discussion have been illustrated from actual use in projects directed by the author. Readers are cautioned to adapt devices and materials to the needs of the groups they lead: no two groups are alike, and a technique which works well in one group may fail miserably in a comparable group. Ingenuity and versatility on the part of the leader is essential. Not only is the leader obligated to consider the interest-needs of individual group members, but also he should stimulate *new* interests, attitudes, and appreciations which can help personal growth. In this regard, groups of neurotic and psychotic patients present the greatest challenge.

XI

THE BRIEFING AND EVALUATION INTERVIEWS

INDIVIDUAL COUNSELING BY THE LEADER in multiple counseling projects includes a minimum of two leisurely conferences: a preliminary "get acquainted" interview and a summary interview which may require as long as two hours. Individual conferences with the leader during the course of the group project are held at the request of participants; some participants need reassurance in short chats, others become upset over discussions, behavior of group members, or their own performance in the group; they wish to talk things over in a full-length counseling interview. Because these intermediary chats or interviews are unstructured they will not be analyzed in this chapter. The briefing and summary interviews, however, follow a prescribed pattern in order to give to, and receive from the participant, definite information.

There are two types of briefing interview: in one, the prospective group member knows nothing about the project and is not a referral from a counselor; in the other, he has been urged by his counselor to join the project as a supplement to the counseling program. Thus the group leader may have little or no information about the first applicant while knowing a great deal about the second one (from conferring with the counselor or reading his case history). The first applicant is easier to interview than the second, since he has come to join the group project through some strong incentive — on his own — so to speak. On the other hand, the second type of applicant may be disinterested and fearful: his counselor may have put pressure on him to join the project. Often the group leader must use a "velvet glove" approach in this briefing interview.

First the structure of a briefing interview for the non-counselee is described. The sequence of conversation units consist of:

1. Questions by leader as to applicant's reasons for joining project.

2. Information from leader as to purposes, procedures in the project.

3. Questions by leader re "how it sounds" to applicant.

191

4. Information from leader as to other members in group, permissiveness and confidential nature of group.

5. Leader presents list of discussion topics to applicant to check and to add other topics.

6. Discussion of topics, if applicant is interested.

7. Leader presents questionnaire re 5 categories, 4 structures, 2 approaches. He explains the questionnaire as the applicant looks it over, after which applicant checks his choices.

8. Leader draws out applicant to talk about himself, using cues from answers on questionnaire.

9. If insufficient self-description is given in (8), leader gives participant the information blank to fill in before the first session.

10. If applicant is uncertain about group membership the leader suggests that he think it over, decide within a few days. Emphasis is given to the importance of equal numbers of males and females, limited membership. Leader may encourage applicant, reassuring him that he can make a real contribution to the group because of some feature of his background, etc.

11. If applicant is uncertain, requesting permission to try one group session, he should be allowed to do so.

The briefing interview for the counselee can be shorter because information has been given the leader by the attending counselor. The approach in this interview is to get the applicant to do the talking. In other words, the leader lets the applicant, especially a reluctant one, talk himself into group membership. He is allowed to take the initiative throughout the interview. His questions are answered to his satisfaction with the exception of those which demand full description of "exactly what he will get out of this group." Answering this, the leader tries to make clear to him that he will get out of the group experience what he *wants* to get out of it: each individual should gain in self-understanding and acceptance; in understanding others better. The leader cannot predict the direction, or amount of learning: usually the group experience helps a participant to gain social skills (if he needs this) and to get reassurance and support in personal problems.

A counselee-interview uses the following sequence:

1. Answering questions from the counselee.

2. Giving information as to other members of the group; explanation of permissive atmosphere and strict confidence in group.

3. Asking the counselee if he wishes to try the group, at least for one meeting. If answer is affirmative, list of topics is presented, which counselee checks.

4. Topics are discussed and additional ones such as religion and sex may start self-revelation.

5. After counselee finishes talking, present questionnaire on 5 categories, 4 structures, 2 approaches. Discuss as fully as counselee wishes.

6. If counselee has not talked about himself, open the door for confidential information by saying,

"Although your counselor has told me a little about you, I'd like to have you tell me anything you think I should know — especially anything which you do not wish to discuss in group sessions. I want to avoid embarrassing you in the group by asking questions which you don't want to answer. If there are any topics which you prefer not to discuss in the group, it's a good idea for me to know about it."

7. End the interview after the counselee's response to (6), reassuring him that you will confer with his counselor regularly, and will help him in the group activity in any way he wishes. Assure him that you will be available for chats and conferences when he needs them. Repeat the time and place of the meeting, emphasizing the importance of all group members being present in the first session.

A sample interview with a non-counselee illustrates leader's questions and activity in the three parts of an interview: warm-up, body, and conclusion.

Warm-up:

1. Tell me, how did you hear about the group project?

2. Do you have some special reason for wanting to join the group?

   (*Leader gives explanation of group purposes, membership, etc.*).

3. How does it sound to you?

Body:

   (*Further explanations of permissive atmosphere, confidential nature of the project, etc.*).

4. I'd like to have you help suggest topics for the meetings, subjects you are interested in discussing. Will you look over this list and check five which you prefer.

   (*While applicant is studying the sheet*).

5. If you have a topic in mind which is not listed, will you write it in at the bottom. We like to have extra suggestions. Sometimes they are more popular than those listed.

   (*If applicant writes in a suggestion, discussion of it is held*).

193

6. Which topic would you like to be sure of being discussed in the group?

   (*Applicant may talk about this, giving reasons for his interest*).

7. Now I have another check sheet I'd like to have you look over. Notice the five categories of reasons we've found for group members joining a project. Some analyze themselves as coming under as many as four headings. I'd like you to check the ones where you think you belong.

   (*Discussion may follow, in which applicant talks about his needs, or feelings of inadequacy*).

8. Now will you check one of the four group structures: the first is most like a class with a teacher leading the group. The fourth is like a bull-session, without any leader. The ones in between will be made clear as you read the descriptions. Will you check the one you think you'd enjoy the most?

   (*Discussion may follow because the applicant is undecided, wanting to check somewhere between (3) and (4). A note to that effect is made on the sheet*).

9. The last thing I'd like to get your opinion on is whether you'd like the group to be very frank, with everyone telling his personal problems and being very confidential. Or would you rather have discussions kept on an impersonal level, so that we talk about problems in general, and other people's rather than our own?

   (*The applicant may reveal himself in his answer. Often the more maladjusted persons do not want to have "the personal approach." However, often the applicant thinks he will get more out of the group if it has frank, personal discussions*).

10. Even if you don't want to talk about yourself you may check "personal approach" if you wish. Often after getting acquainted in the group, members find they do want to talk about themselves. You will not be forced to, anyway — that's what we mean by a permissive atmosphere — we want you to act the way you feel, say what you want to, keep quiet when you want to.

    (*Discussion of this may follow*).

11. Is there anything special about yourself that you do want me to know, which you prefer not to have known by the group? I can be more helpful and tactful — avoid asking you questions in the sessions which might be embarrassing — if I know more about you.

    (*The applicant may deny any problem area or he may give detailed information about his difficulties. If so, a full discussion is held. The leader points questions toward ways the applicant hopes to be helped by the group project.*)

Conclusion:

   (*If insufficient information has been given regarding family relationships, personal goals, etc.*).

12. I have an information blank here for you to fill out before the first session. It will help me get better acquainted with you. You may consider it confidential since no one else will see it.

(The leader ends the interview in a warm, friendly fashion: he is glad the applicant plans to join the group because he can make a real contribution to it; he assures the applicant that it will be an enjoyable, worthwhile experience from which a lot can be learned. The leader's availability for interviews is explained. Finally, the applicant is reminded again of the time and place of the first meeting: emphasis is given to the importance of all members attending the opening session).

The structure for an interview with a counselee includes the warm-up, body, and conclusion but it is client-centered. Leader-activity is limited to answering questions and securing questionnaire responses from the applicant. The interview may be short (when the applicant won't talk) or lengthy (when the applicant wants to talk).

When the applicant is uncertain about group membership at the end of the interview the leader asks him if he'd like to try it for one meeting with the understanding that he can drop out after that meeting. The leader emphasizes the importance of equal numbers of males and females, limited membership: thus another applicant will be selected if the client does not want a place in the group.

If the client decides not to join, and his counselor believes group membership is important for him, the briefing interview may serve as a step toward the client's change of mind during the next few weeks. Often other groups are available at a later date so that the applicant may be reassured by the leader that — when he is ready for it — a place will be made for him.

Substitutes for the Briefing Interview

When it is impossible to arrange briefing interviews, the preliminaries are accomplished in the first group meeting. Illustrations of leader-explanations, questionnaires on topics, structure, and approach were given in Chapter III. In place of the 5 categories, group members are asked to write their reasons for joining the project and what they hope to get out of it. An information blank is distributed, which the participants fill in at home and return to the leader in the second session. A simple information blank which was found useful in high school and college projects is given on the next pages:

195

INFORMATION BLANK (Discussion Group Members)

Directions: A clear picture of you as an individual can be obtained only if you answer the questions as frankly and completely as possible. All information is confidential and will not be released to anyone without your consent.

Name.................... Age............ Date of birth....................

Address...
         local   tel.   home

Place of birth....................Elementary and H. S.........................

Father's age...........Education...............Occupation.................

Mother's age...........Education...............Occupation.................

Brothers and sisters, living and deceased. (Eldest given first)

NAME	AGE	MARRIED (Yes—No)	OCCUPATION
1.			
2.			
3.			
4.			
5.			
6.			

YOUR ACTIVITIES AND INTERESTS

In High School   *In College*   *In the Community*

Literary..

Dramatics..

Debating...

(Discussion)...

Music — Art..

Athletics..

Group Organ-...

izations...

Other activities...

....

196

YOUR HEALTH

List any serious accidents, illnesses or defects in childhood (give approx. age of occurrence)..

....

....

List any recent accidents, illnesses or defects (chronic complaints)....................

....

EDUCATIONAL INTERESTS

Type of course in H. S....................Preparation for.........................

Type of course in College................Preparation for.........................

Name of subjects taken in H. S. according to the following categories:

2 Best Marks	2 Worst Marks	2 Best Liked	2 Least Liked
1...............	....	....	....
2...............	....	....	....

Name of subjects in College or post-high school course according to the categories above:

1...............	....	....	....
2...............	....	....	....

VOCATIONAL EXPERIENCE AND INTERESTS

List in chronological order your five most important work experiences up-to-date:

Nature of Work	From-To Yr.-Mos.	Firm	Salary per Month
1.			
2.			
3.			
4.			
5.			

Which of these jobs did you like the best? ....

Why? ....

....

List in order of preference, five occupations in which you would like to earn a living:

Occupation	Reason for Your Interest
1.	. . . .
2.	. . . .
3.	. . . .
4.	. . . .
5.	. . . .

Have you made a vocational choice? . . . . . . If so, what is it?. . . . .

Why did you make this choice? (check reasons)

. . . . . . Family suggestions or tradition	. . . . . Long personal interest in it
. . . . . . Friends' or teachers' advice	. . . . . . Profitably, financially
. . . . . . The vocation of someone I respect or admire	. . . . . . Best suited to my abilities
	. . . . . . Most interesting to me
. . . . . . Suggested by study in school	. . . . . . Only thing I know
. . . . . . Suggested by work experience	. . . .

How certain are you that this occupation is the one you really want?
(check) Very certain. . . . . . Somewhat certain. . . . . . Very uncertain. . . . . .

How much information have you on this vocation? (check) None. . Some. . Extensive. .

Where did you get this information? (Specify books, talks with people, lectures, work experience, acquaintances working in the occupation, etc.). . . . .
. . . .

What has been your most important achievement related to this vocation? (activities, grades in school, work experience, etc.). . . . .
. . . .

If you were free from all restrictions (if you could do what you wish) — what would you want to be doing 10 or 15 years from now?. . . . .
. . . .

What additional information can you give as to your skills and interests? What topics of discussion are of special interest to you which would enable the counselor to help you with your problems?. . . . .
. . . .

The Summary Interview

The summary interview is structured to provide (1) test results and report of behavior observations (2) full discussion of these results and observations (3) oral questionnaire of 12 key questions to get the reactions of the participant to the group project (4) counseling of the participant.

The approach in the summary interview is client-centered through allowing the interviewee to spend much or little time on various parts of the interview. For instance (1) may be omitted entirely if the client is not interested in hearing test and sociogram results, or observations of his behavior in the group. Likewise, the oral questionnaire may bring forth laconic answers without elaboration or discussion. Such a client may be waiting for the opportunity to discuss something of greater significance to him. Thus (4) becomes the main body of the interview, and the client may reveal a serious personal problem for which he needs intensive counseling. If the leader is qualified to provide such counseling, it is started in the summary interview; if he is not qualified, referral and a definite appointment with a counselor or psychiatrist are made.

Usually the leader knows the client well enough to predict the structure of the summary interview: some participants enjoy test interpretation and behavior reports; others like to analyze the project, including definite discussions, social interactions, and personal relationships which made impressions on them. Occasionally a participant dwells on self-assessment in terms of his personal strengths and weaknesses for a greater part of the interview. More often he focusses attention on ways to solve immediate or long-range problems concerned with vocations, social, marital, or family maladjustments.

In the case of a maladjusted client the value of the summary interview as a connecting link between counseling in the past (the group project itself) and counseling in the future is great. Referral to a qualified counselor or psychiatrist if the leader cannot provide it (so that there is no break in supportive influences) may be the chief value of the summary interview.

When the results of tests and observations turn out as expected by the participant, showing that he has an accurate picture of himself as an individual and as a group member, the summary interview usually lasts about 50 minutes. If, however, there are discrepancies between the participant's self-concept and his ratings on tests, sociograms, and behavior observations, the conference will be much longer. When the participant is upset by the discrepancies and needs extensive discussion of himself and his behavior, a second appointment may be needed. In general, the summary interview should not run over one and one-half hours. If the discussion is not ended to the satisfaction of the participant, it should be continued in another conference.

The summary interview may be the start of counseling interviews to help the participant with problems which have come to light through the group project, or which — at the last possible minute — he divulges. This happens rather frequently as a matter of fact: the participant has learned to enjoy the support of the group and the leader; when the project comes to an end, he feels the need of continuing the counseling contact. If it is necessary for him to produce a valid reason for continuing the individual counseling, he will do so. However, except in the case of serious personality deviations, two or three extra counseling interviews after the end of the project usually suffice to straighten out the problem or to provide props until the participant is ready to stand on his own feet.

(Even when the summary interview appears to fill the counseling needs of the participant, a follow-up contact of some kind should be made. Depending upon the circumstances, the follow-up may be planned a month or several months after the summary interview. It may be in the form of a "progress report" interview, a casual chat, a telephone conversation, or a letter with a questionnaire inclosure. The purpose of the follow-up is to assure the participant that the leader has him in mind and is available for counseling aid if needed. The general plan of the follow-up is an inquiry of "how things are going": has the group project experience proved to be helpful in personal and social adjustments during the intervening months; can the leader help the counselee in any way).

Leader-activity in the summary interview purports to draw from the client *his* ideas of himself as a person and of the ways in which he can work for personal growth and satisfactory life-adjustments. The client is asked to estimate his own performance in tests, sociograms, behavioral reports: his self-concept may be accurate or distorted. The initiative for a discussion of discrepancies is given to the client.

Also the leader uses "how do you feel about —" questions to stimulate the client's ideas for planning future personal growth and satisfactory life adjustments.

An illustration of client-initiative in the summary interview is taken from the case summary of Josie, group 1:

Leader: Well, Josie, this is your chance to find out things about yourself from the tests, what Mr. G— and I wrote into our observational reports of you, and anything else you'd like to discuss with me. First, about the tests — did the results of the Strong surprise you?

(The profiles had been given out in a meeting and discussed).

Josie: No, I expected to rate high in "office work." Of course I really want to be a housewife, only I am not sure I could stand having a husband.

Leader: Do you think your feeling about fellows has changed during the last six months?

Josie: Yes, it has. I used to hate all of them. I preferred the company of horses to people. Now I've found a couple of fellows that aren't so bad.

Leader: Are you happier at school and in this city, now that you've lived here for awhile?

Josie: Yes, I really do like school and being here. I've changed my mind about joining the Wacs after I graduate. I plan to get a job in the city. As a matter of fact, I'm pretty fond of a fellow, he has a good job bricklaying.

Leader: You certainly have changed a lot from the first group meeting, do you remember how you hated everything and everybody and were quite frank in saying so?

Josie: Yes, I was in an awful state then, I have changed a lot.

Leader: Let's discuss the results of the personality inventory and your own ratings of those 10 behavior traits. Here's your rating sheet for you to look at.

Josie: Yes, I wouldn't give myself the same ratings now.

Leader: What would you change?

(Josie discusses changes in ratings).

Leader: That's good. You would certainly seem to be happier and better adjusted now. Do you think you'd answer the questions on the MMPI the same way now?

Josie: No, I have quite a different outlook. I hated myself and everyone else when I made that thing out.

Leader: I'm glad to hear that. For instance at that time you showed a big chip on your shoulder and a tendency to stay by yourself and to day-dream. Can

201

you explain those traits in terms of what you were like, and how you've changed?

> (*Josie gives good analysis of behavior changes which have taken place: how she used to act in a situation, how she now acts in the same situation, etc.*).

Leader: There is an interesting thing about the MAPS test you took — you remember that one, in which you built up 10 stories with characters.

Josie: Yes, I remember, that was fun.

Leader: Well the results of that test showed that underneath you seemed to be a happy person, and not at all a person who would like to live alone on a farm with a lot of horses.

Josie: I guess that was just a phase I was going through. I was sore at my family for moving to the city, and I guess I wanted to be different from my sister (*a very attractive older sister in college*).

Leader: Is that why you didn't bother to fix your hair, or think much about your clothes. I notice that you look very different now than when I first saw you.

Josie: (*laughing in an embarrassed way*) Well I guess that's the effect my boy friend has had on me. I know I'm not so bad looking, but I didn't used to care. Yes, it's true, I knew I couldn't compete with my sister. I guess that's why I don't want to go to college. All my family have gone and expect me to, but I won't do it.

Leader: Well it's natural for your family to want you to go to college. I see from the psychological tests that you are of college caliber.

Josie: The last thing in the world I want to do is to go to college, and that's that. I think I want to get married.

Leader: It certainly isn't the thing to do if that's the way you feel about it. About marriage — have you decided on this boy friend you're going steady with?

Josie: I don't know — this is the first fella I've ever had.

> (*A discussion of marriage partners followed. The leader asked Josie about her own parents, and her older brother who was married. Personality types which complement each other in marriage were discussed as well as business couples, desirable number of children in a family, etc.*).

comment: The above excerpt constituted the first two parts of the summary interview. The next part consisted of the 12 evaluation questions relating to the group project influence on Josie's behavior changes. The last part contained further self-analysis, statement of personal goals in terms of growth toward maturity, and specific plans for the next year.

Three months later the leader had a follow-up interview of 50 minutes with Josie: a progress report, and evaluation of simmering effects of the group project on Josie's personal growth.

One year later another follow-up was done. Josie, a receptionist in a hospital, was taking university extension courses and was engaged to a fellow student. It looked as though his influence might take her into full-time college work, before or after their marriage.

The twelve evaluation questions with answers and discussion by the participant often take the main portion of interview time. The leader uses a notebook, jotting down the answers and comments of the participant. An explanation of note-taking is given: the leader is trying to improve the group project method and the analysis given by the participant will be helpful. Thus he is urged to give specific ways in which the group experience has affected him, and to be entirely frank in his evaluation. If he believes he learned nothing from it, that information is just as important as things he did learn.

The leader uses an outline form, previously prepared in his notebook so that he can unobtrusively jot down answers and comments under various headings. The subheadings, analyzing the reactions of the participant to various activities in the project, are made into a question, *e.g.*, "Do you recall any of the discussion topics which were particularly interesting or helpful to you?" In order to help the participant recall various meetings (over a six month period, possibly), a typed sheet listing the dates and discussion topics of all the sessions is shown to him. He refers to this as he ponders the questions pertaining to discussion sessions.

An outline of the 12 questions, with subheadings, used in the multiple counseling projects is given below:

EVALUATION OF GROUP PROJECT (statements of the participant)

(*Questions by Counselor*)

A. Changes in self-concept.

  1. *Do you think you understand yourself better because of the group experience? In what way?*

    a. self-assurance, self-confidence, ego-bolstering

    b. acceptance of self, reassurance

    c. ego-deflation, self-dissatisfaction, guilt feelings

  2. *Which discussion topics were most helpful?*

203

3. *Which parts of the group experience were most helpful?*

    a. discussion sessions: talking, arguing, listening, sociodrama and role-taking. friendly-contacts

    b. self-appraisals and tests: autobiography, rating sheets, personality inventories, sociogram

    c. counseling by group leader

B. Changes in understanding and acceptance of others.

1. *Do you think you understand others better because of the group experience?*

    Are you more accepting (tolerant) of others?
    group members
    friends, parents, acquaintances, etc.

2. *Which discussions were most helpful in this?*

3. *Which parts of the group experience were most helpful?*
    (go over points listed in A-3)

C. Changes in behavior.

1. *Did the group experience help you change, help your adjustments?*

    a. changes in feelings, attitudes, ways of acting

    b. improved expression of viewpoint, feeling "at ease" in a group

    c. carryover to other situations or groups

2. *Which discussions were most helpful?*
    (go over points listed in A-3)

D. *Did you enjoy or gain satisfaction from any of the following?*

1. acting the way you felt	7. friendly argument
2. saying what you wanted to	8. winning an argument
3. griping	9. asking leader question he could not answer
4. blowing off steam	10. friendly give-and-take in group
5. relating personal experiences	11. friendly contacts
6. listening rather than talking	12. making jokes, getting laughs from group

E. Influence of the group experience.

1. *Do you think the benefits derived from the group experience are temporary or something you can use in the future?*

F. *Have you some suggestions for improving the group project?*

To facilitate note-taking the outline form may be prepared in advance of the summary interview with plenty of space for filling in verbatim comments of the interviewee. Such an outline, filled in during the conference with a college student who was an unhappy isolate follows:

A-1......Great change — I've never talked to people before . . . saw world in a more friendly light.

  a

  b....Satisfaction with myself . . . assurance that I have some worth within me . . .

  c   I felt good after the meetings, all of them.

A-2......I liked all the discussions . . . being with the kids . . . the subject wasn't important . . . after a few meetings I didn't feel ill at ease . . . could talk back and forth. Jud was worse than I was in breaking in, interrupting others.

A-3-a.....The most important thing was the friendliness — that did most for me.

  b

  c

B-1......Yes, but I can't define it . . . I have always been tolerant of others . . . about the others in the group — I liked all the members, at first without any reason, at the end I had found the reasons for liking them. I'm searching for the same thing Jud is, although I don't agree with his way . . . As to my family, well I don't like my younger brother, I may sound like a sissy but I don't like his dirty jokes and ways, it gets me down. I think I could get to like my parents but I can't live with them. Their ideas are so different from mine . . .

  2......The discussions on sex — I learned a lot. Sex compatibility in marriage hit home with me. My girl, the one I'm engaged to, I have already made up my mind about her (breaking it off).

  3......I got the most from the frank discussions and the friendliness in the group.

C-1-a....Yes there has been a change in my behavior — the world looks less malicious to me, I felt at ease in the group throughout and didn't feel that the kids would talk about me afterwards (I usually do, you know).

  b....I've always thought I was incapable of expression, of getting my ideas across, it went better in this group, they could understand me . . . I know that Jud and I took too much of the time . . . I always wanted to be accepted in a group but I was never liked in high school and it was even worse at the boys' school they sent me to . . . I'd like to have a gang.

  2......The topics weren't important, being with the people, the friendliness was.

  3......Same as I said before — the friendliness — and I liked talking and arguing.

D.......(Checked "friendly argument," "friendly give-and-take in the group," "friendly contacts").

E........A change in my personality is indicated. I certainly don't think I'll turn backwards ... I despise the idea of maturity as being forward ... I think the way they describe "stages of maturity" are artificial.

F........(When asked for suggestions to improve the structure and procedures in the group project, he said he objected to the summaries of discussion content the leader had given: they were "too pat." He then thanked the leader, saying he had learned a great deal. This was the first group activity he had ever really enjoyed).

Conclusion

The briefing and summary interviews are a vital part of a multiple counseling project. In the preliminary interview the stage is set for learning. In the final interview learning is brought into clear focus: incentive for further personal growth is stimulated; help with plans for improved personal and social adjustments is given.

Rapport, essential for counseling, is established in the first interview. The relationship between leader and participant becomes closer during the project; the final interview completes welding the rapport into a permanent relationship. The assurance of a continuing interest in the personal growth of the participant by the leader is affirmed. Even though the two do not meet again for a year or more, when they do meet, the warm relationship built from the shared group experience and counseling is unchanged. The two can pick up where they left off. A sample conversation in a meeting one year after the summary interview follows:

Rose: Hello Miss D, my it's nice to see you again. I've thought about you and that discussion group so many times. I sure did enjoy that.

Miss D: Well, Rose, I've thought of you and the others in the group, too. I've wondered how your teaching went this year.

Rose: Just fine. You know I got so encouraged from the group and what you told me about myself — I'm really getting over that inferiority complex. I took on the job as advisor to the activity program at school. If I do say so, we had a wonderful success this year.

Miss D: I'm sure glad to hear it, not surprised either. What I told you about the impression you made in the group was not malarky, you know. You have real ability in handling people, a sensitivity to them which is mighty important.

Rose: Well, I meant to write you and tell you how fine the year was going, but I never got around to it.

Miss D: I hope you will keep in touch, and if there ever is anything I can help you with, be sure to let me know.

The relationship described above resulted chiefly from the summary interview ending a six-session project (group 12). The interview lasted one and one-half hours. It contained extensive discussion of self-appraisals, personality inventories, behavior observations, sociogram results. Rose told of her inferiority feelings and fear of taking added responsibilities in her teaching position. Ego-bolstering and reassurance by the leader helped her to take an important step forward in her personal growth.

Using John Dewey's simile of the learning adventure as a voyage, the briefing interview helps to launch the boat, the summary interview to prepare for another voyage.

XII

TANGIBLE EVIDENCE OF PERSONAL GROWTH

THE TEST OF AN EFFECTIVE COUNSELING METHOD lies in constructive changes in attitudes and behavior of the clients: attitudes toward oneself and others; behavior which carries these attitudes into significant living and personal growth. This means the growth or maintenance of personal strengths, the diminution of, or adjustment to, personal weaknesses. It means an increase in capacity for new interests, friends, living efficiency: enjoyment, creativity, contribution to society. Growth in empathy and sensitivity to others is essential in personal growth. Growth away from childishness and egocentricity toward adult behavior with its acceptance of societal responsibilities is implicit in the personal growth process. Furthermore, motivation toward sharing with, and helping others, constitutes the dynamic force for personality development.

Evidence of constructive changes in attitude on the part of participants in the multiple counseling projects reported in this book was plentiful. With the exception of six of the one hundred and twenty-one group members, significant learning took place. Evidence of behavior changes attributable, at least in part, to the group experience was found in 98 of the 121 participants, approximately 80%. These results compare favorably with results of individual counseling and psychiatric treatment. However, multiple counseling does not aim as high or as deep as a psychotherapy method: its objectives are primarily "encouragement," "support," or "social rehabilitation" in the case of seriously maladjusted individuals. The method attempts to direct experiential learning in the daily lives of the participants into constructive channels so that personal growth and adjustments can proceed satisfactorily. For the normal individual multiple counseling is an educational activity which aids personal development; for the emotionally ill person it is likewise an educational activity, but it also may have therapeutic value for him.

Summary of Results in Fifteen Multiple Counseling Projects

The first eight group projects directed by the author included 70 participants; there were two teen-age groups, two college groups, and four adult groups. Supposedly, members of the groups were normal individuals in the sense of functioning in society through their school, community, and job participations. These projects might be called personal development, preventive mental hygiene, or human relations study groups. No therapeutic objective was considered because theoretically the group members were mentally healthy persons. However, such was not the case. Nine of the seventy group members (13%) were seriously maladjusted (showing neurotic and other symptoms of mental illness or personality deviation). Eight of these participants were referred to health and psychiatric service agencies, but continued membership in the group projects. They were aided in personal growth and adjustment both by individual treatment and the project experience. For these individuals the group project served as an adjunct to individual counseling and the group leader limited her relationship with these persons to supportive, educational, and vocational guidance areas (3).

The succeeding seven group projects led by the author included three college groups with mixed memberships of normal, maladjusted (counselees), and mentally ill (psychiatric) students. In one group there was a preponderance of normal students; in another, counselees; in the third, psychiatric cases. Next, three groups of psychiatric cases were activated. Last, one group of institutionized mental patients were given the multiple counseling activity. Obviously the majority of the fifty-one participants in these seven projects were mentally or emotionally ill. The shocking fact is: many of these psychiatric patients were not as seriously ill as the majority of the so-called normal participants who were referred to health and psychiatric agencies from the eight high school, college and adult projects. Thus group memberships in personal development and preventive mental hygiene projects included seriously maladjusted individuals although the preponderance of participants were so-called normals while membership in group projects for maladjusted individuals included so-called normal individuals, with a preponderance of emotionally or mentally ill persons.

209

Regardless of the kind of group or characteristics of its membership the same results were secured: the consensus of group members (with the exception of not more than one in each group) was as follows:

1. Enjoyment of group membership and social interaction.

2. Support and reassurance from the group in discussing a personal conflict, worry, or problem.

3. Tension reduction from "talking out" feelings and problems.

4. Clarification of problems, improved attitudes and self-confidence in facing them.

5. Greater objectivity in viewing one's own difficulties, increased understanding and acceptance of self.

6. Improvement in empathy, tolerance, and sympathy for others.

7. Improved skill in interpersonal relationships and social competence.

Of course not all these seven outcomes were found for every participant who gained personal growth through the group experience. According to reports from psychiatrists treating certain group members, "enjoyment of group membership and social interactions" was sufficiently significant to make the group project worthwhile and to aid the therapeutic process. Several group members were deemed by the psychiatric department as unsuitable for psychotherapy and the multiple counseling project was a last resort. These participants "made good" in the group projects: the benefits to them were definitely therapeutic (or socially rehabilitative).

Even though behavior changes often included only improved attitudes and applications in present situations and symptomatic areas such learning is significant, according to many counselors and psychiatrists. For example, Dr. Thorne, in "Principles of Personality Counseling" writes:

"Analysis of present situations is of the greatest importance . . . one of the basic problems of counseling is to secure suitable conditions of emotional stability in the client so that learning can take place (p. 30). . . . In a normal personality (whose behavior is not neurotically determined) there is considerable opportunity for behavior modification on conscious voluntary levels if the *basic attitudes* which determine traits can be identified and manipulated. Given favorable circumstances, it is literally possible to secure any desired alteration of personality by the manipulation of the appropriate attitudes. . . . Some cases will require relatively little work (counseling) to secure the desired changes in attitude (p. 448). . . . In our opinion, it is indicated to deal with symptoms realistically and effectively as part of the total process of case handling . . . situational factors appear to play an important role in almost all personality disorders, and they should not be neglected because of excessive preoccupation with depth factors in personality (p. 165)" (8).

Thus the value of a multiple counseling project for seriously maladjusted participants comes in the improved attitudes and renewed incentives *to face, and to work toward solutions* of their individual personality problems. Dr. Washburne refers to this in the Foreword when she writes:

"the benefits of such an approach to various human problems, has been well demonstrated by the author . . . the results were sufficiently encouraging as to suggest that, not only as a method in itself, but also in combination with private conferences, the period of rehabilitation and recovery may be shortened."

Perhaps we should be more deeply concerned with the seriously maladjusted individuals who cannot afford psychiatric treatment, or who fear the stigma attached to mental illness, thus avoiding psychiatric treatment in any event. Results of the multiple counseling experience for group members in this category were definitely encouraging. In many cases there was evidence of all seven outcomes: the group experience and adjunctive counseling, focussed on present situations and immediate problems, was extremely helpful to these participants. They learned to get along better with themselves and others; to use more effective adjustive techniques; to be encouraged to make the best of themselves in spite of unalterable personal weaknesses.

Case Study Illustrations of Attitude and Behavior Changes

Illustrations showing frequent evidence of changed attitudes and behavior among participants in the fifteen group projects are classified into:

1. Well-adjusted group members who elected the project because they enjoy group discussions.
2. Well-adjusted individuals who want to learn more about personality, human relations, etc.
3. Apparently well-adjusted group members who had hidden conflicts, tensions, and feelings of inadequacy.

211

4. Maladjusted and mentally ill participants who acknowledged their need for personality counseling or psychiatric treatment.

Examples will be given, in addition to the above categories, of participants who failed to gain significant learning from the group experience: in one case a well-adjusted individual, in the other, an individual whose personal growth and adjustments were definitely unsatisfactory.

I. The well-adjusted participants, electing a group project for the fun of it, did not anticipate learning much from the activity. They were satisfied with their personal growth progress and life adjustments, therefore the learning outcomes were unexpected and unpredictable.

Example 1

Doug (Group 4), well-to-do graduate student who had been successful in radio and night club entertainment work, returned to college to get a teaching certificate. He thought he'd try speech and dramatics teaching in a high school for a change. Outgoing, attractive, and popular in his group as well as in college circles, Doug contributed well to the discussions and to the social interactions in the project. He expected to be drafted and hoped to be given an assignment as interpreter, since he was proficient in several languages.

Although Doug had not expected to learn much from the project, his evaluation of influences on his self-concept and understanding of others showed that he had gained important insight and skills in human relations which might prove useful in his tour of duty.

A year later Doug returned on furlough to the campus as a corporal serving as Chaplain's assistant at a large basic training camp. He looked up the group leader and reported significant carryover of learnings from the group project into his job in the Army. He apologized for the fact that he, untrained for the assignment, was "counseling" G.I.'s as well as assisting in difficult problems concerning negro and white troops who were billetted together. The discussions as well as the various personality types within the multiple counseling project had given him a helpful background for his work. Likewise the self-assessment and test results had helped him to analyze his personal strengths and weaknesses. A year later, the summary counseling interview was still fresh in his mind: it had provided motivation "for changing some things about me."

Example 2

Theo (Group 11), an attractive professor of Speech, was more experienced in group dynamics than the group leader. She joined the project because of enjoying group discussion as an activity. An excellent participant, she was popular even though the only college teacher in the group.

212

Although Theo had not expected to learn anything from the project, a very significant clue came to light through the MMPI and projective test which gave her new insight into her personal traits. An extended discussion of her perfectionistic tendencies was held in the summary interview. She appeared to be stunned by the self-analysis, in which she reviewed her habits and reactions and admitted her obsession of orderliness and perfection in details. Then she told the leader that she had come to summer school to get away from her involvement with a fellow professor. She was trying to make up her mind whether or not to accept his proposal of marriage.

A letter written from a foreign country to the leader ten months later in reply to the follow-up questionnaire contained the following:

"Little did I realize how significant it would be for me . . . in my marriage. Many times I have thought of the tests we took which revealed my strong traits for perfection in myself and others. Under the exigencies of travel I have had to give up many ideas of perfection in dress, comfort, time available, etc. It was easier for me to do so when I thought in terms of preconceived ideas, ideas explained in the tests and the discussion with the project director. The same applies to ideas I was almost guilty of forcing on my husband. The discussion project and he, saved me from making us both unhappy.

II. Well-adjusted participants who wanted to learn more about personality, and human relations often elect a multiple counseling project because formal courses in psychology and sociology have not satisfied their need for exchanging viewpoints in discussions, e.g., they desire an *active learning process*. For these participants, learning to understand others better, and to gain new knowledges and appreciations are most frequent outcomes. An outstanding example of this occurred in a college project (group 6) because of the varied backgrounds of the eleven members. The two members who contributed the most, and who gained the most in new knowledges and appreciations were foreign students on exchange scholarships from Germany. Their cases are described below:

Example

Fritz and Margo, aged 22 and 20, respectively, were studying economics and labor relations on one year scholarships at the university. Fritz planned to return to the University of Munich to continue in graduate study of economics and law at the end of the year. Margo, secretary to a labor organization, would return to her position. They were invited by the leader to join a group project of normals, counselees, and psychiatric patients for two reasons: (1) greater heterogeneity and breadth of interests was needed in the group (2) the leader wished to learn the effect of a project on foreign students.

Fritz and Margo became the most popular members of the group. They often had difficulty expressing themselves in "American," although their English allowed them to participate actively in the discussions. They were frank in disagreeing with the American point of view on practically everything. But arguments, violent though they tended to be, were always friendly and tinged with humor. Both Fritz and Margo often got so excited in their attempts to find the right "American" word or phrase to put across their points that they would throw up their hands, tear their hair and jabber to each other in German. Margo usually let Fritz do the talking. The other group members decided she was acting too much like a German woman: she should learn to feel and act the equal of males as American women (at least the college students in this group) do. Therefore, Margo was asked for her opinion frequently; if Fritz tried to answer for her the group would tell him to stop acting like the dominant male — this was America, not Germany.

Excerpts from a discussion on "selecting a mate" illustrate variant viewpoints, earnestly expressed in the effort to gain understanding of one another.

Margo: I certainly don't want to have to push my husband . . . I intend to get one who knows what he's doing. He is the main person, a woman should accept her place.

Duncan: Basically I'll stand on what I said last week, but I'll qualify it. (He had said he wanted a wife who would push him, egg him on to success, etc.). Each couple must make their own adjustment, it varies with the kind of people they are.

Hulda: But one always dominates more than the other — it's impossible otherwise. I think a coöperative plan has to be worked out in marriage so there won't be too much domination.

Bob: In our family the man is the head. That's the way it should be.

Nan: It should not, it should be mutual, 50–50. Although the man earns more money, women can carry on their own careers, too. There are lots of career women who are married.

Margo: We don't have that in Germany so much. The man is the head, the wife helps him in any way he wants. If he wanted her to push him, then the wife pushes him.

Bob: The wife's career should be in the home. I don't want my wife to work. Something's wrong in America; the European way is better.

Hulda: My Sociology professor said yesterday that divorce rates are not caused by the reasons usually given. Women should be able to have careers and be good wives, too. A husband and wife must look over the wife's potentials — perhaps she could work and keep the family going, too.

Bob: There'll be a hurt somewhere —the kids get neglected maybe. I know of a couple in our hometown, her working broke up the marriage.

Hulda: Well it depends on the kind of woman, not on her working.

Charlotte: The ideal is a 50–50 relationship. Domination of man over woman is ridiculous. Everything depends on the capability of the woman. Of course her first responsibility is to her home and children.

Bob: Queen Elizabeth — maybe she is the head of her country but I'll bet her husband rules in the home (bedroom, anyway).

Charlotte: But her husband wouldn't dominate her in infantile aggressiveness.

Duncan: What should be the relationship if the wife feels her ability justifies a career — should that regulate the size of the family?

Charlotte: One can't generalize — it's all relative — each case. Actually a woman is in the labor market twice: before marriage and after the children are grown.

Bob: And she gets in labor in between . . . Ha! Ha!

Duncan: Take the example of a business couple. Both work, but then a child comes. The wife becomes dissatisfied.

Charlotte: I'd say the family is the important thing, not the job.

Fritz: I agree, very much. The family is the main thing. In America you try to make women a partner — in Germany we think of woman as looking up to man, not a partnership.

Charlotte: Can't a woman admire and respect a man without fauning at his feet and being submissive?

Fritz: Not just the physical strength, but something more fundamental — I can't express it in English. Margo, you know what I mean.

Margo: Yes, but I don't think there is an English word for it.

Charlotte: In the eyes of God, woman is equal.

Fritz: If you start quoting from the Bible you defeat your argument. I could give many more things from the Bible on my side. I'll just say man and woman are *different.*

Margo: It depends on woman's status. If working, then there should be equal wages for men and women in the same work. But in the family, it's a different status. Man has his place of authority in the family.

Bob: Yes and don't forget Adam's rib.

Duncan: Well, there is something about domination and coercion that I hate. I could never be that way with a wife. I have to think of marriage as a 50–50 relationship.

Fritz: If you have equal rights between them, what happens when there's a difference of point of view, where compromise is not possible — who decides the thing?

Charlotte: I'll admit the 50–50 is an ideal concept.

215

Bob: Well, take it in a Physics problem. What happens when there is a push of 50 pounds striking head-on?

Duncan: Perhaps the forces are at angles.

Nan: Well, I think compromise is possible. After all there are two different personalities involved in a marriage.

Charlotte: Mustn't we look at the aims of married life. Aren't they to have a family, harmony, happiness, etc.?

Margo: If the stories of American men leaving their wives for the more submissive European women are true, it shows the 50–50 business doesn't work out so well, perhaps.

Nan: Well, we live here and have to work things out the American way. For instance, I go 50–50 on some dates. When the fellow doesn't have any more money than I do I think it's fair for me to pay my own way to the movies, and I do.

Fritz: Speaking of those stories, maybe these dissatisfied American soldiers wanted to get the feeling that they were really worth something — they didn't get enough admiration or dependence from their American wives.

Duncan: I don't think I want a clinging vine wife. I'm sure I don't.

Fritz: How can there be 50–50, how can there be equality in unequal things? Man has always been dominant by nature. He will continue to be.

At the end of the project Fritz and Margo thanked the leader and other group members, invited them to visit their homes in Germany if a European trip was taken. Addresses were exchanged with promises of corresponding.

In the summary interviews both Fritz and Margo analyzed the learning they had gained: understanding American students, the culture, and differences between themselves and the other group members.

Fritz's Evaluation of Learning

1. He got new insight into American students' ideas, attitudes, reasons for their behavior. He gained in understanding and tolerance of the American point of view.

2. A growing affection and friendliness for American students resulted, even though he felt older and more mature. The group experience might influence him in the direction of a teaching career. He was still trying to make up his mind about a profession, having left the seminary where he started training for the priesthood.

3. He had known nothing about defense mechanisms, etc. The extensive discussions on behavior-causes gave him new knowledges, but he still did not believe in psychological tests, personality inventories, etc.

4. He became aware of his own rigidity regarding concepts of personality, determinism, etc. He intended to try to be more open-minded and willing to consider new viewpoints.

216

Fritz said they did not have such discussion groups in Germany and he intended to organize one when he got back to his university. The coeducational aspect was a great surprise to him — he liked it. His last statement, after thanking the leader, was perhaps the most significant evidence of the value of the group experience to him:

"That was the best thing I got from my American visit — I am so grateful for it."

Fritz wrote a long letter to the leader six months after returning to Germany in which he repeated his appreciation for the group experience. He was preparing for his Master's exams in Economics and was still undecided as to a career. He mentioned the counseling given by the leader (she suggested that politics might be a possible field for him), with an implication that a political career might be a longterm goal.

Margo's Evaluation of Learning

1. She gained skill in expressing herself and understanding the American language; this pleased her, and gave her confidence.

2. She gained new insights concerning the democratic way and the value of friendly argument — a completely new experience.

3. She gained much knowledge and appreciation of American people: how they differ, one from another; reasons for differences between Europeans and Americans.

4. She gained in tolerance for different points of view. She admitted she had been rather rigid, probably because she had never participated in free discussions of this type before.

Margo felt sure the learning influenced by the group experience would be permanent and would carry over into interpersonal relationships in Germany. She was particularly impressed with the violent arguments which remained objective and friendly. Like Fritz, she said the discussion group was the most meaningful and enjoyable experience she had had during her year in the United States.

A letter from Margo was received by the leader nine months after she returned to Germany. She again expressed her appreciation, asked the leader to remind various group members to write her, and ended with the news that she had become engaged with marriage intentions in the near future.

comment: It is interesting to note that all other group members mentioned Fritz and Margo as important influences in their enjoyment and learning gained in the group project. This frequently resulted when participants of different nationalities or races were in groups which would have otherwise been narrowly homogeneous.

III. Among the participants who elected the project because of feelings of social inadequacies, many were making excellent occupational and social adjustments. Yet they harbored inner feelings of inferiority and inadequacy of which their colleagues and friends were either unaware, or could not understand.

217

Example 1

Kermit (Group 5), a sophomore transfer, was a brilliant student, conscientious in college and possessing a strong loyalty and affection for his family. He was unhappy on the campus and sought counseling help because of his depressed state, characterized by tension, worry, and dissatisfaction. In spite of his low morale he maintained his high grades and became an active leader in student government. Nevertheless he was under great strain, and obsessed by feelings of inferiority especially when he had to speak in group or committee meetings.

Placed in a mixed group, (3 psychiatric patients, 4 counselees) Kermit had the chance to practice speaking up in a sympathetic group. Comparison of himself with fellow-members, and frank discussion of individual problems among the participants gave him a new perspective. Ventilation and self-assessment in the group as well as in individual counseling interviews helped to lessen his insecure and depressed feelings.

The following year Kermit became a campus leader. Checking up with the counselor, he reported good progress in ability to "meet the public" with less strain, and his depressed state had dissolved; his scholarship record was outstanding. He gave much credit to the group project experience for giving him support, encouragement, and practice in group discussion techniques. It constituted a re-conditioning process which removed his fear of taking active part in committees and planning groups.

In the middle of his senior year Kermit received outstanding recognition for his academic and campus achievements — he won the Rhodes Scholarship.

Example 2

Ella (Group 6), a quiet, attractive college junior felt so insecure in her relationships with the opposite sex that she had sought psychiatric help. Placed in a mixed group (psychiatric patients, counselees, and uncounseled participants) Ella listened more than she talked. However, she liked the five male participants and was able to engage in friendly social interactions with them during the latter part of the project. There were many discussions which brought out sex differences in viewpoints and several frank sessions dealing with sex and marriage.

The influence of the project, especially the personal contacts made with two of the male members, had the desired effect on Ella. According to reports from her psychiatrist and later from Ella herself, her attitude and behavior with the opposite sex changed. Telling the leader about this Ella said, "Believe it or not, I actually played golf in a mixed foursome last Saturday — that shows I'm *really* changed!"

After graduating from the University Ella took her savings and went to Europe, planning to stay with her Army relatives in Paris until she could locate a civil service job as translator there. She admitted she hoped to find some nice American officers or G.I.'s to play around with while in Europe.

Example 3

Virgil (Group 2), a high school senior farm boy, was shy and lacking in self-confidence, even though he was President of the FFA group in the school and

218

successful in academic and social groups. He earned enough money raising blooded livestock to provide a college education for himself. He looked forward to majoring in Physical Education.

Virgil was popular in the group project and improved in verbal expression and social interactions during the 17 meetings. His leadership and high popularity rating in the group became evident.

The summary interview emphasized his improvement in the group, his high ratings by fellow-members, and the occupational inventory results. The counseling in the interview focussed on his vocational plans, supporting his idea of going to college to defer the draft for at least a year. The leader questioned him at length regarding his choice of Physical Education as a major. When he admitted that his interest was based on a desire to be a coach, a job-analysis of coaching, with its pressures and highly competitive nature was discussed. Virgil admitted he had never thought of the position in exactly those terms.

Two years later Virgil had still not been drafted. After one year away at college majoring in Physical Education, he had transferred to the Agricultural School of his home town University where he was making good progress.

comment: Virgil, like many high school seniors in a wartime era, was confused and upset by the threat of being drafted. During the group project he had changed his mind three times regarding plans for the next year: first, he thought he would enlist in the Marines, next, he had expressed his longtime desire to be an agricultural county agent, lastly he decided to major in Physical Education at a college away from home. The discussions of occupations, plans for the next year, and the personality and occupational interests tests were influential in keeping Virgil from enlisting rather than going to college. The leader withheld information regarding results of psychological tests which were not encouraging for college attendance. Such tests sometimes are neither valid nor reliable when a student is highly motivated and conscientious in studying. The prediction for Virgil is that he will graduate from the University and go into business with his father, a live stock breeder, or teach Agriculture in a high school, perhaps eventually to become a county agent.

Example 4

Ronald (Group 13), a high school teacher, was observer-assistant in an adult group project. Thus he was a passive participant in the discussions, but otherwise engaged in all the activities of the multiple counseling project.

Ronald was very interested in all the discussions, and became excited and agitated during the session in which alcoholism was discussed. He told the group leader who was in the observation room at the time, "I wish I could get in there and tell them some facts. I know all about it from my own experience."

In the summary interview Ronald told the leader his story. He "had been a bum, lying around in the gutter not long ago." He had married and "was trying to sublimate his former habits into more socially acceptable behavior." He was most enthusiastic about the effect of the group project, for he had gained in understanding of himself and others. He felt reassured that his personality difficulties had straightened out.

The follow-up questionnaire was sent to Ronald six months later. He returned it with 27 of 32 statements checked regarding learning gained from the project. In other words he had checked all the statements except those concerned with active participation in discussions. An explanatory note to the leader was enclosed. Excerpts from it follow:

> "I gained greater tolerance for colored people from Mr. W's explanation of the negro question . . . appreciated use of humor from the young Physics teacher and his manner of explaining his views . . . Mr. W helped me here (reassurance that others have similar problems) . . . schoolmarms are human, nice, too (thanks to Miss D—) . . . first impressions are quite apt to be wrong (thought Mrs. R was Mr. R's secretary) . . . I think I got most from the MAPS test . . . would have liked more in that line. My interview with Miss D was of great value to me."

IV. The participants who were mentally or emotionally ill formed approximately 30% of the total number in the fifteen group projects. In some groups only one or two members were diagnosed as neurotic, pre-psychotic, or personality deviates. In other groups all members were so diagnosed, and in one group all members were institutionalized for mental illnesses. Effects of a small-group discussion therapy project were expected only in peripheral areas, but in many cases the group experience aided the psychotherapy being given during and following the group project. These results follow the opinions of psychiatrists who believe in the value of group therapy.

With few exceptions, these members showed improved attitudes toward facing and working through their personal problems.

Example 1

Dick (Group 7), a college freshman at the age of 23, had had psychiatric treatment in and out of hospitals since the age of 6. He entered the university without the admissions officers knowing his background of mental illness. In January he tangled with his English instructor and his behavior necessitated referral to the Dean's office. Because of his agitated and uncoöperative manner he was told to report to a counselor before being allowed to continue his English class. Dick demanded a woman counselor and was assigned to the writer. It became evident in the first interview that Dick should be transferred to a psychiatrist, but he refused, promising to coöperate with the university officials and his English instructor if he was allowed to remain a client at the Counseling Center.

Assigned to a group project as part of the counseling process, Dick could not assume his responsibility as a group member, although he tried. He rejected members of the group although they attempted to take him into the intimate circle. Several times during the project Dick came to the counselor (the leader of the group) and said he couldn't stand the sessions, he hated them, and got nothing from them. The subject of a psychiatric referral was again raised, but he refused any consideration of it.

Finally the pressures became too great for Dick: he was unable to get along with fellow students in his rooming house, his depressive state scared him, and the group project seemed to be a last straw. In the summary interview test interpretations and sociogram results showed Dick his emotional instability and isolate-standing in the group; he asked for the psychiatric referral. An appointment was made two days hence, but the next day he phoned his father to come and get him, he had decided to drop out of college. However, his father insisted on staying over for the psychiatric interview and told the psychiatrist the whole history of his son's mental illness.

Dick retained contact with the counselor, writing her and phoning long distance to ask help in gaining admittance to another college. When last heard from, Dick had decided to live at home and commute to a college. Excerpts from his letter:

"I am going to try to share my college experience with my parents. Living at home, I think I can get along better and make a success of college."

comment: The psychiatric diagnosis given for Dick's personality difficulty was congenital infantilism. His inability to "grow up" to give to, or accept love from his parents, and all others with whom he had been associated — was brought sharply to his attention during the group project. The opportunity was given him to make friends and to share his feelings of insecurity, depression, and inadequacy with others in the group. He refused to do this, and his negativism made him feel "different from the others," thus deepening his depressive state. This was the precipitating factor in his decision to accept psychiatric treatment. But it came too late and Dick had to chalk up another failure in the succession of attempts to make satisfactory life-adjustments. However, the prompt action at the time of his breakdown may have prevented a suicide attempt.

This case is presented to show the influence of a group project on "immediate situations," and "attitudes." Perhaps if the group experience had come earlier in the year psychiatric treatment might have started in time to help Dick finish the college year. No one can predict the effects of the encouragement of a successful accomplishment. It is hoped that he will make a success of the new college attempt. As far as intellectual capacity is concerned, he could be a brilliant student.

Example 2

Gertrude (Group 10), a 24-year-old college sophomore had sought psychiatric help for her agitatedly depressed condition. Maladjustment factors included difficulties with her roommate and dormitory membership. She was obsessed by feelings of inferiority and fear, reinforced by her long stay in a sanitorium and thoracic surgery. She could not converse with other students and dreaded meal-time for that reason. Her roommate had threatened to ask for a change, since Gertrude tried to monopolize her time and became angry when she refused to limit her friendships and activities in the dorm.

Placed in a psychiatric group project, Gertrude was fearful that the three men and other two women members would not accept her. In the briefing inter-view the leader advised her not to disclose her age or the fact that she had spent three years in a sanitorium; she should think in the present; she was a college sophomore. After a few sessions Gertrude gained self-confidence and became an excellent participant. She saw herself, by comparison with the others, in a new light. Although personal problems were not similar among members of the group, all of them had great difficulty in self-expression. Gertrude's self-esteem was given a much needed boost through the group experience, since she was superior in verbal expression and was well-liked by the group.

Support and reassurance helped her make a change to another dormitory and a single room. She was able to converse and make friends with girls in the dorm. Her depressed condition disappeared as she learned to face the world as a normal person rather than a cripple. Also, new insight had come regarding her paranoic outlook. From last reports Gertrude was making good progress in overcoming this personal weakness along with improvement in her personal and social adjustments.

Example 3

Alice (Group 15), 36-year-old member of a discussion therapy group in a mental institution, was recovering from a third bout with a depressive phase. Her diagnosis was manic-depressive, and the mental illness was associated with childbirth trauma.

During the 26 group sessions Alice was an active participant, even while taking insulin shock treatments. She was popular with the other members and they respected her judgment and common sense. Alice had never been given individual psychotherapy, due to the crowded conditions of the hospitals in which she had been confined.

Alice engaged in reminiscence and self-revelation frequently in the non-directed discussions and, according to her psychiatrist, gained some psychotherapeutic benefit from her self-assessment.

After hospital discharge Alice was able to go back to college to finish required courses for teaching and from last reports, was making excellent adjustments.

V. The six participants who learned little or nothing from the group experience and adjunctive counseling included well-adjusted, mal-adjusted, and mentally ill persons. Analysis of reasons for the lack of learning in these cases revealed two factors related to "readiness for learning": (1) not feeling a need for learning (2) not wanting to learn.

An example of a well-adjusted participant who was not challenged by the multiple counseling project follows:

Fred (Group 2), a high school senior, joined the group project because of his interest in human relations and interpersonal skills. A leader in the school, he recruited the male members of the group and was the most popular participant among the ten members.

Fred's chief concern was the draft. He couldn't decide whether to enlist, or wait until he should be drafted. He was not interested in college and stated his vocational aim as "I want to have my own business."

In the summary and follow-up interviews Fred said that the group project had not influenced his attitudes or behavior: he had understood himself and was proud of his ability to figure out and get along with others long before the group experience. He had enjoyed the project and was glad he had been able to help others in the group, not only during discussions, but outside.

An example of a maladjusted participant who did not want to face facts or learn to understand himself follows:

Ted (Group 4), a married veteran college junior, 24 years old, joined the group project "as an easy way to do the field work assignment" in conjunction with a teacher-training course.

Although the group gave him a high ranking in the sociogram at the beginning of the project, he received a low ranking at the end. (Leadership, participation, attractiveness, brain-power, etc.) Ted showed great egocentricity and a tendency to boast of his prowess in athletics, and military service. After getting to know him, the group believed him to be rather emotionally unstable and untrustworthy. He missed several meetings, and arrived in the middle of two others, dressed in his air force officer's uniform.

In the summary and follow-up interviews, Ted displayed an unrealistic attitude toward himself, others in the group, his professors, and college officials. Statements he had made concerning attendance and grades at another institution proved to be untrue. He believed he had been the most outstanding participant in the discussion group, refusing to accept the results and comments by fellow members in the final sociogram. Whereas he had been most enthusiastic about his occupational goal of physical education teacher and coach during the project, in the follow-up interview he said he had decided to drop out of school and work in his father's real estate business. This was the fourth change of occupational goal in three years. Meanwhile his wife was pregnant with a second child. He was not worried about finances, because his parents were willing to see him through college and he had sufficient credit under the G.I. bill to finance his teacher-training course.

In his evaluation of group project influences on his self-understanding and understanding of others, he said he had gained nothing; he felt more sophisticated than the others, had always been skillful in interpersonal relationships and tolerant of others. He refused to accept, not only the sociogram results and leader's observational report of his behavior and standing in the group, but also his major professor's report of unsatisfactory work in education courses. He rationalized, placing the blame on others throughout all interviews.

comment: The leader-counselor focussed discussion in the counseling interviews on vocational guidance after seeing that Ted was not ready for a frank self-appraisal. Encouragement was given him regarding sales work since his outgoing personality and nervous energy might prove a great asset in a salesman position. When last heard from, Ted was selling automobiles, and real estate on the side. Quite possibly his responsibilities as head of a family will help him to "settle down" and "grow up."

SUMMARY

Evidence of changes in attitudes and behavior attributable to learning gained in multiple counseling projects were presented in this chapter. A summary of results among 121 participants in 15 miscellaneous group projects was given. Representative case studies among well-adjusted, maladjusted, and mentally ill participants described learning outcomes both predictable and unpredictable. The illustrations show the various facets from which learning may result: discussion content and dynamics, social interactions, self-appraisals, and adjunctive counseling.

Evidence that some participants do not feel sufficient need or desire to learn from the multiple counseling activity was illustrated from two cases: a well-adjusted high school student and a maladjusted veteran college student.

CONCLUSION

INDIVIDUALITY, WE ARE REPEATEDLY TOLD, is seriously threatened by the age and country we live in. Excessive value is ascribed to machines, speed, and power; the assembly lines of mass production threaten to dominate education as well as industry. Size or numbers have become increasingly important in our value system. Whereas in Sweden, government regulations prohibit school populations of more than 500, in the United States we are closing the little red school house and working for high schools of 5000 pupils. The larger the community or city, the more its citizens boast.

Furthermore, we do not use the leisure the machines have supposedly given us to develop our personal and special gifts. We watch. The more leisure we have, the more radio and television programs we may attend, and the larger the audiences at varsity and professional sports events. The result is the submergence of individuality and the growth of inertia; the lessening of our confidence in ourselves and in our individual power to create and to contribute to others.

Psychologically, the suffocation of individuality through mass production and lack of personal creativity is reflected in the alarming increase among us of neuroses and psychoses. The National Association for Mental Health estimates that 10 to 20% of our citizens are mentally or emotionally ill sometime during their life span. Over 50% of all hospital patients in the United States are mentally ill. 50% of the Korean War casualties were psychiatric cases.

Let us consider the so-called mentally healthy individuals in our society. How many people do we know who are living up to their intellectual, creative, or Agape potentials? Even Einstein, according to estimates of neurologists, uses only a part of his brain cell capacity. Yet individuals exist among us who arouse our amazement and admiration in their zest for life and range of creativeness: Toscanini, Grandma Moses, Sir Winston Churchill. But there are today all too many persons lost in the mass, lacking self-confidence, lacking faith in their ability to contribute to society, lacking vision of their responsibility to society. Not only are there thousands of psychotic persons, inside and out of mental institutions, but there are also millions of emotionally ill persons who live ineffectively and unhappily in our society, a prey to frustrations, inner conflicts, feelings of guilt, hostility and bitterness, anxiety and fear.

The responsibility for improving the mental health of our citizenry must be accepted as "part of the job" of all who work with human relations — whether in teaching, social work, youth groups and recreation, industry and labor management, or in the medical and psychological fields focussed on human behavior. We can, and are obligated to, counteract the disintegrating effects of certain aspects of modern society. To use John Dewey's figure of speech, the teacher steers the boat: but he also helps his charges to liberate the energy that propels it. And it must be remembered that we are all embarked together. Not only is the individual of value; he will find his fullest value in the contributions which he as an individual can make to other individuals.

Who can say what effect wise counseling at the right time might have had in the lives of many unhappy persons today? It might have been the fine example and kindly help of a teacher; the support and vision of a minister or priest; or — more pertinent to this book — group membership in a multiple counseling activity where companions in misery could both receive and give.

Multiple counseling provides a learning medium for personal growth for individuals in institutions, schools, and communities. Whether these projects be organized as education and preventive mental hygiene, or social rehabilitative and group therapy, they are focussed on personal growth. They are not a substitute for individual counseling but an enrichment of it. To be able to contribute to his group improves the mental health of a participant and develops his best individuality. In multiple counseling, group members share the responsibility with the leader and in trying to understand and help others, they themselves are helped. This is perhaps the most significant lesson learned in multiple counseling.

APPENDIX

SUMMARIES OF FIFTEEN
MULTIPLE COUNSELING PROJECTS

APPENDIX

Summaries of Fifteen Multiple Counseling Projects

INTRODUCTION

THE SUMMARY DESCRIPTIONS OF THESE PROJECTS show the skeletal framework of knowledges, discussions, and auxiliary activities on which the method is based. The variation with which the structure of each project is developed come from needs and interests within the group. Since there are basic human needs and communicative skills, certain knowledges and activities are common to all projects.

Personal growth levels among the 121 participants in the projects varied from successful, happy high school and college students to incapacitated neurotic and psychotic patients. General outcomes for practically all these participants were significant learning of knowledges, new attitudes, and social skills. The group experiences aided personal growth in the case of well-adjusted individuals and helped remove blocks to personal growth or to satisfactory life adjustments in the case of the maladjusted or mentally ill individuals. Enjoyment of the group activity was a significant factor in the learning; the camaraderie of membership in an intimate group was most important.

The sequence in which the project summaries are presented is the same as shown in the summary chart (p. 35). Some of the projects can be classified as personal development courses, others as social rehabilitation therapy. Common to all projects is the multiple counseling aspect: individual counseling was concommitant with the project. In some cases the counseling was performed by the group leader; in others, by attending psychiatrists or counselors. No participant lacked the opportunity to secure a private interview with the group leader or his counselor when he felt the need of it.

From reading the summaries it becomes evident that group sessions *do* substitute for private interviews: the need for ventilation and for support can often be filled by the group activity. Thus this method proved to be a time-saver for psychiatrists and counselors. The minimum of two interviews per group member for noncounselees filled the needs and "steered the boat" toward further personal growth in the majority of cases.

GROUP 1 — Ten high school seniors: 7 girls, 3 boys (non-counselees)

This project was organized as an activity club for a limited number of senior students who were interested in learning about personality, human relations, and "getting along with people." There were 16 weekly sessions held during the regular school activity period: 15 were discussion sessions, 1 (the last) was used for writing evaluations of the group project. Adjunctive counseling consisted of an average of 2.5 interviews per student.

Chronological list of discussion topics in 15 sessions

1. Getting acquainted: self descriptions.

2. What is an attractive personality: difference of opinion among boys and girls as to desirable traits.

3. Analysis and criticism of a high school poll listing eight characteristics of "a smooth person." Group worked in couples to draw up lists of desirable traits (boy and girl) in rank order.

4. Why do you like or dislike a person. (At end of session the group members rated themselves on nine behavior traits).

5. How do we differ, one from another: nine behavior trait ratings, feeling toward parents, brothers and sisters.

6. Discussion of various work experience and vocational choices of the group members. They guessed at A and C ratings for themselves on the Strong Interests Inventory (recently taken, but not yet scored).

7. What personal traits are characteristic of emotional maturity: a well-balanced life. (Autobiographical outlines distributed, explained).

8. What is a well-adjusted person: a ninth grader, a twelfth grader, an adult. Changes in behavior, likes and dislikes, as one grows up. What about honesty, drinking?

9. Sociograms: Negro and Jew on train. Discussion of racial prejudice and the Negro problem: should a white girl date a Negro if she is not willing to marry one; difficulties of interracial marriages.

230

10. Sociodramas: (1) Jewish nurse applies for job in Catholic hospital (2) Scout master argues with Lutheran clergyman. Discussion: what can we do about prejudices; how can one learn to be more understanding and tolerant.

11. Discussion on "being outstanding": what would you be in life if you could have your wish.

12. Sociodramas: (1) the wrong way to apply for a job (2) the right way. Discussion: analysis of errors of behavior in applicant; unrealistic behavior of employer in second scene.

13. Why do people act the way they do: be-boppers, alcoholics, the under dog. Influence of four basic drives in causing behavior. Second discussion: what would you do if a bomb dropped today, wiping out your family and home?

14. Defense mechanisms (typed sheets with simple definitions and examples of identification, projection, sublimation, rationalization, compensation). Discussion: examples of defensive behavior in everyday life of group members.

15. Can defense mechanisms be used in a good way: huddles discussed this and reported back to group with examples. Discussion: is rationalizing really lying?

Sociometry of group

A close knit group of four girls; two other girls who were friends; one girl isolate; two boys who were acquaintances but not friends; one boy isolate.

Group structure, dynamics, leadership

Structure 4 (leaderless free discussion) was used as often as possible, and the assistant leader (a male graduate student) participated in group discussions in support of the three male members. The leader started sessions with a short talk, a springboard question, or typed material. Most frequently the free discussion was allowed to go in any direction and the leader exerted controls only when violent arguments or "ganging up on one member" became disruptive.

The chief characteristics of the discussions were the outgoing behavior, frank self-revelations, strong feeling-expressions used by the

231

dominant members (four girls and one boy). Boy-girl competition and antagonisms decreased after six sessions.

Auxiliary activities

Self-appraisal devices consisted of autobiographies, self-ratings on nine behavior traits, the MMPI, Strong, and MAPS. Role-playing was used as the main activity in three sessions. Written evaluations of the project took up one session.

Adjunctive counseling

There was no briefing interview. The summary interview was held immediately following the conclusion of the group project; the follow-up interview two to three months later. Before or after the administration of the projective test (MAPS) a short conference with each participant revealed reactions to the project, personal problems, etc. Several of the group members were counseled during the year following the end of the project.

Outcomes

The general outcomes for the majority of the group were:

1. Improvement of discussive and social skills.

2. Reduction of tensions; satisfaction from ventilation.

3. Support and reassurance regarding worthiness as a person.

4. Motivation toward improvement of personal weaknesses.

Results of the questions asked in the written evaluation were as follows:

	Yes	No	?
1. Do you think you understand yourself better because of participation in Personology Club..............................	8	1	1
(affirmative answers require explanation)			
2. Do you think the discussions, role-playing, tests, etc., helped you understand and accept others better......................	8	0	2
(affirmative answer requires explanation)			

	Yes	No	?
3. Do you think there may be any carryover in the future to make you more understanding and tolerant of others.............. (*affirmative answer requires explanation*)	4	1	5
4. Did you find the role-playing helpful.....	7	3	0
5. Were you helped in vocational guidance areas.................................	9	1	0

Results of the summary interview and the follow-up conference usually substantiated answers given in the written evaluation, especially in regard to the influence which implemented the learning. For example, one participant repeated his appreciation of test results and comments of fellow members. Another gave evidence that changes in attitude and behavior were influenced by her discovering others had similar problems of rebellion against parental control. While the majority of the group had been upset, confused, and unhappy at the beginning of the project (beginning of the senior year), many of their "growing up" problems were dissipating by the end of the year. The frank discussions, mutual problem-sharing, and influence of adult leader-counselors, helped them through a difficult growth period.

GROUP 2 — Ten high school seniors: 5 girls, 5 boys (non-counselees)

This project was organized as an activity club for a limited number of seniors in the second semester following Project 1. Thus students who had not been able to gain membership during the first semester could elect the group project. It was publicized in the same way as the first project: "students interested in learning more about human relations, personality, and 'getting along with people'." There were 17 weekly sessions held during the regular activity period; 16 were discussion sessions, 1 (the last) was used for writing evaluations of the group project. Adjunctive counseling consisted of an average of 2 interviews per student.

Chronological list of discussion topics in 16 sessions
  1. Getting acquainted. Discussion: should women be drafted into the AF as well as men?

233

2. Continuation of discussion: which is preferable, Army, Navy, Air Force or Marines. New topic: what makes for high school popularity and leadership.

3. Do boys and girls agree on personality traits which are most desirable in the opposite sex; in their own sex.

4. What makes a good teacher; a poor one. (Examples within the school).

5. What kind of a date do you like; dislike.
New topic: are girls smarter than boys.

6. Do people fit into certain jobs because they are extroverts; introverts. What kind of a job would you enjoy most if you like to work with people, with things.
New topic: do people choose their mates because of similar traits or differences in personality.

7. What is your idea of success in life; what would you like to be in ten years.

8. What is happiness; what is the definition of a well-adjusted person.

9. Which is the most important basic drive (to live, to love, to belong, to be recognized). Which is most important to you, personally.

10. Why do people go to college: for prestige, to find a mate, or to train for a job. Is college worthwhile or can you do better, training on the job.

11. Sociodramas: (1) principal with unruly student (2) mother with uncooperative daughter (3) high school girl arguing with boy friend that he should not enlist. Discussion: what are the reasons for these people feeling the way they do. Who is right?

12. Sociodramas: (1) father reprimanding son for drinking, not doing chores, etc. (2) two co-eds, one has flunked out and must face irate parents (3) two naval boot camp trainees arguing about gold-bricking. Discussion: which of the basic drives and emotions cause the feelings and actions; do girls

and fellows differ in their expressions of anger; does anyone ever develop a real dislike for a parent?

13. How much parental control is fair in the case of high school seniors; how much rebellion and freedom of action can be taken by a senior and still be fair to his parents; is it all right to stay out all night after prom.

14. How do different people react when they feel inferior; how would you act if you were a Negro in this high school.

15. How do we use defense mechanisms. (Typed definitions and illustrations used as point of reference).

16. Continuation of discussion: defense mechanisms, good and poor adjustive techniques.

Sociometric pattern of group

None of the five girls were close friends, but all were friendly except one who tended to be an isolate. One of the boys was dominant, having brought three of his friends into the project. One boy was an isolate. There were no antagonisms within the group, nor strong attractions.

Group structure, dynamics, leadership

The structure was seminar-type; leaderless discussions were few. Dynamics were low-level: emotionally colored interactions, and arguments were infrequent. The group waited for the leader to initiate most discussions which remained on intellectual, unemotional level, dominated by the opinions of the boy leader. There was comparatively little self-revelation or griping.

Auxiliary activities

Self-appraisal devices consisted of autobiographies, self-ratings on nine behavior traits, the MMPI, Strong, and MAPS. Role-playing was used as the main activity in two sessions. A sociogram of first, second, and third choices on six personal traits was done at the beginning and end of project. Written evaluations of the project took up all of the final session.

Adjunctive counseling

There was no briefing interview. The summary interviews were held the week following the conclusion of the project; follow-up interviews one to two months later. A short conference with each participant accompanied the administration of the MAPS (projective test).

Outcomes

The general outcomes for the majority of the group were in terms of self-assessment and vocational guidance. Written evaluations followed much the same pattern as in group 1. Results of the summary interview and follow-up conference showed that only three of the ten participants had definite personal and social adjustment problems; the group project and individual counseling was helpful to these students. For the other seven members, learning was significant in assessing their personal strengths and weaknesses in terms of plans for the next year. An important group influence steered in the direction of further education rather than enlisting in the AF.

GROUP 3 — Eight college juniors: 4 women, 4 men (non-counselees)

This project was organized as an elective in field work in conjunction with a teacher-training course. No grade or exam was given for the project. There were 18 one-hour sessions held twice a week during one semester: 17 were discussions, 1 (next to last) was used for writing evaluations of the project and of each other. Adjunctive counseling consisted of 2 interviews per student.

Chronological list of discussion topics in 17 sessions

1. Getting acquainted: self-descriptions. Discussion: what is emotional stability.

2. Debate, four against four: is heredity or environment more important in molding personality.

3. Nondirected discussion: individual differences.

4. Sociodrama: G.I. Joe and Korean girl. Discussion: can mixed marriages succeed; is one love forever.

5. Where do you stand on the Negro question; what can an individual do to ameliorate discriminatory practices.

6. Sociodrama: two Negro students come north to college. Discussion: behavior causes, aggressiveness, prejudices.

7. What is a feeling of security; how do we get it, keep it, lose it.

8. Defense mechanisms. Discussion of definitions and illustrations from daily life.

9. Psychodramas: defense mechanisms. Discussion: clarification of behavior causes.

10. Why do people act the way they do: group versus individual behavior; individual differences in reacting to the same situation.

11. Sex differences: kind of behavior a teacher may expect from high school boys and girls; why co-eds act the way they do; college men.

12. When and where should children get their sex education.

13. Which are the most valuable personal traits for success in teaching.

14. Psychodrama: professor and disgruntled student. Discussion: case studies of difficult situations to be handled by the teacher.

15. Sociodrama: Principal and social science teacher. Discussion: reasons for selecting teaching as a career; difficulties which must be faced.

16. Social competence: how can one improve his personality and ability.

17. Has this group project been as valuable as practical field work (leading a youth group) would have been in gaining social competence.

Sociometric pattern

None of the group were acquainted prior to the project even though several were in the same section of the education course. There were no signs of antagonisms among the participants and no strong attachments developed. However, a strong camaraderie grew up and all members became friendly during the project.

237

Group structure, dynamics, leadership

Equal proportions of leaderless discussions, student-led discussions, and seminar-type sessions were included. Informational talks, psychodramas, and typed question sheets were used as springboards to discussion. Six of the eight participants were active discussants throughout; two men and one woman vied for dominance in the discussions. The atmosphere of the group was intimate, friendly, light-humored, except when a serious discussion was underway.

Auxiliary activities

Self-appraisal devices consisted of autobiographies, self-ratings on nine behavior traits, the MMPI, Strong, and MAPS. A sociogram was done at the beginning and end of the project. Role-playing was used as springboard to discussions in five sessions. Written evaluations embraced both the project and fellow members.

Adjunctive counseling

There were no briefing interviews, but the professor in charge of the teacher-training course talked with prospective participants, discussing them with the leader who advised on selection of the eight students for group membership. Summary and follow-up interviews were held with all participants. There was a short conference before or after the administration of the projective test. Short chats were held with individual group members before or after some group sessions.

Outcomes

The majority of these participants were transfers from other colleges; they were dissatisfied with their adjustments on the campus, and uncertain of vocational choices. They were aided in their college adjustments and vocational choices by the group project. According to written evaluations, substantiated in summary and follow-up interviews, the general outcomes were:

1. Better understanding and acceptance of personal strengths and weaknesses.

2. Better understanding and tolerance of others.

3. Improved discussive skill.

4. Motivation toward improving social competence.

5. Support and reassurance regarding vocational choice or change to another field.

Two illustrative cases

The first example whom we shall call John, illustrates a type of college student who gains more from the self-appraisal devices than from the discussion activity. The meaningful discussions for him were held in private interviews, and he continued the counseling contact after the project ended. John was a "listener." He felt different from the others who were younger and also he differed from a fellow veteran in the group who was married. John was the only physical education major; he had wanted to be a professional baseball player, but a physical disability from the war prevented that career. John had tried electric engineering after army discharge but was unsuccessful in it. When it became evident that he could not make his grades at the university, counseling focussed on self-assessment in terms of another vocational choice. He was dropped from school but could be re-admitted after working for a semester. During this period he corresponded with the counselor and came in for an interview. He became engaged to a social worker who was anxious for him to finish college but wanted him to stay near her. At last report John was re-admitted to the University and was taking courses at the extension center in his girl's home city.

The second example whom we shall call Marie, illustrates a type of college student who gained much from the social interactions and discussion activity. Adjunctive counseling was relatively unimportant in her case. Marie had always wanted to be a lawyer like her brother, but her family discouraged her, insisting that teaching was the best vocation for a girl. Marie was a brilliant student but a quiet, non-gregarious type who at first felt insecure in the mixed discussion group. Comparing herself with the others she found she was outstanding in discussions: her logic, concise expression, skill in debate was appreciated by all the other group members. They all liked Marie but couldn't imagine her as a high school teacher. She decided that she would try it, changing to graduate work in Political Science, perhaps law school, if she didn't like high school teaching.

A year and a half following Marie's graduation she was back on the campus. Conferring with the leader, Marie said she had tried teaching social studies in high school. Although her teaching was satisfactory, she hadn't liked it, and was now working on her Master's in history and political science. She thought she would like college teaching and if marriage didn't intervene, she might go on with a law career.

Support and reassurance from her fellow group members and the leader helped Marie's self-confidence and determination to make up her own mind about a career.

GROUP 4 — Seven college juniors: 4 women, 3 men (non-counselees)

This project was similar to project 3. Eight students were selected from fifteen who applied for membership (one male student left school after 4 sessions). Selection was based upon the opinions of the professor and group leader as to the students who could best contribute to, and gain from, the group experience. Participation substituted for field work in conjunction with the teacher training course but no exams or grades were given for the project. There were 18 one-hour sessions held twice a week during a semester: 17 were discussions, 1 (the last) was used for writing evaluations of the group project and fellow members. Adjunctive counseling consisted of an average of 2 interviews per student.

Chronological list of discussion topics in 17 sessions

1. Self-descriptions. Discussion: what is emotional maturity.
2. Debate, four against four: is heredity or environment more important in molding personality.
3. Free discussion: individual differences; influence of emotions and drives.
4. Sociodrama: G. I. Joe and Korean girl. Discussion: can mixed marriages succeed; the Negro-white problem.
5. Structured discussion: typed questions on mixed marriages and "is one love forever."
6. Sociodrama: two Negro students come north to college. Discussion: behavior causes, aggressiveness, minority groups.

7. What is a feeling of security; how do we get it, lose it.

8. Behavior causes: aggressive and withdrawing reactions; defense mechanisms.

9. Defense mechanisms: inductive method, seminar-type discussion.

10. Psychodramas: defense mechanisms demonstrated. Clarification of adjustive techniques as important to human behavior.

11. Discussion: which are the most valuable personal traits for successful teaching. Strong profiles analyzed by individual members in comparison with self-concepts.

12. Sex differences: discussion of variant viewpoints of men and women group members regarding opposite sex.

13. When and where should children get their sex education.

14. How can the teacher help. (Case studies of problem pupils in school).

15. Sociodramas (1) principal reprimanding teacher for going in cocktail lounge (2) principal arguing with English teacher regarding importance of grammar. Discussion questions: can a teacher be human; can he maintain his teaching philosophy and keep his job.

16. Social competence: how can one improve his personality and ability to get along with people.

17. Psychodramas: interviews with prospective teachers. Discussion: is the education curriculum too theoretical; is this group project just more theory.

Sociometric pattern

None of the group were previously acquainted. There were no strong attachments or antagonisms. The camaraderie was immediate and lasting but not as strong as in group 3. Four of the participants were aged 22–26; the others were typical undergraduates.

Group structure, dynamics, leadership

The same design was used as in group 3. The influence of the more mature participants produced greater depth and breadth in discussions.   Self-revelation was more frequent and the atmosphere had more emotional coloring.   One participant, a speech major, was highly skilled in discussion leadership.

Auxiliary activities
Identical with those of group 3.

Adjunctive counseling
Although counseling was limited to summary and follow-up interviews in conjunction with the group project, three of the participants continued the counseling contact following the conclusion of the project.   The group project provided an effective impetus for recognition and talking out of personal problems; new incentives toward solutions.   The subsequent counseling aided three counselees to make important decisions concerning vocations as well as to improve attitudes toward themselves and others.

Outcomes
All group members except one showed evidence of the following learning:

1. Better understanding and acceptance of personal strengths and weaknesses; clarification of personal values and goals.
2. Better understanding and tolerance of others; greater appreciation of personality differences.
3. Improved judgment regarding vocational choice or a change to a different field.
4. Increased skill in participating and leading discussions.

GROUP 5

Eight college students : 4 women, 4 men (counselees and psychiatric clients)

This was a group therapy project for maladjusted students who had sought help from university counselors and psychiatrists.   Thus there was concommitant counseling and treatment for the majority of the participants; the group leader served as group therapist in these cases, reporting regularly to the attendant counselors.   There were eleven sessions planned as weekly meetings, but vacation and exam periods interrupted the sequence so that the project extended over three months. Sessions were held in late afternoon, lasting one and one-half hours. Adjunctive counseling by the leader pertained to the group activity and averaged two interviews per student. In the case of four members the number of private interviews with the attending counselor or psychiatrist was cut down during the project: group sessions substituted for some interviews.

Characteristics of group members

The majority of the group were individualistic and lacking in interpersonal skills. Although there was a common meeting ground in the group, viz., a strong feeling of insecurity and social inadequacy, individual problems differed widely among six neurotic members. Heterogeneity was great: two were 18-year-old freshmen, two were 26-year-old ex-teachers; there was a Negro and a Jew in the group; academic and vocational interests were widely divergent. Several members were undependable, and used excuses of illness, depression, or study pressure as reasons for not attending sessions regularly.

Chronological list of discussion topics in 11 sessions

1. Self-descriptions. Discussion: difficulties in adjusting to college.

2. Sociodrama: interviews with a secure and an insecure person. Discussion: what are the elements of a feeling of security.

3. Sociodrama: a friend tries to help an alcoholic. Discussion: reasons for losing one's feeling of security; ways to regain it.

4. Case conference session: around-the-table recitation of worries, needs, personal goals.

5. Leaderless discussion: what is a mature person.

6. Review of book "The Mature Mind": Discussion: what is emotional maturity.

7. Psychodramas: (1) Instructor and uncoöperative student (2) irate father and flunking son. Discussion: self centeredness as a quality of immaturity; family relationships.

8. Differences in family relationships in various cultures; difficulties of adolescents in American society, especially college

students whose independence from parental control is impossible.

9. Criteria of college success. Discussion: criticism of the university as atheistic; vocational training emphasis rather than personal growth.

10. Defense mechanisms. Discussion: does a mature person use them.

11. Racial discrimination: what is the responsibility of a college student in combatting it.

Sociometric pattern

None of the group were previously acquainted. There were no signs of antagonisms and the four members who attended regularly developed a close camaraderie which carried over to outside contacts.

Group structure, dynamics, leadership

In general a seminar-type or case-conference structure was used. The leader gave informational talks or presented sociodramas as springboards to discussion. Two dominant members were so concerned with their personal problems that leader control was necessary to prevent sessions from deteriorating into self-pity soliloquies. There was no internal leadership among group members.

Auxiliary activities

Role-playing was the only activity aside from the discussions.

Adjunctive counseling

Counseling by the group leader was limited to the summary and follow-up interviews. Concomitant counseling by the attendant counselor or psychiatrist used the group activity to foster self-assessments and incentives. The group therapy was considered to be helpful as a ventilating and supportive activity, thus expediting the counseling.

Outcomes

The chief value of the project for the group members was blowing off steam, griping, frank self-revelation. The comparison of oneself with others, and a newborn desire to help others were important outcomes for several of the egocentric members. Practice of empathy and awareness of others' problems aided personal growth of all members who attended regularly.

According to evaluations of group members and their attending counselors, general outcomes were:

1. Tension reduction through ventilation.

2. Support and reassurance of being a worthy person.

3. New interest in helping others, being less self-centered.

4. New motivation to coöperate with attending counselor or psychiatrist in working through to problem solutions.

NOTE: The most beneficial effects of the group project were in the case of two members who thought "they were going nuts." Through group support and talking out their fears in the group they gained sufficient emotional balance to finish the semester rather than dropping out of college. Also they were able to plan and carry through second semester programs. The two psychiatrists believed the group influence, coming at a time of crisis, was the deciding factor.

GROUP 6 — Eleven college students: 6 women, 5 men (non-counselees, counselees, psychiatric clients)

This project combined well-adjusted students with maladjusted and neurotic students as follows: 3 well-adjusted, 3 counselees under treatment by the group leader, 5 psychiatric clients referred by a university psychiatrist. Concomitant counseling was continued during the project, but the number of private interviews was cut down in the case of five participants when group sessions were found to fill counseling needs. There were 12 weekly sessions of one and one-half hour each. Adjunctive counseling by the group leader averaged two interviews per member.

Characteristics of group members

Great heterogeneity in age, academic classification, cultural background, and personal need, was characteristic of this group. It included one Negro woman graduate assistant, one male graduate student, two exchange students from Germany, as well as freshmen, sophomore, junior, and senior students. The common meeting ground was a desire to gain understanding of oneself and others; to become more socially competent.

245

Chronological list of discussion topics in 12 sessions

1. Self-descriptions. Discussion of topics in which group members were interested.

2. What is a feeling of security and how does one achieve it.

3. Parent-child relationships during the growing-up process: should college students rebel, concur, or compromise with parents.

4. Should children follow parents' advice: when, how, what, why.

5. Sociodrama: G.I. Joe and the Korean girl. Discussion: can mixed marriages succeed.

6. Discussions: (1) communism *vs.* democracy (2) sex differences.

7. What makes for success in marriage.

8. What is emotional maturity.

9. Differences in religious faiths.

10. Defense mechanisms.

11. Defensive behavior; effect of primary needs and emotions on behavior.

12. Is personality modify-able.

Sociometric pattern

The two German students were acquainted prior to the project; the other members were not. A close camaraderie sprang up quickly and included all members even though two women members were aggressively antagonistic toward people and the college in general. Camaraderie among group members increased during the project. The final meeting contained regretful farewells, promises to see one another, and to write to the German students who were soon to return to their country. The two antagonistically inclined participants were among the most enthusiastic group members at the end of the project.

Group structure, dynamics, leadership

There were equal proportions of (1) leaderless discussions (2) seminar-type meetings (3) discussions moderated by the leader. Internal leadership by three male participants was skillfully done, with the

246

German student taking responsibility for keeping the discussion focussed on the topic of the day. Disrupting influences by two rather disturbed psychiatric clients were occasionally controlled by the leader. All eleven participants contributed to the discussions although two tended to be "listeners."

Auxiliary activities

Self-appraisal devices consisted of self-ratings on nine behavior traits and seventeen personal characteristics. MMPI's were given the counselees and psychiatric clients. A sociogram was done at the end of the project. Role-playing was used in one session.

Adjunctive counseling

Summary and follow-up interviews were held with all participants. Counselees averaged 3 appointments during the 3-month period of the group project; psychiatric clients averaged 8 appointments with their psychiatrists. Several of the participants continued a counseling contact related to peripheral areas with the group leader after the project ended.

Outcomes

According to evidence from the participants and observations of the group leader and psychiatrist, all group members benefitted from the group experience. Normal members gained in understanding of individual differences and tolerance of conflicting viewpoints; in empathy and appreciation of human relation problems. Maladjusted and emotionally ill participants were aided either in their social adjustments or in self acceptance. Specifically, the combination of individual counseling and group therapy had excellent results for six seriously maladjusted students.

In general the influence of the group experience consisted of:

1. Improved understanding and acceptance of individual differences, especially European and American viewpoints.
2. Support and reassurance of being a worthy person.
3. Tension reduction through ventilation.
4. Enjoyment of discussion group activity.

GROUP 7— Eight college students: 5 women, 3 men (2 non-counselees, 5 counselees, 1 psychiatric client)

This project combined normal, maladjusted, and psychiatric clients in a group where the two well-adjusted students served as assistants to the leader, attempting to help the three male participants. Concomitant counseling for one counselee and the psychiatric client was continued during the project. Group sessions substituted for private interviews in the case of the other counselees. There were 7 weekly sessions of one and one-half hour each over a two-month period. The group leader was also the attending counselor. The average number of counseling interviews per student was 4, including summary and follow-up interviews with all participants.

Characteristics of group members

Heterogeneity within the group was great, especially regarding personalities and felt needs. One male student was found to be psychotic; another student with schizophrenic manifestations had been screened by the psychiatric department as a birth injury case. The third male student was a sixteen-year-old prodigy. The women participants were older and more aggressive than the male members. Thus a common language of experience, feelings, values, and goals was not found during the seven sessions.

Sociometric pattern

No camaraderie developed even though there were attempts of mutual help and friendship among several of the participants. The aggressiveness of two women members was resented by the male participants.

Chronological list of discussion topics in 7 sessions

1. Self-descriptions. Discussion: what is good adjustment in college.

2. What is a feeling of security: how do we get it, keep it, lose it.

3. What is the meaning of a mature person.

4. Book review "The Mature Mind." Discussion: what is emotional maturity.

5. Defense mechanisms (typed sheets of definitions). Discussion to clarify and illustrate common usage.

6. Defensive behavior, adjustive techniques, behavior causes.

7. What do students get from a college education.

Group structure, dynamics, leadership

The sessions were equally divided between leaderless discussions and seminar-type meetings. Internal leadership was shared by two dominant women participants who tended to engage in verbal duels. Both leaders, however, attempted to bring breadth and depth in the discussions; they often asked for opinions from the other members. Disagreements were frequent and many of the discussions were lively, but there was a minimum of self-revelation although griping was common. There was a close relationship between individual members and the leader.

Auxiliary activities

Self-appraisal devices consisted of rating sheets on nine behavior traits and seventeen personal characteristics, nine criteria of college success, a test of lovability. A sociogram was done at the end of the the project.

Adjunctive counseling

All but one member either were former counselees of the leader or were present counselees. The psychiatric client continued weekly interviews with her doctor. Group sessions substituted for weekly interviews in the case of three counselees. Four continued the counseling contact after the project ended.

Outcomes

With the exception of one participant the group members showed evidence of meaningful learning in the project. They gained understanding and acceptance of personal strengths and weaknesses; improved social skills; appreciation of individual differences; clarification of values and goals. Follow-up of these students in the year after the conclusion of the group project showed improved personal and social adjustments in all cases except one. (This psychotic student had refused psychiatric referral and was harmless, so he was allowed to participate in the group project).

The two well-adjusted students who served as assistants gained fully as much from the group project as the maladjusted members. For them it was a course in applied psychology.

Comments made by group members in summary or follow-up interviews included the following:

"Comparing myself with the others bolstered my ego and helped clear away my longtime inferiority complex."

"I could see how very intolerant I've been of other people. In this group I was able to react emotionally to the others' problems, when they told about them. I never did that before."

"I appreciated the opportunity to say what I really think. You don't do that in other groups. Also I got to know myself better, and I don't like what I see. There have got to be some changes made."

"I know now that I need 'serious help' (psychiatrist). I was too different from the others in the group. . . . I didn't feel I belonged with them, they didn't know what I was talking about. . . . I couldn't make them understand how I felt."

"I felt at ease in the group. . . . gained confidence so I can talk up in my quiz sections."

"I can understand my mother better . . . get along better with her. I enjoyed the group, wished I could have got a date with J. I became dissatisfied with myself, I need to mature. I am very shy but got to feeling at ease in the group. I wish I could make more friendly contacts like that."

NOTE: This last comment was made by the male student who was a birth injury victim. He did not reveal his bizarre ideas in group meetings and only one of the group knew his background. This was the first time he had ever been accepted in an intimate group.

GROUP 8 — Six college students (3 women, 3 men, all receiving psychiatric treatment)

This group therapy project was organized at the request of the psychiatric department to supplement the weekly interviews in the case of five clients; to substitute for individual appointments in the case of one client who had not benefitted from psychotherapeutic treatment. There were 11 weekly sessions of one and one-half hour in length. Adjunctive counseling by the group leader averaged 3 interviews per member over a three-month period.

Characteristics of group members

With one exception the participants were upper classmen with excellent scholastic standing. Tentative diagnoses included neuroses, pre-schizophrenia, congenital infantilism. Conflict with, or rejection of, parents was common to all participants. Personalities included two aggressive men, two girls who tended to be listeners. There were two Jews, one Catholic, and three Protestants, but all except one had rejected the faith of their fathers and were seeking a new faith or philosophy of life. One of the men was a Negro.

Chronological list of discussion topics in 11 sessions

1. Self-descriptions. Discussion: is love essential to a feeling of security.

2. Continuation Questions: is it possible to feel secure in an insecure world; which of the four basic drives is most important to you.

3. Case conference: One of the members presented her own case and the group discussed it. Second discussion: how does one work toward emotional maturity and free oneself from parental domination.

4. Emotional maturity, continued. Discussion: relationships of group members with their parents; problems concerned with them.

5. Sociodrama: G.I. Joe and the Korean girl. Discussion: can mixed marriages succeed; is one love forever.

6. Different concepts of love: brotherly love, filial love, sexual attraction and married love.

7. How important is sexual compatibility as a basis for marriage. Second discussion: defense mechanisms.

8. Why do people act the way they do: be-boppers, alcoholics, aggressive or withdrawing behavior.

9. Case studies illustrating different adjustive techniques, aggressive and withdrawing behavior; group *vs.* individual reactions to situations.

10. Discussion: nine criteria of college success; does our university encourage students to gain the nine competences.

11. Discussion: (1) is a religious conviction basic to a well-adjusted personality (2) Since there is agreement on this, what are you doing to work toward spiritual growth.

251

Group structure, dynamics, leadership

The sessions were divided between nondirected discussions and seminar-type meetings. The two aggressive male participants objected to the latter but were so monopolistic in nondirected sessions that the other members became disgusted and threatened to drop out of the project. Moderation by the leader was necessary in order to give the four other members a chance to participate in the discussions. Discussions were always lively; arguments were common; self-revelation and frank expression of feelings were characteristic of all sessions.

Auxiliary activities

Self-appraisal devices consisted of self-rating sheets on likes and dislikes. A sociogram was done at the end of the project, using the nine criteria of college success for rank order of all group members, including oneself. Role-playing was used in one session.

Adjunctive counseling

The group averaged three individual interviews with the leader: briefing, intermediary, and summary. Five members had regular psychiatric interviews, weekly or biweekly with their doctors; one member had been dropped from psychiatric treatment because of lack of coöperation with the doctor.

Outcomes

The group therapy was judged by both the participants and their psychiatrists to have aided personal and social adjustments. In general the group influences helped in the following ways:

1. Improved self-understanding and acceptance; reassurance that he (she) was a worthy person in spite of weaknesses.

2. Support and reassurance from fellow members concerning similar conflicts and guilt feelings concerned with family relationships.

3. Tension reduction from griping and ventilation.

4. A new understanding and appreciation of individual differences, especially related to masculine and feminine viewpoints on sex mores and marriage concepts.

252

An analysis of answers given by participants to evaluation questions in summary interviews with the leader or psychiatrist follows:

Summary of outcomes from statements in summary interview

	Joy	Arlene	Hulda	Mike	Jud	Elliot
Self-understanding:						
Ego-building (self-confidence)...........		√		√		
Reassurance (self-acceptance)..........	√		√	√	√	
Ego-deflation (self-acceptance).........		√				√
Understanding and acceptance of others:						
Improved tolerance....................	√	√	√		√	
Improved acceptance.................	√	√	√	√	√	√
Change in behavior:						
Attitude toward self..................	√	√	√	√	√	√
Attitude toward others (specific)........		√	√	√	√	
Tension reduction.....................		√	√	√		
Improved verbal expression in groups and general conversation..............		√			√	√
Improvement in self and social adjustments:						
Daily habits of thought, activity, etc.....	√	√	√			
Interpersonal relationships.............	√	√	√		√	
Enjoyment or satisfaction from the participation:						
Acting the way you felt................	√	√				
Saying what you wanted...............	√	√				
Griping..............................			√			
Blowing off steam....................						
Relating personal experiences..........	√				√	
Listening rather than talking..........	√				√	
Friendly argument....................	√	√	√	√	√	√
Winning an argument.................						
Saying something funny...............				√	√	
Friendly give-and-take in the group......	√		√	√		
Social interactions, friendly contacts.....	√	√	√	√		√
Belief that benefits from the group experience will influence personal growth in the future..	?	√	√	√	√	√

GROUP 9

Six college students: 3 women, 3 men (all receiving psychiatric treatment)

This group therapy project was organized at the request of the psychiatric department to supplement individual psychotherapy. All

253

the clients needed an intimate group in which they could get support and reassurance. There were 15 weekly sessions over a four-month period. A relaxed, social atmosphere was implemented by late afternoon sessions lasting one and one-half hour; group members took turns bringing refreshments.

Characteristics of group members

These were older students, ranging in age from 20 to 31: three were working for Masters or Ph.D. degrees, one was a veteran who had worked for six years before starting college, one was an elementary school teacher who had been in a sanatorium for several years, one was a husband and father. The common meeting ground for group members was a depressed state and need to ventilate feelings of resentment, hostility, fear and worry.

Chronological list of discussion topics for 15 sessions

1. Self-descriptions. Discussion: what is a feeling of security.

2. Discussion continued: elements essential to feeling of security. Question: which of the four basic drives is most important to you.

3. Discussion continued: importance of self-esteem in a feeling of security.

4. Sociodrama: English girl, engaged to American G.I., argues with mother. Discussion: when should parental control cease.

5. Discussion: what is the maturity concept; what are elements of maturity.

6. Non-directive session without topic or leadership. (Ventilation, griping).

7. Discussion: does our University encourage growth in the nine competences listed as criteria for college success.

8. Discussion: what should one get out of college; what am I getting from it.

9. Seminar-type meeting: listing and discussion of pet gripes.

10. Discussion of gripes, continued.

254

11. Seminar-type meeting: defense mechanisms defined and explained. Group members gave illustrations from own experience.

12. Sociodrama: the professor and disgruntled student. Enacted three times with three different couples, role reversal included. (*Practice in reacting spontaneously in a conflict situation*).

13. Discussion: how and where should one get his sex education.

14. Case conference type: exchange of frank opinions of, and questions to, each other.

15. Truth party continued in first 30 minutes. Sociodrama: interviews of an Atheist, Catholic, Protestant. Discussion: how important is a religious faith to developing an integrated personality.

Sociometric pattern

One girl had had an unsuccessful blind date with one of the male participants previously, and she was in the same course with another woman member although they had never formed a friendship. Otherwise members of the group were not acquainted.

Friendships sprang up between several of the participants which continued during and after the group project. All members liked each other with the exception of one who was an isolate by his own choice. The other five members became irritated with him and were openly antagonistic to him in some sessions.

Group structure, dynamics, leadership

With the exception of three sessions nondirective leadership was used. Internal leadership was provided by two members, a man and a woman. Frequently the leader gave information, book reviews or case studies as springboards to discussion, after which she withdrew into an observer or passive participant role. The dynamics were restrained in early sessions but boiled over into frank reactions, expressions of feeling, and self-revelation in later sessions. The two dominant members assisted by the leader succeeded in breaking down the ego-defenses and cover-up behavior of other members so that the last four sessions resembled "truth parties."

255

Auxiliary activities

Self-appraisal devices consisted of a structured self-analysis of personal philosophy, goals, strengths and weaknesses; a sociogram which rated oneself and others on nine criteria of college success. Role-playing was used in three sessions.

Adjunctive counseling

In addition to the regular psychiatric interviews provided by the attending psychiatrists, group members averaged two interviews with the group leader (exception was one woman member who had four interviews). However, several group members conferred with the group leader before or after group sessions because of concern regarding their performance in the session. Counseling by the leader was confined to the group activity and certain areas defined by the psychiatrists.

Outcomes

Five of the six members were benefitted by the group activity both in personal adjustment on the campus and in expediting psychotherapy. Evidence of meaningful learning was given both by the clients and their psychiatrists. The sixth participant had dropped psychiatric treatment before the start of the project, changing to a university counselor. He showed no signs of progress in recognizing or facing his serious personality weakness either in group sessions or individual counseling.

In general the outcomes were the following:

1. Improved understanding and acceptance of oneself.
2. Tension reduction from ventilation, griping and arguments.
3. Encouragement and help from fellow members in meeting present situations and facing future problems.
4. Improved incentive and ability to benefit from psychotherapy.

GROUP 10 — Six college students: (1 drop-out)
3 women, 3 men, (5 psychiatric clients, 1 counselee)

This group therapy project supplemented, and in two cases, substituted for regular psychiatric interviews. The male student who dropped out after the fourth session also discontinued individual psychotherapy at the same time. There were 12 weekly sessions of one and one-half hour each over a three-month period. Adjunctive counseling by the leader averaged two interviews per participant plus short chats.

Characteristics of group members

Heterogeneity in the group was great: ages ranged from 18 to 27 years, academic rank from freshman to graduate assistant. Tentative diagnoses included pre-schizophrenia, neurosis, and retarded growth toward maturity. The common problem of group members was a lack of social adequacy and communicative skills. While one member was overly aggressive and talkative, the others were noncommunicative and inarticulate.

Chronological list of discussion topics in 12 sessions

1. Case conference (only three present). Discussion: where did you get your self-concept; how did it change through the years.

2. Seminar-type session. Discussion of self-concept continued. New discussion: in what way do you feel socially inadequate in groups; how and when did your fears and feelings of inferiority begin.

3. Discussion: how much conformity is necessary in order to feel well-adjusted in society; in college.

4. Seminar-type session: listing and discussion of pet gripes.

5. Discussion: tracing the origin of pet gripes; ventilation of painful or embarrassing situations in one's life.

6. Discussion: love and sex mores at college and in our society.

7. Discussion: which of the four basic drives is most important to you.

8. Discussion: "this I believe" (personal philosophy, values, goals).

9. Continuation: analysis of personal values and goals with statement of "what I should try to do now" (around-the-table recitation).

257

10. Truth party: questions to each other including "what do you think of me," "what do you think I should try to do to improve myself."

11. Discussion: sex differences, homosexuality, compatibility in marriage, selection of mate.

12. Sociodrama: interviews with Atheist, Catholic, Protestant. Discussion: how important is a religious belief in a well-balanced life.

Sociometric pattern

One man and one woman knew each other from participation in another group therapy project: they liked each other. All members liked each other with the exception of the male student who dropped out. He had been an isolate through his own choice. There were no antagonisms although one member was irritated by the monopoly of the aggressive male participant. This monopolist was well liked even though other members felt sorry for him because of his eccentricity.

Group structure, dynamics, leadership

This group was very dependent upon the leader. There was no internal leadership. Interview-type sessions consisting of round-the-table recitations were most frequently used: there was a dearth of group dynamics and lively discussions. Except for one member self-revelation and expression of feelings was frequent. The teacher-pupil relationship was maintained throughout the project because of the failure of group members to take responsibility (with the exception of the aggressive member who usually failed in his attempt at leadership and turned to the group leader for help).

Auxiliary activities

Self-appraisal devices consisted of a structured analysis of likes and dislikes; self-assessment of personal beliefs, values, goals, strengths and weaknesses; a sociogram giving self-ratings as well as rank order within the group on nine criteria of college success. Role-playing was used in one session.

Adjunctive counseling

Four of the five members were having weekly psychiatric interviews, while one had been dropped because of his inability to benefit from psychotherapy. The group leader, counseling only in areas recommended by the doctors, held an average of two interviews per member plus short chats.

Outcomes

Four of the five participants and their psychiatrists believed the project had helped them in social skills and amenability to psychotherapeutic treatment. According to individual evaluations the benefits included:

1. Reassurance that others have similar problems; new incentive to face and solve personal problems.
2. Improvement in verbal skill and group participation.
3. Tension reduction from ventilation and griping.
4. Better understanding and acceptance of the opposite sex.

Examples of interactions and attempts to support or reassure fellow members are taken from recordings and leader's notes:

Gertrude: I get embarrassed when you talk about Hollywood models as being what men want for wives.

Elbert: Well I think that is bunk. Most fellows, like myself, don't care what a girl looks like, it's her personality that counts. You girls shouldn't worry so much about your not looking like movie stars, that isn't important.

Judy: I think the reason I can't talk in groups is I'm afraid of what the others will think of me. It will show how dumb I am.

Ardith: But you aren't dumb and look at us, we are interested in hearing your opinions. Other groups are the same, when they ask you questions it's because they are interested in you.

Mike: I'm trying to keep my mouth shut, but I always have to jump in and mess things up. I'm sorry if I was too inquisitive, Judy.

Ardith: Well, you have improved, Mike. There is a big change in you from the other group we were in.

Elbert: Maybe I'm crazy to want to be a college professor, but that's my goal.

Gertrude: I think you'd make a good one. You express things so clearly, and are so logical and keen minded. You could give a lecture better right now than some of my professors do.

259

GROUPS 11-14

Four projects for normal adults (teachers, school administrators, athletic coaches, music directors)

The four discussion groups were organized from volunteers in an Educational Psychology course during a college summer session. The projects included 35 adult students interested in learning more about group dynamics, interpersonal skills, and personality. The projects substituted for laboratory learning experiments but no exams or grades were given for membership in the group projects. Each group met twice weekly for an hour totalling six meetings in the three-week period. Adjunctive counseling by the group leader was combined with academic advisement, since the leader was also the teaching assistant in the course.

Organization of groups; characteristics of members

Eight participants were placed in each group and a ninth student was assigned as observer-recorder (passive participant). There were three coeducational groups (11, 12, 14) and one group of men (13). Heterogeneity among group members pertained to type of school work, marital status, age, educational, religious and family background. There were two Negroes and one American Indian. About two-thirds of the whole group were well-adjusted in their jobs and living situations while one-third were dissatisfied with some aspect of their professional or personal lives. Three (8.6%) either had had psychiatric treatment or were referred to Student Health service for help with emotional problems. They were not incapacitated and continued membership in the group project.

Group structure, dynamics, and leadership

Groups 11 and 12 planned the topics they wished to discuss and rotated discussion leadership within the group. Groups 13 and 14 did not plan the discussions, which were leaderless (structure 4). The project director served as resource person and gave informational talks at the beginning of two sessions in each group project. The following chart gives an outline of the discussion topics in the six sessions of the four groups:

260

CHRONOLOGICAL LIST OF DISCUSSION TOPICS IN SIX SESSIONS

Session	Group 11	Group 12	Group 13	Group 14
1	Planning topics, procedures, leadership	Same as 11	Discussion: definitions and meaning of "personality"	Same as 13
2	Discussion: "motivation"	Discussion: "minority groups"	Discussion: "unpredictable behavior"	Discussion: "effect of broken homes on children"
3	Discussion: "discipline problems"	Discussion: "reasons for prejudices"	Discussion: "is personality inherited"	Discussion: "what are causes and treatment of dishonesty"
4	Discussion: "personality traits of teachers"	Discussion: "maladjusted children"	*Talk by project director followed by discussion: "defense mechanisms"	*Same as 13
5	*Talk by project director followed by discussion: "defense mechanisms." Then discussion: "improving teacher-pupil relationships"	*Talk by project director followed by discussion: "defense mechanisms"	**Discussion: "alcoholism and its relation to defense mechanisms"	**Discussion: "alcoholism, cause and treatment"
6	**Discussion: "defense mechanism"; "tolerance"	**Discussion: "defense mechanism"; "tolerance"	Discussion: "tolerance and ability to sympathize with others"	Discussion: "tolerance; the Negro problem"

* In these sessions the project director distributed typed sheets of definitions of defense mechanisms and asked each group to discuss that subject, using personal illustrations whenever possible. In groups 11 and 12 the project director answered questions and gave clarifying illustrations for half the discussion period. In groups 13 and 14 the director left the groups "on their own" for the full discussion period.

** In these sessions the project director asked the groups to discuss a definite subject: "tolerance" in groups 11, 12; "alcoholism" in groups 13, 14 (these two groups had shown interest in the subject of alcoholism; the director suggested they relate it to defense mechanisms).

Sociometric patterns

Since all members of the four groups were in the academic course together, a cohesiveness and camaraderie was apparent from the start. Also, no exams or grades were given for participation in the group activity, so there was no pressure of competition.

The only antagonisms displayed in the groups were toward school administrators. Several teachers disliked school principals and superintendents in general; they "took a crack" at members of their groups who were school officials whenever an opportunity presented itself.

The three teachers given the most attention by their fellow members were a Negro teacher from the South, the American Indian teacher, and a young college instructor who disclosed the fact that he had been a diabetic since the age of seven.

There were three isolates, by their own choice. One woman teacher felt inferior to others in her group. A music director in the all male group felt different from the others in the group. A young woman teacher disliked teaching and rejected identification with "teachers"; she wanted to feel that she was different from the others in her group. In none of the three cases did the group reject the member, but rather, fellow members tried to bring the withdrawn person into the discussions and social interactions.

Comparison of group dynamics and leadership in four groups

Quantitative as well as qualitative records were kept of participation units and individual behavior of group members. The groups using structures 1 or 2 (seminar-type sessions) showed a higher average participation per member than did the structure 4 (leaderless) groups. The following chart analyzes the group dynamics, individual participation, and internal leadership in the four groups.

Group members were almost unanimous in their opinion that a skilled leader from outside the group was desirable; they would have liked either the professor in charge of the course, or the project director (teaching assistant) as moderators of discussions. This viewpoint was characteristic of the structured groups (who had excellent student leaders) as well as the leaderless groups. The participants believed "they would have learned more "with such a leader. In the case of the all male group, the participants missed a coeducational atmosphere; they thought the feminine point of view was needed in their discussions.

COMPARISON OF GROUP DYNAMICS IN FOUR GROUPS

	Structured		Unstructured	
Group dynamics	Group 11	Group 12	Group 13	Group 14
Average number of participations per minute during free discussions.	3	2.4	1.89	1.79
Assigned leadership	Project director in first session; rotating leadership within group for other sessions	(same as 11)	no leaders	no leaders
Internal leadership; steering discussions, filling in silences, etc.	shared by three	shared by three	shared by five (no domination)	shared by three (dominated by one)
Interactions among group members	Among seven (one inactive participant)	Among seven (one inactive participant)	Among seven (total group)	Among seven (one inactive participant)
Controversial dynamics: arguments, aggressiveness, etc.	two members (occasionally)	none	none	none

NOTE: This was a new experience for all but two of the participants: free discussion without strict moderation which used an inductive method of learning did not give them the usual "props." Yet their enthusiasm for the group experience was immediate and lasting.

Auxiliary activities

Self-appraisal devices consisted of autobiographies, self-ratings on nine behavior traits, the MMPI and MAPS. Evaluations of learning gained through the group experience were written three weeks after the projects ended. A follow-up questionnaire evaluating the project after 4–10 months was returned by 83% of the total group. All 29 reported excellent carryover of project influences.

Adjunctive counseling

All 35 participants had two scheduled appointments for private interviews with the project director. In the first the MAPS was administered either before or after a short counseling session. The second appointment was the summary interview which lasted from one to one and a half hours. In three cases another appointment was made at the request of the student to finish the discussion of a personal problem.

All participants were extremely interested in the results of the personality inventories: 75% confided personal problems, worries, fears, or idiosyncracies. The implications were clear: adults as well as teen-agers need counseling and eagerly seek it when there is an opportunity; self-assessment of personal strengths and weaknesses may be fully as meaningful to well-adjusted persons as to the maladjusted. Interest in personal growth does not have to cease with "the mature years."

Outcomes

1. *The attitudes of group members were favorably affected*

The intimate atmosphere in the discussion groups and the rapport between participants and the project director influenced attitudes toward the academic course and the professor in charge. Enthusiasm for the course was far greater on the part of the thirty-five participants than in the case of the other forty-five students in the class. In the words of several representative participants, "The group discussions gave more meaning to the course and gave us personal relationships which are not possible in a large lecture class; we made real friends of some of the class members and we felt much closer to the professor and teaching assistant."

(*The other forty-five class members had learning laboratory assignments, such as learning a series of unassociated words, motor coördination, etc.*).

2. *Participants gained in self-understanding and acceptance.*

In response to the question, "Do you think you understand yourself better because of your participation in the group discussion project," 34 of the 35 group members answered in the affirmative both in their written evaluations and the summary interviews. Their reasons could be classified (1) self-analysis of personal traits (2) new attitudes or appreciations (3) interpersonal skills. A total of 43 statements describing the learning were given by group members, for example,

"It helped to give new insight and new knowledge of self; how my mind works, thinking processes, why I do some of the things I do."

"It gave me a better understanding of personality; what it is, what influences help to shape it, how to judge it, how it can be improved."

"It gave me a better understanding of group dynamics and interpersonal skills, sensitivity to others."

3. *Participants gained in understanding and tolerance of others.*

In response to the question, "Do you think you understand the behavior of other people better because of your participation in the group discussion project," 34 of the 35 participants answered in the affirmative, both in written evaluations and the summary interview. 46 statements described their reasons for their answers. These could be classified into (1) increased knowledges (2) new attitudes or appreciations (3) improved skill in human relations. Examples of representative statements are:

"I understand individual differences and defense mechanisms much better, also alcoholism."

"I found that group members were sensitive, had keen insight, sincerity, ambition; it gave me new faith in mankind."

"I understand behavior causes in problem children much better and am working out better methods in handling them."

GROUP 15 — Seven women mental patients (insulin shock treatment cases, without individual psychotherapy)

The discussion therapy project was organized under the supervision of the attending psychiatrist for seven women patients in the treatment ward. No regular psychiatric interviews were held with the patients during the project, although the doctor had short conferences occasionally with them on the ward. All seven patients looked forward to hospital discharge within the next few months; the purpose of the project was to help them to understand and accept themselves and the problems to be faced after leaving the hospital. Thus the group activity was encouragement, supportive, or social rehabilitative in nature. It also could be called educational therapy because a teacher-pupil relationship was maintained throughout the project. There were 26 sessions over a three-month period. The group met in the library of their building after lunch for one and one-half hour sessions two or three times a week. This activity was scheduled as part of their treatment program.

Characteristics of group members

Heterogeneity among group members was notable. Ages ranged from 23 to 53. Five were married, two were single. Of the wives, two had been living with their husbands at the onset of their mental illness, one was separated and seeked a divorce, one was a widow; four of the five had children. Educational backgrounds ranged from tenth grade to college graduates. Past occupations included tavern waitress, saleslady, teacher, civil service supervisor. Diagnoses of mental illness included two manic-depressives, one character disorder, one simple schizophrenic, three paranoid schizophrenics. Three of the patients had been hospitalized one or more times previous to the present commitment. All the patients were responding well to the insulin shock series which varied from 50–95 treatments. All but one were on the two last weeks of shock treatment when the group project started.

Chronological list of discussion topics in 26 sessions

1. Personality: how we differ one from another. Question: what childhood influences are important in molding one's personality.

2. Personality cont'd. Childhood influences; relative importance of heredity and environment in personality growth.

3. Basic drives: to live, to love, to belong, to be recognized. Which one seems most important to you.

4. Basic drives, cont'd. Personal goals influenced by basic drives.

5. Emotions and their influence on behavior. Debate: does man have free will.

6. Discussion: how to increase love, diminish hate.

7. Kinds of love: love in the family, between children and parents, husband and wife, brothers and sisters. How does love sometimes change to hate.

8. Feelings of anger, hostility, resentment. Psychodrama: the discharged mental patient and her curious neighbor.

9. Self-understanding and acceptance; planning for the future after hospital discharge.

10. Recognition of mental illness in oneself and others. The continuum of personal traits that make for illness or health.

11. Discussion: what have you learned from your hospital experience.

12. What is peace of mind and how does one get it.

13. Alcoholism: why do people drink. Psychodrama: Lola and her alcoholic friend. Discussion: ways in which we use defense mechanisms.

14. Symptoms and degrees of mental illness: case conference, self-analysis by three members.

15. Defensive behavior: good and poor use of defense mechanisms.

16. Discussion: how I feel on a weekend home visit: toward myself and others.

17. Effects on one's feelings and behavior of bottling up fears, worries, and resentments.

18. Alcoholism: physical and psychological effects of drinking. Discussion: how I feel when I drink; why I drink.

19. Family relationships: sibling rivalry; difficulties mothers have in being impartial and fair to their children.

20. Self-understanding. Question: do you feel ready to go back home. If not, why not.

21. Question: is a convalescent period essential in mental illness just as it is necessary in a physical illness.

22. What kind of a convalescent period do you think would be good for you.

23. Is it possible for a person to really understand himself. Should we rely upon the judgments of our families and friends as well as the doctor.

24. Getting well: what can a person do to gain strength.

25. Differences in personality: flexible and rigid personalities. How can a person achieve better adaptability or avoid too heavy pressures.

26. Question: what should I try to do. (Plans, attitudes, new behavior patterns analyzed by individual group members).

Sociometric pattern

The group members were previously acquainted since they had lived on the same ward and had their shock treatments together. Camaraderie in the group was keen from the start. With the exception of one member the patients were proud to have been selected from the group of 21 ward inmates who were interviewed concerning possible membership in the therapy group. A sociogram had been done in order to determine the personal attractions and repulsions in the ward. The seven members had, in many cases, voted for each other as desirable companions in an intimate group.

Group structure, dynamics, leadership

The participants thought of the project as a class, with the group leader in the role of teacher. However, many of the sessions were nondirected discussions following an introductory talk by the leader. In these sessions the leader withdrew from the discussion circle (psychologically) after presenting a question for discussion. At the end of the session the leader took control, summarizing or interpreting the content of the discussion in preparation for the next session. Often group members suggested a topic or were asked to think over the discussion and bring something of interest to the next session.

Interview therapy techniques were used in at least one-third of the sessions. Thus the leader stayed in the discussion circle and questioned individual members or stimulated questioning of each other regarding feelings, attitudes, assessment of personal strengths and weaknesses. In these sessions the leader, along with group members, gave support and reassurance to the participant "who told his story."

Two of the group members assumed responsibility for steering discussions, filling in pauses, etc. Nondirected discussions were successful because of internal leadership.

There was one aggressive, hypomanic group member who sometimes disrupted the discussions through her long, tangential soliloquies. It was necessary to use direct tactics with this participant, asking her to let the others say something. Another member was so withdrawn and blocked in verbal expression that the leader assisted her with contributions to the discussions. Sometimes the whole group would sit quietly for several minutes while this participant worked through her psychological block to answer questions asked her by the leader. Once the block was removed this member often could take active part in the discussion during the remainder of the session. The other group members were very understanding, tactful, and effective in helping her to "come out of herself."

Auxiliary activities

The only auxiliary activity was role-playing which was used in two of the 26 sessions.

Adjunctive counseling

The group leader held briefing, summary, and follow-up interviews with five of the seven patients (two left the hospital before the end of the group project). Intermediate conferences were held on the ward, before or after group sessions. Rapport between group members and the leader was close. It continued in a permanent "friendly" relationship long after the patients were discharged and returned to their homes.

Outcomes

Evaluation of the group experience by the participants and their doctors showed that encouragement, support and reassurance were chief values. The patients believed they understood themselves better and felt more confident in facing the world after discharge. They gained in self-esteem and were prepared to take up their lives with lessened guilt feelings in connection with their illnesses. They accepted their personal weaknesses and the possibility of reoccurrences of their illnesses; incentives to prevent this were strengthened.

269

Five of the seven participants disclosed facts, thoughts, and feelings in group sessions which were cathartic. The tension reduction coupled with greater objectivity in self-assessment was at least preparation for greater insight. Since individual psychotherapy was not given to these patients, the value of the group activity as adjunctive treatment in psychotherapy is not known.

Changes in attitudes were the most significant learning, auguring well for personal adjustments after discharge. Sample statements made in the summary or follow-up interview follow:

"I understand my husband better, also my sister-in-law and the trouble I've had with her. . . . I know I must keep away from the old places and people, if I go back to that town I'd get running around to the same taverns. I'd get into trouble again. . . . I want to take the practical nursing course and settle in this city."

"I don't feel so guilty about what I did. Now I understand mental illness better. . . . I'm going to be careful not to get overtired and I'll tell my husband everything. I can trust him to know how I really am, if I go haywire I'll come back here on the double."

"The discussions helped me understand the relationship between my dad and me. . . . I'm going to lead my own life and not feel guilty if he disapproves of what I do. I don't think I'm as bad a person as I did before . . . the others in the group helped. It reassured me. . . . I can see now that my mental illness has been spread over the years. I never got over it the first time I had to come to the hospital. Now I will keep being cautious and fearful, trying to avoid letting it happen again. I'm going to check up with a psychiatrist regularly after I leave here . . . my daughter knows me better than I do myself and she can tell when I start to slip, whether I'm too high or low."

"It's going to be better if I talk more. . . . I should talk right back to my husband . . . he never wants to go anywhere but the tavern. I know I'm better off not drinking and wish I could get him to do other things, like picnics and church affairs where we can take the children. We ought to do things as a family. The kids love him and would enjoy it . . . no, I've decided I wouldn't divorce him even if the gossip is true, I must think of the children first."

"The group had the greatest influence in the world on me. I started to talk, I haven't talked about myself to anyone. I'm going to try to keep on talking, I know it's good to get things out. . . . I was encouraged, that I could express myself so well in the group. . . . I can see that holding in one's feelings is bad. Most people can get rid of them by talking to others but I have never been able to."

Six months later the new attitudes of these five patients had been translated into action. One was preparing to take the practical nursing course; one was making an excellent adjustment with her husband and infant son; one was attending college in a refresher course for teaching; one was making a valiant attempt to keep her family together although the odds were against her. The fifth, still at the hospital, was working as typist and file clerk in one of the offices.

Implications of this therapy project

According to the doctor in charge of the women admissions ward, there are hundreds of patients each year who would benefit in the same way as the participants in this project if the opportunity for discussion group therapy were given to them. The ability of the group members to carry on lucid discussions and to enjoy mental activity and group dynamics on the same days that they received insulin shock therapy appears to be significant. It shows the potentials of such patients for initiating new behavior patterns. The fact that these patients could recall specific discussions several months later and could trace changes in their self-understanding directly to the group experience shows that meaningful learning did take place.

271

LIST OF REFERENCES

Chapter I

1. Bloom, M. T. "Boston Psycho Breaks the Rules and Cures the Patient." *Readers Digest*, Jan. 1954. (Condensation from *Today's Health Magazine* article, Jan. 1954).

2. Buttrick, G. A. *Faith and Education* (p. 26). New York, Abingdon-Cokesbury Press, 1952.

3. Cantor, Nathaniel. *The Dynamics of Learning*. Buffalo, N. Y., Foster & Stewart, 1946.

4. Dreikurs, R., Mosak, H., and Shulman, B. "Patient-therapist Relationship in Multiple Psychotherapy." *Psychiatr. Quart.*, 1952–26:590–596.

5. Driver, H. I. *Group Discussion as an Aid in Self-Evaluation and Social Competence*. Madison, Wis. 1951. (Unpublished Ph.D. dissertation available through University of Wisconsin Library loan service).

6. Fisher, J. T., and Hawley, L. *A Few Buttons Missing*. Philadelphia, Lippincott Co., 1951.

7. Fromm, Eric. *Psychoanalysis and Religion*. New Haven, Yale University Press, 1950.

8. Harrison, G. R. "Faith and the Scientist" (p. 53). *Atlantic Monthly*, Dec. 1953.

9. Hartwell, S. W. *Practical Psychiatry and Mental Hygiene* (p. 396). New York, McGraw-Hill, 1947.

10. Hinckley, R. G., and Hermann, L. *Group Treatment in Psychotherapy* (p. 132). Minneapolis, Univ. of Minnesota Press, 1951.

11. Hoppock, R. *Group Guidance: Principles, Techniques, Evaluation* (pp. 221, 222). New York, McGraw-Hill, 1949.

12. Hulse, W. C. "The Role of Group Therapy in Preventive Psychiatry" (pp. 531–547). *Mental Hygiene*, Oct. 1952, 34:4.

13. Jones, M. et al. *The Therapeutic Community*. New York, Basic Books, Inc.,1953.

14. Low, A. A. *Mental Health through Will Training*. Chicago, Recovery, Inc., 1950.

15. May, R. *Man's Search for Himself*. New York, W. W. Norton & Co., 1953.

16. Mead, M. "What Psychoanalysis Does for You," *Look Magazine*, May, 1953.

17. Menninger, K., and Leaf, M. *You and Psychiatry*. New York, Charles Schribner Co., 1948.

18. Montagu, A. *On Being Human*. New York, Henry Schuman Co., 1950.

19. Moreno, J. L. *Who Shall Survive.* New York, Beacon House, Inc., 1953.

20. Murro, Edward (Ed). *This I Believe.* New York, Simon & Schuster, 1952.

21. National Association for Mental Health. "Mental Health is 1-2-3." Pamphlet published by National Association for Mental Health, 1951.

22. Oman, J. B. "No Barred Windows nor Locked Doors" (pp. 5 fol). *Christian Advocate,* Aug. 20, 1953.

23. Overstreet, H. A. *The Mature Mind.* New York, W. W. Norton and Co., 1949.

24. Peale, N. V. *The Power of Positive Thinking.* New York, Prentice-Hall, 1952.

25. Powdermaker, F. B., and Frank, J. D. *Group Psychotherapy* (Chap. 3). Cambridge, Harvard University Press, 1953.

26. Pratt, J. H. "The Group Method and the Treatment of Psychosomatic Disorders." Psychodrama Monograph No. 19. New York, Beacon House, Inc., 1945.

27. Redl. F., and Wattenburg, W. W. *Mental Hygiene for Teaching.* New York, Harcourt, Brace, 1951.

28. Sears, R. Address at APA Convention reported in The American Psychologist, Dec. 1951.

29. Slavson, S. E. "Group Bases for Mental Health" (pp. 280–292), *Mental Hygiene,* April, 1949–33.

30. Stevenson, I. "Why People Change," *Harper's Magazine,* Dec., 1953 (p. 59).

31. Strang, R. *Counseling Technics in College and Secondary School,* rev. ed., (Chap. IX). New York, Harpers & Bros., 1949.

32. Taba, H., and Elkins, D. *With Focus on Human Relations.* Washington, D. C., American Council of Education, 1950.

33. Taylor, G. A. *The Sober Faith: Religion and Alcoholic Anonymous,* New York, Macmillan, 1954.

Chapter II

1. Allison, S. G. "Nondirective Group Therapy of Alcoholics in a State Hospital," *Quarterly Journal of Studies of Alcohol,* 13: 596–601.

2. Andrews, J. A. "Directive Psychotherapy: Reassurance," *Journal of Clinical Psychology,* Jan., 1945, Vol. I, No. 1, p. 52.

3. Ansbacher, H. L. "The History of the Leaderless Group Discussion Technique," *Psychol. Bull.,* Sept., 1951., Vol. 48, No. 5, pp. 383–391.

4. Bierer, J. (ed). *Therapeutic Social Clubs.* Institute of Social Psychiatry, London, Eng. Publisher, H. K. Lewis & Co. 1948.

5. Bullis, J. E. "Teach Our Children How To Live" (pp. 20–22), *Health,* Nov.-Dec., 1950. (*Bimonthly Bulletin of Wisconsin State Board of Health*).

6. Courtney, D. "Clinical Psychology in Public Schools," *Journal of Clinical Psychology*, April, 1951, Vol. VII, No. 2, p. 171 fol.

7. Foulkes, S. H. *Introduction to Group-Analytic Psychotherapy.* London, Wm. Heinemann Co., 1948.

8. Grant, M. "The Group Approach for Weight Control," *Journal of Group Psychotherapy*, Dec., 1951, Vol. IV, No. 3, pp. 156–165.

9. Gorlow, L., Hoch, E. L., Telschow, E. F. *The Nature of Nondirective Group Psychotherapy.* New York Teachers College, Columbia University, 1952.

10. Haas, R. B. (ed). *Psychodrama and Sociodrama in American Education.* New York, Beacon House Press, 1949.

11. Herrold, K. J. "Evaluation and Research in Group Dynamics," *Edn. & Psychol. Meas.*, 1950, Vol. 10, No. 3, pp. 492–504.

12. Hertz, D. R., Lesser, S. L. "People in Groups," *Scientific American*, Feb., 1951, pp. 26–28.

13. Hinckley, R. G., Hermann, L. *Group Treatment in Psychotherapy.* Minneapolis, Univ. of Minnesota Press, 1951.

14. Jones, M. et al. *The Therapeutic Community*, New York, Basic Books, Inc., 1953.

15. *Look Magazine.* "Troubled People Meet," Dec. 18, 1951, pp. 75 fol. (report of group therapy at the Henry Phipps Psychiatric Clinic, Johns Hopkins University).

16. Low, A. A. *The Techniques of Self-Help in Psychiatric After-Care.* Chicago, Recovery, Inc., 1943.

17. McCann, W. H., Almada, A. A. "Round-Table Psychotherapy," *Journal of Consulting Psych.*, Dec., 1950, Vol. 14, No. 6, pp. 421–451.

18. Moreno, J. L. (ed). *Group Psychotherapy: A Symposium.* New York, Beacon House Press, 1945.

19. Neugarten, B. L. *Discovering Myself.* New York, National Forum, Inc., 1946.

20. Parry, D. "Teaching Self-Adjustment to Socially Handicapped Girls," *Journal of Exceptional Children*, Dec., 1949, Vol. 16, No. 3, pp. 73–76.

21. Powdermaker, F. B., Frank, J. D. *Group Psychotherapy.* Cambridge, Harvard University Press, 1953.

22. Pratt, J. H. *The Group Method and the Treatment of Psychosomatic Disorders.* Psychodrama Monographs No. 19, Beacon House Press, New York, 1945.

23. Slavson, S. R. *Creative Group Education.* New York, Association Press, 1948.

24. Slavson, S. R. *The Practice of Group Therapy.* New York, International Universities Press, 1947.

25. Taylor, F. K. "On Some Principles of Group Therapy," *British Journal of Medical Psychology*, 1952, Vol. 25:128–134.

274

26. *Time Magazine.* "Husband of the Patient," May 12, 1953. (Digest of talk by Dr. Gene Gordon at meeting of California Medical Association: group therapy experiment for husbands of mentally-ill patients).

27. Torrance, P. "Getting Mental Hygiene Practices into Action through a College Class," *Mental Hygiene,* Jan., 1951, p. 88–95.

Chapter IV

1. Bales, R. F. *Interactive Process Analysis.* Cambridge, Addison-Wesley Press, 1950.

2. Driver, H. I. "Gripe Sessions Lead to Better Understanding," *Wisconsin State Edn. Assn. Journal,* Oct., 1952.

3. May, R. *Man's Search for Himself* (p. 276). New York, W. W. Norton & Co., 1953.

4. McBurney, J. H., Hance, K. G. *Principles and Methods of Discussion.* New York, Harpers & Bros., 1939.

5. Moreno, J. L. *Who Shall Survive* (p. 42), Beacon, N. Y. Beacon House, Inc., 1953.

6. Overstreet, H. A. *The Great Enterprise* (Chapter 7). New York, W. W. Norton & Co., 1952.

Chapter V

1. Cantor, N. *The Dynamics of Learning.* Buffalo, N. Y., Foster and Stewart Co., 1946.

2. Cantor, N. *The Teaching-Learning Process.* New York, Dryden Press, 1953.

3. Rogers, C. *Counseling and Psychotherapy.* Boston, Houghton Mifflin Co., 1942.

4. Rothney, J. W. M., Roens, B. A. *Counseling the Individual Student.* New York, William Sloane Associates, Inc., 1949.

Chapter VI

1. Cameron, N. and Magaret, A. *Behavior Pathology* (pp. 114–122, 575). Boston, Houghton Mifflin Co., 1951.

2. Dymond, R. F. "Personality and Empathy," *Journal of Consulting Psychology,* Oct., 1950, Vol. 14, No. 5, pp. 343–350.

3. Moreno, J. L. (ed). *Group Psychotherapy: A Symposium* (p. 161). New York, Beacon House, 1945.

4. Moreno, J. L. *Psychodrama.* New York, Beacon House, 1946.

5. Strang, R. *Counseling Technics in College and Secondary School,* rev. ed. (Chap. IX). New York, Harpers & Bros., 1949.

Chapter VII

1. Cameron, N., Magaret, A., *Behavior Pathology* (pp. 589–91). Boston, Houghton Mifflin Co., 1951.

2. Fantal, E. "Counseling for industrial adjustment," *Sociatry*, 1948, No. 2.

3. Franks, T. W. "Role-playing in an industrial setting," *Group Psychotherapy*, 1952, No. 5.

4. French, J. R. P. "Role-playing as a method for training foremen," *Sociatry*, 1947, No. 1.

5. Hass, R. B. *Psychodrama and Sociodrama in American Education.* New York, Beacon House, 1949.

6. Hagan, M., Kenworthy, M. "The use of psychodrama as a training device for professional groups working in the field of human relations," *Group Psychotherapy*, 1952, No. 5.

7. Hulse, W. C. "The role of group therapy in preventive psychiatry," *Mental Hygiene*, Oct. 1952, Vol. 34, No. 4, pp. 544–5.

8. Jones, M. *The Therapeutic Community* (pp. 63–66). New York, Basic Books, Inc., 1953. This book is printed in England under the name of *Social Psychiatry*.

9. Liveright, A. A. "Role-playing in leadership training," *Personnel*, 1951, Vol. 29, pp. 412–16.

10. Moreno, J. L. *Psychodrama*, Vol. I. New York, Beacon House, Inc., 1946.

11. Moreno, J. L. *Who Shall Survive* (pp. 81–89). Beacon, N. Y., Beacon House, Inc., 1953.

12. Parrish, M. M. "Psychodrama: description of application and review of techniques," *Group Psychotherapy*, May-August, 1953, pp. 63–89.

13. Toeman, Z. "Role analysis and audience structure," *Psychodrama Monograph*, 1944, No. 12.

Chapter VIII

1. Corey, S. M. "Introduction," *The Teaching-Learning Process*, by N. Cantor, published by The Dryden Press, N. Y., 1953.

2. Haddon, S. B. "Treatment of Neurotics by Class Technic," *Annals of Internal Medicine*, Vol. 16, pp. 33–37. Also Dr. Haddon's paper given at Symposium on Group Psychotherapy, 1944, reported in *Group Psychotherapy: a Symposium* (pp. 68–76). New York, Beacon House, 1945.

3. Jersild, A. T. "Self-Understanding in Childhood and Adolescence," *The American Psychologist*, April, 1951, (pp. 122–126), Vol. 6, No. 4.

4. Lewis, C. S. *The Screwtape Letters.* New York, Macmillan Company, 1952. (Reprint of letters appearing in *The Manchester Guardian*).

5. McBurney, J. H., Hance, K. G. *The Principles and Methods of Discussion* (Chapters I, II). New York, Harpers & Bros., 1939.

6. Mowrer, O. H. *Learning Theory and Personality Dynamics.* New York, Ronald Press, 1950.

7. Mowrer, O. H. *Psychotherapy: Theory and Research.* New York, Ronald Press, 1953.

8. Raths, L. E., "Education as Process," in Part I of *Psychodrama and Sociodrama in American Education*, edited by R. B. Haas, published by Beacon House, N. Y., 1946.

9. Saul, L. J. *Emotional Maturity* (p. 305). Philadelphia, J. B. Lippincott Co., 1947.

10. Slavson, S. R. *Creative Group Education* (Chap. V). New York, Association Press, 1948.

11. Stevenson, I. "Why People Change" (p. 56), *Harper's Magazine*, Dec., 1953.

12. Strang, R. *Counseling Technics in College and Secondary School*, rev. ed. (Chap. I). New York, Harpers & Bros., 1949.

Chapter IX

1. Allport, G. W. *The Use of Personal Documents in Psychological Science.* New York, Social Science Research Council, 1942.

2. Bullis, H. E. *Human Relations in the Classroom* (Vol. I). Wilmington, Del., Delaware State Mental Hygiene Society, 1940.

3. Chamberlin, Drought, Scott. *Did They Succeed in College.* New York, Harpers & Bros., 1942.

4. Cronbach, L. J. *Essentials of Psychological Testing* (Chapters 14, 15). New York, Harpers & Bros., 1949.

5. Harmon, L. R., Wiener, D. N. "Use of the Minnesota Multiphasic Personality Inventory in Vocational Advisement," *J. Applied Psychol.*, 1945, Vol. 29, pp. 132–141.

6. Peale, N. V., Blanton, S. *The Art of Real Happiness.* New York, Prentice-Hall, 1950.

7. Rothney, J. W. M., Roens, B. A. *Counseling the Individual Student* (pp. 105-126). New York, Wm. Sloane Associates, Inc., 1949.

8. Super, D. E. "The Kuder Preference Record in Vocational Diagnosis," *J. Consult. Psychol.*, 1947, Vol. 11, pp. 184–193.

9. Strong, E. K., Jr. *Vocational Interests of Men and Women* (pp. 412–482). Stanford Univ., Stanford University Press, 1943.

Chapter XII

1. Carrol, H. A. *Mental Hygiene.* New York, Prentice-Hall Co., 1951.

2. Deutsch, A. *The Mentally Ill in America.* 2nd rev. ed. New York, Columbia University Press, 1949.

3. Driver, H. I. *Group Discussion as an Aid to Self-Evaluation and Social Competence* (pp. 153–175). Madison, Wis. University Loan Library Service, Ph.D. Theses Division.

4. Slotkin, J. S. *Personality Development.* New York, Harpers Bros., 1952.

5. Symond, P. M. *Dynamic Psychology.* New York, Appleton-Century-Crofts, Inc., 1949.

6. Travers, R. M. "A Critical Review of Techniques for Evaluating Guidance," *Ed. and Psychol. Measurement,* summer issue, 1949, Vol. 9, No. 2.

7. Tyson, R. "Current M. H. Practice," *J. Clinical Psychol.,* Jan., 1951, Vol. 7, No. 1, pp. 87–89.

8. Thorne, F. C. *Principles of Personality Counseling.* Brandon, Vt., J. of Clin. Psychol. Press, 1951.

9. Zlatchin, P. "Controlled Evaluation of Group Therapy with Adolescent Deviates," *The American Psychologist,* July, 1951, Vol. 6, No. 7, pp. 381–82.

General References: Personality and Human Behavior

Leader-counselors need an eclectic frame of reference in order to understand individual differences and learning found in a group process. Many experts in the field of learning and human behavior agree with Hilgard that no one psychological theory has proved satisfactory. It is advisable to take helpful material wherever it is found rather than "taking sides" with behaviorists, psychoanalysts, individualistic or interactivistic advocates. In "Theories of Learning," Hilgard draws the truce line as follows:

"How can psychologists be helpful to other social scientists or to practical people when they disagree among themselves on these fundamental matters (theories of learning) . . . there are no laws of learning which can be taught with confidence (p. 326) . . . a social psychology of learning would almost certainly be called for if a fresh start were made in the study of learning (p. 327) . . . the price to be paid for overmuch experimentation with animals is to neglect the fact that human subjects are brighter, and are

278

able to use language — *and probably learn differently because of these advantages over lower animals. Only if a process demonstrable in human learning can also be demonstrated in lower animals is the comparable method useful in studying it"* (p. 329).

A new psychology, aptly called "personology" by R. B. Cattell, is slowly emerging. New directions for research and applications of psychological and sociological theories were skillfully outlined by R. R. Sears in the President's Address, American Psychological Association, September, 1951.

The following list of references has been selected to help readers gain perspective of contributions made by psychologists, sociologists, and educators to a new science of personality, human relations, and learning.

GENERAL REFERENCES

Allport, G. W. *Personality, a Psychological Interpretation.* New York, Henry Holt, 1937.

Anastasi, A. *Differential Psychology: Individual and Group Differences in Behavior.* New York, MacMillan, 1937.

Asch, S. E. *Social Psychology.* New York, Prentice-Hall, 1952.

Beers, C. W. *A Mind that Found Itself.* New York, Longmans, Green, 1908.

Brill, A. *The Basic Writings of Sigmund Freud: Translated and Edited, with an Introduction.* New York, Modern Library, 1938.

Brubacher, J. S. (ed). *Eclectic Philosophy of Education: a Book of Readings.* New York, Prentice-Hall, 1951.

Buttrick, G. A. *Faith and Education.* New York, Abingdon-Cokesbury, 1952.

Cameron, N. and Magaret, A. *Behavior Pathology.* New York, Houghton Mifflin, 1951.

Carroll, H. A. *Mental Hygiene: The Dynamics of Adjustment,* 2nd ed. New York, Prentice-Hall, 1951.

Cattell, R. B. *An Introduction to Personality Study.* London, Hutchinson's University Library, 1950.

Dewey, J. *How We Think.* Boston, Heath, 1933.

Eysenck, H. J. *Dimensions of Personality.* London, Routledge and Kegan Paul, 1950.

Faris, R. E. L. *Social Psychology* New York, Ronald Press, 1952.

Fromm, E. *Psychoanalysis and Religion.* New Haven, Yale Univ. Press, 1950.

Hartley, E. L. and Hartley, R. E. *Fundamentals of Social Psychology.* New York, Knopf, 1952.

Hilgard, E. R. *Theories of Learning.* New York, Appleton-Century-Crofts, 1948.

Hull, C. L. *Principles of Behavior.* New York, Appleton-Century, 1943.

Hunt, J. M. *Personality and the Behavior Disorders,* Vol. I, II. New York, Ronald Press, 1944.

Kilpatrick, W. H. *Philosophy of Education.* New York, Macmillan, 1949.

Koffka, K. *Principles of Gestalt Psychology.* New York, Harcourt Brace, 1935.

Krech, D., and Crutchfield, R. S. *Theory and Practice of Social Psychology.* New York, Dryden Press, 1949.

Lewin, K. *A Dynamic Theory of Personality.* New York, McGraw-Hill, 1935.

Liebman, J. *Psychiatry and Religion.* Boston, Beacon Press, 1953.

Linton, R. *The Cultural Background of Personality.* New York, Appleton-Century, 1945.

May, R. *Man's Search for Himself.* New York, Ronald Press, 1953.

McGeogh, J. A. *The Psychology of Human Learning.* New York, Longmans, Green, 1942.

Mead, M. *Male and Female: a Study of the Sexes in a Changing World.* Wm. Morrow, 1949.

Menninger, K. A. *Man Against Himself.* New York, Harcourt, Brace, 1938.

Miller, N. E. and Dollard, J. *Social Learning and Imitation.* New Haven, Yale Univ. Press, 1941.

Moreno, J. L. *Who Shall Survive.* Beacon, N. Y., Beacon House, 1953.

Mowrer, O. W. *Learning Theory and Personality Dynamics.* New York, Ronald Press, 1950.

Murray, H. A. *Explorations in Personality.* New York, Oxford Univ. Press, 1938.

Overstreet, H. A. *The Mature Mind.* New York, W. W. Norton, 1949.

Overstreet, H. A., and Overstreet, B. W. *The Mind Alive.* W. W. Norton, 1954.

Pavlov, L. P. *Conditioned Reflexes.* New York, Oxford Univ. Press, 1927.

Ragsdale, C. E. *Modern Psychologies and Education.* New York, Macmillan, 1932.

Sargent, S. S. *Social Psychology.* New York, Ronald Press, 1950.

Sears, R. R. "A theoretical framework for personality and social behavior," *American Psychologist,* Sept., 1951.

Skinner, C. E. (ed). *Educational Psychology,* 3rd ed. New York, Prentice-Hall, 1951.

Slotkin, J. S. *Personality Development.* New York, Harpers, 1952.

Sorokin, P. A. *Society, Culture, and Personality,* New York, Harpers, 1947.

Symonds, P. M. *Dynamic Psychology.* New York, Appleton-Century-Crofts, 1949.

Thorne, F. C. *Principles of Personality Counseling, an Eclectic Viewpoint.* Brandon, Vt., J. of Clinical Psychol. Press, 1950.

Watson, J. B. *Behaviorism.* New York, W. W. Norton, 1925.

SECTION II
SYMPOSIUM

SMALL-GROUP DISCUSSION AS AN
AID IN COUNSELING, TRAINING AND TREATMENT

Thirty-nine articles by professional leaders in the fields of elementary and secondary public schools, colleges and universities, theological seminaries, Veterans Administration and mental hospitals, correctional institutions, alcoholic treatment centers, public and private counseling centers, Christian education and mental health organizations.

PART 1 — *School Children and Youth: Group Projects for Personal and Social Adjustment*

Nine articles dealing mostly with under-achieving or pre-delinquent pupils.

PART 2 — *College Programs: Orientation, Courses, and Leadership Training*

Five articles describing orientation and psychology courses, student leadership.

PART 3 — *Professional Training and Research: Small-Group Discussion as a Learning Medium*

Eleven articles showing a wide range of group discussion methods.

PART 4 — *Community Mental Health and Parent Education Programs: Small-Group Discussion Methods for Education, Counseling and Training*

Six articles mainly concerned with leadership training and mental health programs.

PART 5 — *Group Psychotherapy, Rehabilitation, and Counseling Programs: The Value of The Intimate Group*

Eight articles describing a variety of group therapy and counseling methods.

REHEARSAL FOR ORIGINAL PLAYLET — CREATIVE DRAMA CLUB
(see article 8)

INTRODUCTION

The adaptability of a multiple counseling method combining group and individual counseling is clearly illustrated in the following articles which were generously contributed by professional leaders in the fields of education, religion, psychiatry and psychology, mental health, counseling and guidance.

For the most part, the teaching-learning process used by the group leaders focuses on the personal growth of group members. Attitude-changes followed by behavior-changes are sought. Two change-agents are operative: (1) the group process and interpersonal relationships (2) the influence of the leader (counselor, teacher). Although the SYMPOSIUM contributors are modest in withholding credit from themselves for the progress of group members, one can read between the lines of their writings and see *the group leader as the key to the success of the group project.*

In the case of children and youth, and also mentally-ill adults, a mature adult leader is prerequisite. This leader may represent in the minds of members of the group a parent-substitute, a worthy authority-symbol, or some other object of identification. The leader is above all a friendly counselor whom the group members can trust, confide in, go to for help.

A second quality of the leader is his ability to manipulate the learning climate for maximum benefit to all members of the group. At times when the group itself is unable to fill the needs of an individual member, the leader provides individual counseling (teaching) for this purpose. Just as some students in a class require extra tutoring, so some individuals may need special help from the counselor or teacher.

Thus the leader exerts a three-pronged influence in the teaching-learning process. First, he arranges the program and climate of the group for maximum benefit to all members. Second, he uses his own skills and resources in the group process — moderator, teacher, member, catalyst, resource person. Third, he provides opportunities for individual conferences with members of the group who need additional support and help.

The thirty-nine articles of the SYMPOSIUM cover a wide range of subjects and purpose classified into five groups according to special interests: Children and Youth; College Programs; Professional Training and Research; Mental Health and Parent Education; Group Psychotherapy and Counseling Programs. The common core of group discussion as a learning medium is found in all of them. The value of "the intimate group" is propounded over and over again. Furthermore, the value of small-group discussion in college classes, leadership training programs, in-service or practicum courses for teachers, pastors and counselors is convincingly presented.

This distinguished collection of articles was made possible through the generous cooperation of the thirty-seven contributors, several of whom asked to remain anonymous. Their enthusiasm for the task exceeded all expectations. The Editor gratefully acknowledges their generosity and assures them that the wave of appreciation will continually widen as other professional persons make use of the valuable knowledges and experiences they have described.

HELEN I. DRIVER ·

283

Courtesy of Mrs. Theora Standing, San Bernardino Public Schools

SECTION II — SYMPOSIUM

PART ONE

SCHOOL CHILDREN AND YOUTH: GROUP PROJECTS FOR PERSONAL AND SOCIAL ADJUSTMENT

List of Articles

1

SMALL-GROUP COUNSELING FOR UNDER-ACHIEVING PRIMARY SCHOOL CHILDREN
by Dr. Gale E. Jensen, *Program Director and Associate Professor of Education*
School of Education, University of Michigan

2

A MULTIPLE COUNSELING PROJECT FOR UNDER-ACHIEVING SIXTH GRADERS
by Mrs. Leona Ney, *Counselor*
Sombra del Monte Elementary School, Albuquerque, New Mexico

3

A MULTIPLE COUNSELING PROJECT FOR PRE-DELINQUENT EIGHTH GRADE GIRLS
by Quentin R. Bryan and Edna M. Younker
Inglewood Unified School District, Inglewood, California

4

REACHING YOUNG TEENS THROUGH GROUP COUNSELING
by Althea M. Brach, *Teacher-Counselor*
Washington Junior High School, Racine, Wisconsin

5

MULTIPLE COUNSELING: EIGHT OVER-AGE BOYS, NINTH GRADE
Anonymous

6

A SEMANTIC APPROACH IN GROUP COUNSELING
by Reverend J. N. Kelly, Jr.
Christian Church, Harrodsburg, Ky.

7

A SMALL-GROUP COUNSELING PROGRAM FOR PUPILS, PARENTS, TEACHERS
reported by Dr. Helen I. Driver, *Consultant in Mental Hygiene*

8

PERSONAL COUNSELING THROUGH A CREATIVE DRAMA CLUB
by Mrs. Theora Standing, *School Psychologist*
San Bernardino City Schools, Calif.

9

A DISCIPLINARY GROUP GUIDANCE PROJECT
by Paul Crawford, *Counselor*
La Cumbre Junior High School, Santa Barbara, Calif.

The nine articles in this Part include projects for children in primary and intermediate grades, junior and senior high school. The use of the intimate group and concomitant individual counseling is described. Children and youth grouped together because of a common problem of under-achievement, non-conformity and delinquency, are able to change attitudes and behavior patterns. As time goes on we believe special group work of this type will become common practice in schools. It can be a significant part of the educational process for emotionally disturbed children; early detection and treatment can prevent wasted lives caused by emotional and mental illnesses, delinquent and criminal behavior patterns.

1

SMALL-GROUP COUNSELING FOR UNDER-ACHIEVING
PRIMARY SCHOOL CHILDREN

by DR. GALE E. JENSEN, *Program Director and Associate Professor of Education*
SCHOOL OF EDUCATION, UNIVERSITY OF MICHIGAN

One of the most persistent and tantalizing problems with which teachers and school administrators are faced today are under-achieving pupils — those who are intelligent enough to progress satisfactorily in school, but who don't.

One explanation of under-achievement asserts that interpersonal or social relationships of the pupils are so unsatisfactory that most of the pupils' energy are diverted to work on these problems. Thus there is little or no time and energy left for working on the learning tasks in school.

The implications of this explanation for personality development and future academic progress are gravely serious. As time passes and the learnings to be acquired through participation in the school work are not realized, these pupils are caught in a vicious circle. With each succeeding year in school, the pupils fall further behind; they do not possess the skills, assumed to have been acquired from previous school work, which are essential to acquiring more complex or higher level abilities. This creates a situation in which the expectations of the teachers and administrators are not met, since such expectations are based on the number of years spent in school rather than the actual amount of learning assimilated by these pupils. The fact is, the under-achievers do not possess the knowledge and problem-solving skills because the major share of the time and energies of these pupils has been given to their interpersonal and social relations problems.

The project to be described in the following paragraphs was developed to cope with this situation. It was undertaken by the clinic school (a part-time school designed to deal with problems of under-achieving students) of a college engaged in teacher education.

The project had two chief purposes: (1) To discover the social relationships in the classroom group (and to some extent the family group) that were disturbing some pupils to the extent of blocking their academic achievement (2) To enable these students to acquire insight and understanding of the relationships so as to provide a chance to change them in such a way that the energies of the pupils can be re-directed into their class work.

Three illustrative case studies are given to show the kinds of problems these children have:

1. Jimmie was greatly concerned about the fact that he had lost the attention of his mother because of the demands made by numerous younger children in the family. Strong dependency needs for his mother, unsatisfied, had led him to become extremely apathetic and passive. He was inclined to show regressive tendencies whenever confronted with difficult tasks concerned with developing independency. He had "lost out" to other children in the family for so long and to such an extent that he was in no way surprised by his "losing out" in the classroom. As a matter of fact, he more or less expected that this would be the case. At the time he started participating in the small counseling groups he was unaware of how his family relationships had affected his activity in the classroom.

287

2. Bobbie was tightly controlled by his father who set extremely high standards for him to meet. Failure to meet the standards resulted in strong disapproval from the father. This was extremely upsetting to the boy since he admired his father greatly and desired to do nothing that would make his father disapprove of him. Because of this relationship he was extremely cautious about making mistakes. No overt effort was ever made until he was certain that it would be "right". This had so slowed down his class work that he was unable to keep up with the other pupils. Urging him to "go faster" only caused him to become extremely anxious and confused.

3. Harry suffered from an extreme loss of esteem from his fellow classmates because of something that had happened to a member of his family. He was extremely upset by this loss of esteem and made exaggerated efforts to recope the loss. His boasting and antics had caused him further loss of esteem: he was perceived as an obnoxious person by his classmates. This led him to spend most of his time in class being greatly concerned about his relationships to the others with the result that little energy was left for class work.

Small-group counseling was the chief method used to diagnose the disturbing relationships and to give the pupils the essential understanding of them.

The subjects involved in the project were ten children enrolled in the second, third, and fourth grades of three public elementary schools.[1] Their teachers were about ready to "give up", or at least decrease the amount of attention given to these children's difficulties. Although the native intelligence involved was judged by test data and observable behavior to be normal, the classroom performance of the children was not conducive to effective learning. Behavior ranged from silent withdrawal to hyper-active, disruptive participation.

The children were removed from their regular school for two hours each morning for four days per week. In general the children engaged in the special program from sixty to eighty periods during the year. On each of the four days of the week the pupils were given special academic remedial instruction for one hour and group counseling during the other hour. The latter sometimes incorporated a group task such as music, art, drama, and dance "therapy". The counseling groups varied from two to six pupils.

To make individual social relation problems visible and understandable, the counseling group membership was changed from one session to another. The first five or six sessions were conducted for the

---

[1] These grade levels were chosen because they afforded the best situations in which the conditions described above could be easily observed and identified.

purpose of identifying or uncovering the nature of the problem.[2] The rest of the sessions were structured to help the pupils gain insight and understanding of their own individual problems. For example, Jimmie, concerned about his inability to obtain the attention of his mother, was encouraged to examine this family situation to discover how a child who "lost out" would be affected and how this might be related to "giving up" in the classroom. Bobbie, so tightly controlled by his father and fearful of making mistakes, was given an opportunity to examine and discuss how fear to make mistakes develops and how this might affect work in the classroom. Harry, who suffered from the extreme loss of esteem, was given a chance to discover how a "vicious cycle" results from over-reacting in such a way as to become obnoxious and troublesome to his friends and classmates.

Sometimes the members of these small counseling groups were given tasks which required them to work together as a group. At other times the counselor (group leader) simply would initiate discussion designed to produce analysis and discussion about social relationship problems that might apply to some of the group members. Regardless of the particular procedure employed, the purpose was always to enable these children to have a counseling experience which would leave them in a better position to understand and possibly to do something about their social relationship difficulties.

As the project progressed, the children were observed for changes in participation, both in their academic remedial group and their regular classroom group. Academic progress in the remedial group was measured periodically.[3]

Also, their teachers were asked to report periodically on changes occurring in academic achievement or ability.

RESULTS

Eight of the ten pupils benefited from this program. (One was dropped from the project after two months because of irregular attendance and lack of family cooperation. Another was referred for psychiatric treatment.)

---

[2]The framework for this analysis was taken from:
Jensen, G. E. "The Social Structure of The Classroom Group: An Observational Framework", *J. of Educational Psychology*, Vol. 46, No. 6, Oct. 1955, pp. 364-374.

[3]Both standardized and informal achievement tests relevant to the areas of academic deficiency were used for this.

Data collected regarding academic achievement and improved social relationships showed the following:

1. Gains in reading, writing and spelling ranged from one to three grade level advancement. (Measured by standardized and informal tests)
2. Improvement in ability to do independent work and to apply newly acquired academic skills in the classroom.
3. A positive relationship was found between the ability of the pupil to engage satisfactorily in the group task of the small counseling group (through improved social relationships) and his ability in classroom work.
4. Personal discouragement and dissatisfaction with classroom work tended to increase when failure in social relationships in the counseling groups occurred.
5. Changes in work relationships in the small counseling groups were affected by ability of the pupils to assume roles required by the group situation. And achievement of pupils dropped appreciably when interpersonal difficulties occurred.
6. Successful organization for accomplishing group tasks in the small counseling groups appeared to carry over into more successful performance in group tasks in the classroom.

CONCLUSIONS AND RECOMMENDATIONS

1. With respect to school achievement problems, a school faculty should develop an organizational structure that uncovers those pupils whose arrested progress is primarily due to, or affected by, social relationship problems.
2. These pupils should never be placed in remedial groups with pupils whose school progress is being affected by some organic or physical shortcoming, mental deficiency, or serious neurotic or psychotic difficulty.
3. Pupils whose progress is being affected by social relationship problems can be "restored" to adequate classroom performance within relatively short periods of time if the *right* counseling is given at the *right* time.
4. The identification and diagnosis of those pupils whose progress is being affected primarily by social relationship problems must be done by skillful and competent personnel.
5. The small-group counselor should be a person who is trained in school counseling and guidance work.
6. The remedial teacher (for reading, mathematics, etc.) must be very skillful at locating and defining a child's academic difficulties; be able to prescribe instructional activities in accordance with this analysis.
7. The small-group counselor and the remedial teacher must be in close communication and working relationship throughout the duration of the project.

2

A MULTIPLE COUNSELING PROJECT FOR
UNDER-ACHIEVING SIXTH GRADERS

by MRS. LEONA NEY, *Counselor*

SOMBRA DEL MONTE ELEMENTARY SCHOOL, ALBUQUERQUE, NEW MEXICO

Preface

Sombra del Monte is one of the sixty-seven semi-autonomous schools in the Albuquerque City-County Public School System. Administratively, school counselors are responsible to their principals. However, they may request leadership and assistance from a staff of guidance specialists in the Guidance Services Department of the Central Administrative Offices. Group methods are being attempted in many different situations in the system in an attempt to solve a variety of problems. Mrs. Ney here describes the use of multiple counseling to prepare sixth grade pupils for Junior High School.

HENRY P. LAMPMAN, *Director of Guidance*

Counseling in our elementary school of 1350 pupils is a non-disciplinary situation in which the counselor and pupil strive together for a more effective understanding by the counselee of the problems he faces, the ends which he desires, and the means by which he can attain them. The counselor restrains himself from telling the pupil what to do and from stressing difficulties which the pupil is likely to encounter. Although "advice" does not usually bother the stable pupil, it can be a threat to the child who is already having difficulty making adjustments.

One part of our guidance program concerns the sixth-grade pupils preparing for Junior High School. Those who have not made satisfactory adjustments in elementary school need more specialized guidance than those who have proved their adjustability. However, all pupils getting ready for the "big step" need help, and our schools give this help through the guidance program.

For sixth graders with definite adjustment problems, multiple counseling projects are organized within the following framework:[1]

1. Groups include from six to ten pupils who have been recommended for special guidance by their teachers.
2. A common problem among the pupils forms the basis for a cohesive group. However, the membership is coeducational and heterogeneity is sought, not only in terms of family, racial and cultural backgrounds but also in personality types. Not more than two aggressive pupils in a group.

---

[1]Driver, H. I., *Multiple Counseling*, Chap. II

3. Briefing interviews are held by the counselor-leader with all pupils to establish rapport and to explain the purpose, time, place, length and number of sessions.
4. The counselor-leader arranges the meeting place, seating with name plates for each pupil on the table, paper and pencils, etc. Shy pupils are placed near the leader, the two aggressive ones next to each other.
5. The first meeting is used to get acquainted and to plan discussion topics for successive meetings.
6. The successive meetings are structured so that
   a. Leadership comes from within the group as much as possible.
   b. The shy ones are brought out, the aggressive ones kept under control.
   c. Summaries of the preceding sessions are duplicated and given to members of the group to keep.
   d. Activities not found among the educational projects of the regular classroom are used, for instance, role-playing.
   e. Individual counseling interviews with the pupils are held and the anecdotal report of group sessions (written up after each meeting by the leader) are used for reference.

An example of a group project for ten under-achieving sixth graders follows:

The group members, five boys and five girls, had from average to above average intelligence. They had failed to make a good adjustment to school, according to opinions of teachers and parents. Seven showed aggressive behavior patterns; three were shy and withdrawn (two of these were girls).

There were twelve weekly sessions held during the regular school day and an average of three individual interviews per pupil during this period. Conferences between the counselor and teachers averaged five per teacher.

The meetings were forty minutes in length. Most of the time the atmosphere was permissive. In the opening sessions many differences of opinions and arguments developed. However, the pupils could always agree on two or three pertinent points made during the discussion. When the discussions strayed from the topic of the day, the leader did not attempt to bring it back except for summary purposes.

The topics of discussion selected by the group (some topics were discussed two or three times) were:

1. What are we expecting in Junior High.
2. What we would change about school if we had the power.
3. How to study.
4. What qualities we like and dislike in our friends.
5. Problems we have with our parents.

A follow-up of eight of the group members after they had attended Junior High for four months secured their opinion and reaction to the group experience. They looked back on it as an enjoyable experience and thought all sixth-grade pupils should have the opportunity to participate in discussion groups. Thus more of the same type of group projects should be set up and pupils should try to get more information about what Junior High would be like. They thought sixth graders

292

should form the habit of doing homework every night. They were critical of the permissive atmosphere of the group and believed more order should be maintained.

Follow-up interviews with the teachers involved brought out the following:

1. The pupils showed pride in bringing back to class the opinions of the group.
2. The pupils felt they had had a hand in helping to solve common pupil problems. (A feeling of leadership)
3. Often the pupils seemed more settled in their class work on the days that the group met.

In evaluating the group project, the leader decided that a group could profit by including a member or two who were well-adjusted pupils so that the internal leadership would be improved. Thus the need to "maintain order" on the part of the counselor-leader would not be so great, and the focus or direction of the discussion could be helped by the internal leadership. This membership combination is now being used, and works out well. Although the counselor-leader attempts to maintain a nondirective role, sixth-graders need the security of structure. About four meetings are needed for the group members to settle down; to have regard for the opinion of others; to gain considerateness so that a member can present his personal problem for solution.

Auxiliary activities which proved to be of interest and benefit in the group project are autobiographies, an essay, "How I feel", oral reports on Science Research Associates booklets, role-playing. Psychographs prepared by the leader proved to be helpful in both pupil and teachers conferences.

Further experimentation and research are needed to continue to find effective methods for helping the elementary counselee understand the problem he faces, the ends he desires, and the means by which he can attain them.

3
A MULTIPLE COUNSELING PROJECT FOR
PRE-DELINQUENT EIGHTH-GRADE GIRLS
by QUENTIN R. BRYAN and EDNA M. YOUNKER
INGLEWOOD UNIFIED SCHOOL DISTRICT, INGLEWOOD, CALIFORNIA

This project describes the efforts of an eighth-grade teacher to provide an adequate counseling program for her pupils. A high percentage of adolescents in her class had problems of running away from home, truancy, anti-social behavior, drinking, and sexual promiscuousness. Individual counseling during the lunch hour and before-and-after school proved inadequate because of the shortage of time. Also the severity of the problems required additional professional help, so the teacher consulted the school psychologist. A partial answer to this dilemma came with the organization of a group project for six of the girls with the most serious problems.

The standards for member selection were:

1. Homogeneous sex grouping.
2. Pupils who suffer from strained relationships with parents.
3. Interest of the girls in attacking their problems and participating in group counseling.

The objectives were to help these girls become more self-directive (to face, understand, and work out their own problems) and to understand themselves and other people better.

The school psychologist served as leader of the group and the teacher was recorder, as well as continuing her individual counseling function under the supervision of the school psychologist. All school records, as well as the girls' written assignments concerning themselves and their feelings toward others, classroom sociometric data, were available to the leader.

No contact was made with the girls' parents before the project began, since the school's privilege and responsibility to counsel pupils was assumed. The psychologist cleared the project with the school principal and arrangements were made for the girls to be excused from physical education for one forty-five minute period each week.

Eleven very informal group sessions were held in a small conference room. The girls, leader, and recorder sat around a large table. A completely permissive atmosphere was maintained: the girls were encouraged to talk freely of their problems. The structure of the meetings and the content of the discussion were left to the girls' discretion.

Since these girls had originally taken their problems to the classroom teacher, the effect of her presence seemed positive. Unless she was directly approached by the girls or the leader, she did not enter into the discussions. The teacher spent approximately a half hour a week counseling each participant individually.

Weekly group counseling sessions with the parents of the girls were considered, but only one such meeting was held due to scheduling difficulties. This meeting was held with the girls' knowledge and permission. Although it was scheduled as a forty-five minute session, the session lasted two and one-half hours. In addition, twenty individual conferences were held with the parents of these girls.

RESULTS

A follow-up, six months after the end of the group project, showed that the girls were maintaining the growth they had demonstrated as a result of this program. Evaluations were done by observational and anecdotal records of before-and-after behavior of the girls by (a) the group leader (b) the teacher-recorder (c) teachers who had the girls in classes (d) the vice-principal (e) fellow group members (f) the parents (g) the girl herself. These evaluations pointed out the following:

1. There was no evidence of regression in any case.
2. As a direct outcome of the multiple counseling program one girl was screened for private psychiatric help.
3. The greatest changes occurred in increasing ability to cope with problems; adaptability in terms of reacting to frustrating home experiences.
4. Members understood themselves better, which led to increased understanding of others: realization that each girl wasn't the only teen-ager with a problem.
5. Members developed ability to view their problems more objectively; to understand parental attitudes; to be more accepting of others.
6. Ventilation and clarification of problems seemed to reduce tensions in the classroom.
7. Most members found they had developed more self-reliance and self control; other people found the girls had improved in responsibility and co-operativeness.

This experiment points out one method of helping teen-agers with their personal and home-relationship problems. The authors emphasize the fact that additional group counseling sessions with the girls and also with their parents would have increased the value of the program. An essential factor is the full support and co-operation of the school administration and faculty.

This multiple counseling experience was a dynamic phase in the learning processes of these girls during the school year. The results as outlined above, indicate the significance and value of such a program at the junior high school level. Sample statements from the evaluations of two of the group members illustrate the positive influences:

Student "B"

Physical education teacher: By the end of the year, B's hostile attitude toward the teacher changed to a very good relationship.

The vice-principal: B really worked out her basic problems amazingly well for her low mentality. The group helped her, for she couldn't have worked out these things for herself.

Core teacher: B showed extreme hostility toward her parents, her home and her step-sister at the beginning of the school year. She has come to accept the fact

295

that she really loves and needs her step-father, and she has developed a protective-ness toward her step-sister . . . Her former complaints of bad health and emotional dizzy spells disappeared completely . . . She sees her parents as individuals . . . has made amazing growth through this counseling program.

B's parents: This year has made a big change in B and her attitude toward home. The multiple counseling was of great importance to us, to B, and to the home atmosphere in general.

The group leader: B was the most amazing one of the group in terms of her develop-ment and insight . . . She has grown from complete self-absorption to a state where she can deal with other people and their problems.

Student "C" (now receiving psychiatric treatment)

Physical education teacher: C has always been very dependable and reliable. Now she seems to feel more at home in the class, is cheerful, and to all appearances, she's much happier.

The group leader: The worthwhile outcome was in getting her to a private psychia-trist. This probably never would have happened without the awareness of the parents of the girl's problem, and this was achieved through the multiple counsel-ing project.

A fellow group member: All along, none of these meetings could help C. I think her problem is much bigger than we think.

The private psychiatrist: If psychotherapy had not been started, C as well as her parents, would have definitely been in serious personality difficulties.

BIBLIOGRAPHY

A. Books

1. Arbuckle, Dugald S. *Teacher Counseling.* Cambridge: Addison-Wesley Press, Inc., 1950.
2. Bennett, Margaret E. *Guidance in Groups.* New York: McGraw-Hill Book Co., Inc., 1955.
3. Bullis, H. Edmond, O'Malley, Emily E. *Human Relations in the Classroom.* Two volumes. Wilmington: The Delaware State Society for Mental Hygiene, 1947-48.
4. Driver, Helen I. *Multiple Counseling — A Small-group Discussion Method for Personal Growth.* Madison, Wisconsin: Monona Publications, 1954. (Section I of this book)
5. Frank, Lawrence K. *This is the Adolescent,* New York: The National Committee for Mental Hygiene, 1949.
6. Hinckley, R. G., Hermann, Lydia. *Group Treatment in Psychotherapy.* Minneapolis: University of Minnesota Press, 1951.
7. Powdermaker, F. B., Frank, J. D. *Group Psychotherapy: Studies in Methodology of Research and Therapy.* Cambridge: Harvard University Press, 1953.
8. Rogers, Carl R. *Client-Centered Therapy.* New York: Houghton Mifflin Co., 1951.

B. Periodicals

9. Driver, Helen I. "Small Group Discussion as a Aid in Counseling", *School Review,* 59:525-30 (December, 1951).

10. Froehlich, Clifford P. "Group Guidance Approaches in Educational Institutions," *Review of Educational Research*, 24:140-159 (April, 1954).
11. Gabriel, Betty. "Group Treatment for Adolescent Girls," *American Journal of Orthopsychiatry*, XXV (October, 1944) pp. 513-602.
12. Jersild, A. T. "Self-Understanding in Childhood and Adolescence," *The American Psychologist*, VI, Number 4 (April, 1951) pp. 122-126.
13. Lifton, Walter M. "Group Therapy in Educational Institutions," *Review of Educational Research on Guidance, Counseling and Pupil Personnel*, XXIV (April, 1954) pp. 156-65.
14. Pepinsky, Harold B. "An Experimental Approach to Group Therapy in a Counseling Center," *Occupations*, XXVIII (October, 1949) pp. 35-40.

4

REACHING YOUNG TEENS THROUGH GROUP COUNSELING

by ALTHEA M. BRACH, *Teacher-Counselor*
WASHINGTON JUNIOR HIGH SCHOOL, RACINE, WISCONSIN

Pupils in the 13-15 year age range often have growing pains and confusion regarding their roles in our culture. They want to be considered near grown-ups but often feel like children. They face in two directions like the middle child in a family. One day his parents say to him, "You're too big for that kind of behavior", and the next day, "You'll have to wait for that until you're older."

The junior high school pupil also is plagued by problems of many "firsts". Thus he begins to have contacts with many teachers in one school day; he starts elective subjects; he begins to plan a vocational goal; gets his first job, first date, first conflict with parents in regard to keeping hours. In spite of all that wise parents and schools can do, problems are bound to arise. Frequently added to these problems are the pupil's worries because of an insecure home situation — the short supply of money and clothing or other material things considered important in his peer group constantly bother him. He is unable to prove himself a capable person in a useful area. He may be misunderstood by the adults in his life and consequently feels upset and unworthy.

The problem of the teacher-counselor is to reach these troubled young people through counseling in spite of the limitations of time and pupil accessibility. Many of the pupils have had such bad relationships with adults that they resist counseling. However, in a group the youngster feels more secure: he can take refuge in the group identification.

In the first of two experiments in multiple counseling, five boys from the seventh grade were selected by the homeroom teacher on the basis of poor adjustment in homeroom and class activities. Four were trouble-makers in all classes. One refused to put forth effort in school work, although he was not an active behavior problem. All were from one to three years over-age for the seventh grade and considered of low-average mental ability.

The boys were told by the principal that the group meetings would be an opportunity to talk over problems and to learn more about themselves. They were given a choice as to whether they were willing to give up two study periods a week for this purpose. (One is not surprised to hear that they were glad to do this.) The counselor-leader was their class teacher in one subject. The group met for seven sessions of approximately forty minutes each.

The atmosphere of the sessions was as permissive as possible, although the leader did, occasionally, have to take a firm stand when the good of the group was involved. At times the behavior of one or more members became disturbing. In these cases the leader gave an interpretation of the behavior, and the reasons back of the behavior became the subject of the discussion. (This is the Adlerian approach.) In this way the boy causing the disturbance became a participating group member once more. The leader had to prove to the group that she knew more about the reasons for various types of behavior than the boys did. She also had to structure the discussions to avoid boredom and lapses of attention. Effective aids were a careful use of interpretations, a friendly atmosphere of give-and-take and the leader's personal interest and respect for the boys as shown in the support given to each member. She often pointed out to them that each was a capable person, but they had not yet learned to use their capabilities in ways most beneficial to themselves.

The first session began with the leader's explanation of the difference between this group activity and a class: the chief purpose was to help each other. Each boy introduced himself by telling something of his family, his place in the family, his present interests, and his earliest recollections.

Succeeding discussion centered largely around purposes of behavior[1] which in the Adlerian orientation consists of attention getting, power, revenge, or demonstration of inadequacy. The boys were asked why they were doing what was done. Of course, they did not know, or they would give some rationalization. Then the leader, trained in

---

[1]Dreikurs, Dr. Rudolph, "Psychology in the Classroom," N. Y., Harpers & Sons, 1957

Adlerian procedures, could make an interpretation of the purpose of the behavior. This helped the boys to gain insight into their own problems.

An illustration is given from the notes of one session to show how these behavior purposes were discussed by the boys:

Session 3 (The discussion during the previous sessions centered around how it feels to be oldest in a family)

The points of the previous session were reviewed. Then the leader asked, "How does it feel to be youngest in a family"? B, who has four older sisters, commented that everybody makes you do things. He said, "My family say things like 'He is the baby of the family'. How I hate that!" Q, who is the youngest of three boys, said, "You get more privileges. Your mother takes you along because it seems like she likes you 'cause you're littler."

The leader asked if boys liked being treated big or little. The group agreed they wanted to be considered big. In answer to the question, "How do you show people you want to be big?", comments were given such as "by wearing engineer boots", "wearing your pants real low", "wising off", "trying to make people real mad". Other comments were "You can fight a kid and win and feel bigger", "Even if you lose you feel good if you know you fought good and hard."

B commented that Q tried to be big on Sunday and Monday. After much hesitation Q told of running away from home because of fear of what his father would do about his getting a bike traffic ticket. Then he added, "I did it for fun. They had detectives out and everything." The leader asked how it had worked out; had he got the fun and attention he wanted? Q replied that when he came back, the boys had asked if he had fun and he had said sure. But then he added, "It wasn't so much fun because I was alone so much."

The discussion that followed centered on reasons for running away. The group agreed that it is a way to keep people busy with them, or showing other people they want to be the boss, or maybe getting even with someone. They also talked about how they could run away in their minds by not listening to parents or teachers who talked to them. F said that when he got a headache he could usually have his own way and not have to do what people told him to do.

Disclosures of these purposes at each group session seemed to release a flood of things the boys wanted to talk about. Questions of special interest came from them periodically and were discussed as they came along. Some examples were "Why do police ask you about dope? Why are girls grown up at sixteen and boys aren't? Why do some people have to swear so much?"

At one of the last sessions B said he wanted to tell how he almost ran away the night before, but had not done so. He described the thinking he went through as he worked on this problem by himself.

A springboard to a discussion of constructive membership in a class or group brought volunteer suggestions from the boys. Very specific actions were listed, such as "I could go into Miss M's class and just be myself — not big and not a baby."

During and following the seven sessions there was a decided improvement in the behavior of three of the boys, both in classes and in the sessions. One boy appeared interested in the discussions but showed little improvement in classes. The problem of the quiet boy was so deep-seated that the group experience seemed not to touch him.

A second group experiment was carried out with ninth grade girls. Six of the girls were selected by homeroom teachers as being the most troublesome. A seventh girl was added at the suggestion of the girls themselves. They were all of average or above-average ability.

Conferences were held with mothers of five of the girls. Although the counselor did not have the girls in class, she had had some counseling contacts with four of them previously.

Six sessions, similar to those of the boys' group, were held. The pattern and group dynamics were much the same. However, the common problem for the girls tended to center on conflicts with parents over dating and keeping hours, conflicts with sisters, and worry over what others think of them.

The evaluation of the group experience at the end of the project was done through unsigned notes by the girls. They all expressed the feeling that they had learned a great deal about themselves and had gained a better understanding of parents and teachers. A typical comment was, "It helps to have a chance to talk about problems without getting a lecture."

Evaluations by the parents gave enthusiastic reports of improvement in their daughters which they attributed to the group counseling project.

CONCLUSIONS

Our experience with this type of group counseling for junior high pupils is extremely limited, but nevertheless we feel it is a method well suited to this age group; it fills a serious need. We believe the larger the number of sessions the greater the chance for success. At least six sessions are necessary before any improvement can be expected.

Improvement in the method could be effected by working more closely with both parents and pupils in individual conferences. Also it would be beneficial to spend some time discussing the feelings of pupils who do change their behavior: will other pupils still like them; will such changes appear cowardly; what are some of the acceptable methods for remaining a part of the group? These considerations often seem to affect a teen-ager's attempts to change his behavior pattern.

5

MULTIPLE COUNSELING: EIGHT OVER-AGE BOYS, GRADE NINE

Editor's Note:

The anonymity of the leader-counselor and the school was requested because the group project is part of on-going research. The problem concerns pupils who are sent on to high school in spite of the fact that they lack the necessary knowledges and skills for high school work. Poor reading ability, lack of simple mathematical concepts, and lack of self-confidence made the pupils antagonistic toward both school and community. The need to straighten out these boys is obvious. Perhaps they are salvageable now, but not later.

This group project was organized on the recommendation of the school psychologist. Sixteen weekly sessions were held, with individual interviews with each of the eight boys at least bi-weekly. Since these boys would not have accepted membership in a therapy group, the project was presented to them as a series of lessons to help them become acquainted with their new school. They would get ideas for entering activities and achieving greater success than they had in their previous school experience. All were eager to participate.

Only two discussion topics were chosen by the counselor-leader: (1) Differences between high school and elementary school (2) Who's who in our high school. In the rest of the sessions the boys decided in advance what they would like to discuss. Although the wording in the listing of the fourteen topics is that of the author, the ideas are entirely the boys':

1. Study techniques. (Why should every student have a study schedule?) (What is the best study schedule for you?)
2. Study techniques. (How can one know which are the most important facts in a history lesson? How to remember them?)
3. Study techniques. (What is the best way to study an English lesson?)
4. Extra-curricular activities. (What activities are open to freshmen boys? How can a boy get into them?)
5. Reading techniques. (What is the best way to read a lesson to be able to recite on it?)
6. Reading for pleasure. (What are some good books?)
7. Use of the library. (How does one find books in the library?) (What does a pupil do to take a book out of the library?)
8. Vocations. (What jobs are available for boys who leave school after the eighth grade?)
9. Vocations. (What jobs are available for boys who finish high school?)
10. Methods of test preparation. (What is a good way to study for a test?)
11. Curriculum. (What high school courses are open to sophomores?)
12. Curriculum. (What high school courses are open to juniors and seniors?)
13. Extra-curricular activities. (What is done in various clubs? How does one get into them?)
14. General questions and discussion.

301

The common problem of group members was their non-conformity and lack of success in school. Where most students were happy, prepared their lessons willingly and eagerly participated in any suggested activity, these boys behaved in an acceptable way only because their teachers required them to do so. They seldom prepared assignments, sulked, and resented any authority. Their attitude toward school and society was antagonistic. Although they had more native ability than some who did acceptable work, these pupils failed. They had been assigned to the high school building because their physical development made it unwise to keep them with younger children. Each had repeated one or two grades.

The structure of the group sessions was the same throughout; the leader started the discussion of the topic selected for the day. As soon as the boys "caught the ball" she let them run with it — in any direction they wished. At the beginning the group members did not pick up the discussion and take it onto another track, but after the fifth or sixth session the topic became just a point of departure: the boys took over the discussion with expressions of desires, antagonisms and grievances. They talked more freely to each other, even in the leader's presence, than they had in individual interviews with the same leader. Following many of the sessions one or more of the boys came to the counselor's office for further help.

Only in the two sessions concerned with vocations did the group stay close to the subject. The reason for this was their deep interest in available jobs. These two discussions — more than any others — showed the leader what the boys wanted to know and hoped to do. Following each of these sessions the counselor held individual conferences with all the boys.

RESULTS

Changes in the boys did not show up during the semester when the project was held. However, during the following semester, improvement in attitudes became apparent: attendance improved and all but one of the group made a definite effort to succeed in school. They did succeed to the extent of earning high school credits in all courses they were taking except history. Because of extremely deficient reading skills they could not handle this subject.

The change in attitudes extended far enough to influence the boys' behavior in positive directions. All the boys seemed more happy in school and several decided they wanted to go on to graduate. Two are tutoring in the history which they failed. All are interested in extra-curricular activities, and seem far less antagonistic to society in general.

During the semester following the group sessions the leader met each boy at least once in two weeks for individual counseling. With but a few exceptions the boys came voluntarily to discuss problems or report successes.

In evaluating the multiple counseling project the leader-counselor believed there was sufficient evidence in behavior changes of the boys to show beneficial influences were operative, but qualified the statement — the improvements may or may not be due to the group project and/or the adjunctive individual counseling. The leader made the suggestion that more might have been accomplished if one or two well-adjusted students had been included in the group.

6
A SEMANTIC APPROACH IN GROUP COUNSELING
by REVEREND J. N. KELLY, JR.
CHRISTIAN CHURCH, HARRODSBURG, KENTUCKY

A semantics approach in group discussions has been used by the author with excellent results both for the purpose of problem solving and for counseling. Projects with problem-solving goals have been held with administrative groups of the church. Another project concerned five young businessmen who met to discuss the anxiety elements in their business relationships. This served as a springboard for individual counseling with the pastor. The discussions filled in the background for further discussions and seemed to remove any embarrassment in private interviews. In fact, the author has become so convinced of the importance of small-group discussion as preparation for individual counseling that he invites those who want counseling to engage in the group activity prior to individual interviews.

An illustration of the semantics approach in counseling consists of a group project, led by the author at the request of the Youth Council, for five high school students, three girls and two boys. A number of such discussion groups had been organized by the Community Youth Council because of the large number of authority-defying youth in the region. "Drag racing" had become popular; the attitude of hostility toward parents, police, and other representatives of authority was a serious problem. Thus the purpose of the small-group projects was the reduction of hostility and resentment against authority. Six weekly sessions were held. The entire series of meetings centered around a study of key words.

The group members consisted of two sixteen-year-old girls who were daughters of a dentist and Army officer, respectively; a seventeen-year-old girl, daughter of a textile plant employee; a boy of sixteen, son of an attorney; a boy of seventeen, son of the manager of a chain store. Since the group members knew each other and the leader through youth activities in the church, including dances and social events, there was a fair degree of permissiveness in the discussions from the beginning.

The leader opened each session by writing certain words on the blackboard — "parents and authority", "police and authority", etc. The group members were asked to give spontaneously their thoughts and feelings which were freely associated with the key words. The leader wrote these words or phrases on the board as they were suggested. Members were asked to define the word both as to its meaning for each member and its dictionary meaning. When a word was suggested that carried an obvious emotional load for any member of the group, the others were requested to discuss the meaning it seemed to carry for the one suggesting it. For instance, the word "cop" brought out into the open a wide range of hostile feelings toward law enforcement officers.

This device for starting a discussion in the group regarding the emotional connotation of a word suggested by a group member forced that member to examine his own understanding and attitude. Frequently he attempted to justify his use of the term, but usually found his own weakness in the process. In following sessions the member who was challenged would bring up the word again to show that he had done some thinking on the subject during the week.

Each session ended with the leader reviewing the words which had been discussed and the apparent meaning they had for the members of the group.

In the sixth and final session, the leader attempted to recall the meanings originally suggested when the authority words were first used. The group discussed the difference between past and present connotations. A phrase frequently used in the last session was, "I used to think," indicating changes in thought and meaning in the present. It is significant that the word "cop" had been replaced in the later sessions by the word "police". Drag racing actually ceased to be a serious problem with the group members. This may have happened by itself, or our group discussions may have had something to do with the situation.

The small-group discussion project led quite naturally into individual counseling, requested by various members of the group. For example, the conflict with parents due to the demands of the youth for increasing independence of action became the subject of discussion in private interviews. It seemed that the key to the family car is a symbol of developing maturity and adulthood. It stands for the authority that the parents must give up, and the responsibility that the young persons must assume. Keeping these two processes in balance was easier to accomplish against a background of the learning gained in the group project and counseling interviews.

OUTCOMES

Specific changes in attitudes and behavior, influenced at least in part by the group project, were found in all five group members as follows:

1. There was a conscious change in the attitude toward authority. It was considered less of an "edict" handed down from above, and more a social invention arrived at through necessity in a democratic society.
2. Sharing of the new attitude with other students in the high school took place. For instance, the author was asked by the student council to lead a study of the "whys" of drag racing.
3. As a carry-over, the author and other group counselors were asked to lead discussions regarding the young people's relationships with each other, and with school and parent conflict situations.

CONCLUSIONS

It is believed that this word-study approach is excellent to use in group counseling or problem-solving groups where the situation involves emotion-laden words. In the southern setting, the recent race problems connected with de-segregation would lend themselves to this type of approach.

LIST OF REFERENCES

A. *For background reading on the importance of words in living relationships.*
  1. *Language in Thought and Action.* S. I. Hayakawa, Harcourt, Brace Co., 1939.
  2. *Language, Thought and Reality.* B. L. Whorf, Wiley and Sons, 1956.
  3. *People in Quandaries.* W. Johnson, Harpers and Sons, 1946.
  4. "The Semantic Approach in Counseling", W. H. Pemberton, *J. of International Society for General Semantics*, Winter issue, 1955-56.
  5. *The Tyranny of Words.* Stuart Chase, Harcourt, Brace Co., 1938.

B. *For background and practical suggestions on small-group discussion methods.*
   1. *Client Centered Therapy.* C. R. Rogers, Houghton Mifflin Co., 1951.
   2. *The Group Work Shop in the Church.* P. F. Douglass, Association Press, 1956.
   3. *How to Lead Discussions.* Leadership Pamphlet No. 1, Adult Education Assn. of the U. S. A., Chicago.
   4. *Understanding How Groups Work.* Leadership Pamphlet No. 4 (above).
   5. *Intensive Group Psychotherapy.* G. R. Bach, Ronald Press, 1954.
   6. *Multiple Counseling.* H. I. Driver, Monona Publications, 1954. (Section I of this book.)
   7. *The Practice of Group Therapy,* S. R. Slavson, International University Press, 1947.

7

A SMALL-GROUP COUNSELING PROGRAM FOR
PUPILS, PARENTS, TEACHERS

reported by

DR. HELEN I. DRIVER, *Consultant in Mental Hygiene*

School programs of mental hygiene for pupils, parents, and teachers are being activated by professional workers in this field, as members of school faculties in public school systems. Professional personnel include school social workers, psychologists, and trained counselors. They can provide special counseling for pupils who are unable to adjust adequately in classroom situations and can coordinate efforts of parents, teachers and other key people to help the "child with a problem".

The intimate group is being used as the medium for treatment and counseling, not only for pupils but also for their parents and for teachers. An illustration of small-group discussion therapy, led by the school psychologist, is found in a small city high school in New England. Of 1200 pupils in the school 110 were failing one or more courses. Some of these were trouble-makers, truants, or deemed incorrigible by their teachers. The parents of these maladjusted pupils needed therapy along with their children. And teachers need some safe place to air their grievances, to "blow off steam". Too often teachers are forced into a restrictive behavior mold which is not mentally healthy in order to serve as "examples to pupils". The school psychologist carried out a program of group counseling which met the needs of pupils, parents, teachers.

An example of one of the groups consisted of twelve Senior boys and girls who had no idea what to do after graduation. At the end of twelve weekly discussion sessions everyone in the group had made a satisfactory decision. In several cases the support of the counselor and the group helped the pupil to make up his own mind instead of giving in to the will of a parent.

Another pupil project was organized for under-achievers. It was a voluntary group, but the psychologist devised a clever promotional scheme so that no stigma was attached to those who signed up. A good majority of the under-achieving pupils joined the activity and a number of small discussion groups were organized. The pupils were eager to engage in a discussion group where "you can talk about anything you want — school subjects, teachers (as long as they aren't identified), grievances, problems etc." Signs on the bulletin board had advertised the discussion groups with questions that struck an appealing note:

Do you have examination blues?
Do you waste your time?
Do you fear school failures?
Do you find it impossible to resist TV?
Do you think you are a dope?

The assumption is made that feelings influence all actions and a child works or acts in school according to how he feels about himself and others. Satisfactory emotional relationships at home and among his peers allow the child to put his energies into the task at hand, namely, his school work. Under-achievers, brought together in small discussion groups, are encouraged to talk freely of their feelings, of the things that bother them. The emotional reasons for their inability to study and put forth real effort are discovered. Once the problem is out in the open, the psychologist, teachers and parents can help the pupil with it. *Almost without exception, the grades and school adjustment improved after the pupils had engaged in the group therapy project.*

Often the parents of a troubled child need therapy more than the child. The school is in a strategic position to work with these parents when there is a school psychologist. In the great majority of cases the cooperation of the parents is secured. As long as the parents meet in groups — and the fact that it is a therapy group is carefully hidden — much can be done to give them better understanding of parent-child relationships, and to help them change their attitudes and behavior toward their children. The parents are encouraged to bring up any question or problem for discussion; private interviews with the psychologist are available to them also. In our illustration the school psychologist was successful in carrying out a parent project which helped materially in "straightening out" a number of confused, rebellious teen-agers.

In providing a group project for teachers, the voluntary enrollment aspect plus the fact of providing professional advice to teachers who have "pupils with problems" are important. Thus the psychologist offers service which many teachers desire: a time and place to talk over both teacher and pupil problems. Skillfully led, such a group of teachers becomes a therapy group as time goes on. The warmth and permissiveness of an intimate group where the leader is respected and trusted can de-frost the group members to the point of discussing personal feelings and problems. Here again, once the problem is "on the table", something can be done about it.

CONCLUSION

The school, through its specialized guidance personnel, is admirably suited to the task of providing programs of mental hygiene for pupils, parents, and teachers. The efforts of therapist, parents, teachers and community agencies can be coordinated into an effective preventive, or early-treatment program for emotionally disturbed or maladjusted pupils.

8
PERSONAL COUNSELING THROUGH A CREATIVE DRAMA CLUB

by MRS. THEORA STANDING, *School Psychologist*
SAN BERNARDINO PUBLIC SCHOOLS, CALIFORNIA

The Club members consisted of nine Senior High boys and girls with ages ranging from fourteen to sixteen. They called themselves the Creative Drama Club and met weekly during the school year for a total of forty sessions. The advisor and coach was the school psychologist.

The participants had been selected by the advisor and invited to form the Club because of their great need for understanding and guidance. All had emotional problems ranging from the withdrawn, deeply disturbed personality, to the dramatic show-off whose tensions could only be reduced by finding a more acceptable way of gaining recognition and approval.

In the first meeting of the club the members decided the purpose should be to create opportunities for personal growth and satisfaction by the presentation of plays and the study of drama. All members felt a need for success-experiences that might raise their social status and feelings of self-esteem. It was not long, however, before they became aware of the fact that a deeper, more meaningful purpose had superseded the first.

The school psychologist assumed the role of friend and advisor; the project remained group-centered from beginning to end. However, the individual concomitant counseling was important. Opportunities for individual interviews were available to all members in casual, informal settings for the most part. For example, the leader often manipulated the transportation of the group so that the member needing counseling found himself alone with the counselor in a favorable setting such as a scenic mountain road or near a place where refreshments could be enjoyed.

PERSONAL COUNSELING BY GROUP LEADER IS FACILITATED IN INFORMAL SETTINGS.

The situation seemed to "prime" feelings of warmth and expressions of confidence. Many troublesome problems were revealed, and effective counseling could be done while riding through a place of natural beauty or eating a luscious sundae.

The drama activity acted as a springboard for the discussions, individual ventilations and revelations. The projection into areas of sensitivity called for deeper understanding and analysis on the part of the group; they accepted and met the challenge, gaining not only in understanding of the "member with a problem" but in self-understanding as well.

The presentation of the drama was of secondary importance in the group. Interactions and the personal growth of each member were of prime importance. At first the members with fewer adjustment problems assumed roles of leadership. As the group became more intimate, these students were the first to sense the deeper and hidden

309

meaning of the club. They accepted a "mutual-help" relationship with others whose problems were more evident, and gained a depth of satisfaction, a feeling of strength and self-discovery. As leaders, they exhibited qualities of understanding and kindness that were in direct contrast to their past attitudes and behaviors.

As the glow of friendship and approval was felt by the withdrawn, more deeply disturbed members, they grew more confident and capable. Before the project ended the roles of leadership had been transferred to them through adroit manipulation of the original leaders.

Several examples will describe the group activity and its influence on individual members.

Case No. 1

A girl member, twelve years of age, weighed two hundred pounds and had a history of psychosomatic and hysterical disorders. Her physician requested that she be admitted to the group for therapeutic reasons. She had been withdrawn from school because of poor motor coordination and a complete lack of adjustment to school routine. She walked with a staggering gait much as though she were inebriated. She frequently became lost and dazed. Home conditions were fraught with father-daughter conflicts and the father had refused to cooperate in the counseling process.

This girl became oriented and active in the group due to the patience and kindness of fellow members. They seemed to feel a solemn but unspoken challenge to help her solve her problem. They made her feel important and necessary to the success of the group project. She wrote an original play based on the story of Kate Smith and cast herself as the lead. The research connected with this endeavor served as stimulus for much significant discussion. It motivated other members to talk about their hidden fears and anxieties.

This girl resolved her own problems so well that she was re-admitted to school and overcame the psychosomatic disorder that plagued her. Although her father remained unchanged, she learned to be more tactful with him and the whole family atmosphere improved.

The result was a determination on the part of the girl to accept herself as she was. Moreover, she was able to take off many pounds, to find a husband and establish her own home through an early marriage.

Case No. 2

An unusually tall teenage boy drooped his shoulders and wanted to hide. He was chosen by the group to be the lead in a play —

310

Abraham Lincoln, no less! The characteristic that had caused him to shrink from general group participation was changed to an asset and he was even envied by others.

His new feeling of self-respect developed an attitude which "snowballed" into other fields of success such as basketball and track. The new attitude helped him to be accepted socially. He finally understood the fact that he could be outstanding and unusual because of his tallness; his self-esteem grew to the point that he felt secure and at peace with himself.

Case No. 3

Two sisters whose sibling rivalry had reached dangerous proportions were invited to join the club. They were 13 and 14 years old. The older sister was accepted by the family, popular with friends, while the younger one was rejected and labeled as incorrigible. She was defiant to society in general and to her family in particular. She was acting out her frustrations by reckless and aggressive hostility that caused her to sink deeper into negative patterns of adjustment and lowered self-esteem.

Many group discussions centered upon the younger sister's problems. Significant individual counseling was included in the events that led up to a seeming miracle. The younger sister was chosen to be the lead in a club production. Her attitudes of hostility and feelings of being rejected seemed to melt away and she emerged as a most benevolent and lovable personality. Her desertion of the rebel-role appeared to be absolute and complete. She radiated talent and attractiveness. The family looked upon her in a new light and the two sisters became agreeable companions.

CONCLUSION

The dramatic activity with the group discussions constituted the whole content of the group project. However, intelligence and projective tests, and personality inventories were given all group members. The leader, as school psychologist, could measure status and progress through these and provide the individual counseling interviews which accompanied and followed the project. The fact that five years later, all group members were continuing the improved life-adjustment patterns found in the Drama Club is perhaps the real test of the values of such a multiple counseling activity.

9
A DISCIPLINARY GROUP GUIDANCE PROJECT
by PAUL CRAWFORD, *Counselor*
LA CUMBRE JUNIOR HIGH SCHOOL, SANTA BARBARA, CALIFORNIA

Emphasis on rehabilitation rather than punishment for "law breakers" in schools has been attempted through a group guidance project in La Cumbre Junior High School. This was tried because of the almost complete lack of success of the conventional after-school detention period for the "hopeless" repeaters in our school. We wanted to give a positive, rehabilitative emphasis to an essentially penal instrument. The method and results are reported forthwith.

A guidance group was established to meet weekly at the time of the school assembly. All pupils who showed too many demerits and/or incorrigible behavior in assemblies were required to report to this group. In general the pupils assigned to the guidance group were unable to adjust to conventional behavior when not under the direct control of a teacher.

Ideally the group would contain eight to twelve pupils in order to have full participation in discussions. However at times there would be as many as twenty boys and girls in the group. The counselor-leaders were able to handle the larger number with a minimum of difficulty and discussion participation was well spread over the group.

The common problem for group members was learning to live with people and accept their individual places and responsibilities in school. Often a change of attitude was essential and a discussion of this was the springboard to the sessions that followed. The counselor asked the group to decide the minimum length of time in which a change of attitude would become evident to the principal's office and the teachers. Usually the pupils agreed that two weeks could be sufficient. It was understood that the pupils would initiate proposals for release from the guidance groups. They could come to the counselor for individual conferences anytime they felt they deserved to be released. This gave the counselor many opportunities for individual counseling with the pupils who needed it most. The group also agreed that the rules must be flexible and each case settled on its own merits.

Many of the "good" kids who slip once are released after one group session. Others have stayed a whole semester. In general, we feel it is better to get a pupil to try it "on the outside" and fail, rather than to stay in the security of the group without a try. Of course they must be ready for the try. And all final disposition of a case is between the child and the counselor.

312

The counselor establishes rapport with each pupil in a very direct way. The counselor is his friend, believes in him as a "good kid" who sometimes does things that are unacceptable. Since the school cannot permit its rules to be broken, the pupil must show by his actions that there is a reasonable chance of his conforming to the acceptable behavior pattern before being released from the guidance group. The counselor will listen to, and accept each pupil and his feelings, but he cannot accept the kind of actions that brought about the assignment to the disciplinary group. The counselor tells the pupils that he knows he can *make* them behave, but that is not the important thing. They are old enough to take over the responsibility for their own behavior — *they must do the change themselves.*

When the pupils are assigned to the guidance group, their merit record comes with them. The first thing they do is to fill out an enrollment sheet. This includes necessary school data plus the reason they were sent in, and, most important to the counselor, how they feel about it. Later, and periodically, they write progress reports in the group sessions. These may be on how they feel, how they are progressing, or anything else they feel like writing or drawing. Often the revelations of the reports help the counselor to structure the individual counseling interviews.

One of the first discussion activities in the group relates to the merit reports (which are given to each pupil) and the whole citizenship program. The pupils are considerably interested in this discussion. Most of them claim they know nothing at all of the system. This is probably true, but when it affects them to the point of making them lose out on assembly programs, they become deeply interested in the program and especially their own past records.

The chief activity of the group sessions is free discussion, with time out for writing progress reports. When a common problem of current interest emerges, such as cutting or excessive tardiness, the discussion is lively, with group members suggesting ways to improve. Most of the time the counselor does not need to prepare a "springboard" to discussion, for strong feelings of anger against the vice-principal (because he assigned them to the group) or against teachers, or the world in general, are expressed quite freely by these junior high youngsters. They always start their questions before the leader is ready, for example, "How can I get out of here?", "How many demerits have I got?", "What do you think of a teacher who won't let you go to the washroom when you have to go?" Sometimes a number of topics are touched on in a single session, other times the group will not finish with one topic in a period. The discussions always show up the need for more knowledge of the basic human needs and feelings. For this we use "Human Relations in the Classroom" by Bullis and O'Malley, which contains information for the group leader, stories, discussion materials, etc. Another good source is the folder, "Mental Health is 1, 2, 3" published by the National Association for Mental Health. It includes characteristics of persons with good mental health in three areas: oneself, relations with others, demands of life.

Topics of interest are often seasonal, for example, grades, teachers, report cards, tardies, cuts, citizenship, vice-principals, bullies, boy-friends, dates, parents, graduation, promotion.

The pupils decide for themselves when they think they are ready for release. This cannot be wishful-thinking, but must be backed up by concrete evidence of changed behavior: merit records, classroom citizenship, changes as reported to the counselor in interviews with teachers and the vice-principal. The pupils must take the responsibility of seeking out the counselor when they think they can demonstrate their readiness for release.

The results of this guidance group have been good. However, there is a tremendous potential in this type of individual-group counseling program which has not been tapped. The counselors feel strongly that this type of program is one of the answers to problems of discipline, but certainly not the solution. In the present program there is no opportunity for depth counseling: to try to treat and "cure" these pupils. All the counselors are able to do is attempt to help the pupils change their attitudes and behavior enough to meet minimum requirements for school participation.

The change of attitudes and behavior on the part of pupils is shown by the following sample cases, reported in the counselor's notes:

"Joe" — Case 1 (1 session)

3-15   Assigned by Mr. Brown. Reason: too many tardies. How do you feel? "I deserve my punishment and I'll live up to it."

3-20   Joe came in to see me about a release. The tardies came from not sitting down in class. He says he'll take care of it. Released.

      Comments: Joe is a good boy but sometimes immature and pesty. He's never been reassigned.

"Jim" — Case 2 (6 sessions)

10-28   Assigned by Mr. Brown. Reason: "I lost too many merits." How do you feel? "I think it was a dirty deal, and I don't think I deserve this punishment. IT WAS A DIRTY DEAL! (etc., etc.)"

314

     Comments: Jim seemed very earnest and innocent. He tried hard to get the undivided attention of the counselor and badly wanted his case heard. He was definitely not to blame — he said! A boy with reasonably good home and looks to be a successful case. Immature and quite a bit spoiled. His merit record shows five unexcused tardies and one case of disobedience to a teacher. A tough bump now and he should be O.K.

10-31   Jim came to the counselor's office to be released as he was not to blame for anything. A good conference, but a long one. He talked much and didn't want to face anything. He was told he'd have to prove himself by actions and not words. He'll be back next week with some suggestions.

11-6   Good conference, not so cocky. Will try to go five weeks without demerits and will get O.K. from his teachers.

12-7   Jim had taken a tracer around to his teachers: two good citizenship ratings and five satisfactories. He had no demerits in five weeks. He had cleared with Mr. Brown. Chastened, but good attitude. Can still grin. Released.

     Comment: Jim stayed out of trouble the rest of the year and all the next year.

"Jane" — *Case 3 (3 sessions, released, 3 sessions)*

12-9   Assigned by Miss Jones. Reason: too many tardies. How do you feel? "All my tardies except two have been after gym. And not because of walking in the halls. I'll try to be on time to my fifth period class."

1-16   Came in for conference. Good attitude. No tardies for three weeks. Took tracer to teachers and Miss Jones.

1-19   All her teachers notice improvement and feel she should have a chance. Released.

5-18   Reassigned for too many tardies. 3 more. "I don't know what to say except the reason I've been getting so many tardies is because of daylight savings time."

     Comment: This is a different situation — A.M. tardies. She hasn't the ability to cope with new situations rapidly. Released the last two weeks because of good attitude.

"Charles" — *Case 4 (10 sessions)*

2-3   Assigned by Mr. Brown. Reason: too many demerits. How do you feel? "I think it was the right thing to do. I think I should have been kicked out (assemblies) a long time ago."

     Comment: Charles goofed last year and started out this year with very few merits between him and graduation. Broken home. Mother the helpless type. Charles is easy-going, pleasant, but easily led.

2-15   Charles came to conference, but said he thought he'd better stay in the group. Doesn't want to risk graduation and feels this will be a reminder. We discussed his case in the group. They admired him for his decision but most felt they would have tried it "on the outside." Charles liked the attention very much.

Comment: This is probably the only place Charles can feel he is being punished and not have to put forth any effort. He enjoys the comfortable limitations on his actions. (He is free to roam every night — and does.)

3-3   He is much too happy here. Called him into office and urged him to try going out on his own as he has lost no more demerits. He says he doesn't want to.

Comment: Will see him about this again.

3-15   He will accept alternate weeks at assembly. Released, but free to return if he wants to.

Follow-up: Charles returned occasionally. He lost two more merits, but graduated with his class. A year later he cut a high school class to visit the counselor. Says his citizenship is down so low that he is going to have to have a special conference on procedure for next year. Still wants to finish high school.

It is evident in these sample cases that youngsters need a counselor in whom they can confide, and who can support them in their personal growth, self-discipline and feeling of worth. Unfortunately the limitations of time, schedules, pupil-load, prevent real personal counseling for pupils who desperately need it at this particular time in their maturing process.

Our program is still developing and expanding. The principal is, as always, the key person in a guidance program. His understanding and backing must be secured. Also the vice-principals must be in sympathy and work in close cooperation. And, of course, the teachers are all-important. Working together as a team, members of the guidance department, school administration, and teaching staff can exert lasting influences on the personal development of pupils. We have been most fortunate in the cooperation given in this group guidance program. The team work is the chief reason for its success.

SECTION II — SYMPOSIUM

The five articles in Part 2 illustrate various methods whereby college orientation programs can be personalized; student leadership utilized; psychology courses combined with multiple counseling. Readers will find materials and ideas that can be adapted to different purposes in colleges and universities: counseling, teaching, and student activities.

317

1

A JUNIOR COLLEGE GUIDANCE PROGRAM
WITH A TEAM APPROACH*

by VINCENT F. CALIA, *Assistant Professor*
JUNIOR COLLEGE, BOSTON UNIVERSITY

The psychology and guidance program in the Junior College, Boston University, is a result of five years of developmental planning and experimentation. (8) It combines lectures, group seminars, small-group discussions and individual counseling in a year's course of three required meetings weekly for three hours of academic credit. This two-year program of general education in Boston University Junior College involves a student body of approximately 900 and a professionally trained counseling staff of 8 persons.

The course is divided into four major content areas: (1)

A. Orientation to College.
B. Psychological foundations of self-analysis.
C. Self-analysis and self-understanding.
D. Occupational and educational planning.

Thus the course parallels the changing needs of the student during his first year of college. The Sophomore course is a more standardized mental hygiene and adjustment course in Psychology.

The structure of the Freshman course includes three group-contact hours per week: a lecture, a team seminar, and a small-group discussion session. (6)

Lecture Hour

This is primarily informational with emphasis on content. General principles and concepts are stressed. Areas involved are:

1. You and your college
2. Learning and college
3. The causation of behavior
4. Learning theories
5. Personality
6. Individual differences
7. Motivation, values, emotions
8. Vocational interests and aptitudes
9. Intelligence and scholastic aptitudes
10. Personality and self-analysis
11. Self-analysis, occupational and educational planning
12. Occupational and educational information
13. An occupational and educational research paper

*Condensation of article "A Group Guidance Program in Action", by author, April issue of *Junior College Journal*, 1957.

Team Psychology Seminar

A series of highly structured situations are presented to illustrate the lecture material and to provoke discussion. Psychodrama, panels of students and instructors, audio-visual aids, case studies are used to reconstruct the lecture material in reality situations. For example, a lecture on motivation might include a presentation of psychological and social concepts. The seminar hour might present a student-faculty panel which discusses the problem of student motivation in college. Such a panel may then be open for general student discussion. The team approach (4) uses instructors from five subject matter areas: humanities; social relations; science; communication; and psychology and guidance. Each member of the team teaches the same section and hence the same students as the other four members. Thus instructors can discuss the day-to-day problems arising in teaching. They can view problems of integration at close range and avoid repetition in subject matter presentation. Focus of the seminar on problems and needs of students as they arise is practical, realistic, and of great benefit to the students.

Staff and student syllabi have been developed so that anticipation and preparation for the weekly demonstration hours (the seminar presentations) are made possible. There is enough flexibility within the framework of the syllabus so that problems and needs can be met, and spontaneity maintained. The Staff Syllabus includes objectives of the unit, design, materials. The Student Syllabus uses the following outline:

1. Lecture topic
2. Reading assignment
3. Description of the seminar program
   a. objectives; b. procedures; c. special features to observe d. suggestions for small-group discussions; e. special terms to study.

Small-Group Discussion

The third weekly meeting consists of small groups of ten or twelve students who discuss lecture, seminar, and personal problems. These groups are structured so that they meet with their counselor on alternate weeks, and in student-led groups in-between. Leadership and recorder roles are rotated among the group members. Student-led groups are assigned specific tasks beforehand, usually a case study which is to be discussed.

319

As time goes on, the small-group discussions take on a more affective and personal tone, moving away from the informational and cognitive type. As the group becomes more cohesive, the students learn to verbalize and to discuss their problems in small groups, led by either a fellow student or the counselor.

Individual Counseling

The levels or dimensions of the entire program contribute to the process of individual counseling. The lecture material helps to establish facts, knowledge, and concrete learnings; the seminar or group guidance program illustrates and extends student learnings; small-group discussions bring learnings into a personal frame of reference and individual involvement. Individual counseling provides the direct one-to-one personal relationship and process for problem solving.

CONCLUSION

The value of this multi-dimensional guidance program for freshmen in a Junior College has been proved over a number of years at Boston University. The learning and personal growth of participating students during their first year of college justify the efforts and time devoted to the guidance course by the counselor-instructors. This is an active teaching-learning process through a sound group-individual counseling method. It is gratifying and satisfying to both the "counselors" and "counselees".

Bibliography and Sources

The unique program of Boston University Junior College demanded special sources. The textbook developed for this course was published by Boston University Press and currently by Allyn and Bacon Company of Boston and New York. Reprints of many of the listed articles are available as are copies of unpublished studies and articles. Requests should be directed to Chairman, Psychology and Guidance Division, Boston University Junior College.

BOOKS AND PAMPHLETS

1. Glanz, Edward C. and Walston, E. B. *Psychology and Critical Thinking, A New Approach to Guidance.* N. Y., Allyn and Bacon, 1957.
2. Butler, J. R., et al. *For Those Who Want An Education — A Program in Humane Studies.* Boston, Boston University Press, 1956. 56 pp.
3. *General Education at the Junior College.* Boston University Junior College, 1957. 96 pp.
   (Actual curriculum of all Divisions including Psychology and Guidance)

ARTICLES

4. Anthony, V. A.; Liversey, C.; Richter, P.; Russell, C. "The Team Approach to General Education". *Junior College Journal*, XXVI, No. 6, 319-327; No. 7, 405-410.
5. Calia, Vincent F. "The Guidance Counselor — Miracle Man in Education?", *School Review*, LXIII, 1955.
6. Calia, Vincent F. "A Group Guidance Program in Action", *Junior College Journal*, April, 1957.
7. Glanz, Edward C. "The Faculty Team in General Education", *Journal of Higher Education*, XXVII, No. 7, Oct. 1956.
8. Glanz, Edward C. "A Guidance Program in Action" (unpublished study), Boston University Junior College, 1956. 41 pp.

2

A GROUP DISCUSSION APPROACH
IN FRESHMAN ORIENTATION

by RAY A. FARMER, *Dean of Students*
NEW MEXICO HIGHLANDS UNIVERSITY, LAS VEGAS, N. M.

Much has been said and written regarding the desirability of having upper classmen plan an active part in Freshman orientation. To check the advantage of greater student participation and find better methods of instruction, we decided to make the subject of "Campus Courtesies" a student-centered project.

Our Freshman Orientation Class meets twice a week during the first quarter; the group averages 250-300 students. Different topics of the course are handled in a variety of ways. In order to institute the student-centered method for "Campus Courtesies", the help of the fraternities and sororities was solicited.

A joint meeting of the Inter-Fraternity and Panhellenic Councils was called to consider the problem of helping entering Freshmen adjust to the social life of the campus. The group agreed on the following standards for student leaders in the project:

Attractive in appearance and dress.

Ability to speak and think on their feet.

Ability to gain the respect of the Freshmen.

Deeply interested in making this contribution.

Each fraternity and sorority agreed to send a number of members willing to act as panel members. The representatives were duly selected and a meeting was set to discuss the sub-topics under the heading

"Campus Courtesies" and effective methods of presenting them. The group selected these areas: table manners, dating, dress and etiquette. The scope of the subject matter was sufficient to warrant the scheduling of three separate sessions:

Session	Group	Topic	Leaders
1	All freshmen men	Table Manners	Home Ec. Dept. & women conference leaders
1	All freshmen girls	What I want in the girl I go with.	Men conference leaders
2	Mixed groups of 30	Correct dress (everyday, semi-formal, formal)	Mixed panel of four
3	Mixed groups of 30	Etiquette	Mixed panel of four

When the magnitude of the project began to reveal itself, the students who had agreed to act as group leaders expressed a desire for assistance and instruction in methods of leading a group and in presenting their projects. It was agreed to hold two training periods. A number of articles and books, particularly the pamphlet "Conference Leadership" printed by the Esso Company, proved most helpful.

During the training sessions, there was a discussion on the definition of a conference, qualities of a leader, his preparation and methods of presentation, and the results that could be expected. The group leaders wanted various types of aids such as outlines, charts, case-studies for illustration, etc. Wherever possible these were secured for the leaders. It was decided that each panel should prepare or select the aids it wanted and the Dean of Students' Office helped in the preparation of materials.

The first session for the Freshmen men was handled in the following way:

1. Tables seating ten students were set up. A demonstration table with china, silver, etc. ready to lay in the center of the room. At the front of the room a piano and the head table with four panelists and the moderator sitting around it.

2. After the Freshmen men were seated at the round-tables, a trio of girls entered and sang the following song to the tune of "Sweet Betsy from Pike":

> "There was a young man came to NMHU,
>   he always thought that he knew what to do;
> But when he sat down in the big dining hall,
>   he suddenly knew that he didn't at all.

322

Oh my good gracious, just how do I eat?
What is the deal now on cutting up meat?
How shall I butter this bread in my hand?
By hector, it's easier to live off the land.
So our new student faced real misery
'cause he'd forgot what his manner should be.
His mother had taught him but he'd always thought
'twas much more important to lick what he'd fought.
Now listen you he-men who've come here to school —
there's never a reason to feel like a fool,
For dining is simple and apt to be fun,
So if you will listen you'll hear how it's done."

3. The men were asked to write down (paper and pencils had been provided) any questions they might have had about table manners in either public or private dining places. The slips were collected.

4. The moderator asked the groups to think about some particularly objectionable table manners they had noticed in others. The groups were to select a chairman, to discuss this for five minutes and then have their chairman report for the group.

5. Reports were made from the groups after five minutes.

6. The panel discussed and answered representative questions from the slips that had been collected from the groups.

7. Demonstration and practice in the proper setting of the dinner table was the final part of the program.

The first session for the Freshmen women students was handled by a panel of men. They had decided to call their subject "What I want in the girl I go with". This was an outstandingly successful meeting! Although a forty-five minute meeting had been planned, the girls insisted on asking questions and after one and a half hours the session had to be called to a halt. Some girls stayed later to ask personal questions; they even made appointments to talk with panel members the next day.

In the second session the following material was to be covered:

Correct Dress	*Etiquette*
Everyday	Introductions
Semi-formal	Dating-Dancing-Dining
Formal	Respect for others
Care of clothing	Dormitory life
	Conduct on and off campus
	Drinking
	Chaperones and their treatment
	Cutting dining hall line
	Conduct at games

323

A representative plan which was used by one group of 30 with a panel of 4 follows:

1. The moderator introduced the subject of "appropriateness in dress" and outlined the information to be covered: appropriate dress for everyday, semi-formal and formal occasions, poor taste in clothing and a sample wardrobe.

2. The moderator stationed fellow-leaders at four corners of the room and instructed the men to divide themselves into two groups with men leaders; the women students into two groups with women leaders.

3. The men's groups were given assignments to plan one-minute skits showing pet peeves in women's dress; the women's groups were given paper and pencils with which to concoct comic valentines of pet peeves in men's dress.

4. The men presented the skits and the women students gave them the valentines. Each of the panelists then summarized the "pet peeves" of his groups.

5. The moderator next introduced the subject of appropriate clothing. Three panelists each presented a short report on the types of clothing to be considered: everyday, semi-formal and formal. Mimeographed sheets on necessary and optional items that might be included in each category, with prices, were then given to the freshmen.

6. A question period followed.

A representative plan used for the second session, mixed group of 30, with 4 panelists and a cast of role-players is as follows:

1. The moderator had placed in front of the room a large sign listing the sub-topics to be discussed:

Introductions	Drinking
Dating-Dancing-Dining	Chaperones and their treatment
Respect for others	Cutting dining hall line
Dormitory life	Conduct at games
Conduct on and off campus	

2. Role-playing situations involving a number of the sub-topics were enacted. After the psychodrama the moderator turned the discussion to the group. Each panel member was responsible for summarizing the discussion on one or more of the psychodramas.

RESULTS

The results of the student leadership in the unit "Campus Courtesies" were most gratifying. This unit was conceded to be the most successful one in the Orientation Course. The enthusiasm of the Freshmen for the method of handling this unit assured us that it should be continued. Results on the final examination showed proportionately fewer errors on material covered than ever before; they compared very favorably with results on other units. A further value, not anticipated by the Dean of Students, was the improved relations among the various Greek organizations. A feeling of pride and responsibility for "orienting" the Freshman class was in keeping with a democratic, student-centered process.

We are now planning to encourage the students to accept the responsibility of assisting with other units of the Orientation Course, especially the subjects of "Student Activities" and "Scholarship". In order to avoid criticism of taking students away from their work and to cover the campus we are inviting service organizations and some of the advanced education students to participate.

Certainly an important goal in an Orientation Course is the effective assimilation of new students into University life, with high standards held up by leadership from the student body. In my estimation, this project was a significant contribution to the effective assimilation of our Freshmen at New Mexico Highlands University.

REFERENCES

1. Baird, A. C., *Discussion Principles and Types*, 1st ed. N. Y. McGraw-Hill Co., 1943.
2. Boaman, L. E., *How to Head a Discussion*. A Guide for the Use of Group Leaders. The Woman's Press, 1947.
3. McBurney, J. H., Hance, K. G., *Principles and Methods of Discussion*. N. Y. Harpers & Bros., 1939.
4. *Conference Leadership:* Esso Training Center Publication, 1949

3

A TRAINING PROGRAM FOR
JUNIOR STUDENT COUNSELORS

by MARY MORTON, *Dean of Women*
LAWRENCE COLLEGE, APPLETON, WIS.

Because Juniors are used as Freshman dormitory leaders in our College — with heavy responsibilities in terms of leadership, giving a good example to the Freshmen under their charge, handling human relationship problems with a mature touch — a training course is given those selected in the spring term of the year preceding their term of office. The Dean of Women serves as advisor and counselor to the dormitory leaders during the year in which they serve. In addition to individual counseling, group meetings are held during the academic year for the purpose of discussing problems the leaders face.

The leader-role in the dormitories is shared by two Juniors for each section of Freshmen. As well as serving as counselors for their own groups the Junior leaders also serve as officers of student government. They are counselors not only in an information-giving sense, but also in helping the younger girls to understand themselves and to progress toward maturity. At the same time the Junior Counselors are in the role of learners, themselves. They are attempting to become more adept as leaders and counselors; they are progressing toward maturity also. This latter aim is apparent in the group meetings with the Dean of Women.

The group process and its learning benefits for the younger counselors proved of great value in the personal growth of these Junior students. The observer can see immediately in the first meetings in the spring that the girls are chiefly concerned with the law-enforcement aspect of the job. They ask, "If the Freshmen don't want to dress for Wednesday night dinners, how can we make them"? Some of the more perceptive members of the group help to focus the emphasis where it belongs: how to draw the new girls into the social program so that they wish to take part. Usually several girls ask about personal privileges which they, as counselors, may receive. The query, "Do we get any extra late permissions?", is followed by an embarrassed giggle, indicating that the question stressed the external rewards of counseling more than the rest of the group deemed appropriate.

In the fall, after the first two hectic weeks of orientation and sorority rushing, everyone settles down to a normal pace. Counselors begin to see their section as a group for whose morale they are responsible.

Also their counselees have many questions and often tears which they must, sometimes literally, dry. At the Counselors' meetings, someone tells about a section party for a homesick freshman who had a birthday, and someone else describes the fun her section had going to a football game together. The concept grows that looking after one's section is the acceptable thing to do and that it gives a warm satisfaction to the counselor.

At the early fall meetings, however, the counselors themselves are not a cohesive group in any real sense. Each girl, or at best, each pair of roommates seems distracted by her own problems and those of "our section". The Staff leader finds it difficult to maneuver the group into any kind of coherent discussion. Problems brought up are likely to involve enforcement of quiet hours and other minor disciplinary matters. The counselors find that living among Freshmen is not easy and their attempts to subdue the animal spirits of the young often seem to be based on self defense. The leader points out some of the psychological causes of adolescent behavior, and suggests acceptable ways in which these needs can be met. Soon some of the Juniors start to express concern for the personal adjustment of their individual charges and can tell the rest of the group the methods they used successfully to help the Freshmen "grow up".

RESULTS

After three monthly meetings the counselors are a recognizable, cohesive group. By then they have accumulated common experiences and have adopted a common goal, namely, helping the freshman progress toward maturity. They have become aware of the qualities of a good counselor, regardless of the wide variations in many personal traits. Among other things, the counselor must put her duties ahead of purely social affairs: she must even arrange her academic life so as to leave time for her counseling duties. If one of the counselors leaves a group meeting early "to study for a test", glances are exchanged, and the culprit usually does her studying early the next time, or postpones her date! Eventually they come to the point of telling one of their number about her shortcomings in front of the group.

Thus the counselors learn and teach each other in and through their own group. By learning to understand each other, by seeing that there is more than one way to solve a problem satisfactorily, they improve in understanding and skill in dealing with the growing pains of the freshman girls. Through the creation of a genuine group spirit they become more effective in democratic participation in community life. At the

327

same time the personal growth of the counselors shows the positive influence of the group and leadership experiences.

4

A COMBINATION PSYCHOLOGY CLASS AND
MULTIPLE COUNSELING PROJECT

by PROFESSOR WILLIAM L. PATTY

LOS ANGELES CITY COLLEGE

In the seven sections of the semester Psychology course which deals with personality and personal adjustment we use the first half-semester for the exposition of the favored foundations in scientific study of personality. The second half-semester consists of a multiple counseling program devoted to the topics of courtship adjustments, family adjustments of the students to their own families (whether marital or paternal), male or female role, self-concept, and adjustments to the controls encountered in the community.

Multiple counseling may be thought of on a scale from the highly structured extreme that a college class sometimes exemplifies to the other extreme of a therapy group with a minimum of structuring. Our use of the latter in the second half-semester is possible because of the informational basis established in the first half of the semester. The therapy aspects produce valuable adjustment outcomes for individual students which, we believe, could never be achieved in a formal class setting.

This course, Psychology 3: *Personal and Social Adjustment* is the second semester of a basic year course in Psychology. It was revised in 1946 into a realistic framework of learning based on the assumption that students must understand the processes of life adjustment in order to self-direct their own personal growth and life adjustments. We reduced content to a necessary minimum and placed the multiple counseling activity in the second half of the second semester for maximum application of subject matter to real life situations. We wished to avoid preachment and advice-giving. Over the years effective techniques have been developed from the client-centered group activity in the second half-semester, which averages twenty-two sessions, since the class meets three times a week. Class age ranges from 18 to 35 in day classes; 19 to "senility" in evening classes. Class size averages 30 students.

The four objectives of the course are:
1. Introduction to the variety and extent of human personality problems.
2. Improvement of insight into the processes of life adjustment, i.e. perception, psychosomatics, social-cultural constructs, personality dynamics, such as self-expression and integration.
3. Development of a framework of understanding for major areas of adjustment, i.e. courtship, family and home, male-female roles, socio-economic status and mobility, handicaps such as minority group membership or old age, etc.
4. The adjustment area (called "delinquency") where the real concern is adjustments of authority-submission which have become emotionally charged to the point that normal processes of empathy and intellect cannot work toward satisfying human relationships.

A general, underlying purpose for the entire course is the improvement of objective verbalizations, both individually and in groups. Probably no process is more rewarding than group thinking about the emotionally charged frustrations of daily living. This kind of verbal expression is, in our opinion, "normal multiple counseling".

For content and a basic framework a textbook had to be constructed, since other texts were tried out and found to be unsuitable to either the viewpoint or the dual arrangement of the course.[1] Students are pressured by frequent quizzes, given according to an assignment sheet covering the entire semester, but allowing for content materials to be concentrated in the first half-semester. Collateral reading is required in various psychological journals and in the Journal of Marriage and Family Living, according to student choice. A second book is read in its entirety in the library.[2] Class periods are used by students as a service to their reading. Consequently the instructor-leader avoids rehash of material which should have been read before the class period started. However, illustrations from newspapers, magazines, and journals are often given.

The room arrangement is a pair of concentric horseshoes with a table or desk at the open end. Films, classroom demonstrations, test-inventories, and the like are used to help get thoughts and feelings out into the open for verbalization during the content-oriented stage of the

---

[1]Patty, W. L. and Johnson, *Personality and Adjustment*. N. Y. McGraw-Hill Co., 1953. Also the teaching manual.

[2]White, R. W., *Lives in Progress*. N. Y. Dryden Press, 1954.

course. Later, class periods are devoted to buzz-group work which leads into the more serious multiple counseling process in which each buzz-group presents its conclusions to the class for evaluation.

Each buzz-group of four or five students has an area of adjustment within which its work is confined, i.e. courtship, home and family, etc. The instructor-leader meets with each group, rotating around the classroom according to invitation and serves as both motivation and resource person. He gives guidance which encourages the students to consider their own experiences, to discuss in terms of the concepts and research findings of earlier class meetings, and to carry the discussions outside the classroom to the coffee shop or into the home. Five or six buzz-groups work in the classroom at once. During the time a buzz-group is presenting its conclusions for class evaluation, speeches are ruled out. No person may speak longer than two minutes at any one time. The entire buzz-group is expected to reach agreement, avoiding minority reports before presenting itself. Discussion is vigorous, purposeful and with good understanding of feelings and needs of individuals involved. The instructor-leader strives to center attention on the buzz-group but is constantly active during these evaluation periods. Need for skill at this stage must not be overlooked.

OUTCOMES

Outcomes for the whole group are best illustrated in the frequency and intensity with which the group takes hold of its own members when one expresses feelings indicative of poor emotional insight. Understanding, considerateness, and a wish to be helpful seem to develop objectivity in the discussions.

Individual members are, by the end of the semester, typically able to read the books on personality dynamics, to help each other analyze approaches to problems as well as to recognize egocentric reactions with fair reliability.

Such achievements are frequently mentioned by students as their expectation when they come to register for the second semester of psychology. The appearance of younger brothers and sisters in these classes in later semesters (at the urging of former students) is also noteworthy.

One buzz-group took on permanent status and now, three years after, is still meeting about once a month. Its members feel greater personal competence, having discovered a means of resolving tensions through the verbal process of group thinking and the satisfying security of understanding effective communication.

5

A MULTIPLE COUNSELING APPROACH IN AN
EDUCATIONAL PSYCHOLOGY COURSE

by PROFESSOR CARLETON P. MENGE

UNIVERSITY OF NEW HAMPSHIRE

The one semester course has as its purpose for the students who plan to go into the teaching field, a self-examination of personal value structures and improved understanding of teaching, education, and life in general. Emphasis is placed upon individual interpretations and feelings of the students relating to the subject matter and its application in reality situations.

The students in this course are chiefly sophomores considering teaching as a vocation. Teacher candidates are screened in the Junior year and one year of Educational Psychology is prerequisite. Immediately upon entrance to the course, students have individual interviews with the instructor and summary conferences are held at the end of the semester. During the semester the instructor is available eighteen hours a week for counseling interviews with members of the group. Enrollment in the course runs from ten to twenty-five students who meet three times a week for fifty-minute periods.

Course content follows the usual chronological sequence of human growth and development: prenatal influences, early infant characteristics, childhood, adolescence, and early adulthood. The major concepts in Educational Psychology as given by Skinner[1] are developed: creative experiencing, pupil-purposing, continuous growth, social functioning, goal-seeking, and intelligent self-direction.

While the above outline of developmental psychology forms the subject matter, the major emphasis is placed on the student's realization of the concepts within himself — past, present, and future. Students write self-evaluations around the ideas that they feel "working" within themselves. There are no textbooks and reading assignments vary year by year. A list of references used for reading assignments in a recent course included:

Wolfe, "Look Homeward, Angel"; Gesell, "Infant and Child in the Culture of Today"; Huxley, "Brave New World"; Montagu, "On Being Human"; Carroll, "Christmas without Johnny"; Baruch, "New Ways in Discipline"; Gesell, "The Child from Five to Ten"; Saroyan, "The Human Comedy"; Jersild, "In Search of Self"; Moravia, "Two Adolescents"; Rogers, "Client-Centered Therapy"; Hurlock, "Adolescent Development"; Salinger, "Catcher in the Rye"; Snygg and

---

[1]Skinner, C. S. (ed.) *Educational Psychology*, 3rd ed. N. Y. Prentice-Hall, 1951.

331

Coombs, "Individual Behavior"; Fromm, "Escape from Freedom"; May, "Man's Search for Himself"; Jersild, "When Teachers Face Themselves".

Four films used in the course were: "Life with Baby", "Learning to Understand Children", "Angry Boy", and "Passion for Life".

An example of the integration of subject matter, reading assignments, and application is as follows: the instructor introduced the cliché "Competition is the spice of life". The group discusses this in relation to college life, American society, the nature of man. Montagu's "On Being Human" is assigned. In a succeeding class period his views, their authenticity, other data from psychology and sociology are examined. Then group members re-examine themselves in terms of their individual concepts and attitudes.

In lieu of a final examination, research projects are selected by class members according to their interests. These projects may be academic or intensely personal. Some examples of choices are:

1. The general problem of mental health in the United States was studied by a girl who couldn't face herself because her father was in a mental institution.
2. Parental domination was studied by a boy whose father was headmaster in a private school.
3. Information on Alcoholic Anonymous was sought by a girl whose parents were alcoholics.
4. Natural childbirth was studied by a pregnant student.

Although class performance affected the final grade, the permissive atmosphere established by the instructor minimized the importance of verbal skill in discussions. The seminar paper and evidence of learning from the reading assignments were used in grading. And the student's own self-ratings plus the instructor's estimate of personal growth influenced the final grades heavily. Appraisal of personal growth was in line with the objectives of the course, viz, to demonstrate the living concepts of personal growth, not merely state them as psychological possibilities. Real change in behavior — chiefly attitudes — is the proof of a successful semester.

The role of the instructor as group leader and counselor was based on concepts of nondirective and group-centered teaching roles developed by Axelrod.[2] The leader's chief concern is the growth of individual class members. He shifts leadership from himself to class members without formal or obvious devices. He changes his own roles continually, according to the appropriateness: resource person, participating member, interested observer and so on.

[2]Axelrod, Joseph, "Group Dynamics, Nondirective Therapy, and College Teaching", *The Journal of Higher Education*, April, 1955.

When class members need the support of the leader he provides this, but only on a temporary basis and not to fill an excessive need for affection, support, power over others or other ego needs. Students who need depth counseling are referred to the student counseling center.

When the group bogs down or suffers discomfort in some other way, the leader attempts to alleviate the situation, using clarification and interpretation. He also tries, when essential to class progress and member growth, to sharpen issues facing the group without himself acting as judge or using authority to influence the group viewpoint. Likewise he does not use his authority status in dealing with deviant behavior among class members.

An evaluating device was developed in order that individual students could assess their progress and performance in the course. It was used for discussion in the summary conference with the student and also for assigning the final grade. A replica is shown below:

GROWTH PROFILE IN EDUCATION

for_____

	A	B	C	D	F	No Evidence
1. Self-recorded average (final self-evaluation)............						
2. Treatment of ideas presented in readings, as reported in self-evaluations:........................						
(1) Quality						
(2) Quantity						
3. Treatment of ideas presented in class, as reported in self-evaluations:........................						
(1) Quality						
(2) Quantity						
4. Effectiveness of self-evaluations in analyzing own personal philosophy and psychology...............						
5. Personal value, depth and quality of research paper......						
6. Pursuit of ideas beyond the class situation						
7. Class participation:...............................						
(1) Quality						
(2) Quantity						
8. Social responsibility as revealed by type of class participation						
9. Effectiveness of communication:......................						
(1) Oral						
(2) Written						
10. Free exchange of ideas in conference....................						
11. Learning demeanor: approach to projects requiring analysis (e.g. writing in class)						
12. Degree of involvement, "blood-letting", "pants dropping"						
13. General quality of growth in terms of ability and pertinent environmental factors......................						

Grade_____

N.B. Any point that you feel needs clarification please use the reverse side of this sheet.

Confusion and conflict arise in individual students when faced with complete freedom from quizzes and exams and from compulsory attendance at classes. Pressure on them to face themselves as they are and to grow into a mature person in so far as they are able is something new. A course of this kind is a change-agent. It "floors" some students and "challenges" others. Examples of different effects on students are found in excerpts from self-evaluations: (written at different times during the course).

STUDENT I — *An eighteen-year-old Sophomore girl, majoring in Biology.*

"Being a student in Ed. 41 is really a torturous experience, provided one obtains everything from the course that is expected. Since the objective of this course is to provide profound experiences that will produce change within each student, the course is one of those labeled 'a gut course'. Changing and facing reality are two very hard tasks.

"It would seem that the students fall into three groups . . . those with blasé attitudes . . . a second group which changed to varying degrees although none of them were outstanding in their change . . . many remained greatly confused . . . A third group represents those who were fortunate enough to be able to become involved deeply and yet to overcome the confusement and change for the better. It was in this group that the remarkable changes can be seen — sometimes it is in ideas, but these ideas can affect the attitudes and actual appearance of the student.

"Never before have I partaken in such a controversial affair as this Ed. 41 course . . . It seems though that what this course does is *speed up the psychological growth* that would have come about sooner or later anyway. Is it necessary to take a course to think about matters which we think about every day anyway in order to become teachers? Also, is it good to have confused teachers molding the minds of the youth?"

STUDENT 2 — *A twenty-year-old Sophomore, majoring in secretarial studies.*

Oct. — "I am not sure I understand what you want on these papers, but as I see it, you want them to be spontaneous, an extemporaneous reaction to what we have been discussing in class and what we have been reading . . . My first reaction in regard to Brave New World — as Savage said, 'I don't want comfort. I want God, I want poetry, I want real danger, I want freedom, I want sin.' This is exactly how I feel. I think it was good for me to read this book. It's the type I never would have read of my own accord."

Jan. — "There were three difficulties I came back to school with this year (1) A defensive attitude toward my father's illness . . . (2) a feeling of self-consciousness, that is, a fear of speaking up to people, and (3) a desire to date more as I had never dated much. These three difficulties have resolved themselves to a considerable degree in this one semester of school . . .

"The last and final thing that I found extremely beneficial was the open and free attitude of discussions in class . . . as others began to voice their feelings, I loosened up. I now realize there is nothing to be ashamed of . . . Moreover, the thinking which was provoked in class extended outside of class . . . even my family became involved . . ."

STUDENT 3 — *A twenty-four-year-old married veteran, majoring in Vocational Agriculture.*

Feb. — "The first day of school after four years absence . . . I had heard about progressive education — most information was not favorable but I was interested to see it working and to take part in it . . .

"One guy, talking about class today, said it had no point, no conclusion; I agree. It was stimulating in a different way, but I haven't figured it out . . ."

April — "This period since the last self-evaluation paper has, for the most part, left me discouraged in class . . .

"The class discussion concerned the fact that we should take a stand and be able to support our beliefs. We should get excited about things and say or act our feelings. This is all very well but very hard to do . . .

"These last few days I have been excited, not about the topics especially, but the class itself. I go in, sit down and feel like there is going to be an hour exam or something I know nothing about. Yet I know there is no reason for the feeling, still it remains."

May — "One of the most outstanding factors, and forms the most important part of the course, has been the individual appointments with Menge. Even when my interest in the class lagged, and I even became disgusted, these interviews continued to stimulate my interest and ideas . . .

"As I got more interested in my particular topic of teaching, it seemed that I became more interested in each class in Education as well as my other subjects."

OUTCOMES

The outcomes of the course in Educational Psychology — from instructor and student evaluations over the years — can be generalized as follows:

1. *The whole group:* enjoyment of learning; specific awareness of group process and dynamics; broadened concepts of life, education, teaching, and self; growth of social responsibility for group direction.

2. *The individual:* self-appraisal, improved understanding of self and others; improved concept of vocational goal and commitment to it; improved interactive skills and self-integration.

3. *Carryover:* students sought other courses that yield more than information; they used counseling services more freely and frequently.

IMPLICATIONS AND ADVICE TO OTHER COLLEGE TEACHERS

This type of course is valuable and successful in proportion to the awareness of the individual of himself and his society. His motivation must be based in a desire for personal growth. The larger the group, the less benefit to the individual members. Thus a group of 25 shows diminished returns over a group of 10. For the success of the course, external signs of progress must not be stressed, and "working for grades" in the usual sense must be eliminated from the course design.

A T-GROUP IN AN EARLY SESSION. THE DISCUSSION PRODUCED SOME FACTS THE GROUP AGREED ON. SUMMARY ON THE BLACKBOARD LISTS (A) WE DON'T HAVE A WAY OF INTRODUCING A QUESTION (B) NEED FACTS BEFORE CONSENSUS (C) WE ACCEPT AN UNCLEAR UNDERSTANDING OF THE QUESTION. *(see article 2)*

SECTION II — SYMPOSIUM

PART THREE

PROFESSIONAL TRAINING
AND RESEARCH: USE OF SMALL-GROUP DISCUSSION

List of Articles

1

A GRADUATE COURSE IN GROUP TECHNIQUES IN GUIDANCE
by Professor George L. Keppers, *Director of Counselor Training*
University of New Mexico, Albuquerque, N. M.

2

THE T-GROUP: A LEARNING LABORATORY FOR LEADERSHIP SKILLS
by Helen Driver, *Delegate, Bethel Session*
The National Training Laboratories in Group Development

3

THE THERAPEUTIC GROUP EXPERIENCE AS A COURSE
IN THE THEOLOGICAL SCHOOL CURRICULUM
by Professor Robert C. Leslie, Pacific School of Religion, Berkeley, Calif.

4

RESOLVING THE RESISTANCE OF INTELLECTUALIZATION
IN SEMINARY STUDENTS
by Chaplain Robert G. Foulkes, The Presbyterian Hospital, Philadelphia, Pa.

5

A TRAINING COURSE IN PASTORAL COUNSELING
by Professor Paul E. Johnson,
Boston University School of Theology, Boston, Mass.

6

A GROUP DISCUSSION APPROACH IN TRAINING COURSES FOR NURSES
AND RELIGIOUS COUNSELORS
by Chaplain W. B. Bristow, Glendale Sanitarium and Hospital, Glendale, Calif.

337

7

INFORMAL DISCUSSION GROUPS FOR GRADUATE STUDENTS
IN CHRISTIAN EDUCATION
from The General Assembly's Training School
Presbyterian Church, U. S. A., Richmond, Va.

8

THE NAVY CHARACTER EDUCATION PROGRAM: USE OF DISCUSSION GROUPS
by F. H. Wickham, LCDR, CHC, USN, San Francisco, Calif.

9

SOLVING A DE-SEGREGATION PROBLEM THROUGH SMALL-GROUP ACTIVITY
by Frank C. Mabee, Jr., *Director of Christian Education*
Texas Board of Christian Churches, Fort Worth, Texas

10

RESEARCH INTO BUZZ-GROUP METHOD WITH
IN-SERVICE CLASSES FOR TEACHERS
by Professor Jjuji Misumi, Kyushu University, Japan

11

TRAINING PROGRAM ON CONFERENCE LEADERSHIP IN INDUSTRY
by Dr. Harold R. Burke, *Coordinator of Academic Counseling*
University of Connecticut

Training courses for many professional workers often include learning in the field of human relations. The personal growth of the trainee is important: better understanding of himself and others; empathetic and interpersonal skills; ability to be an effective group member and leader.

The eleven articles in Part 3 present many unique illustrations of the use of the intimate group and small-group discussion in professional training courses.

1

A GRADUATE COURSE IN GROUP TECHNIQUES IN GUIDANCE

by PROFESSOR GEORGE L. KEPPERS, *Director of Counselor Training*
UNIVERSITY OF NEW MEXICO

An effective teaching-learning method in a graduate summer school at the University of Colorado used the classroom as a laboratory for experience and practice of group techniques in guidance. There were nineteen students, eight women and eleven men, with varying backgrounds as follows: one director of guidance, five secondary school counselors, eight teachers (various subjects), four teacher-counselors, one elementary school counselor. Twelve students were candidates for the Masters degree; seven were doctoral candidates. The class met one hour daily for five weeks, a total of twenty-five meetings.

The first day was devoted to orienting the students, securing biographical data, and briefing the group on suggested readings: Bennett's "Guidance in Groups", Driver's "Multiple Counseling", Gibb's "Dynamics of Participative Groups", Hoppock's "Group Guidance Principles: Techniques and Evaluation", and Moreno's "Who Shall Survive". The readings were to provide a basis for discussion as well as an understanding of group techniques.

The second meeting, and for the duration of the five weeks, the seats were arranged in the form of a circle. As a get-acquainted device, the members of the class were divided at random into groups of three. Each trio was given four minutes to learn as many facts as possible about its members. Then, instead of self-reports or introductions, the students gave reports of each other. The class liked this procedure and it was the consensus that whenever possible, group techniques be learned by using them in the class. The instructor raised the question of what techniques the group wished to study. To pursue this question the class was divided into small groups and given five minutes to list as many group techniques used in Guidance as they could. The following topics were listed, and a selection was made from the list for the individual and group work of the course:

Buzz sessions	Multiple counseling	Field trips
Panel discussions	Case studies	Career and college days
Debates	Sociometrics	Class in Occupations
Role-playing	Audio-visual aids	

The instructor as group leader assumed various roles during the 24 sessions. These varied from being very directive to that of being nondirective, if one can assume there is such a continuum. To be more specific, the instructor at times gave specific reading assignments — especially at the beginning of the course. At other times, he was a listener, interrogator, clarifier, dissenter, observer, played the role of a father, a junior high student, or just one of the group working through a mutual or personal problem.

At times, the students assumed the leadership for group activities. A typical illustration had to do with the techniques of sociodrama and

339

sociometrics. One of the students assumed the role of an eighth-grade teacher and the group assumed roles of the pupils. The sociodrama and resulting sociogram provided some very down-to-earth discussion of the use of these techniques in studying the structure of interpersonal relationships within a group. The sociogram developed out of the sociodrama when the teacher wished to form sub-groups and asked the pupils to indicate the three they would like to work with (1st, 2nd, and 3rd choice).

When the class activity was role-playing, whoever was leader at the time took the initiative in getting others to play various roles. It was most difficult to get the full cooperation of the students. There was considerable apprehension regarding the value of the technique and participating in it. Several of the group refused to participate actively in role-playing. However, the others who did take roles reported they felt much better toward the group and the role-playing activity as a result of participating. In one particular situation one of the "actors" stopped the role-playing as she said to the person playing the father-role, "You remind me too much of my father." In general, the group and the instructor found that role-playing situations led into discussions effectively, and the advantages or disadvantages of the activity for various groups, in and out of school, were fully discussed.

In some sessions the group made considerable progress in discussing their own personal and job problems. This usually developed spontaneously. However, the instructor used some structuring to encourage this activity by announcing that personal, pseudo, or real pupil problems could be brought up for discussion and assistance with solutions.

On several occasions the group member around whom the discussion centered would appear at the instructor's office after the session for further help. Often a counseling interview would be arranged.

One member of the class, on his own volition, made a modified quantitative analysis of the group participation by checking the number of times each member responded during a session. All but three members contributed and the number of responses was well distributed with the exception of the leader who talked too much that day. This fact pointed up the compulsion on the part of the instructor for keeping the discussion moving in order that various techniques could be introduced and discussed. Perhaps this is a weakness of structure and method in an "experimental laboratory" course: not as much material can be covered as in a traditional-type course.

Student Evaluations

An evaluation of the course came from the students during the last few sessions. They felt quite free to express their reactions and to criticize the laboratory method in any way they wished. The following is a summary of verbal and written statements:

— When I first came to this class I just knew I wouldn't enjoy it but I have since been able to "talk out" and I feel much better.

— I think role-playing is O. K. but I don't want to do it myself. I would like to try it with some Junior High pupils who aren't so inhibited.

— The greatest value of this course has been its lesson in the amazing effectiveness of group discussion techniques. It has been of considerable interest to watch quite good interpersonal relationships develop in so short a time.

— The amount of personal revelation which occurred is indicative of the acceptance of the members of each other.

— From a group of strangers nodding perfunctory greetings five weeks ago, we have emerged a friendly bunch, genuinely interested in the problems of the others and sincerely concerned with offering advice or suggestions to help in some way.

— Our class of graduate students had a tendency to drift. At other times individuals would tend to monopolize the discussion and then others would not speak out on their views. Yet we seemed to get at a great many different and important topics. On days when we seemed to drift, it appeared that we accomplished a great deal. For one accustomed to being in a very highly structured classroom, the group participation approach was very new.

— There is more threat to the security of the individual in group work since it encourages more student participation. This may cause some to try to shrink within themselves.

— It was actually seeing group techniques used in our class that made them meaningful.

— My attitude toward group techniques is one of cautious enthusiasm and is reflected in the desire to try out these methods in my classes next year.

— I have learned to appreciate the group atmosphere and this, I believe, is the one most important result of the course. I can now appreciate the apprehension of a group and the problems of the leader.

— I learned how different people react in a group situation. It was interesting to see how different students "behaved": there was the listener, tension-reducer, dissenter, and others.

— Teachers want immediate results; they are in a hurry; they must meet a schedule. All of these are to a degree contrary to the nature of group procedures.

— I have learned to be more patient and not expect sudden results.

— Knowing myself, I think I can use group procedures in a limited way only. I will attempt group techniques only where I am somewhat sure of good results. By gaining confidence in these small areas, I or any other teacher with similar reservations, may be able to grow with the group and thus gain confidence in using more varied techniques.

341

Instructor Evaluation

The instructor of the course — group leader — gave the following evaluation points:

1. Using the techniques to learn the techniques is an active teaching-learning process.
2. A heterogeneous group adds variety (and depth) to the discussions.
3. The leader must be capable of playing many roles.
4. The sessions should be frequent enough to permit continuity of discussion. (A minimum of three meetings per week.)
5. If the leader has confidence in the students, they will develop into a functioning group.
6. A small amount of structuring is sufficient.
7. The leader must control his compulsion to get things done in a hurry and to feel that every topic must be covered.
8. The leader must be informal and gain acceptance as a member of the group. Yet he must keep the respect of the group as a resource person.

2

THE T-GROUP: A LEARNING LABORATORY FOR LEADERSHIP SKILLS

by HELEN DRIVER, *Delegate, Bethel Session*

NATIONAL TRAINING LABORATORY IN GROUP DEVELOPMENT

Training programs in human relations and group development use small-group discussion as the activity to teach trainees problem-solving techniques in groups. Understanding of oneself and others in the group, the various leadership roles, aids and blocks to group progress — these knowledges are basic to skill development. Through participation in a problem-solving group the trainee learns not only how to become a more effective group member but also how to lead a group more skillfully.

The laboratory group is called the T-Group, consisting of 15-17 students, assisted by a staff member. The group meets for two-hour sessions daily during the three-week summer session of the National Training Laboratories. There is no leader, no agenda, no procedure in the group activity. All group members have equal status regardless of the position or prestige in back-home life. Each member hopes he will learn something to help him in his job or other human relations. Usually these hopes relate to committees, boards of directors, industrial conference or subordinate groups, church organizations and the like. For in the T-Group may be ministers, industrial executives, school administrators and teachers, supervisors of nursing, social workers, etc.

The goals of individual group members relate in varying degrees to one or more of the four objectives of human relations institutes and workshops:

1. *Diagnostic sensitivity* — awareness of one's own feelings and the feelings of others; ability to analyze interactions and performance in a problem-solving group.

2. *Group development concepts* — group dynamics, change-agents in groups, factors favoring or preventing progress in group problem-solving.

3. *Behavioral skill in groups* — how group members fill the needed roles of participation and leadership.

4. *Carryover of knowledges and skills* — how to put them to work in back-home situations.

The task of the T-Group is explained in the first session by the staff member: to develop its own leadership; define the problems it wants to work on; agree on procedures; initiate and carry out the activities in line with the goal; test progress; finally, to evaluate the results.

The group must first weld itself into an effective problem-solving organization. Usually it spends all three weeks trying to do just that. The obstacles purposely built into the structure of the "laboratory" consist of too large a group, too great heterogeneity among the membership, absence of rules and regulations, no steps of progression or guideposts to follow, no assigned task for the group to accomplish.

Agreement (and consensus of all members is usually sought) on anything is almost impossible to achieve. Each individual has his own idea about goals, methods, procedures, evaluation, according to his professional background. Feelings of hostility, anxiety, frustration become rampant as the group struggles to become a group instead of an aggregate of individuals. One after another, the courageous attempts of members to assume leadership and "get something done" are beaten down in a storm of disagreements and expressions of dissatisfaction. One learns much about himself and the others in the group during this painful experience, viz, diagnostic sensitivity.

Learning to listen to and interpret correctly the verbal contribution of a group member is difficult because of the necessity of understanding the feelings as well as the word meanings involved. It takes many group sessions to become well acquainted with fellow members so as to understand their reactions and behavior in the group. This is an important skill, useful in all kinds of human relations situations.

The surface behavior of members of a problem-solving group may be classified into eighteen verbal actions, as follows:

Defining and stating a problem	Supporting fellow members
Asking for opinion	Opposing fellow members
Giving opinion	Setting up and invoking rules
Asking for information	Testing for feasibility
Giving information	Aiding members to participate
Asking for clarification	Taking consensus
Giving clarification	Summarizing
Asking for problem solutions	Compromising
Suggesting problem solutions	Harmonizing

Many of us have had the unpleasant experience of serving on a committee where the authoritarian chairman did all the work and railroaded through an agenda without the committee members having a chance to perform any of the problem-solving functions essential to a democratic group. On the other hand, the skilled chairman allows his committee members to take responsibility for filling needed roles in the problem-solving process, to the satisfaction of the whole group.

In the T-Group the members *must* assume the leadership functions. According to Dr. Robert Blake, staff instructor at the Bethel Laboratory Session:

"In T-Groups we are now having the opportunity of learning when these roles need to be supplied, how to supply them, and the consequence for the development of the group when they are inadequately represented. This approach constitutes the microscopic view. The challenge of effective group membership is to be able skillfully to act in the role requirements that must be supplied for effective action."

An illustration of the difficulty in reaching agreement in the leaderless T-Group concerned a proposal by the staff member that group members take turns in observing the group, since the observations might help the group to see what is happening as far as blocks or aids to progress are concerned. During the discussion the group became hopelessly split into two factions: one believed the group should follow the suggestion, the other believed it was better for everyone to participate and observe at the same time. The battle for consensus went on for an hour and a half, ending in a stalemate. To the outsider this would seem to be a great waste of time; to the T-Group it was fraught with meaningful learning. The various leadership and blocking roles played by individuals were seen and understood; the strong feelings and head-on clashes helped group members to understand themselves and others better. The fact that all seventeen members were emotionally involved in the problem at hand helped each to learn something.

Thus the T-Group provides group action in slow-motion, with a chance to "play back" past performances for the purpose of analyzing and evaluating both individual and group behavior. The staff member encourages the group to stop action and consider what is happening in the group. Tape recordings are made of all sessions, so that a play-back of any part of a discussion can be done. Often it will be found that a majority of the group are bored, disgruntled or unhappy with the topic under discussion but no one was quite ready to do anything about it. Sometimes it takes a lot of courage to break into the rolling momentum of a group discussion even when one is convinced of the wrong direction.

The T-Group resembles a therapy group for the length of time needed for clear understanding of fellow members' motivational and personality characteristics. Ideally this is accomplished before an effective problem-solving group is achieved. Actually it doesn't happen in a T-Group: usually there are two or three members who never fully expose themselves and their feelings sufficiently to become "in-all-over" participants.

A succinct explanation of the T-Group was given in a summary session of a Bethel workshop by Dr. Leland Bradford, Director of the National Training Laboratory in Group Development:

> "*The T-Group training provides fluid, unstructured groups in which every person becomes deeply involved; in which problems of leadership, decision-making, interpersonal problems, hidden agenda (so typical of all staff meetings) are seen in slow motion.*
>
> *In such a group the individual becomes more diagnostically sensitive to what happens in groups; becomes aware of the ways in which groups grow; gains in self-awareness.*
>
> *The group provides opportunity for trainees to behave; to secure feed-back on their behavior; to experiment with new ideas of leadership and membership . . . to get — on the 'feeling' as well as 'intellectual' level — a real awareness of the problems of group organization, functioning and growth.*"

The T-Group method, originating in the work of Kurt Lewin, has been developed and expanded by the National Training Laboratories.[1] It is widely used as a core activity in training institutes and workshops for human relations. Usually such training courses also include lectures, group experiments, demonstrations of large as well as small group activities. However, participants in these training courses tend to agree that the T-Group experience is the most unique and meaningful part of the learning.

---

[1]National Training Laboratories in Group Development. *Explorations in Human Relations Training, 1947–53.* Washington, D. C., 1955.

3

THE THERAPEUTIC GROUP EXPERIENCE AS A COURSE
IN THE THEOLOGICAL SCHOOL CURRICULUM

by PROFESSOR ROBERT C. LESLIE

PACIFIC SCHOOL OF RELIGION, BERKELEY, CALIFORNIA

The training of ministers has only recently included the study of interpersonal relationships and even then the work has usually been done as an academic exercise, as in a seminar dealing with Harry Stack Sullivan, or in an institutional setting, as in programs of clinical pastoral training. It is this writer's conviction that there is a place within the theological school curriculum for regular courses stressing the dynamic relationships that exist between people in groups and that such courses need to be developed as group experiences that have many of the characteristics of therapy groups.

The need for the minister's deeper understanding of emotional involvement in group activity is quite apparent. The contemporary church calls for leadership that is group-centered more often than individual-centered, since the complexity of the minister's role makes intimate individual contacts with all his parishioners virtually impossible. *To seek to accomplish therapeutic purposes indirectly through developing an adequate emotional climate for productive growth throughout the group organization of the church seems to be a more realistic goal than an ambitious program of direct personal counseling.*

To help students to sense what is involved in creating a therapeutic atmosphere in group activity, at Pacific School of Religion we include in the regular curriculum an elective course carrying two quarter-hour credits called "Group Therapy and Mental Health." Limited in enrollment to twelve, the course has no prerequisite but is clearly announced as a therapeutic group experience. At least three goals are sought in such a seminary course.

Course Objectives

The first goal is to study what happens whenever people come together in group activity so that it becomes possible to identify barriers to real communication. Thus, for example, a seminary group was encouraged to discuss reactions felt by the men present when they found two women enrolled in the group. Prejudices about women in seminary were explored, tendencies toward rivalry for the girls' favors were considered, and the inclination to consider the two women as a unit rather

346

than as two individuals was thoroughly discussed. Such discussion helped to clear the way for freer communication that did not overlook sex differences but accepted them and moved beyond them.

Another goal of the seminary group is to recognize the determining role played by feelings, especially negative feelings. Thus, for instance, when a member came in late, the whole group discussed their reactions to being interrupted, and then went on to try to understand the late-comer's feelings. Next they explored the meaning of promptness and tardiness in other areas in their lives.

A third goal is to sense the primary significance of the leader's role in any group. By helping the group to identify and explore their feelings toward the leader when he ignored the usual class pattern of taking a break after the first fifty minutes, the leader in one group enabled the members to realize that they needed to work through these and similar feelings toward the leader before their progress as a group could move forward.

Procedures

With such goals in mind, the seminary group meets once a week for two-hour sessions during the twelve-week quarter. The course follows no agenda, has no outline, and has no goal other than an increased awareness of what happens between group members as they try to relate to each other and to the leader in a meaningful way. The focus of attention is kept on the immediate current situation; nothing has higher priority than what is happening at the moment in the group itself. Tangential excursions, however interesting, are discouraged as the leader helps the group to keep to its central task of exploring what is happening in the group and encouraging the expression of personal feelings. For instance, in the opening session of one group meeting in the Fall, the leader directed attention away from personal reminiscing about summer travel to the immediate situation: the pattern of seating, note-taking, meeting strangers, relating to the leader.

To sharpen sensitivity in observation and to stimulate investigation into the meaning of observed behavior, each member of the group serves in turn as observer. A brief (eight minute) report of verbal and non-verbal interactions is written up and read aloud by the observer in the succeeding meeting. The group gives its reactions to the report. Sometimes an observer will choose to diagram lines of verbal interaction; another may prefer to concentrate on what he believed were the real attitudes being conveyed non-verbally (as in alert or reclining postures) and in verbal participation (ranging from clarifying to ridiculing). These written reports become the record of the work of the group and are available for individual discussion with the instructor and for comparing the seminary group with other groups discussed in the literature.

Leadership Role

Basic in such a project is the kind of leadership employed. A major goal is to demonstrate leadership that exercises authority without being authoritarian. This means that the leader accepts the responsibility for providing a clear structure within which the group is to work, but refuses to be cast as the authority with specific answers. Thus, for example, when a group member tells an irrelevant story, the leader reminds the group that story-telling is not the purpose of the group. He then invites the group to consider what prompted the telling of the story, how typical it was of the story-teller to assume that particular role, and what the reaction of each person was to the story-telling. Refusing to supply answers himself, the leader provides encouraging support as the group members search out answers to illumine the behavior just observed. Often they can draw from their own experiences in similar situations. In this fashion the leader plays a role that goes beyond friendly interest to therapeutic concern, that confronts behavior realistically but with the intent of understanding rather than condemning.

RESULTS

Results achieved in such a program are difficult to evaluate, especially in the brief span of a single quarter. Some students, more resistant to the therapeutic orientation than others, have a hard time sharing their feelings. They tend to withhold emotional investment in the project and so can make little progress in personal growth and in the understanding of others. On the whole, however, several specific gains can be noted as a result of the therapeutic group experience. The support of the group often brings to light expression of feelings that are interfering with real communication. These feelings are pretty carefully hidden so that their expression comes as a considerable surprise to the group. For example, these feelings may relate to such matters as the perception of leadership, or to ease of participation, or to anxieties about minority group members, or to discomfort in an agendaless group discussion. The obvious implication is that such feelings are always present in any group and that until they are handled, good communication will be difficult.

348

Group members gain in sensitivity to others. A heightened awareness of the high degree of interaction going on in even the apparently passive type of group makes for significant learning. Not only recognizing and handling feelings, but learning to catch the cues, both verbal and non-verbal, is important. Thus one becomes sensitized to what is really going on and the group members become more confident about working with people rather than depending on an agenda. One group, for example, discussing the apparent withdrawal of a member, told of similar situations in which they had withdrawn for reasons that were important to them but unknown to the group.

Another important outcome is a new confidence in the group process which results when the members experience working through tension-situations rather than taking the more common path of evasion. Under good leadership touchy subjects are dealt with openly, and, indeed, are lifted up for examination if they do not come up naturally. For example, a group member became so angry with the group that she left abruptly, slamming the door. The group focussed on what had happened that prompted her behavior and considered ways of helping her back into rapport with the group. Because the leader demonstrated his confidence in the capacity of the group to handle this emotional explosion, the group met the issue head-on and worked it through to a meaningful solution.

An allied outcome, close to the group confidence in itself, is learning that a group can do much more in changing personal patterns through its acceptance of individuals than by pressuring them. Every student group in my experience has attempted to compel a group member to change his pattern of relatedness to others in the group. In each instance the group discovers how futile such an approach really is. The implications for preaching and for pastoral counseling are very obvious here.

A final achievement gained through the group experience is the awareness on the part of each individual of his own customary pattern in group activity, and of the typical roles emerging in a group. Thus a group becomes aware of the fact that one member habitually handles tensions with a humorous story, whereas another avoids the situation by denial of any recognition of stress. One member may habitually attack the leader while another customarily defends him; one member tends to ask questions while another participates by quoting an authority. Although little time is available for attempts at modifying roles, the groundwork for modification is laid.

A realistic carryover of the experiential learning was described by a student who had taken the course in another school under the leadership of the present writer:

"This work has meant more to me than any other course in seminary. This week, for the first time, I was able to pray with some sense of prayer being real. I think the reason was that I have begun to understand people better and to accept myself more. I was able to accept the hostility of a parishioner without getting upset, and over the week-end my wife and I were able to discuss why each of us has had to be so defensive with each other, leading to constant quarreling. All this has been made possible because I first was able to participate freely in our student group."

4

RESOLVING THE RESISTANCE OF INTELLECTUALIZATION
IN SEMINARY STUDENTS

by CHAPLAIN ROBERT G. FOULKES

THE PRESBYTERIAN HOSPITAL, PHILADELPHIA, PA.

A program in Hospital Ministry is held at our hospital for Princeton Theological Seminary students who spend each Saturday here during the school year exclusive of exam periods and vacations. This is a total of twenty-five sessions distributed from October to May. The group is limited to six students who are selected by the Chaplain through personal interviews with interested applicants. They receive remuneration and Field Work Credit, a specified number of such credits being required for graduation.

The day is divided into two parts, half for patient visitation and half for discussion sessions. Private interviews with the Chaplain may be arranged in addition to the general discussion periods by students who wish it. Also special features are introduced from time to time: observation of operations, post mortems, participation in planned recreation with psychotic patients (at another hospital), discussions with doctors in such specialties as surgery, obstetrics and gynecology, anesthesiology, radiology, etc.

One of the important goals in training seminary students in hospital visitation is to increase the student's sensitivity to the emotional and spiritual need of the patient and to encourage his own flexibility in responding to these needs.

Group discussion of the material is the primary medium for such learning but constantly faces the problem imposed by the students' tendency to over-intellectualize. This natural trend is heightened by the academic seminary environment and poses a difficult barrier to dynamic sharing and understanding.

In order to deepen both the level of discussion and the emphasis on interpersonal relationships, a technique aimed at *resolving the resistance* has been used for several years as follows:

1. At the beginning of the discussion period a student or the leader will present an account of an actual visitation situation.
2. Next, the group is asked to free-associate to the problem presented, writing these thoughts down on paper. There is no time limit set and when the last person seems to be "written out", the leader closes the period of writing.
3. Then, each person in turn, including the leader, reads aloud exactly what he has written. No one is to comment on what is read and the reader must not edit his reading in any way.
4. Now the whole process of association, writing, and reading is repeated. (The stimulus for this round involves the first-round readings.)
5. This procedure is repeated until the leader senses a sufficient break-through of feeling responses (taking over for the academic ones.)
6. Now a discussion begins: the importance of feelings; what different feelings mean to members of the group and what they mean to patients, etc.

The shift from academic material and stylized responses to personal feelings and responses becomes obvious to all through this approach.

In analyzing the change that takes place we find, almost consistently, that the first round of associations and writing is filled with definite content suggestions, problem-solving statements, and considerable philosophical and theological speculation. Most of this is irrelevant to the emotional involvement of the student and the patient he has visited. Each successive round begins to include more and more personal material and comment as well as intra-group reactions.

Examples of first-round comments are:
— I think this person has a faulty understanding of prayer.
— Wouldn't it help to find out if the person is a regular church attender?
— I don't think I would want to read the Scripture to the patient.
— Where is the priestly function of the minister if cordial greetings are all that are exchanged?

Examples of second-round comments are:
— I feel uncomfortable when a patient has tubes coming out from under the bed covers.
— What would I do if the doctor continued to stand there when I was about to pray?
— I think John would have done well to pray with the patient.
— Why did Tom use the particular Scripture he did?

The third-round brought comments such as:

— Boy, does Charles get uneasy around real sick people.

— I think it is unfair to the person to have it all figured out just what you are going to say to him.

— I'm glad John didn't stop to analyze the situation. His spontaneity was great.

Further rounds began to bring out such comments as:

— I wonder why Charles looks out the window so much when the rest of us are writing?

— I'm getting thirsty, I'd like to get out of here and get a coke.

— Man, have we strayed from the subject. What happened, aren't we interested in the patient any more?

— Why am I so reluctant to say what I really feel?

— I'm glad we are beginning to talk about ourselves more.

Other alternatives to the stimulus described above, which are also helpful in breaking through the intellectualization barrier, are either for the leader to read some provocative literary excerpt or for him to omit the initial stimulus entirely. (A nondirective approach)

CONCLUSION

The chief value of the free-association method for changing the tone and pace of the discussion activity lies in (1) the freedom of not being interrupted or criticized in the middle of a reflective process (2) the knowledge that all products have an equal opportunity for reception when read (3) the leisure and permissive silence provided for such introspection.

5

A TRAINING COURSE IN PASTORAL COUNSELING

by PROFESSOR PAUL E. JOHNSON

BOSTON UNIVERSITY SCHOOL OF THEOLOGY

An intern type of training course for theological graduate students at the Boston State Hospital (psychiatric) provides an opportunity for personal growth as well as knowledge and practice in pastoral counseling.

In the semester course for pastoral counselors, the twenty class members met at the hospital on fifteen successive Fridays from 8:30 A.M. to 4:30 P.M. The students from the Boston University School of Theology ranged in age from 24 to 36 years. There were 16 men, 4 women. Several had experience in the parish ministry, one had missionary experience in Asia, and others had experience of group leadership in summer and part-time church projects. They came from different Protestant denominations and all desired to learn to be pastoral counselors.

The first hour at the hospital brought all students together for discussions of pastoral counseling, led alternately by the academic professor and the hospital chaplain. Students asked questions from their readings and experience in counseling situations at the hospital and elsewhere. The leaders tended to be eclectic, varying from silence and reflection to clarification and interpretation, information and suggestions.

Next came the counseling hour, when each student interviewed a hospital patient. These interviews were written up as verbatim as possible with introduction (known facts, observation, preparation) and conclusion (analysis of what happened, self-criticism, and plans for the future). Supervisor's comments were added on the wide margin at the right of the page, and returned to the student the following week.

At eleven o'clock the students who interviewed women patients met as a group with the psychiatrist in charge of the female service, and the students who interviewed men patients met with the psychiatrist in charge of male service. Students asked questions about their patients, the diagnostic interpretations, and the treatment program.

At noon the students formed spontaneous groupings around lunch tables in the cafeteria where lunch was served. Comparing notes and experiences sometimes appeared to be more important than eating during this period.

At one o'clock a psychiatrist presented a lecture demonstration, interviewing patients to show behavior types and therapeutic approach. The two hours in this session allowed time for questions and discussion following the demonstration interviews.

At three o'clock the students met in groups of ten on the male and female service for discussion of interviews. These discussion groups used role-playing to present their interviews. Discussions that followed were spontaneous and unstructured, a nondirective approach being followed for the most part by the leaders (professor and chaplain).

Outcomes for Groups and Individuals

The total group acted like an academic class when meeting in the first hour of the morning and afternoon. The three o'clock discussions of interviews were dynamic, confessional, supportive and insightful.

353

The individual students became more emotionally involved than in academic classes. Interviewing mental patients caused anxiety and this experience was disturbing enough to penetrate defenses and to open deeper levels within most of the students. It was evident in group discussions as well as individual conferences with supervisors that the students were working on unresolved problems of their own. Several students asked for personal counseling and pursued intensive reconstruction of personality and relationships to family and/or others.

Evaluation

The students revealed some facets of what the experiences meant to them in their final written evaluations. Some sample statements follow:

— I have learned a great deal about myself and the way in which I relate to other persons.

— I have begun to feel the importance of seeing the other person's problems through his own eyes.

— For the first time in my life I have been able to look squarely at myself and evaluate myself.

— A healthful relationship is focused more upon the sharing of interests and feelings than it is upon digging up problems.

— During this semester I have grown emotionally and thus have become a more mature Christian.

— This to me was a real workshop in which much of what I have talked about in theology was put to the test.

The students felt, however, that the day was too crowded, and they would have liked more time to assimilate the meaning of their clinical experiences. Much preferred is the summer training course where students spend five days a week at the hospital for a total of twelve weeks.

CONCLUSION

The value of a practicum-type course in pastoral counseling at a mental hospital is so great that many schools of theology throughout the country are providing this experience as a required part of the curriculum. Pastors and religious workers are included in many community mental health programs so that understanding and skill related to mentally and emotionally ill persons are expected from these professional persons.

REFERENCES

1. Freud, S. *A General Introduction to Psychoanalysis.* N. Y. Boni and Liveright, 1920.
2. Garrett, A. *Interviewing: Its Principles and Methods.* N. Y. Family Welfare Assn., 1942.

3. Hiltner, S. *Pastoral Counseling.* N. Y. Abingdon, 1948.
4. Johnson, P. E., *Psychology of Pastoral Care.* N. Y. Abingdon, 1953.
5. Rogers, C. R. *Counseling and Psychotherapy.* Boston. Houghton-Mifflin, 1942.
6. Rogers, C. R. *Client-Centered Therapy.* Boston. Houghton-Mifflin, 1952.
7. Sullivan, H. S. *The Psychiatric Interview.* N. Y. Norton, 1954.
8. Wise, C. A. *Pastoral Counseling: Its Theory and Practice.* N. Y. Harper, 1951.

6

A GROUP DISCUSSION APPROACH IN TRAINING COURSES
FOR NURSES AND RELIGIOUS COUNSELORS

by CHAPLAIN W. B. BRISTOW

GLENDALE SANITARIUM AND HOSPITAL, GLENDALE, CALIF.

Our hospital makes use of a small-group discussion method in training courses in three different areas (1) Pastoral Counselor Training (2) Demonstration-treatment Project (3) Student nurse course: *Psychological Problems of the Sick.*

The teaching uses a Christian frame of reference, since the hospital is church-related and the student nurses and religious counselors are associated with this denomination. Likewise the Chaplain and the clinical psychologist who teach the courses have the same Christian frame of reference.

Pastoral Counselor Training

One unit of the pastoral counseling course consists of twelve weekly meetings with the clinical psychologist. Group discussion is the primary activity. The purpose is to provide a personal development project to strengthen the emotional stability of religious workers through a mutual sharing of thoughts, feelings, and problems arising in their work as ministers and religious counselors.

In this twelve-session unit there are no textbooks. The instructor starts each meeting with a short talk on the topic of the day. A wide range of subjects is covered, pertaining for the most part to psychological problems of patients and parishioners and their relationship to the church. Since each group member is occupied in some type of counseling situation there is a wealth of case material for discussion in the class.

The chief value of this project, aside from the factual material regarding psychological problems provided by the instructor, is the added feeling of security gained by the group members. This field of counseling is difficult for even the highly skilled; religious counselors need reassurance and guidance in dealing with emotionally disturbed or mentally ill persons.

Demonstration-Treatment Project

A second project which held significant learning for this group of ministers and religious counselors was the demonstration-treatment of a mentally ill patient by the psychologist. The treatment interviews were conducted before the group, twice a week for a period of six weeks; once a week for six weeks; once every two weeks for six weeks — a total of twenty-one sessions. This was a unique experience in that each member of the observation group was primarily interested in counseling from the Christian viewpoint. The patient's problem was diagnosed as basically related to religion and the psychotherapist's approach to the problem was in line with Christian counseling.

Following each treatment interview the group could ask questions of the psychotherapist; there was a free discussion of methods, techniques and procedures. Verbatim reports of each treatment session were transcribed and given to group members for study. The dynamics of the counseling process could be perceived and understood better when such oral reviews in print were made available to the trainees. The psychotherapist had clarified the therapeutic goal for the group, viz., to free the patient from her basic fears. This helped the trainees to follow the progress of the interviews with greater understanding.

The results of the twenty-one session treatment were excellent, both for the patient and the trainees. The patient was sufficiently helped that she was restored to normal activity in the home; family relationships were happy once more, and she became pregnant. She visited the hospital on several occasions to express her appreciation to the psychotherapist and the group. One of the group members, a religious counselor, had continued the contact with the patient in her home, maintaining friendly social relationships.

In evaluating the group experience the students believed it was invaluable: they had seen at first hand the dynamics at work in a patient-doctor counseling relationship. They thought their own personal growth had benefited; that the knowledges and understanding gained in the discussion period following each treatment-interview were too great to be measured.

Student Nurse Course

The course for student nurses called "Psychological Problems of the Sick" had as its primary goal the emotional development of the students in judgment, morals, and personal relationships. This course was taught by the Chaplain and a discussion-group structure was used. Students were given the opportunity to discuss any subject of interest to them, in any way they chose. The class met twice weekly for six weeks.

The Chaplain maintained a nondirective role for the first twenty-five minutes of each session. The subject and discussion emerged from the group, according to the needs and interests of the students on that particular day. Much of the discussion revolved around hospital cases which concerned the student nurses. Since the Chaplain was closely associated with these cases — "patients with problems" — it was possible for him to give guidance to the nurses connected with the cases.

Each student nurse had a counseling interview with the Chaplain prior to entering the course. Encouragement was given the students to come to the Chaplain for further counseling interviews during the duration of their nurses' training.

Benefits to individual student nurses from this intimate group activity were a healthy growth in emotional stability, judgment and personal relationships. As a group the camaraderie carried over into a feeling of "belonging" and loyalty. School activities benefited and the general tone of the student body improved. Projects such as the swimming pool fund drive, Red Cross, etc. were taken on with added zeal. Several of the group volunteered for special projects concerned with the patients-with-problems.

CONCLUSION

There is no doubt in the minds of the instructors that a group discussion method aids learning over and above the traditional lecture method. Similarly the trainees and student nurses are enthusiastic advocates of the informal discussion approach, endorsing it both for learning and for enjoyment.

357

7

INFORMAL DISCUSSION GROUPS FOR GRADUATE STUDENTS
IN CHRISTIAN EDUCATION

FROM THE GENERAL ASSEMBLY'S TRAINING SCHOOL
PRESBYTERIAN CHURCH, U. S. A.

The need for a closer relationship with professors than afforded by the traditional university system is felt by many students, especially on the graduate level. Small discussion groups, with the professor in the role of resource person, serve this need effectively in our institution. Each year groups of ten or twelve students from the senior class organize for weekly meetings in the home of a professor living close to the campus. Participation in the group is at their own request or on invitation of other students for the purpose of discussing informally problems that arise in class or on campus during the course of the year. These groups meet for two-hour sessions each week, thus totalling thirty or more meetings during the year.

Group Organization and Leadership

Leadership comes from the students themselves, who take the initiative in organizing the group, providing the refreshments, choosing the discussion topics. The professor serves only as the resource person. In some groups leadership is rotated at each meeting; in other groups a chairman is appointed for a half semester and questions for discussion are referred to her as they arise in the minds of other students in the group.

The students are largely young women, because the student body is predominately women, although occasionally a young man becomes a part of the group. Often there will be a foreign student or two. Thus there have been a Brazilian, Japanese, German, in addition to Negroes. Most of the students are preparing for a church-related vocation, equipping themselves to be a director of Christian Education, teacher, missionary, etc.

Although there is no plan for individual conferences with the professor in connection with the discussion group, often such conferences are requested and held, as a result of the meetings.

Sociometric Patterns; Group Dynamics

Most of the members of a group are close friends. Occasionally an individual is invited into a group who is not intimate with any of

358

the other members. Often this is a foreign student who enjoys participation as a part of her experience in a foreign country.

In general, group members participate freely and discussion is lively. Often one or more tend to assume leadership in the groups; one or two can be counted on to have a barrage of questions for discussion; one or more have little to say, even though they attend regularly and seem to enjoy non-verbal participation. Usually no antagonisms arise in the group, nor are any strong attachments apparent.

Discussion Topics

The questions proposed for discussion often refer back to those raised in the student's mind in lecture classes where there was insufficient time for full discussion. An example of the kinds of topics discussed during one fall quarter follows:

The meaning of salvation.

The nature of sin, the doctrine of "imputation".

Prayer: intercessory prayer; the plans for prayer groups on campus.

The techniques of dealing with the race question in Southern Churches.

The nature of human freedom.

Interpersonal relations; the techniques of counseling.

The problem of counseling in relation to controversial issues.

Campus problems of interpersonal relationships.

The adjustment of the unmarried woman.

The philosophy of the curriculum in Christian Education.

It is apparent that no design is followed in selecting or arranging topics, but discussion centers around whatever topic is uppermost in the thinking of the group. Occasionally it is proposed that the group undertake a systematic study of some book, or some topic over a period of several weeks, but even though the idea may appeal at first thought, the group is seldom willing to follow through on it. The importance of a time for discussing urgent problems that arise from week to week apparently far outweighs the value of a more systematic study of a single large topic. It might be concluded that the classroom itself provides sufficient opportunity for consistent and planned study, and the greater need, from the student's point of view, is for the more informal kind of discussion.

OUTCOMES

The students gain a deep satisfaction as well as increased understanding of academic subject matter from these informal meetings with the professor.

Although not a therapy group, supportive and "ventilating" benefits result from the freedom for unlimited expression in discussion in an intimate, trusting atmosphere.

The great value of this type of discussion group is the opportunity for frank exploration of feelings of uncertainty; for coming to grips with theological and social issues in a way not possible in the lecture room. A healthy experience results when a student is able to differ sharply with another student within a common faith, when "heretical" answers may be tried out on one another, when real understanding of abstract theological and biblical concepts is gained.

This warm social climate allows problems to be presented which no one individual dares to present outside the group. Doubts and fears can be verbalized. Group members can project themselves into the future to prepare for leadership in such a group as this, and to develop an at-homeness with such discussions.

In summary, the discussion group aids the personal growth of the graduate students and provides a laboratory for significant learning, useful in the present and for the future.

Students in commenting in later years on their participation in these groups, always refer to the values of the free, unhampered discussion, of hearing opposing points of view expressed, of hearing their own opinions both respected and rejected. They find that such an experience strengthens their faith in the religious beliefs in which they have been nurtured, and prepares them for leading other people in their quest for religious certainty.

8
THE NAVY CHARACTER EDUCATION PROGRAM
USES GROUP DISCUSSION

by f. h. WICKHAM, LCDR, CHC, USN[1]

From the lee of turret No. 3 came the question: "How can you keep squared-away, as far as women are concerned, while in the Navy?"

"By staying away from two-bit bars," chirps a smooth cheeked seaman with a sheepish grin.

"Find niceeee . . . . girls to date, *when* — and *if* you can," complained an "old salt" of nineteen.

---

[1]The views of this article are those of the writer and are not to be construed officially as those of the U. S. Navy.

From such small beginnings constructive conclusions have been developed in five separate character education discussion topics participated in by thirty-four groups during the year. Positive antidotes, applicable to the daily lives of the men, were determined and agreed upon in each group. Selected were such topics as "My Moral Responsibilities as a Driver", "My Attitude toward the Opposite Sex", and "What am I going to do with my Life." Workable conclusions help to develop convictions which lead to positive action. Thus the first objective, to raise the moral standard of the individual Navy-man, is accomplished.

The character education objective and program are not unique: it is a concentrated Navy-wide program developed by the Navy Chaplains Corps. However, the need for greater leadership-example was met by the development of a secondary objective obtained by a particular method of implementation and participation of group leaders described forthwith.

The group leaders were Navy chiefs and first class petty officers. They were almost completely lacking in any extensive specialized training normally deemed necessary for leaders of guided discussion groups. Their training as instructors, as required by their rate, includes a rudimentary knowledge of guided discussion techniques, but largely was the direct product of the Navy's school of experience and hard knocks.

The course outline, guide for leaders, and other materials were developed by the Navy Chaplains Corps.[2] The materials have been most effectively tailored to the average seaman's needs and interests. And the built-in discussion group techniques have proved sufficiently trustworthy to assure the desired responses from the group, thus eliminating the necessity of specialized training of the group leaders.

The second objective of the program concerns the leaders: first, to further develop the leadership qualities of the petty officers; second, to develop moral leadership so that the petty officers offer a good example to the men, both on and off duty. Traditionally the character development of non-rated men has been the prerogative and responsibility of the petty officers. This responsibility was usurped during and immediately following World War II. Now, through a formal pro-

[2]Materials include:
Our Moral and Spiritual Growth — NAVPERS 91962
This is My Life — NAVPERS 15884
Because of You — NAVPERS 15874
My Life in the Far East — NAVPERS 15881

gram, this responsibility is returned to the petty officers, re-emphasizing the moral implications inherent in military leadership.

How well has this program succeeded? Results have been deemed satisfactory both in the case of the men and the petty officers. The program has served as a yardstick to measure the effectiveness of leadership abilities on a broader scale rather than being confined to the petty officer's professional specialty. Leadership-example has greatly improved. The non-rated men's conduct has shown an upward trend as reflected in a low percentage of disciplinary problems and the non-existence of venereal disease among the group members who participated in the program.

It is believed that similar results can be achieved, and that the program is applicable, in any type military command. All Navy Chaplains have received copies of the materials used.

Procedures used in organizing the program follow:

1. Appointment of group leaders by immediate superior officer; one leader for each twenty men or fraction thereof.
2. Program director reviews basic techniques of directed discussion leadership with appointed leaders.[3]
3. Program director distributes and discusses materials with group leaders.
4. Immediate superior officers schedule group meetings, assuring one hundred percent participation. Two months are given in which to accomplish the assigned responsibility for each subject covered in the program, allowing complete control of the men's time by their immediate superior. Thus the discussion groups may be held at times which will avoid disruption of daily work schedules required to accomplish primary military missions.

---

[3]Materials include:

Manual for Navy Instructors — NAVPERS 16103-B

Leadership and the Protection of Moral Standards and Character Education Program, by Lt. J. J. O'Connor, CHC, USN. Navy Chaplains Bulletin, Spring, 1955.

Protection of Moral Standards and Character Education Program — NAVPERS (no. not assigned) Part II, Chapter XIII.

9

SOLVING A DE-SEGREGATION PROBLEM THROUGH SMALL-GROUP ACTIVITY

by FRANK C. MABEE, JR., *Director of Christian Education*
TEXAS BOARD OF CHRISTIAN CHURCHES, FORT WORTH, TEXAS

We have adopted the small-group discussion method for programs of Christian Education on all age levels. We are emphasizing this approach particularly in our adult Church School classes. And the entire program of outdoor camping — junior camps for grade school children and intermediate camps for junior high students — uses the small group as its organizational base.

All of our state youth activities on the college level are integrated programs which use small-group discussion activity. And the camp and conference training program for directors and youth leaders have included Negro members for three years.

Recently we tried a new type of organization for a state-wide training program for teachers and counselors of all age levels. The purpose of the program was to introduce advanced techniques and methods in adapting the small-group procedure to all our camping programs. Before the new plan was inaugurated, the Negro leaders had not appeared to gain much from the conferences that they could use in their church programs. In searching for reasons for this failure to meet the needs of our Negro leaders, we found that they could not adapt the materials and methods to the work of their churches. The information was not what they wanted, or was not presented in terms which had meaning for them.

The addition of a State Director of Negro work to our staff helped with the problem. He was present and shared in the planning sessions which we hold several times during the year. The new approach at camp conferences, utilizing "the intimate group" and small-group discussion, gave the Negro educational leaders the right setting. In this they could feel the acceptance of the group, talk freely of their back-home problems, and learn how to adapt materials and methods in their work.

The new organization of camp conferences included the following:

1. The entire five-day training session was set up on a small-group basis, with all regimentation omitted. When each person arrived, he found no registration lines, but rather, an informal fellowship which was begun earlier in the day by the faculty.

2. Freedom was given to find bunks and get settled as individuals, instead of attending an orientation meeting. The first "get-together" was the evening meal where, in an informal atmosphere, needed explanations were given. The conferees were told: "There will be no bells, schedules or required sessions. But we have planned that while you are here you will receive help for setting up and conducting the camps and conferences you have scheduled for this summer."

3. Each person was assigned to a small group on the basis of his need. The high school conference directors were together, as were the adult, junior high, and grade school camp directors.

4. The small groups planned their own daily schedules around the three mealtimes. During the week, each group had a cook-out and their own evening program. It was in these small groups that the Negro directors were accepted and were able to identify their own problems the same as the others. They felt free to stop the discussion at any time, to ask such questions as "How does this work in my situation"? Thus they were partners in the planning and training programs — not outsiders invited in to observe.

Results

By the end of the week, the Negro leaders showed evidence of growth which had never before been achieved. They were able to accept many of the ideas about camping which they had previously rejected as being impossible for their groups. This learning never would have taken place in a formal lecture-type training session. It was only in the small group that acceptance was possible so they could identify themselves with the group and realize that the training session held much for them in terms of learning and problem solutions for their Negro groups.

Conclusion

Two basic factors appeared to be important in the new organization of conference programs: (1) A Negro leader was present at the planning sessions. This fact was known to the Negro directors before they came to the conference. (2) The Negroes were accepted as individuals who had problems in their camps and conferences, no more or less than anyone else present. Because of this acceptance they were able to be receptive to learning and help which had meaning for them as individuals.

Not only the Negro leaders, but also the white directors gained more in this small-group organization of the conference than in the traditional type of conference structure. For this reason we have adopted the method as a permanent procedure in all our state-wide training conferences.

IMPLICATIONS

The many Christian groups who are concerned with making the Christian faith relevant to the integration problem may find part of the answer in the use of small-group discussion activity. This would also be true for our public schools which now teach and use democratic procedures. They would find that integration is facilitated when Negroes and whites serve on small committees together, and participate in small-group discussion activity as a part of the educative process. Use of the small-group discussion method is applicable to the basic faith about man that is primary to Christianity and democracy.

10

RESEARCH INTO BUZZ-GROUP METHOD WITH
IN-SERVICE CLASSES FOR TEACHERS

by PROFESSOR JJUJI MISUMI, KYUSHU UNIVERSITY, JAPAN

Editor's Note:

Professor Misumi, an Educational Psychologist, has experimented with various teaching-learning methods for some years. It is interesting to note that he is now engaged in translating Driver's MULTIPLE COUNSELING into Japanese so that it may be used in counseling programs in Japanese schools.

The purpose of the experimental study of methods in the Government teacher-training school for the Fukoka Prefecture was to make the traditional lecture-type meetings more dynamic and productive. Formerly the lecture was followed by a question period, but the latter was deemed ineffectual and done away with.

We applied the buzz-method to a certain stage of the class period and tried to verify its usefulness experimentally. In such an experiment in 1952 it was clearly demonstrated that the buzz-method was more effective than the traditional lecture-type method.[1] In the experiments reported herein, a control group was compared with an experimental group. In the experimental group buzz-sessions were held for six minutes of each class period, while in the control group a lecture followed by a question period was used. The buzz-groups consisted of about six members. There were 61 teachers in the experimental group and 77 in the control group.

---

[1]Misumi, J. "Theory and Practice of Group Dynamics", *Educational Statistics*, No. 22, pp. 21-23

365

The first hypothesis consisted of the assumption that the buzz-groups would bring more ego-involvement of participants than the question period, resulting in greater enthusiasm and motivation.

The second hypothesis consisted of the assumption that the buzz-session method is more effective for assimilating content of the lecture than is the question period.

The third hypothesis is that the homogeneous groupings in the buzz-groups are more productive than heterogeneous groups. In this case the groupings were primary, secondary, and high school teachers. Along with this, separating the sexes in buzz-groups is assumed to produce better results than the heterogeneity of the large group.

TIME SCHEDULE OF EXPERIMENTAL AND CONTROL GROUPS

Buzz-Method (Experimental) 61 teachers	*Lecture-Method* (Control) 77 teachers
Orientation................. 5 min.	Lecture..........70 min.
Lecture.....................70 min.	Question period....25 min.
Buzz-meeting.................10 min.	
Symposium.................. 5 min.	
Discussion of all participants....10 min.	

Procedure in the Experimental Group

The time for orientation was devoted to clarifying the buzz-method for the attending teachers; then the 70-minute lecture on educational psychology was delivered. After the lecture the teachers, who had been given number cards assigning them to groups, gathered in buzz-sessions containing 6 or 7 members. The leaders of the buzz-groups were automatically appointed by a designated card number. Discussion concerning the lecture was carried on for 6 minutes, and results were summarized by the leader. Leaders from the groups then proceeded to the stage for the symposium. After the reports from group leaders, a general discussion was held by the leaders and the audience.

Procedure in the Control Group

The lecture (same as in the experimental class) was delivered and then the speaker asked the audience: "Are there any questions"? During the 25-minute question period, when nobody has a question, the lecturer further detailed the content of his lecture. This occurred for about half of the period.

The two procedures outlined above, were carried out in the same groups twice a day for three days, with a final class meeting in the morning of the fourth day. Thus there were seven class meetings for each group. However, the final meeting was taken up with a multiple-choice test and a questionnaire related to an evaluation of certain aspects of the lecture meeting and the buzz-group.

Results of the Experiment

1. The buzz-group did better than the lecture group in the objective test.
2. The opinion-poll concerned understanding of the lecture material; like or dislike of lecture and/or buzz-method; interest in the class meetings; carryover into discussions after the class period ended.
   a. Although the control group thought they understood the lecture better than the experimental group, this was not the fact. The experimental group got better grades on the final test.
   b. The experimental group were more in favor of changing the traditional lecture method into the new method than were the control group.
   c. The experimental group made more friends during the seminar sessions than did the control group.

A second experiment, similar to the above described design, was tried with 58 in the experimental group, 74 in the control group. The one difference was the use of age-groupings for the buzz-groups, rather than teaching levels. Thus the buzz-groups were formed on the basis of teachers' ages: those in the 20's, 30's, and 40's (or older).

Again the results were similar: degree of comprehension of the lecture material was greater in the experimental group; experimental group preferred the buzz-method structure to the traditional lecture structure; more friends were made in the experimental group. However, the age-groupings dissatisfied many of the members of the experimental group.

CONCLUSIONS AND IMPLICATIONS

The results of the experiments with teaching-learning methods in in-service training classes for teachers are clear; they should have implications for planners and lecturers in such courses. *Students tend to get more from the lectures when they have a chance to discuss the material among themselves. They become more interested in the subject matter and participate more actively when discussion in small-groups is a part of the class period.*

There is sufficient evidence to show that replacement of the traditional question period following a lecture by small-group discussions, a symposium, and general discussion by the whole class is to be highly recommended.

367

11
TRAINING PROGRAM ON CONFERENCE LEADERSHIP IN INDUSTRY
by DR. HAROLD R. BURKE, *Coordinator of Academic Counseling*
UNIVERSITY OF CONNECTICUT

The title of the course given for supervisory personnel in the Chandler-Evans Division of Pratt and Whitney Company was *Conference Leadership for Plant Foremen*. The primary goal of the course was to teach methods of group conference leadership to plant foremen and to provide them with practical experience in handling group discussions. The class members were responsible for the operation of departments in which they served as foremen. Each had several supervisors in his department. Twelve departments were represented ranging from experimental manufacturing to assembly and experimental testing. The course consisted of ten two-hour sessions over a period of five weeks. Meetings were held in the plant at West Hartford, Conn.

Resumé of the Ten Sessions

The instructor (author) conducted the course in a manner which called for creative participation by all twelve members. The first meeting was structured in that the instructor presented information on group characteristics and individual differences. Discussion of the material was encouraged, but there was an obvious hesitancy on the part of group members to risk their ideas and opinions before fellow workers. At the second meeting a buzz-session technique was employed to determine the type of visual aids the group members wanted to utilize in meetings. Throughout the first two meetings there was an undercurrent of disbelief that group discussion could be used as a method for seeking solutions to particular problems. The idea was not readily accepted that the discussion leader (foreman in this instance) could risk letting the workers engage in suggestions and discussion about problems of money, equipment, safety and work schedules. Their general notion seemed to be that the leader (foreman) should come to the discussion with his own ideas as to what the solution should be, and then proceed to manipulate group discussion so as to bring about his preconceived solution. However, this should be done in a way that would cause group members to feel that they themselves created the solution. When the instructor began to suggest that genuinely creative thinking by group members might prove more productive than manipulative discussion control by the leader, the members challenged the instructor to demonstrate his opinion by leading the class through a discussion of a knotty problem which they were facing daily. Plant Cleanliness was the problem for which they had found no solution. The instructor accepted the challenge and the stage was set for what turned out to be the most significant period of the course. It was a test of the instructor by a group of men who were accustomed to obtaining results: if the instructor couldn't "produce", then he would lose the status essential for the effective teacher. The time for the demonstration was fixed for the following class period and the class selected an evaluation committee to rate the effectiveness of the demonstration.

Two class periods were devoted to the topic of Plant Cleanliness. The instructor organized the discussion by employing a phase-space analysis approach. By liberal use of the blackboard, he displayed for all to see the many ideas submitted by group members as they tried to explain forces within their industrial organization which operated to encourage or retard plant cleanliness. The topic, one of genuine concern to all foremen in the group, proved so exciting that the two-hour session ended before all the pros and cons had been listed. The discussion leader (instructor) then suggested that members divide into four subcommittees, two to study the forces encouraging plant cleanliness, and two to study those discouraging plant cleanliness. The subcommittees would be ready at the next meeting to suggest constructive ways and means for handling those forces. The suggestion was accepted willingly and committees were formed. At the following meeting committee reports were presented and discussion of them was heated, to say the least. However, class members were observed to be making notes of ideas which presumably they would try out in their own departments.

At the instructor's suggestion in this second session on plant cleanliness an evaluation of the experience thus far was made. He reviewed and explained the methods he had employed as discussion leader. The committee on evaluation rated him high on the forty-two item scale which they had devised for checking discussion leadership effectiveness. Lastly, group members agreed that they would be willing to try leading the class in discussions. As an evidence of rapport-establishment, several foremen invited the instructor to visit their departments.

The remaining meetings of the course were planned and conducted to allow each member opportunities to lead the group in a twenty to thirty minute discussion of a predetermined topic and to conduct a ten to fifteen minute discussion on a topic not previously assigned, to be handled extemporaneously. Topics discussed were chosen for relevancy to plant operation, for example: union relationships, worker recreation programs, orientation of new workers, increasing production, reducing waste, etc. Visual aids were introduced at appropriate times; evaluation of class progress was made periodically.

During the final session of the course the instructor presented a review of principles, methods and techniques covered in the course. A general discussion including questions and answers followed. Insight into human behavior was well demonstrated by the members in this summary discussion.

INSTRUCTOR'S EVALUATION

Relationships between an organization of higher learning and an organization of industrial production were strengthened by this group project. In this instance it was a case of transferring principles of group and individual psychology from a setting of study and research to a setting of functional usefulness. Academic principles had to retain their essential character and also to be stripped of misunderstandable and extraneous terminology. Theory and principles had to stand the test and be judged on a severe action level. The teacher-learning experience was devoid of educational trappings, viz, textbooks, testing, grading, and credit requirements. In one sense it was a sink-or-swim experience, with complete dependence upon group dynamics and creative contributions of group members for its success. It is the writer's belief that such experiences do much to bridge the gaps between classroom study and daily living; they serve also to hasten the expansion of ideas to match emerging opportunities.

SECTION II — SYMPOSIUM

PART FOUR

COMMUNITY MENTAL HEALTH AND PARENT EDUCATION PROGRAMS: SMALL-GROUP DISCUSSION FOR EDUCATION, COUNSELING, AND TRAINING

List of Articles

371

The activities in the six articles show the efforts of mental health and educational agencies to help parents to understand themselves and their children better. Through educational, counseling, and lay-leadership programs, opportunities are presented wherein parents can gain needed insights and skills for personal growth and effective parenthood.

1

A TRAINING COURSE FOR LEADERS IN THE MENTAL HEALTH ASSOCIATION

by DR. HAROLD R. BURKE, *Coordinator of Academic Counseling*
UNIVERSITY OF CONNECTICUT

Colleges and universities need to expand their services beyond the traditional semester-hour programs if they are to meet the needs of adult groups. An example of such a need concerns leadership training courses in the Mental Health Association. Thus the Waterbury Chapter of the Mental Health Association requested that such a course be organized through the University Adult Education Division and the author planned and taught the course. It was a non-credit course, entitled *Techniques of Discussion Leadership*, and was structured for the specific materials and program of the Mental Health Association. Eighteen potential leaders were enrolled and the class met for eight two-hour sessions.

The Mental Health Association regularly sponsors series of discussion meetings with interested social and educational groups in the greater Waterbury community. The Mental Health programs are requested by PTAs, church groups, and other social, civic and educational organizations; the Mental Health Association provides the leadership and program materials for such meetings. Thus trained discussion leaders representing MHA are sent out to group meetings to lead discussions based on movies or playlets depicting various aspects of mental health. The films used include: A Place to Live, Fears of Children, Social-Sex Attitudes in Adolescence, Meeting the Needs of Adolescents. Playlets used are: Random Target and You Never Know. Other audio-visual aids may be used, according to the theme and special interest of the group meeting.

The Mental Health Association paid all expenses involved in conducting the course: renting films and plays, cost of instruction and other related items of expense. Candidates for the course were screened carefully for interest, availability, discussion leadership potential, and experience. Nineteen men and women, representing several professional and semi-professional occupation groups, attended the first meeting of the course. One person withdrew after the second meeting and eighteen finished the course.

The course was conducted informally in a classroom with movable chairs arranged usually in semi-circular fashion. The instructor used blackboard outlines, mimeographed materials and other audio-visual aids in his teaching. The course included the following topics, listed in chronological order:

1. Orientation to Mental Health Association work and objectives.
2. The dynamics of group functioning.
3. Techniques of discussion leadership.
4. Use of films and plays in group discussion.
5. Observation and evaluation of discussion leaders.
6. Practical problems in leading discussions and how to handle them.
7. Review and re-evaluation of group leadership — clinical approach to individual problems.
8. Observations and try-out experiences.

A major effort was made to provide class and field experiences which would be illustrative of points covered in discussions. At appropriate times group members conducted class discussions using buzz-groups and panel presentations. Informal group discussions proved a favorite means of inter-communication. The instructor occasionally interrupted group members to encourage drawing conclusions about application of theoretical points to discussion leadership.

When viewing a mental health film or play, group members discussed their observations and reactions to establish conclusions concerning the usefulness and application of media employed and content covered. As meetings progressed there was a noticeable change in member participation. Ways were developed for speaking frankly and for sharing constructive criticism. Feeling of camaraderie became evident by the third meeting; discussions became more realistic and frank. Knowing that each person would soon be "on his own", handling discussion problems, seemed a sobering influence which encouraged members to focus on basic issues rather than superficialities.

There are three conclusions gained from this experience in training for discussion leadership:

1. Theoretical knowledge and group experience may be combined effectively through careful definition and utilization of interdependent roles of instructor and learner. The instructor assumed responsibility for presenting theoretical knowledge and information; the group assumed leadership in determining the how, when, and where of the application to problems at hand. The broad outline for the course is best developed through conferences involving representatives of the Mental Health Association and the course instructor. Candidates should be briefed carefully on course outline before acceptance, and must promise to take responsibility as future discussion leaders in the organization.

2. Procedures which tie together theory with both classroom and field experiences in discussion leadership help the members to improve their understanding and their effectiveness in action. Specific needs of a special group, such as this, require imaginative use of educational resources: materials must be designed and adapted to the group needs. Consequently the traditional semester-hour credit courses cannot be used because they fill none of the needs of such a group.

3. There is no point in giving credit for such an adult course: the class members do not want credit, they want to reach certain practical goals with as much understanding and skill as possible. It would seem that educational institutions could improve their contributions to community well-being by providing more service to adult groups through specifically designed courses, both inside and outside the framework of traditional semester-hour credit courses.

ADDITUM: *Course Outline and Sample of Materials*

Plan of Classes for Discussion Leadership Course

Eight Meetings 2 hours each (evening course, 7-9 pm). Under direction of Dr. Harold Burke, University Counselor, Division of University Personnel.

1st Meeting Orientation to course. Why are we here? What do we
Thurs. Nov. 1 plan to accomplish and through what means? What is mental health? The Mental Health Association?

374

What does it accomplish and hope to do? (Panel discussion between representatives of the local and state Association and a member of the Medical Advisory Committee)

2nd Meeting Role of the discussion leader in the MH educational
Thurs. Nov. 8 program. Principles of group dynamics. Techniques of discussion. Pattern of a meeting (1) welcome (2) introduction (3) the discussion tool (4) the discussion (5) summary.
(The above content is to be drawn from the group by a group process with a minimum of lecturing.)

3rd Meeting The use of the film as a discussion tool in successful
Thurs. Nov. 15 group discussions. Film such as "Meeting the Needs of Adolescence" is presented in order to (1) get a thorough understanding of films — what they attempt to portray, conflicts they may create in the audience, reactions of discussion leaders to films. (2) Viewing of film from standpoint of group discussion techniques: how can the film be used most effectively to elicit group discussion.

4th Meeting Continuation of discussion of use of films. At this
Thurs. Nov. 29 meeting a psychiatrist explains and demonstrates discussion techniques.
Note: After this meeting, student discussion leaders will actually start out in the field accompanied by someone who has previously served as a discussion leader.

5th Meeting Use of Mental Health play as a discussion tool in
Dec. 6 group discussion. Purpose and plan similar to 2nd and 3rd meetings.

6th Meeting Use of play, continued. Resource person as in the 4th
Dec. 13 meeting.

7th Meeting Practical problems of leading a discussion: the heckler,
Dec. 20 the long-winded talker, what to do about questions, what to do when discussion lags, etc.

8th Meeting Clinic on discussion techniques: what problems were
End of Jan. encountered? Where is more help needed?

375

Example of Specific Materials

Questions discussed in buzz-groups prior to showing of the film "Meeting the Needs of Adolescence" were as follows:

1. Does the picture furnish standards for parents to evaluate their own guidance approach?
2. Would discussion leaders be expected to have resource materials available?
3. Is this film an *ideal* situation or does it go into religious matters at a practical level — such as mixed marriages, etc.?
4. Should social life of the adolescent be met in the home — how far can parents go?
5. How to identify and meet the needs of parents in their relationship to the adolescent?
6. What about the responsibility the child has to his family?
7. Do we agree that parents should accept the child to the extent suggested by the film?
8. Should the parents help to select friends of their children?
9. How much should parents actively participate in activities of their adolescent children?

2

A TRAINING PROJECT FOR LAY LEADERS OF CHILDREN'S PLAY GROUPS

by MRS. ELBA CRUM, *Consultant, Family Life Education*
SEATTLE PUBLIC SCHOOLS

Our community program in Family Life Education sponsors and supervises parent-operated Play Groups (nursery schools). Classes for parent leaders are held so that the eighty or more Play Groups can be adequately staffed with trained personnel. The leadership training courses are called "Workshops for Leaders" and usually consist of eight sessions of two hours each. The course may be telescoped into a two-week period with the mothers meeting both morning and afternoon on two days of each week. A typical class has fifty members.

The first two hours each day (9:30–11:30) are spent observing in certain designated Play Groups. The trainees received a briefing sheet to guide their observations and the instructors were on hand to interpret and guide their learning. Then the group meets for lunch, with instructors distributed among group members so that informal discussions could be part of the learning experience. The afternoon session begins at 12:30 with the group divided according to experience, and a staff person assigned as discussion leader of each small-group. Content includes observations and reactions of the trainees to the Play Groups with interpretations and applications of basic fundamental facts and philosophy given by the leader. There was no attempt on the part of the leader to solve problems for the participants — only to help them apply what they have seen. The leader uses such comments as: "What do you think might happen if . . . ; what was your experience? Mrs. X solved her problem this way, Mrs. Y another — your answers may be different from theirs." Thus the leader's role was to stimulate and to guide the discussion.

The Workshop Guide manual outlines the observation, tasks, and discussion topics for each day, as shown below:

First Day: An Over-All Look at a Play Group in Action

— List the many kinds of activities you see.
— Pick out one piece of equipment and note how many different ways it was used and by how many children.
— How was the time divided between active play and quiet activities?
— How was the group divided for various activities?
— How many children for each adult present?

Second Day: Children's Play

— Observe and describe examples of:
Solitary Play (one child playing alone)
Parallel Play (two or more children playing side by side but not together)
Cooperative Play (children sharing the same activity, sharing ideas and equipment)
— Observe a three-year-old for ten minutes and describe how many things he did during this time and for how long.
— Observe a four-year-old child in the same way.

Third Day: Social Relationships Between Children

— Describe one instance of two children sharing a piece of equipment and the verbalization used, if any.
— Pick out a child who seems to be a leader in the group and try to record one incident that demonstrates why he holds this position.
— Describe one child who seems to be shy and record his activities for a fifteen minute period.
— Describe one incident where two children were in a conflict situation and tell what happened.

377

Fourth Day: The Mother's Role in the Group

— Did the mothers have definitely assigned duties?
— Was there a mother supervising each activity?
— Give one example of good supervision on the part of a mother.
— Did the mothers enjoy their morning?
— Describe an incidence of guidance by a mother.
— Describe an example of a Children's Leader helping a mother to do a better job, or giving her needed direction.

Workshop members are urged to continue their study of children through the adult classes in childhood development and Family Life Education. The laboratory sessions of the Workshop provide excellent motivation for further study. Most of the mothers continue to attend regular classes in their own neighborhood throughout the school year, and to assist in the Play Groups. The fact that these parents enroll not one child, but the second, third and fourth child as well, attests to the carry-over and interest on the part of the "student" mothers.

The mothers can continue their studies and win a basic certificate in Family Life Education. The requirements for the certificate consist of the following:

1. *Attend nine classes* in Family Life Education. These can include: Neighborhood Classes, the Tuesday Night Class, and Workshop Sessions.
2. *Read six books* from the bibliography on Family Life Education and turn in a brief written report on each book.
3. *Make a personality study* of one child based on nine hours of written observation (one hour per week for nine weeks). These observations should be made both in a group situation and in the home, if possible.
4. *Make nine two-hour observations* in Neighborhood Play Groups or in a nursery school. These should be written in narrative form, leaving space for your comments and evaluation in the margins. These are turned in weekly, and conferences with instructors and staff members will provide maximum learning for the observer.
5. *Observe at least one session* in a Demonstration Play Group, accompanied by an instructor or staff member.
6. *Write a summary* of the insights and understandings you have gained — from your reading, observations, personality study and classes attended.

Classes for young adults and parents offered by the Family Life Education Division of the Seattle Public Schools include community and inservice classes in special fields. Observations and group discussions are basic learning methods used in the adult classes. Content is provided as needed through lectures, films, and other audio-visual aids. To meet the needs of the many community groups which request help, the following class offerings have developed:

Film Nites for Expectant Parents	Teen-Agers Must Try Their Wings
Toddler Observation Groups	Learning to Work Together
Guiding Children's Growth	Marriage and Preparation for Marriage
Helping Your Child in School	Solo Parents: Doing the Job Alone
Pre-adolescents: What Makes Them Tick	Workshop for Discussion Group Leaders
Film Series for Parents	Workshop in Group Development

RESULTS

In a large city there are many intangibles contributing to the success or failure of Neighborhood Play Groups and the Family Life Education program. Over a period of seventeen years the community response and cooperation of various groups in the community have been increasingly gratifying. Now the Seattle Council on Family Relations, composed of people from most agencies in the community which provide education or services for families, serves in an advisory capacity to correlate, evaluate, and promote Family Life Education in Seattle. And so the Program may now be considered as all-community (rather than isolated in one division of the City Public Schools).

CONCLUSION

Without the professional staff provided by the Public Schools, the program could not exist; neither could it survive and flourish without the cooperation of PTA's and other cooperating organizations and agencies within the city. This is an example of "grass roots" adult education which not only meets the needs of parents and children but also fills the need for an ever larger reservoir of lay leadership in the field of Family Life Education.

3

A SCHOOL MENTAL HEALTH PROJECT

by Mrs. Theora Standing, *Psychologist*, San Bernardino Public Schools

The mental health plays, *Fresh Variable Winds*, *Scattered Showers*, and *High Pressure Area*, have rich value both for teen-agers and for parents or adults dealing with teen-agers. A better understanding of sibling rivalry, reasons for rebellion against parents, inferiority feelings, is gained from the presentation of these plays. And we believe the plays should be produced and acted by the teen-agers themselves.

379

A scene from a Mental Health Play dealing with family relationships. Members of the cast are school pupils who enjoy their contribution to the community mental health education program. Both children and parents learn much from play presentations.

— *Courtesy of the San Bernardino Public Schools*

A school project, directed by the author, was designed to involve those youngsters whose problems were similar to the play-themes. Thus it combined therapy for the students with a constructive community activity, viz, mental health programs for PTA and civic groups. The drama group realized that they were giving parents and other adults a clearer understanding of teen-agers: how they "tick". They knew the desperate need for this understanding in our confusing modern age. And the therapeutic benefits accruing to the members of the casts were gratifying.

The plays serve as springboards for discussions, both for the casts and for audiences. They often open the way for many private conferences dealing with the more serious and intimate problems which teen-agers and their parents have. All the cast seemed to profit by "exposure" to emotionally-fraught situations. Through role-playing and subsequent discussion, club members and their parents often were alerted to their own individual problems; often they found helpful suggestions and support for problem solutions.

Role-playing leads to the minimization of guilt feelings and a lessening of feelings of fear which pupils had previously thought to be peculiar to themselves. While portraying a character with similar adjustment problems, many could see their own problems more objectively.

Some pupils who were invited to join the drama group had well-adjusted personalities. However, it was believed that they had a higher potential than they were achieving. In these cases the activity provided benefits of assurance, self confidence, and development of talent and leadership qualities.

Three different groups of students prepared the mental health plays. The age range varied from nine to sixteen years. Each play was presented numerous times during a three-year period. New cast members were added as needed, with careful screening by the director. Cohesiveness of the groups was maintained during the three-year period. While the players were in rehearsal stage, several group meetings were held weekly. After the plays were ready, the sessions were limited to times when rehearsals were needed, and to the play nights. Refreshments and discussions were included. Individual counseling was made available to members of the cast and to parents, as well as others in the audience at public showings. The director, as school psychologist, considered the counseling conferences with those who sought them an important part of her work.

Perfection of the drama presentation was not sought, but rather, the personal growth of the cast and members of the audience who discussed the problems presented in the plays. As long as the play was realistic and stimulating for audience discussion, the objective was reached.

The effect on parent-child relationships was the prime factor in the project. Most of the group members felt insecure because of insufficient insight and cooperation within their own family constellations. As a result of the drama project rapport with parents was reported. In fact, family pride and status grew as the adolescent in the family gained favorable recognition and identification with a successful, active student group. In several cases the pupil was able to influence a change in parental attitude where the group leader in her capacity as school psychologist had tried and failed. And frequently the pupil's own improved understanding and tolerance of the family situation caused a happy change.

"WORRY, WORRY, WORRY!" — Three high school students portray the roles of worried mothers in the mental health play, "Scattered Showers". This is one of the three plays presented as a contribution to the city and county mental health education program.

—*Courtesy of the San Bernardino Public Schools*

Parent reactions to their child's role-playing varied from an aloof, sophisticated attitude, deep feelings of guilt, to keen appreciation. Some were amused with the similarity of their own handling of family problems and action in the play. They conceded that they had broken most of the "rules of the book". Some parents sought counseling and gained much from it.

The general attitude of group members was one of dedication to the worthwhile cause of helping each other to gain insight into his own problems through the effective medium of the plays. When the desire for recognition and approval had been satisfied, each member was content to be less concerned with self. And the contribution to the community mental health program made by these youngsters should be noted as an important education influence in the city and the county.

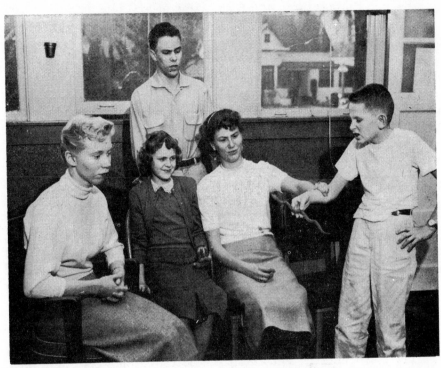

"OHHHH, GO AWAY!" — A scene from the Mental Health Play, "Fresh Variable Showers", with high school students taking the roles in this problem play.
— *Courtesy of the San Bernardino Public Schools*

CONCLUSION

This school mental health project shows the value of coordinating school, parent, and community educational programs. There is a rich reservoir of talent and leadership within the schools of any community for effective presentation of the excellent mental health plays. Leadership of audience discussions is important and provision for counseling parents and children should be made. When the school psychologist or guidance worker is "on the team", an opportunity is given for multiple counseling and for extending counseling services throughout the community.

4

A MENTAL HEALTH ASSOCIATION LAY DISCUSSION PROGRAM

by Dr. Milton Freedman, *Executive Director*
Mental Health Association of St. Louis

Since 1949 the St. Louis Mental Health Association has been training lay people to lead mental health discussions in the community[1]. Leaders, using films and skits as springboards for discussion, conduct about 300 discussion meetings a year in PTAs, church groups, and other community organizations. Over a period of a year these groups will hold from one to eight discussion sessions, with the area of parent-child relationships predominating.

An example of a series of meetings for a group of pre-school parents will illustrate the procedures:

Six monthly mental health discussions were planned and organized through the PTA committee. Two discussion leaders, a man and a woman, agreed to lead the group. A tentative schedule of plays and films was made. An average of twenty parents attended the meetings.

The film "Mental Health" was used in the first meeting. Discussion was lively and a lot of areas were mentioned, but not explored thoroughly. Ideas about raising kids were brought out but the general tone of the meeting was enjoyment of sharing mutual problems and opinions.

In the weeks that followed, such films as "Shyness" and "The Fears of Children" and the play "Scattered Showers" were presented. As time went on, the group found itself no longer formally discussing matters, but delving more deeply into problems and solutions for more effective child-raising.

The role of the discussion leaders in this group was to stimulate discussion; to give everyone a chance to "speak his piece"; to clarify and summarize points made in the films or play (if appropriate to the needs of the group).

Leadership Methods

Because of the varied types of discussion group projects, the methods and techniques used by the group leaders differ according to

[1]Brashear, E. L., Kenney, E. T., Buchmueller, A. D., Gilden, M.C. "A Community Program of Mental Health Education Using Group Discussion Methods", *Am. J. of Orthopsychiatry*, Vol. XXIV, No. 3, July 1954.

Scene from mental health play "The Ins and Outs". The members of the cast were from a local high school and coached by their dramatics teacher. This play presentation is widely used in Mental Health discussion meetings.

— Courtesy of the Mental Health Association of St. Louis

the needs and interests of the particular group. Some leaders are non-directive in their approach while others tend to structure their roles quite differently, using techniques such as role-playing and buzz-groups. There is common agreement that the expertness of the leader is confined to leadership skills and not to the knowledge of mental health. The leader gives no answers to the many questions and problems raised by participants. He is not a "resource person".

Training of Leaders

The key to the success of the St. Louis program is the training of the discussion leaders. The first course is an orientation to the field of mental health which any interested person can attend. In six meetings led by lay leaders the group experiences the kind of mental health program that is given in the community. Of the approximately one hundred people who participate in one of the four sections of the course, twenty are invited to take the basic workshop training. Not all of these are interested in becoming leaders, particularly since active leaders cover from six to twelve assignments a year. For this reason some other well-qualified persons are invited to participate in the training workshop. Some of these are mental health professionals who are willing to lead as lay people in this program.

The basic workshop consists of six weekly meetings plus observational assignments in the community. The trainer is professionally qualified in both mental health and discussion leadership. The groups experience the warmth and reward of discussing mutual problems together, while frequently stopping to analyze what has been going on and what the trainer has been doing. In addition, time is given to an explanation of the Association and the administration of the discussion program. At times one of the group may take over as discussion leader.

Following the basic workshop, leaders are sent to lead groups that require little help, or to groups where an experienced leader can supervise and support the new leader. At this point leaders frequently avail themselves of the help of the office staff, dropping in or calling to talk about this job of leading.

Advanced training consists of a variety of workshops and special meetings. Skill-training sessions, review of films, practice leading sessions, and study groups of unexplored areas of mental health are among the many sessions that are offered. In the course of a year, 90% of our 50 most active leaders will attend some kind of advanced training program. Many will attend several different courses.

386

RESULTS

Although no scientific evaluation of the community discussion program is yet available, the Mental Health Association Office has systematically collected evaluations of each meeting from the leader and program chairman. These have helped to improve the program over the years. And each year the demand for programs has increased over the previous year.

In addition to the anticipated problems of occasional poor physical arrangements and misunderstanding of the nature of the program, the main concern has been to maintain and improve the quality of the leadership as the program expands. Through the selection process after the orientation course and a self-elimination that goes on throughout training, a fairly high standard is maintained. Moreover, special care is taken to assign leaders to groups where it is believed the relationship will be a good one.

REFERENCES

1. Benne, K. D. "Finding Time for Citizenship", *Adult Leadership*, Vol. II, No. 5, Oct. 1953.
2. Hickey, M. "A Community Promotes Mental Health", *Ladies' Home Journal*, April 1954.
3. Kotinsky, R., Witmer, H. (editors). *Community Programs for Mental Health.* Harvard University Press, 1955.

5

ORGANIZING A LARGE MEETING FOR INDIVIDUAL PARTICIPATION

by DR. HELEN I. DRIVER, *Program Consultant*
WISCONSIN ASSOCIATION FOR MENTAL HEALTH

The day of the spell-binding lecturer seems to have gone: television and radio programs provide vicarious emotional binges aplenty and educational features must have an air of entertainment about them in order to hold their audiences. Even preachers nowadays wisely limit their sermons to minutes instead of hours as in the old days.

The effective program planner arranges his large meetings to include the popular audio-visual activities: films and dramatizations. Talks or lectures are slipped in as part of the show, but these must be shortened sufficiently to fit the extremely short attention span of the modern audience.

Participation Methods

The educator, following the principle that *learning is doing*, tries to get his audience emotionally involved and actively participating in the program of the large meeting. The techniques used for active participation of the audience members are round-table discussion groups, buzz-groups, planning committees and the like. Vicarious or participation-by-identification can be effected by panels, debates, films or role-playing (followed by discussion), town-meeting or open forum structures. In such activities audience members may identify themselves or their opinions with the "main characters" who carry the active roles. The prerequisite of audience participation is a common problem or subject of strong interest to members of the audience.

Let us take the example of a PTA meeting of elementary school parents. A common problem and strong interest is there: child-rearing and learning to become better parents. A recording of the talk given by Dr. Spock at the White House Conference on "The Personality of the Child" is to be heard and then discussed by the parents. There is a program director, resource person (psychologist), and lay leaders to handle the discussion groups. The program sequence is as follows:

15 min. Short business meeting.

15 min. Explanation of the program, how the discussion groups will be organized, the use of Dr. Spock's talk as a springboard for the discussion. Recording is played.

40 min. Discussion groups organized around four tables according to age-level interests of the parents. Assigned leaders give out typed slips containing the two discussion questions. 15 minutes for each question, with group opinion or conclusion to be reported by a representative from the group.

a. The leader secures a volunteer recorder from the group, then allows free discussion of the questions, serving as a moderator.

b. During the progress of the discussion period each leader secures a representative from the group to serve as summarizer and reporter.

10 min. After 30 minutes of discussion a bell is rung and the program director requests the groups to send their representatives to the main table. Here a panel formation of representatives, program director and resource person is made around the table.

15 min. An informal presentation of group reports is given, with the program director summarizing. Then the resource person is asked to comment.

15 min. The discussion is thrown open to the audience and an open forum is started, with members of the audience, panelists, and resource person involved. The program director serves as moderator.

5 min. The meeting is closed with a summary by the program director.

This two-hour program was run off with dispatch and a minimum of confusion because of the careful planning and provision for all essential arrangements, leadership, physical expeditors (name tags, labeled group areas, round-tables with sufficient seating, typed question slips, paper and pencils, etc.).

In this program all audience members participated and there was a complete absence of passivity and inertia often characteristic of large meetings.

A second illustration of a large meeting organized for individual participation is taken from a Bethel summer workshop of the National Training Laboratory in Group Development. The program was planned by a committee of delegates to utilize every minute of the hour and a half assigned to the project. Role-playing, buzz-groups, panel of experts, and an open forum were included.

The subject of the meeting was *How can we explain effectively the Bethel experience to people back home?* This was a question close to the hearts of the seventy delegates, many of whom had been sent to the Workshop by their corporations or organizations. In a few days the delegates were to leave for home and the inevitable questions — so hard to answer.

The planning committee had secured the services of a highly skilled staff member to serve as "master of ceremonies" (program director and moderator). This skill included ability to organize a large meeting, giving clear explanations and succinct interpretations or summaries. Also the ability to adjust quickly to changes in the program, needed when plans go wrong or timing is off, is essential in the program director.

The sequence of events was as follows:

5 min. Explanation of the program, outline of events for evening.

5 min. Psychodrama: "Telling the Boss about Bethel". After five minutes of the conversation between boss and employee, the program director stops the action.

6 min.	Buzz-groups of 6–8, with assigned leaders, discuss how the employee can improve her explanation of Bethel to the boss.
5 min.	Reports from the eleven buzz-groups in one phrase or sentence.
5 min.	Psychodrama continued and concluded.
5 min.	Interview of role-players by director to find out their opinions and feelings in the psychodrama.
10 min.	Buzz-groups continued with new task: preparing questions for panel of experts to discuss, relative to difficulties and clarifications of ways to best explain the Bethel experience to people back home.
10 min.	Questions written on board.
30 min.	Panel discussion of questions. About half-way through, the director opened the discussion to the floor and a semi-open forum resulted.
3 min.	Summary by the director.

84 minutes, plus scene-changing time of about 15 minutes total.

This program was an excellent demonstration of involvement and participation of all members of a large audience.

SUMMARY

Successful programs which provide individual participation for members of large audiences are accomplished by careful planning, split-second timing, and skilled leadership, both in the director and in the assigned group leaders. Strong interest in a common problem is essential to satisfaction on the part of participants.

6

GROUP COUNSELING IN FAMILY LIVING

by Mrs. Roberta Lovell, *Director*

Duarte Family Counseling Service, Duarte, California

The Duarte Family Health Center, a Community Chest organization, has been in operation since 1951. The Health Committee of the Community Service Council organized the Duarte Family Counseling Service in 1952 on a trial basis for six months, subsidized by private donations. Sixty-six families were served during this period, and then the Counseling Service became a part of the community service program partially financed through the Community Chest. Counseling and guidance were offered to those having family and personal difficulties. Starting with one part-time counselor, the service now includes a full-time counselor and three part-time specialists from the fields of child guidance and family finance.

390

MRS. ROBERTA LOVELL
Family Relations Counselor
Duarte Family Health Center

The program includes both individual and group counseling. Either method or a combination of the two are used according to the needs and inclinations of the clients. One member of the family may participate in the program, or both parents and one or more of the children are counseled, depending upon the family situation. Adult groups for individuals with common problems and for persons without specific problems have been organized for those who are interested in improving their self-understanding and their understanding of others. The groups include Mothers of Teen-agers, the Young Mothers' Group, the Men's Group, and a Group for women of more mature age and experience. The content of group discussions depends upon the needs and interests of the members.

Group Counseling Method

The method developed for group sessions is unique in that each meeting is a unit in itself: the content and experience is complete and independent. This plan was evolved because each session tends to have different membership. Although some members participate in a group over a period of months — sometimes as long as two years — attendance is not regular, and strict continuity of content is not attempted for this reason.

The materials and content of the group meetings are on a practical, reality-facing level because most group members have little if any education beyond high school and are not usually oriented nor prepared for therapy. Reading is limited, and the members' most expressed grievance is a feeling of harassment common to young people who are ill-prepared to undertake all the responsibilities that go with raising several children, managing a limited family income and maintaining a home, including all the pressures that go with home ownership. Single group meetings, if self-propelled under these circumstances, often tend to deteriorate into gripe sessions leading nowhere, so the role of the counselor-leader and the structuring of the group sessions have proved crucial. Likewise, the counselor's skill is challenged to handle the needs of the old-timer and the nervous first-timer.

Unless a particular subject is requested by a member or the group as a whole, the leader initiates the group counseling process by starting with a "stimulator" for the particular group session. This fits into a flexible plan of group education, subject to adjustment to the growth or problems of the group membership. Each member is supplied with a notebook which is kept at the Center. Pencils and writing boards are distributed as the group members convene. The leader, at the beginning of the session, suggests that ten or fifteen minutes be taken in which the feelings about the particular subject for that session are written down by each participant. Next, usually, is the reading of all the write-ups by group members. Then the session is open for discussion. Members question each other, comment on what others have said, or explore the significance of their own contributions. Only when the participants have exhausted their spontaneous reactions does the leader start asking questions (prepared in advance) to stimulate the group's interactions and deeper understanding of the subject.

An illustration of the method follows:

SUBJECT: *What is Your Definition of Success?*

(The group write their feelings about this, read each statement, start discussion.)

Counselor's Questions:

1. What do you think caused your definition to be different from those of others in the group?
2. How does your definition of success compare with that of your parents?
3. How does your mate's feeling about success compare with yours?
4. Do you feel that you are or can be a success in line with your definition?
5. What differences can you see in your present definition and what it might be at other times in your life?
6. Do you think you should influence your children to develop a certain attitude toward success?

Leader's Role: A dual role is played by the counselor-leader because she is not only the moderator but also the resource person. Ideally, as a democratic leader, she turns back direct questions for the group to discuss. However, when information-giving appears to be constructive, she makes a direct answer. The leader's action is guided by the principle that the purpose of the group is to stimulate individual members into finding their own answers to questions and problems at the same time providing them with as many tools as possible to help them to do so.

Group Standards: Threatened feelings are usually handled in individual counseling interviews rather than acted out in the group. Thus this type of group counseling is not group psychotherapy according to the classical form. In these counseling groups the leader takes an active, stimulating role. At the same time she usually guides manifestations of extreme negative emotions away from the group and encourages shy members to participate (or gives them recognition for their presence in the group until they are ready to take a more active part). The level of interaction usually is maintained somewhere between class participation and group therapy.

In spite of the changing membership each group has a personality of its own due to the core of regular members and to the choice of subjects selected to meet the needs of the group. Following are examples of three types of stimulators and insights that have developed in the course of discussing these subjects:

A. Concept of Self

Written question: What was your position in your family, and how do you think it affected your attitude toward yourself?

Insight example: "Every other group member who was oldest in her family has said she has a tendency to be bossy. I hate to admit this, but I think this may be true of me, too."

Counselor's questions:

1. What special privileges or disadvantages do you think resulted from your position in the family?
2. Did your parents (or other relatives) have any special reaction to your position in the family?
3. If given the opportunity, what position would you have chosen?

Other "Self" stimulators: How important is the opinion of others to you? How do you feel different from other people? What would you like to change about yourself? How do you feel about failing?

B. Family Relations

Written question: How can a wife help her husband?

Insight example: "I've been so busy complaining about my husband's shortcomings and praising myself for all the fine things I feel I do that I haven't given much thought to how much I should, or could, help my husband."

Counselor's questions:

1. Do you agree there is a woman behind every successful man?
2. Was your mother an asset to your father?
3. When your husband achieves something special are you jealous or do you feel it is partially your success?

393

Other "Family" stimulators: What are the things your children do which irritate you the most? What is your definition of a good home? Why do you feel some marriages fail? Why should your husband love you?

C. Relationships with Others

Written question: How do you feel about giving and taking orders?

Insight example: "I've told myself the reason I don't get promoted is because my supervisor has no confidence in me. The truth is, I don't have enough confidence in myself to give the orders necessary in a more responsible job than I have now."

Counselor's questions:

1. Was your childhood home democratic or was discipline rigid?
2. Do you seek or avoid responsibility?
3. Are most of your friends leaders or followers?
4. How does your mate react to giving and taking orders?

Other "Relationship" stimulators: How should we judge other people? What kind of people bore you? What is human nature? What rights does an individual have?

In addition to the subject stimulators, as illustrated above, other techniques are used for variety: pictures, sentence completions, role-playing, defense mechanism study, tests and inventories. Examples of these devices, with accompanying typical insights, are as follows:

1. **Pictures:** Each group member is asked to write the first story that comes to mind while viewing a picture of one or more individuals expressing emotion. (Magazine illustrations often serve as good stimulators.) The result of finding as many different stories — as many as there are individuals in the group — often proves to be a significant learning experience in regard to individual differences. Personality patterns are often brought into focus by the moods and details contained in the stories.

   Insight example: "I will never again be surprised when others don't see things as I do after listening to eight different stories about this one picture."

2. **Sentence Completion:** Sentence stimulators refer to a specific subject (mother, self, success, worry, etc.). Comparison of completions shows wide individual differences in a group. In addition to individual provocative completions, an individual can often see a pattern in his own completions as well as finding food for thought in the significant answers of others.

   Insight example: When three members of her group indicated a desire for violent behavior in finishing the sentence "When my child nags me all day . . .", one woman was relieved of much guilt and said, "Well, I guess I'm not so bad after all!"

3. **Role-playing:** Problems relating to family or job relationships make good themes for role-playing. Re-enactment of conflict situations brings into play much spontaneity and relief of tension.

   Insight example: "I learned more about how my son must feel by taking his role in our argument than I ever have by people talking to me."

394

4. Study of Defense Mechanisms: Mimeographed sheets with the definition, explanation and every-day examples of defense mechanisms are given to group members to read over and study. Then during the period of written assignment they are asked to recall a time when they used a particular mechanism and another time when someone else used it. (At first members often feel they cannot do this, but as time goes by they usually recall very significant examples.)

Insight example: "Not only does this mechanism explain why I got mad at my son last night but it probably explains a lot of other times I've gotten mad without real cause. If I can figure them out maybe I won't be so disagreeable all the time."

5. Tests: Simple self-administered psychological and popular personality tests help to open up new approaches to an individual's problems. Also, the variation in normal patterns can be reassuring to many group members.

Insight example: "My husband and I usually take the various tests in newspapers and magazines. Secretly I've been unhappy because we always answered the questions so differently. Now I can see that what is important is why we answered as we did, and it is not necessary for us to be the same."

Leader Role

The key skill essential for the counselor-leader is to maintain a balance between stimulating yet not forcing insights beyond the readiness of group members. The right timing for "the light touch" — a joke, anecdote or factual material — may make the difference between an assimilated insight and unconstructive aggravation of anxiety. The sensitive use of kindly humor can often help individuals to release tension and reduce self-defeating anxieties.

The personality and skill of the counselor-leader probably are the major factors in the group counseling program at Duarte as in all successful counseling. Not only are permissiveness and acceptance crucial, but a sensitivity to the needs of each group member is basic. The counselor keeps the individual's participation in balance by giving support and adjunctive personal counseling to those who become anxious through insights and guilt feelings aggravated in the group sessions.

CONCLUSION

Group counseling, like all counseling, is a never-ending challenge. Both the leader and the group members should grow. And with this growth the dynamic experience is most rewarding to all participants. Experience in Duarte has shown, regardless of the age or background of the participants, great satisfaction and progress is possible in this approach to learning and growth stimulation.

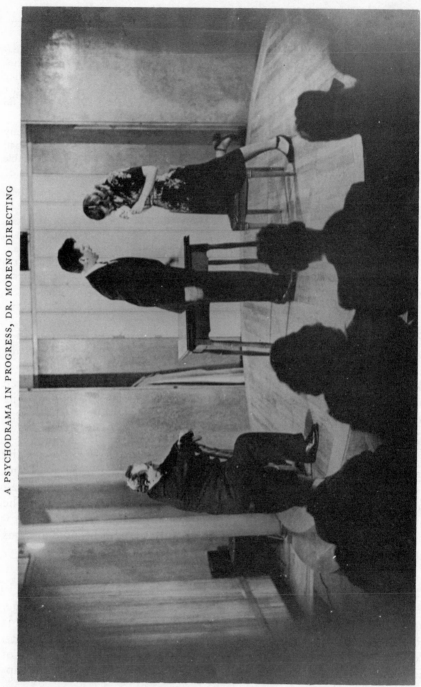

SECTION II — SYMPOSIUM

PART FIVE

GROUP PSYCHOTHERAPY, REHABILITATION, AND COUNSELING PROGRAMS: VALUE OF THE INTIMATE GROUP

List of Articles

1

PSYCHODRAMA AS A TREATMENT METHOD IN A CORRECTIONAL INSTITUTION
by Dr. Michael M. Miller, *Consulting Psychiatrist*
Boys Village, Cheltenham, Maryland

2

MULTIPLE COUNSELING WITH DELINQUENT ADOLESCENTS
by Dr. Gordon K. Higginson, *Director, Psychological Services*
University of Portland, Portland, Oregon

3

GROUP PSYCHOTHERAPY AND AFTER CARE FOR ALCOHOLIC PATIENTS
Charles E. Thompson, Ph.D. and William P. Kolb, M.D.
Veterans Administration Hospital, North Little Rock, Ark.

4

REHABILITATIVE THERAPY FOR CONVALESCENT MENTAL PATIENTS
by Dr. Theodore H. Salzberg, *Counseling Psychologist*
Brentwood Hospital, Veterans Administration Center, Los Angeles, Calif.

5

GROUP THERAPY FOR ALCOHOLICS
by Dr. Vernelle Fox, *Physician in Charge*
Georgian Clinic, Atlanta, Georgia

6

A GROUP PSYCHOTHERAPY PROJECT: *Learning to Live Together*
by Ray W. Dutcher, *Counseling Psychologist*
San Bernardino, Calif.

7

AN EXPERIMENT IN GROUP GUIDANCE FOR LATER MATURITY
reported by Dr. Iona Logie, *Adult Counseling Service*
San Francisco Public Schools

8

GROUP PSYCHOTHERAPY FOR THE AGING
by Dr. Maurice E. Linden, *Director*
Division of Mental Health, Philadelphia Department of Public Health

The value of the intimate group as a therapeutic agent as well as a learning medium is shown in the eight articles of Part 5. Small-group discussion under skilled leadership — especially when the leader is also the therapist — expedites changes in attitudes and behavior. The support of the group and the leader helps individuals face and solve their personal problems. Modern treatment methods for juvenile offenders, alcoholics, mental patients, and the aging are aptly described in the articles which follow.

1

PSYCHODRAMA AS A TREATMENT METHOD IN A CORRECTIONAL INSTITUTION

by DR. MICHAEL M. MILLER, *Consulting Psychiatrist*
BOYS VILLAGE, CHELTENHAM, MARYLAND

Boys Village is a reform school for Negro boys between the ages of eight and eighteen who have been given various court commitments ranging from several months to indefinite sentences until they are eighteen years of age. Offences range from truancy to murder. There are 250–300 boys in the school, contained in eight cottages with 30–40 boys in each unit. Each cottage has "cottage parents" who attempt to establish a friendly, family-like parental relationship with the boys, along with their role as supervisors.

The boys come largely from sub-marginal homes in the slums of Baltimore and from various counties of Maryland. Environmental influences, including the parents, contribute greatly to the outlaw behavior of the children. Because many of the boys return home from school to find nothing to eat, no warmth or love there, they go out on the streets to steal food and find fellowship in gangs made up of others like themselves. So quite naturally they get into trouble with the law.

398

And often their motivation can be "getting even" with those who they feel are rejecting them and treating them unfairly.

The purpose of the psychodrama sessions is to let the boys spontaneously act out their feelings of hostility and other emotions associated with traumatic experiences in the past which contributed to the asocial and psychopathic development of their personalities.

The psychodrama sessions are held weekly, with varied age groupings. Attendance is voluntary. A boy volunteers to present his personal problem and to be the protagonist (main character). For example, John, aged 12, who was committed for running away from home and for stealing, re-enacted home situations fraught with conflicts. Scenes included the humiliation he felt when his father slapped him, his refusal to eat the food his mother cooked because he wanted to hurt her. The reasons for his behavior were brought to light in the discussion following the acting out of the various home situations. The underlying cause of his trouble was his feeling of jealousy toward his sister — the belief that his mother was not as loving or attentive to him as to his sister.

A second use of psychodrama at Boys Village has been to improve the insight and skill of staff members. They have learned to improve their techniques in handling the boys through lessons learned in the psychodramas. For example, a boy wished to act out the role of his male cottage-parent. He did so in a demonstrative, loud and authoritative manner, shouting and shaking his fist at the other boys until they assumed cowed, submissive attitudes. When he finished he was asked by the Director (psychiatrist) if that was the way Mr. S— had acted. One large lad came forward, his face drawn with anger, eyes flashing. He said, "No, Doctor, it ain't quite like that — I'll show you." He asked for a leather glove and roughly pulled the shirt off another boy. Then he simulated a severe blow in the area of the heart. "You see," he boasted, "That's what you get when you cross me — and my glove leaves few marks, so watch your step!" The other boy cowered, for he had actually been subjected to this kind of treatment. It so happened that the cottage master in question was present in the audience. His embarrassment at the situation re-enactment in front of the other staff members was apparent. But, more important, his seeing himself as others saw him made a deep impression, leading to what appeared to be a rather fundamental change in his behavior with the boys. He stopped using this disciplinary method and has since made attempts to use more humane procedures in dealing with his charges.

Another example of the insight gained through psychodrama for staff members occurred in the case of a boy acting out his feelings about running away from the school. He seemed to center his attention on a certain staff member. The boy had inquired about the possibility of obtaining a weekend furlough and release from the school in the near future. The staff member had painted a rather hopeless picture of the possibilities. The boy in role-reversal acted out the part of the staff member in the conference, and then portrayed himself as feeling desperately unhappy, homesick and despairing of getting home. Then only did he make the decision to run away. He did so, was caught and underwent disciplinary action including prolongation of his incarceration. In the discussion following the psychodrama the boy broke down, cried, saying, "Why didn't he tell me the truth — that I was up for a weekend furlough and was being considered for release? Why did he want to torment me and drive me to do it?" The staff member involved was deeply impressed with this psychodrama and outburst. He saw how he had been unconsciously hurting others as well as this boy in the same way. The lasting impression was made not only on him but also on other staff members who were present. This carried over into improved relationships with the boys.

For those who wish to use psychodrama for similar purposes in correctional institutions we have the following advice:

1. The therapist should direct the performance, including the selection of and instructions to the auxiliary actors so that they will be able to help the protagonist to re-enact real life situations. Scenes should be short, with assisting actors being briefed before each scene.

2. It helps to have a stage with lighting equipment so the audience can be darkened for each scene. Intense realism is attempted, with language and movement that is dynamic. For instance, the father slaps the son with force and emotion, so that the son feels really humiliated as in the original life situation.

3. Let the protagonist re-experience and re-evaluate the original conflict situation. Often the other boys in the audience can identify with him and thus gain insight from the performance. We often permit boys to spontaneously act out experiences which they recall by identification and association.

4. The Director should encourage spontaneous participation in the discussion following the skit. Use of incisive questions help, for example,

Why was John trying to hurt himself?

Why did he formerly hurt himself by refusing to eat his mother's food?

Why did he get into trouble with the law — was that also to hurt mother?

What is back of this — why does he want to hurt his mother?

Favorable results of the psychodrama activity have been reported by cottage masters, teachers, work supervisors, members of peer groups, social workers, etc. These benefits have been found in cases of boys in the audience in addition to boys who were protagonists.

CONCLUSION

In conclusion, we have found psychodrama to be an effective educational and therapeutic method for helping the boys and staff members to gain insight, especially in the area of adult-boy relationships. Since the philosophy of our school is based upon treatment of the boys as emotionally disturbed children, the place of the cottage parents is most important. They are parent-substitutes, attempting to influence the attitudes and behavior of their "children". Through psychodrama the boys gain an understanding of their ambivalent feelings toward their real parents. They realize that vengeance, hostility, jealousy, often result in their hurting themselves in order to hurt someone else. Group discussions led by a therapist can result in changed attitudes and improved behavior patterns. Psychodrama has the great advantage that larger groups can be treated. In fact, often the larger the participating audience, the greater is the therapeutic impact.

A Note of Caution

The need for helping the boys after they are discharged from the school is very great. The changed attitudes and behavior patterns can deteriorate and dissolve in a short time if the boy is returned to the same environment which pressured him into his delinquent pattern. Constructive forces, initiated during the stay at the training school, must continue to influence him in an improved environment. To fulfill this obligation, the courts, legalistic and social agencies of the community and state must take responsibility for providing necessary changes for disposition of the case after discharge from the school.

2
MULTIPLE COUNSELING WITH DELINQUENT ADOLESCENTS

by DR. GORDON K. HIGGINSON, *Director, Psychological Services*
UNIVERSITY OF PORTLAND, PORTLAND, OREGON

Our clinic serves the Portland area as well as the University. Cases are referred for diagnosis and treatment from the courts, schools, health and welfare agencies. The challenging problem of treating considerable numbers of emotionally disturbed adolescents on an outpatient basis is being handled partially through group psychotherapy in our clinic. The method is one of multiple counseling, in which the group sessions are accompanied by individual counseling. However, we have reason to believe that group therapy is more effective with some adolescents than individual therapy.

An example of the effectiveness of group therapy over individual therapy concerned a number of fifteen-year-old boys, all of whom had been convicted of a taboo-type misdemeanor, viz, exposing themselves in public. Individual counseling with these boys had been unsuccessful. When the six boys were brought together in a group they were informed that each had a similar problem. This seemed to facilitate their ability to discuss their compulsion and what they could do to overcome it. Excellent results were secured. In a matter of a few weeks, these boys were able to show great improvement; they gained almost complete control over the anti-social acts although at times the urges were present. They were able to help one another to arrive at better solutions of handling stimulating situations and each verbalized insight into his problems.

Multiple counseling is used with various groups at our clinic, adult as well as adolescent. Even when a serious common problem in the group is not present, good results are secured in terms of various individual problems of group members. Intensive group therapy, however, is possible only when groups are carefully organized as to common problems where mutual help can be given.

The group project to be described in detail forthwith concerned six seventeen-year-old boys, all of whom were wards of the juvenile court. Their delinquent symptoms varied from habitual truancy to car stealing. They all had I.Q.'s of between 115 and 130. All were failing in every subject or in all subjects but one in their respective schools. We shall call these boys Tom, Dick, Harry, John, Bill, and Pete. The first four mentioned were from broken homes, living with their mothers and step-fathers. The other two, Bill and Pete, were living with their natural parents. None of the boys were able to maintain very satisfactory relationships with their parents.

This was a closed group, with the same membership through its seven months duration, including 29 group sessions. The group was carefully screened with the following questions in mind: (1) Does this particular case meet the criteria for group treatment (2) Would it seem from the dynamics revealed in the tests that this boy could readily become a therapeutic member of the particular group we are organizing. The battery of tests included the Wechsler, Rorschach, Draw-A-Person Projective Test, TAT, and Sack's Sentence Completion Test. Diagnostic interviews with the boys and parents also were held.

Leader Role

The leader's role in an adolescent group differs from that in an adult group, and especially in the case of juvenile offenders. These adolescents need considerable help with the group process, and then increasing encouragement to express their own feelings and ideas and to help one another gain insights. From the author's experience it seems important to withhold interpretations, even in analytically oriented groups of adolescents. For example, positive transference should never be interpreted. And it is equally important for the leader to safeguard the possibility of these boys becoming an intimate group outside the therapy sessions in which they might not be able to control delinquent behavior. In view of this, in building the group into a therapy group, the leader must frequently reward positive movements, insights, and newly-formed attitudes which are verbalized.

The therapist must be completely accepting and at the same time extremely careful that he does not condone delinquent acts (in his attempt to build rapport) so that the boys identify him with a bigger and better delinquent. For example, to offer these boys cigarettes in the therapy sessions when it is forbidden by law is interpreted by the boys as meaning that the therapist really doesn't believe in these laws either.

Thumb-nail sketches of the group members follow:

Tom — the catalyst in the group, with a flair for keeping the discussion going, moving the discussion from one person to another, and of involving many people. Even though he originally used this as a defense from involving himself, he was, none the less, a very important therapeutic agent in the situation.

Bill — a very aggressive boy and he became almost immediately the group leader. He was big, rugged, physically a handsome boy who both verbally and physically displayed his aggression, particularly toward anyone who might be seen as an authority figure.

403

Dick — a passive lad who was willing to agree with anyone in the hope that they in turn would not reject him.

Harry — might be described as a boy of high nuisance value. He was continually in everyone's hair at school, a constant teaser, and very fond of playing practical jokes as long as they were not on himself. He was an excessive talker with very little to say, and he was low man on the totem pole in the group.

John — a very quiet boy who seemed so filled with suppressed aggression that he did not trust himself to talk much for fear these hostile feelings would get out of control. He seemed to have some awareness of his aggression and to be very fearful of its consequences.

Pete — perhaps the most immature member of the group as far as needing a great deal of nurture from his parents was concerned. Physically and socially, he appeared to be a very adequate seventeen-year-old.

I would like to give one example to show the tremendous advantage of multiple counseling over individual therapy in some instances. After this group had been in session for four months — 16 meetings — Pete informed the group that his parents had just told him they were going to get a divorce. Tom, Dick, Harry, and John had all gone through this traumatic experience within the past seven years. They were able to help Pete to express his ambivalent feelings: he wanted to run after his father and beg him to stay and at the same time he wanted to go stand by his mother and tell his father to leave — he would look after his mother. For the next four sessions the boys discussed their feelings at the time of their parents' divorces, working on this problem almost exclusively. It is doubtful that any therapist in individual therapy could have given Pete the empathy and help in gaining insight that the peer group did. At the end of this period, Pete was able to talk to his parents separately and together; he had so convinced them of the importance of keeping the family intact that they decided to make another go of the marriage.

Benefits to the other group members accrued during this period, also. Tom, Harry, and John were able to see how their own feelings had prevented them from accepting their respective step-fathers. They reported not only that they felt better about them, but also that they were able to live with them in a much more compatible arrangement. In addition, these sessions provided release for Bill, who for the first time was able to really talk about his feelings toward his own father and the tremendous hostility that existed between them.

The boys decided that their parents ought to have group sessions, especially their dads. All the fathers except Dick's accepted the leader's invitation to meet in order to talk about their sons' progress. At the end of the first session the dads agreed that they really needed another meeting. In fact, four sessions were held before they decided they now had a better understanding of themselves and their sons.

RESULTS

At the end of the school year the boys decided to end the sessions since all of them had jobs or were going into the service. The results in terms of behavior changes had been noteworthy: *all the boys passed every course in school and none had a cumulative grade less than B.* In view of the fact that all these boys had been failing, this was extremely gratifying. A second result was also impressive: *after the second month of group therapy, none of the boys was ever involved in any way in further delinquent acts.* It is the opinion of the author, who was the therapist, that there were occasions when only the strong group ego gave the boys strength enough to resist the temptation to act out an anti-social impulse. A careful follow-up study conducted two years after termination of the group project revealed that there had been no regression to anti-social behavior and that all the boys are doing commendably in their respective jobs.

At the time of this writing three of the boys are in service, one is working, and two are at college. The latter two have attained high positions in extra-curricular activities.

CONCLUSION

In conclusion it can be said that we have found multiple counseling with some adolescents to be the best method, suited to the needs of many of the disturbed young people referred to us. Many are more readily able to bring out their problems with the support and acceptance of the group. The ego strength that so many of these youths lack is built up early in group sessions by the approval of the members and the interest in each other's problems. Improved attitudes followed by improved behavior come through the group's progress in working through individual problems of members of the group.

3

GROUP PSYCHOTHERAPY AND AFTER CARE FOR ALCOHOLIC PATIENTS

by CHARLES E. THOMPSON, PH.D. and WILLIAM P. KOLB, M.D.[1]

VETERANS ADMINISTRATION HOSPITAL, NORTH LITTLE ROCK, ARKANSAS

The limitations of medicine in the treatment of the alcoholic are widely acknowledged. The success of Alcoholic Anonymous in rehabilitating alcoholics is well-known. The treatment program described herewith has been set up in a Veterans Administration hospital to make use of A.A. through the establishment of a Chapter within the hospital. This program is carried out on the acute-intensive treatment section of psychiatric services and is under the supervision of that service. In addition, posthospital care is provided through the discharged patient's affiliation to A.A. Both local and out-of-state A.A. members are free to visit our hospital group. Thus the obstacle of V.A. regulations which preclude control of patients in the posthospital period except for service-connected cases is overcome in the case of the alcoholic patient. Our hospital, in setting up an A.A. group, accepted the challenge of integrating the alcoholic patient into the A.A. program from the first day of his hospitalization. The intent is that he becomes so strongly attached to the organization that when discharged he continues his active affiliation in a community group.[2]

At the present time, following many years of effort, the hospital's responsibility in alcoholic cases is established as continuing after discharge until civilian rehabilitation is assured. For example, during one year period, 190 patients have, through their own volition, engaged in this posthospital program. Of that number only 19 have been readmitted as a result of excessive alcoholism. The rehabilitation of the discharged patients has been attested by letters, comments relayed to the hospital, and personal contacts from A.A. chapters throughout the area served by this hospital.

Method

The treatment program was accomplished through a progressive hospital administration that sponsored the facilities for such a program. A special room was furnished with appropriate furniture and decora-

[1]The statements and conclusions published by the authors are a result of their own study and do not necessarily reflect the opinion or policy of the Veterans Administration. This article was reviewed in the Veterans Administration and published with the approval of the Chief Medical Director.

[2]*The Community Plan*, Harold W. Sterling, M.D., Manager, VA Hospital, North Little Rock, Ark.

tions for the use of the A.A. group. In accordance with A.A. practice, the chapter was patient-run.

Upon admission to the hospital the alcoholic patient, if accessible, is briefed as to routine in the hospital and to the A.A. group. An invitation to participate in the meetings is extended, with emphasis on the voluntary character of the membership. If the patient is severely debilitated, the invitation is postponed until he is in condition for it. The active A.A. members take the responsibility for recruiting new members, including patients who are not alcoholics. Signs are posted in the admission wards reading "A.A. Welcomes All Those with Alcoholic and Other Problems".

Six days a week at a designated time this group meets for one and a half hour sessions. One night a week those who wish may go to various city A.A. groups. One of these groups has members who were hospital patients, now successfully employed and enjoying reasonable emotional security.

The meetings follow the standard procedure for any A.A. group. A chairman and secretary are elected from the membership. The chairman exercises the power of his office as though he were not a patient. It is interesting to note that on occasions the chairman has requested members to leave until they are in better shape to work constructively with the group. Also, one time the group used its democratic prerogative by suggesting that the chairman retire until he was more emotionally fit to hold the position.

This is more than just an A.A. group, however. A skilled psychotherapist is present at the meetings and he brings a type of group psychotherapy not possible in the usual A.A. meeting. Each active member is held responsible for his past behavior and for the eventual understanding and acceptance of himself without alcoholic indulgence. The serious efforts of members to achieve this new self-understanding and acceptance is illustrated by excerpts of the secretary's minutes given below:

"As in all things, failures are inevitable. The lapses but stress the successes and the necessity to understand and thereby control ourselves. With these conclusions the meeting considered marital relations with the particular case of belligerence toward the wife because of a feeling of insufficient demonstration of love from her — a condition rooted in a father-son relationship years previously. The denial of father's love was expressed in an almost unwarranted aggression toward the wife. We don't need to apologize; understanding is adequate repentance. Shame is but a reticence to face the facts . . ."

407

". . . After the reading and approval of the minutes, discussions began with the analysis of specific incidents leading to emotional variances in several of the members. Almost everyone thinks he is normal, yet his case is unique. We find common ground when this barrier is pierced, and we understand that although no cases are identical, we all have similar problems with the same alcoholic outlet. Events don't happen: we make them happen. What we feel without senses is all of experience. Revenge was discussed as cutting someone else down to size and as retribution for a feeling of a former conscious or subconscious hurt."

The superficial or intellectualized insight gained in the discussion meetings as illustrated in the secretaries' reports above was believed to be important in the improvement of the patients. However, the alcoholic patient has a great need for a personal attachment to someone or to some group. One of the aims of our treatment program is to transfer the patient's attachment away from the hospital group to a community A.A. group. The personality of the therapist is an important factor in this transfer. He must actually play a realistic role as a member of the A.A. group, ready to accept and to help members in emotional crises. The presence of the therapist at such a time may make the difference between success and failure for the patient.

An example of the hospital A.A. group benefiting from a discussion and consensus in the group was the problem of patients demanding sedation and being refused by the physician in charge. This situation was discussed intensively by the group one morning as a result of a complaint of a new member. The group as a whole agreed that sedation following a spree was equivalent to taking another drink, thus prolonging the sobering-up period. They felt it was better to suffer a little more for a shorter period by not taking medication. It was the opinion of the group that the doctor should be the sole judge as to the need of sedation and he should not be swayed by the pleadings and threats of the patient.

It should be made clear that the alcoholic patient in our hospital is not deprived of the other medical and therapy services. In reality, A.A. is but another adjunct to the overall treatment program which includes many activities such as corrective, educational, occupational and physical therapies as well as individual psychotherapy when indicated.

SUMMARY

In summary, this program is not offered as a "cure" but rather as an approach of the hospital to the perplexing and persistent alcoholic dilemma. Emphasis on a continued association with Alcoholic Anonymous following discharge from the hospital and encouragement to maintain contact with the hospital through visits to the hospital A.A. group are "after-care" factors. The excellent assistance of local A.A. chapters through rehabilitated members has filled the needs of recently hospitalized patients and contributed greatly to the success of the program.

4
REHABILITATIVE THERAPY FOR CONVALESCENT MENTAL PATIENTS[1]

by DR. THEODORE H. SALZBERG, *Counseling Psychologist*
BRENTWOOD HOSPITAL, VETERANS ADMINISTRATION CTR., LOS ANGELES, CALIF.

The group discussion project, with weekly sessions for patients who were employed or in vocation-education programs, had a two-fold purpose: (1) To keep administrative contact with patients working outside the hospital (2) To assist the convalescent patients in their reintegration into the community. It was part of the total program of hospital treatment and rehabilitation.

Group Organization

The group members, ranging from eight to fourteen in number, were all engaged in employment or training programs in the community. They remained in the hospital only as night lodgers, so to speak. The composition of the group was quite heterogeneous, and the length of time a member stayed in the group ranged from one session to an indefinite period of months. Diagnostically, all the psychiatric disorders were represented, but all group members were in relatively good remission and contact.

Once admitted to the group, attendance was mandatory because this was the only contact that the hospital staff had for control and management of these patients. Problems common to all members of the group were (1) immediate adjustment to everyday life (2) plans and adjustment after discharge from the hospital.

Group Method

The group discussions were largely unstructured. The leader (counseling psychologist) let problems emerge from the group. Usually some members brought up points and topics concerned with their personal adjustment problems. Occasionally, when there was a lack

---

[1] The opinions in this article should in no way be construed as official policy or practice of the Veterans Administration.

of participation, the leader would introduce a subject for discussion. Feelings of hostility, confusion, insecurity, and the whole gamut of defense mechanisms were freely expressed during the discussion sessions.

A list of the most frequent subjects of discussion follows:

1. Drinking and job stability.
2. Stigma of neuro-psychiatric hospitalization in job placement.
3. Should you acknowledge neuro-psychiatric status on job application?
4. Is it better to go to school or to a job directly after discharge?
5. Income tax refunds.
6. Exploitation of mental hospital dischargees in jobs: low pay, bad hours, menial tasks, etc.
7. Living alone or with others.
8. Leisure time and avocational activities.
9. Relationships with fellow employees and management.
10. Job-seeking procedures.
11. Can a former mental patient pick up where he left off?
12. Do people feel you are different?
13. How can you combat the idea that ex-mental patients are generally dangerous and unpredictable?
14. Family problems because of limited income, low job status.
15. Should I go directly back to work or convalesce for a period?
16. Is it best to go back to friends and family, or start a new life on your own?
17. How to achieve positive goals while at the hospital: work adjustment, work tolerance, habits, etc.
18. Money management.

Participation in discussions of the topics listed above was mostly spontaneous. The more withdrawn members were occasionally encouraged to voice an opinion.

An illustration of the kind of discussion the group members carried on is given below, from a partial protocol of a meeting where the stigma of hospitalization was the topic of discussion:

(Comments of group members)

— No answer for all people . . . some have to lie, some bluntly confess.
— The personnel officer or management should know, but no one else.
— Take a chance and work for a few months before they find out and maybe your good record will convince them to keep you.
— Sometimes you have to tell or get fired for falsifying the record.
— With small employers they are not likely to investigate.
— You have to live with it — might as well admit it.

410

— I get treated as well as anyone else on my job and they know I'm from here. (Almost all the group members agreed with this)

— Hospitals cure people with mental illnesses; employers should accept this.

Adjunctive Counseling

It appears that this type of ventilation, support, and mutual aid in an intimate group, all faced with the same difficult problems, is beneficial to the men. Added to this positive influence was the individual counseling given the patients by the therapist. Vocational counseling involving interviews and testing was done with each participant prior to his joining the group. Concomitant counseling was provided for group members seeking interviews. These were held following the group meetings. Some patients participated frequently in these short chats; others only infrequently.

Outcomes and Follow-Up

Self-evaluations by the patients indicated positive achievement on the part of most participants. Feelings of increased confidence, status, recognition, and other values were commonly noted among those exposed to the group activity over a period of several months. Realistic planning for the future was a significant outcome for those who were to be discharged from the hospital in the near future.

The value of the rehabilitative therapy project was discussed in a weekly group therapy seminar for hospital therapists (psychiatrists, psychologists, social workers). The consensus was that this group activity combined with outside work experience had positive value as an important transitional device for community integration. In addition, the psychiatrists believed that this program seemed to be a realistic application and evaluation of the total hospital program preceding entrance to the group discussion project, e.g. occupational therapy, psychotherapy, industrial therapy, etc.

A follow-up of patients who had been exposed to the group experience at least two months (eight meetings) and who had been employed at least four months was made. Notes from the case histories are given below:

G. D. — *Diagnosis:* Schizophrenic reaction, paranoid and catatonic type. Hospitalized two years. In group two and a half months; outside work five months prior to discharge and over four months since discharge.

Employment: started as box boy at $50 weekly: apprenticeship grocer earning $105 at present and will be promoted to journeyman status after one full year as apprentice. Employer highly gratified with patient's progress and performance.

411

W. W. — *Diagnosis:*   Schizophrenic reaction, paranoid type. Hospitalized one year. In group three months; employed three months prior to discharge; three and one-half months since discharge.

Employment: assembly line, starting wage of $1.45 an hour; current wage $1.70. Personnel office reported "No particular problems, no negative reports, quiet but related well to others." This is a high pressure job and the employees are pushed to produce.

D. B. — *Diagnosis:*   Schizophrenic reaction. In hospital seven months. In group three and one-half months. Employed during this period and three months since discharge.

Employment: assemblyman with starting pay of $1.40 an hour. At present, $1.65. Personnel office reports, "Overall adjustment satisfactory, average production rate, relates well to others."

P. W. — *Diagnosis:*   Schizophrenic reaction, paranoid type. Hospitalized eight years. In group at present (for seven months).

Employment: Sheltered workshop for past seven months: assembly, packing, soldering, etc. Manager of workshop reports significant progress in verbalization, money management, reality awareness.

Prognosis: long term sheltered employment is contemplated possibly on a terminal basis or possibly transfer to private employment after one year at workshop.

W. M. — *Diagnosis:*   passive dependency reaction w/alcoholism. Hospitalized ten months. In group four months; employed four months while hospitalized, one month following discharge. Has abstained from drinking all this time.

Present status: employer's report states he is making satisfactory adjustment at present time.

L. W. — *Diagnosis:*   passive dependent personality; some history of alcoholism. Hospitalized nine months. Employed and in group three months at two different periods.

Employment: Failed on job after one month and left group for one month. Returned to employment and group for two months. Again failed on job and eloped from hospital.

Follow-up: He has secured a job where he is now employed (one month). Although this case might be considered a failure, positive results were noted in saving of earnings and paying off debts incurred prior to hospitalization.

CONCLUSION

These case reports are characteristic for the group. Of the fourteen group members who have been discharged from the hospital, none have sought or had to be readmitted. A longer follow-up period, and larger numbers of patients for adequate evaluation are needed. However, the results to date have been most encouraging.

412

The Georgian Clinic, Atlanta, Georgia. One of the rehabilitation centers of the Georgia Commission on Alcoholism which provides both in-patient and out-patient treatment.

5
GROUP THERAPY FOR ALCOHOLICS
by DR. VERNELLE FOX, *Physician in Charge*
GEORGIAN CLINIC, ATLANTA, GEORGIA

The Georgian Clinic is one of the rehabilitation centers of the Georgia Commission on Alcoholism. It was established in 1953 with both in-patient and out-patient facilities. The requirements for admission are that the individual must be a resident of Georgia, an alcoholic; he must be dry and want help. We are not geared to handle problems of narcotic or barbituate addiction or to sober up the drunk alcoholic.

At the present time we feel that unless the patient himself requests help and is motivated to try to stop drinking, he will not be able to grow sufficiently to obtain real sobriety.

The average in-patient stay is five weeks. He may then become an out-patient. Individuals who live in and around Atlanta frequently are treated as out-patients only. They have an indefinite length of treatment but two years is recommended. A patient is not discharged from the out-patient department. If he no longer feels the need for help, or is not deriving benefit from the program he simply does not come to the clinic. No attempt is made to persuade him to return, but he remains on our mailing list and is sent our monthly paper, homecoming invitations, etc. Some patients have remained in fairly close contact with us for over three years.

Treatment Program
The treatment program at the clinic is aimed at the total life readjustment of the alcoholic to enable him to live without alcohol. We have three basic orientations (1) psychiatric (2) religious (3) medical. Most of our activities combine two or more of these and rarely do we use a pure application of any one of them. Our efforts go into directing these modalities of treatment toward the specific problems of the individual alcoholic. We provide medical and laboratory work-up and treatment of illness resulting from excessive exposure to alcohol. Referrals to appropriate sources are made for other illnesses. Psychiatric evaluation on admission and during treatment are made. Other parts of the program include group therapy, religious counseling, group counseling for families, occupational and recreational therapy, work programs and the like.

414

In September 1955 we began using group therapy and it has proven to be one of the most useful treatment modalities employed. We offer 29 group meetings per week: 14 for in-patient, 13 for out-patient, and 2 for the family. Patients may attend any or all of these at their own discretion. Members of the staff conducting these groups are physicians, ministers, and a psychologist. The design of each group project is left up to the professional leader. Some are highly structured with lectures, audio-visual aids, etc., which are used as springboards to discussion. Other groups are unstructured, with discussion topics emanating from the members rather than from the leader.

It is difficult to describe a "project" or the results of participation in a group because in our set-up the process is continuing and mobile. Individuals are not assigned to specific groups, nor are they required to attend. Over 1500 patients have been treated to date and each has attended from one to several hundred group sessions. The size of the group varies from 6 to 30, with an average of 12-14 in attendance. Whenever possible we prefer to hold these groups to less than fifteen participants. Because the alcoholic so easily feels rejected and is so resistive to anything he might interpret as control, we do not make assignments to groups. If a group becomes too large we simply create a new group at a popular time. Thus the patients redistribute themselves. Although we follow Roger's client-centered techniques more closely than any other, modifications are made to fit the needs of our groups ad lib.

In addition to these classic therapy sessions, we employ a series of basic alcoholic education films with discussion sessions, and a group of religious orientation tape-recordings with discussions. These are aimed to clear up some of the misconceptions of the physical, mental, and spiritual bases and complications of alcoholism. Thus some of the fears the patient has concerning his inability to recover are allayed. He starts looking inside himself for the basis of his problem rather than focusing on outside factors, especially alcohol as the "cause". In these educational groups the size is not too important. We have found informal lectures, with question and answer discussion, are useful. This type of educational group might be considered as an orientation, preparatory to therapy.

Therapy is aimed at personal emotional growth. In order to remain sober, the alcoholic must re-establish his own sense of personal worth; he must grow to be able to tolerate his anxieties and frustrations. In the subsequent non-directive sessions, the patients are encouraged

415

to explore their real feelings to the fullest. The group leader does not pick a topic or make any attempt to guide the subject matter. His role is to "play back", affirm, or clarify the patients' feelings in any way possible to aid the members in their attempt to express themselves. We have employed any technique that seemed appropriate to the moment. Some of these are: tape recording of a session with subsequent replaying of it for their exploration; modified psychodrama; films and published articles to open a subject, etc. We believe that the technique is not as important as the establishment of real group participation and acceptance. Acceptance of a member by the entire group seems to vary fairly directly with the group leader's ability to accept the individual completely. And the growth of the patient depends upon the degree of acceptance he feels.

CONCLUSION

The success of our group therapy program cannot be measured statistically. It is a part of the overall program to which the alcoholic is exposed. However, in the opinion of the staff, the group therapy is one of the most effective portions of the program. In addition to being the soil for personal growth, it is something the patient can hold to without the threat of developing overdependence.

6

A GROUP PSYCHOTHERAPY PROJECT:
LEARNING TO LIVE TOGETHER

by RAY W. DUTCHER, *Counseling Psychologist*
SAN BERNARDINO, CALIFORNIA

In thirteen years of professional counseling experience I have found that clients can learn to accept normal role relationships and to gain personal growth through group processes. Of course individual counseling is needed, but the social interactions of the group experience are essential to round out the total concept of personality. Individual interviews, concomitant with group sessions, allow both client and counselor to review the happenings experienced in the group as well as to prepare for further sessions.

Normalcy — within the wide scope indicated by that term — is the basic objective. The goals of the counseling process include assisting individuals to learn to live and adjust as easily as possible regardless of the trauma, change, difficulties of life, and maturing which is part

416

and parcel of human growth and development. My plan for group psychotherapy is based on the following premise:

The total personality of the individual is the most important factor. When a feeling pervades the individual that everything is not right, a need exists to improve adjustments in a setting similar to home or family which is preferable over any other structured concept. The self analysis centers on the question, "How can I live with others if I can't live with myself?"

Groups are made up of equal numbers of males and females, having from four to eight members. Clients enter and leave the group according to agreed upon relationships of client and counselor. An example of one of the open-end therapy groups is given to describe the methods and results:

Group 631D

Meeting weekly in 67 two-hour sessions over a period of 17 months the group had a membership totalling 15 individuals, with attendance varying from 4 to 10 and an average of 8 per session. No new members were added during the last 32 meetings where unity was at its peak. The group had been planned so that when one member dropped out, another client who could fit into it was added. The age range was from early twenties to the late fifties. Some of the group were single; others divorced; and others were married. Some of the unattached were searching for mates while others had no marital interest at the time of their entry. All members had college training, and nine of them possessed degrees.

The basic philosophy of the therapeutic techniques and methods to be employed had been explained to all clients before they entered the group: *The whole personality must grow* — not just certain areas or specific adjustments were more important than others. The concept of total personality was taken from the Bible, St. Mark 12, verses 28-34: *And thou shalt love the Lord thy God with all thy heart, and with all thy soul, and with all thy mind, and with all thy strength . . . thou shalt love thy neighbor as thyself.*

The rules for the group were as follows:

1. Sessions started at 1 p.m. and ended at 2:50 p.m. Members who were to be absent were to inform the leader in advance.
2. Only first names were to be used. Members could designate any name desired and could change it if they wished to be called by another name.
3. Each member should personalize as much as possible, i.e. translate into personal feelings and experience whatever was happening in the group.

417

4. No one was allowed to put a fellow member on the spot with a direct question, expecting or demanding an answer. However, clarification as to what a person was saying or doing could be requested.

5. Any subject matter was permissible, but any member could change the subject if a feeling existed that the discussion was "too hot to handle."

6. Talking or participating was a personal matter. The group could handle any member who monopolized the conversation, if they wished to.

7. The doors were always available to come or to go as it pleased the individual need.

There was a certain homogeneity in the group: all members had a "burnt-child" background; a feeling of loneliness, and lack of social acceptability. A common characteristic was that of not getting along with people, yet desiring to *belong*. Most had been referred for vocational counseling, marital difficulties, personal maladjustments, and the like. In those cases where the individual was receiving medical care, the physician and psychologist shared mutual information. All but one were attending some kind of religious services at the time of referral. Rapport and preparation for the project had been established prior to the initial session through individual interviews and psychological tests.

Nondirective leadership was used by the counselor-leader. The permissive atmosphere of the intimate group expedited the learning, because each individual was permitted to go at the rate best acceptable to self. Permissive education, in the opinion of this writer, means obtaining knowledge (insight) when it is needed and the client is ready to assimilate it; this is the connecting link between retardation and maturity. Thus, the group experience meant growing together via "osmosis", as it were. The personal growth was something that these clients could not very often accept in just the individual counseling interviews, and the group-peer relationship strengthened newly won gains in habit and adjustment.

Activities in the sessions ran the gamut from ganging up on the leader, hostility, irritation, near panic, and fear. Role playing was prevalent and learning to trust each other took much patient working-through. Problems had to be approached from every conceivable angle: old taboos and negative conditioning were slow to succumb to constructive reality-facing. Many times the leader believed the group had satisfactorily clarified a subject or concept only to find that the pseudo-acceptance was characteristic of those with burnt-child backgrounds. Intellectual acceptance does not mean emotional acceptance, so the learning process (reconditioning and replacement of old habits with new) is slow and laborious.

Sometimes personal problems were brought up in the group which the client had been unable to talk about in private sessions. Conversely, many painful areas could be discussed in private that could not be brought out in the group. Originally almost all action was directed toward the leader for answers. However, as the group developed, members were able to shift the direction toward each other or to take the initiative themselves. As the "at-one-ness" grew, it was noticeable that fewer questions were directed to others and more introspection and thinking out loud was done by various members. Later, the members were able to share more with each other. Similarly, those members who felt they had to control meetings gradually let go the leadership and felt accepted as members of a cohesive group.

This group was unique in that no one acted as a catalyst. Evasiveness was rampant through the 35th session. Hostility was displayed in many ways: coming in late, absenteeism, speech-mumbling or mushiness, talking in a low voice to one person, loud or high-pitched voice, monopolizing or being cliquish, turning back on another, threatening tones and actions, crying, leaving in a huff, etc.

RESULTS

Behavior changes in group participation were most noticeable in two types of persons: the verbal-aggressive (yackety-yack) and the agreeably-passive ones. The former learned to curb their monopoly, to listen, and become interested in others. The latter gained in self expression, and were able to give opinions, as well as take definite stands. It took 32 sessions to accomplish the re-conditioning sufficiently to show that new habits had actually taken the place of old ones.

The closing session was a serious occasion. Success had been achieved in living together as a group of people through tear-packed meetings as well as those that ended with nerves frayed by discussions packed with dynamite. The goal had been constantly before the group during the many months of weekly sessions: *I must learn to live with myself in order to live with others.* Most of the members reflected the adjustment that had gradually developed in each regarding normal societal feelings. And in the period following the end of the project the improved self-concepts and interpersonal relationships were the proof of the pudding.

419

7

AN EXPERIMENT IN GROUP GUIDANCE FOR LATER MATURITY[1]

reported by DR. IONA LOGIE, *Adult Counseling Service*

SAN FRANCISCO PUBLIC SCHOOLS

Since 1949 the adult division of the San Francisco Public Schools has provided adult counseling services with primary emphasis on vocational guidance. In 1954 a project for "persons over fifty" was offered, tentatively titled *Retirement Counseling*. However, it turned out that the title needed to be changed to *Guidance for Later Maturity* because enrollees included persons from the age of 43 to 70-plus. Only 47% were 65 or older, with 53% younger than 60. It was evident that many American men and women realize that they cannot safely wait until the sixties before embarking on programs of further vocational planning and enrichment in living. In general, the persons under sixty are interested in full-time employment, while many of the older counselees wish to find work on a part-time basis.

The variety and frequency of motives mentioned by 113 clients were:

	Times Mentioned
Counseling and information about jobs for older workers	32
Counseling about training and retraining for work after an interval away from the employment market	19
Counseling about choosing hobbies and avocations — where to learn and what to choose in arts and crafts	17
Counseling about further education: high school, college, or special education apart from vocational	14
Counseling on channels for social contacts, e.g., with older persons with similar interests	10
Channels for community service and volunteer work	9
Counseling on personal problems: home life, living arrangements, housing and psychological adjustments to change of status	7
Channels for information on how to start an independent business	5

The counselor in charge designed a plan to fill the demand for socialized group activity, specific information needs, and individual counseling. Seven three-hour sessions were planned for a seven week period. Volunteers from the group served as reception and information committees. Each three-hour session was divided as follows:

1. *6:30 p.m. to 8 p.m.* Reading time for perusal of the books,

---

[1]The above material is a digest of an article published in the *Vocational Guidance Quarterly*, Spring issue, 1955.

pamphlets, newspaper articles on such topics as part-time jobs, hobbies, educational opportunities in the San Francisco adult schools, and volunteer services. During this period the counselor held individual interviews with members of the group, usually four each night. Each client had at least one interview and some had two, especially the more anxious ones who came early or stayed late.

2. *8 p.m. to 9:30 p.m.* Group activity on topics suggested by members or discussions led by an expert in some field of interest, for example, Social Security benefits. Topics suggested by the group were organized as follows:

   a. Job information, with guest speakers from the California State Employment Service and the Forty-Plus organization.
   b. Tests and Interests Blanks, with opportunity for each member who wished to try such measurements as the Brainard Interest Inventory and the Terman-McNamar Test of Mental Ability. (The results of these were used, wherever pertinent, by the counselor in the individual interviews.)
   c. Discussion of hobbies, with guest speakers and members of the group reporting.
   d. Discussion of volunteer services, with a speaker from the Volunteer Bureau, supplemented by personal experiences narrated by members of the group.

The emphases in the individual counseling interviews were in line with personal needs of clients. Often the need concerned personal assessment related to occupational fitness, or potentials for embarking on new training programs.

At the end of the project an anonymous questionnaire was filled in at home by group members and mailed back to the counseling service office. Under the heading "Most beneficial service rendered", the most frequent statements referred to the following:

1. General information sessions, and especially individual counseling on types of work available to older persons and the training or retraining necessary, where training will apply.
2. Information about avocational pursuits which may ultimately prove profitable as well as enjoyable.
3. The social value of meeting with other adults of mature years, with similar interests and problems.
4. The opportunity to use the occupational library of books, pamphlets, news articles, and current advertisements which bear on the problem of aging but active persons.

CONCLUSION

From the continuing experience and experimentation with adult counseling services in this special field of "Guidance for Later Ma-

421

A DISCUSSION GROUP THERAPY SESSION: STATE HOSPITAL, NORRISTOWN, PENNSYLVANIA

— *Reprinted courtesy of PARADE Publications, Inc., 285 Madison Avenue, New York 17, New York*

turity", it appears altogether likely that many communities can and should provide group counseling projects for the increasing numbers of older citizens who wish to work, to learn new skills or hobbies, to contribute to society through volunteer or cultural activities. In short, they should be encouraged and helped to maintain or improve their active citizenship roles.

8

GROUP PSYCHOTHERAPY FOR THE AGING

by DR. MAURICE E. LINDEN, *Director*

DIVISION OF MENTAL HEALTH,

PHILADELPHIA DEPARTMENT OF PUBLIC HEALTH

Many of the unhappy, mentally-ill aging persons, found in increasing numbers in state institutions and homes for the aged, might have

followed a preventive program in their middle years which would have helped maintain their mental health. It is true that many people, in traversing the transitional period from middle age to late age, have a tendency to develop at least a mild-to-moderate degree of emotional maladjustment. Recent research and investigation into aging and the aged have revealed that a significant proportion of these difficulties could have been forestalled by proper emotional preparation earlier in life. There can be little doubt that many of the problems of aging are based upon tragic misinformation, a failure to comprehend human resources, and unrealistic social attitudes toward aging which are based on ignorance and perpetuated errors.

DR. MAURICE E. LINDEN
*Reprinted courtesy of PARADE
Publications, Inc., 285 Madison Ave.
New York 17, New York*

A ten point program, followed by any individual in his earlier years, will buttress him against the crises and difficulties of older maturity:

1. Continue to Develop Your Resources

Popular dogma, largely incorrect, claims that the mental and emotional supplies of the human mind undergo a decline at or near the middle years. Recent studies strongly suggest that the reverse is more likely to be the case. *Psychologists have found that the human mind continues to increase its capacity for comprehending difficult thought processes even into the seventh and eighth decades of life.*

2. Increase Your Social Effectiveness

With age, the decrease in the demands of the primitive drives allows greater attention and channeling or energies for increased social effectiveness. *An expansion rather than a diminution of civic and social enterprises should be the goal.*

3. Enjoy Your Wisdom

One of the never-ending sources of deep satisfaction in the mental mentality is the pleasure obtained from logical behavior. *The increase in sagacity and the values of the senior mind are more in keeping with the realities of human life than at any other time in the life cycle.* This can become a fount of gratification formerly denied the youthful mind which is striving for self-satisfaction that blinds it to the surrounding logic of nature.

4. Carry Forward the Torch of Human Progress

All forward progress engineered by men in the history of mankind has taken place through the cautious and understanding efforts of the older sages. The careful changes in cultural patterns and social attitudes characterizing social evolution have been conveyed from generation to generation by the parental figures.

The desire for change and revolution in society are characteristics of the impulsive and tradition-destroying youthful mind. *The experience of the mature mind, as a rule, gives it an unerring capacity to distinguish the good from the bad.*

5. Externalize Your Interests

The youthful mind tends to be preoccupied with itself, so that the young person often is almost unaware of the occurrences about him. *As the normal person grows older he experiences a reduction in selfishness and develops an increasingly generous and altruistic philosophy which is considerate of the needs of other people.*

This change from self-centeredness to other-centeredness can remove the myopic prisms from the eyes of the senior citizen: it opens up whole new vistas of beauty and natural grandeur which can be a revitalizing and refreshing experience in life.

6. Place Your Values in Quality

The younger person has a tendency, commensurate with his eager and aggressive nature, to place emphasis on quantitative productivity as a be-all and end-all in human endeavor.

The more mature mind values the intrinsic quality of both things and people. Events and things which were formerly insignificant in life can become a great new world of appreciation.

7. Don't Be a Spendthrift of Time

Time, the commodity which is wasted by youth, misspent and unappreciated, is held precious in maturity. A well-spent hour can become an eternity of pleasurable living.

424

8. Make Your Human Relationships Durable

Instincts of aggression and inborn hostility tend to diminish as one grows older. Love, characteristic of the older personality, glows quietly and is capable of a greater degree of sincerity and genuineness. If an older person permits himself to express this most desirable quality of the human mind, *he has the capacity to achieve the friendships and the more perfect love unions which have been his lifelong goals.*

9. Exercise Judicious Independence

Don't follow the cultural tendency for older people to let the younger people make all the decisions. *The older person should use his experience and accumulated knowledge aggressively.* He can assist oncoming leaders to find more direct paths through the vicissitudes of life.

10. Don't Emphasize Dependence

Polls show that 90% of well-adjusted older people prefer to live independently of their children. Only in time of sickness and need, and not as a way of life, should older persons lean on their offspring.

There is now incontrovertible evidence to prove that every stage of life contains a nucleus for enjoyment. Maturity can be an achievement. *If you develop and build upon the infinite number of resources with which you have been endowed by nature, you have the potential for an independent, satisfying future.*

The effectiveness of medical science in the field of Geriatrics now keeps the vast majority of aging persons from becoming physically handicapped: senior citizens can be healthy and energetic. With a foundation of mental health built up over the years, older people can continue active, constructive participation in societal progress. We have many outstanding examples of this: Chancellor Adenauer, Ex-President Hoover, Grandma Moses. Recently an eighty-year-old attorney was elected to the Presidency of the Bar Association in the State of Maine.

Need for Group Psychotherapy

Our state institutions contain many emotionally disturbed or mentally ill patients. Emotional turmoil, existing in a person over the years but camouflaged during the active period of life, is turned loose with retirement and comparative inactivity. In such cases, "senile" actions may express life-long emotional problems which have finally come to a head. There is a common type of aging person who has given in to the will of others. Because he has less strength and vigor than others he tends to let them make decisions for him — he fails to assert himself. This "act of surrender" makes him hate himself. The symptoms we associate with senility often result from such loss of self-respect.

Group psychotherapy for aged patients at the State Hospital at Norristown, Pennsylvania, has been used as a treatment method since

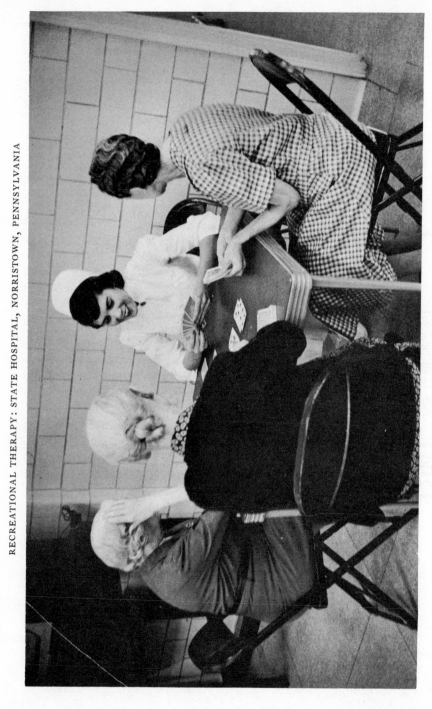

— Reprinted courtesy of PARADE Publications, Inc., 285 Madison Avenue, New York 17, New York

1949. The idea of using discussion groups as the treatment medium for aging patients — those in their 70's, 80's and even 90's — is rather revolutionary. This method allows the group members to work out their emotional conflicts in a "mutual aid" atmosphere. The members help each other to gain an understanding and acceptance of themselves, and to adjust to the shock of growing old.

Group Method

The *intimate group* is a setting where the aged person does not have to oppose the will of others. The group leader (psychiatrist) and assistant (nurse) have already established themselves in the minds of the patients as friends and counselors. A permissive atmosphere is established where members of the group are sympathetic and understanding of each other's problems because they all have similar personal difficulties. In such a social climate the aged person is able to unburden himself, to bare the important emotional problems he faces.

The discussions gradually dissipate the feelings of "oldness" on the part of the group members. Often they have felt old because they have been told over and over that when youth is gone, there is nothing left to live for. Our American society puts such a premium on youth that the influences of our culture — especially TV and advertising — have strongly negative effects on aging persons. These effects and influences are blotted out in a micro-society made up of aged persons who enjoy discussions, games, activities — even affectionate companionship that may end in marriage! And group therapy can actually lead people away from the idea that old age inevitably means "the rocking chair" toward the youthful feeling that *anything can happen.*

RESULTS

Many of the patients who participate in group psychotherapy improve so much that they are able to go back to their homes and resume normal, productive lives. With regained independence, their feeling of self-confidence and capacity to enjoy life are restored.

A case history — let us call it that of Mrs. Brown — will illustrate values of group therapy:

Mrs. Brown, admitted to the hospital at the age of 86, seemed to be losing her memory. She neglected her personal hygiene. She was disturbed, withdrawn, vague. Her son and daughter-in-law, with whom she had lived, believed the end was drawing near.

427

Medical attention built Mrs. Brown up physically and she was able to join a therapeutic group, made up of other women about her own age. After a week or two Mrs. Brown started to "talk out" her problem. She told the group, "There doesn't seem to be anything to live for at home. I felt like a fifth wheel." There were sympathetic murmurings from the other women, for this was a familiar problem. Gradually they, along with the psychiatrist, talked about Mrs. Brown's home life. A discussion of her deep feelings which came out for the first time started her on the road to mental health.

Within weeks Mrs. Brown was a different person, for she regained her self-respect. She became robust and cheerful. Her untidiness disappeared; her memory improved. At the age of 88 she was well enough to go back home. According to reports of her son and daughter-in-law she became again a lovable and helpful member of the family.

Although this case seems sensational, it is not, for similar treatment results are now being secured from group psychotherapy in hospitals and centers for the aging all over the United States.

From our experience at the Norristown State Hospital with aging patients, we believe that good results can be expected from group psychotherapy for persons who show the following signs of so-called "senility":

A feeling of uselessness, lack of interest in friends, tendency to isolation.

Personality changes from happiness to melancholy or from cleanliness to untidiness.

Preoccupation or absent-mindedness.

The patient who forgets current events but remembers remote events.

Too great talkativeness or withdrawal.

Lack of interest in food.

A frightened feeling and inability to sleep.

Even aged patients with real brain degeneration can be helped by group psychotherapy: a measure of happiness and some ability to care for themselves may result from a renewed feeling of self-respect and worthiness. Thus we advocate group psychotherapy for patients with mental deterioration who show the following characteristics:

Hostility, unfriendliness.

Childish behavior.

Indulgence in fantasies which seem real to the patient.

Garbled thoughts, occasional incoherent speech.

Hoarding of sundry items (mostly useless) with the idea that they may come in handy some time.

Excessive restlessness or overactivity.

CONCLUSION

The aging segment of our society will increase in importance as time goes on. Statistics indicate that we may expect one-third of our population to be fifty years of age and older in a few more decades. Educational and preventive programs are needed to help people plan and adjust to the older maturity period. The problem of institutionalization of the so-called "senile" enlarges with the increased older population. We believe a positive approach is to help aging persons maintain feelings of self-respect and ability to make active contributions to society as long as their health permits.

SELECTED BIBLIOGRAPHY

RECENT DECADE

PART I — GENERAL   No. of Refs.

Theories and Philosophies pertaining to Personal Growth and
Learning; Guidance, Counseling and Psychotherapy; Individual and Group Development, Characteristics 138

PART II — GENERAL

Symposia and Reading-Collections, Surveys, Reports, etc. . . 101

PART III — PROGRAM DESCRIPTIONS

Guidance, Counseling and Psychotherapy; Mental Health;
Individual and Group Development 118

PART IV — METHODS

Small-Group Discussion 142

PART V — METHODS

Role-Playing and Psychodrama 100

PART I — THEORIES AND PHILOSOPHIES

Alexander, E. *Psychoanalysis and Psychotherapy: Development in the Therapy, Techniques and Training.* N. Y.; W. W. Norton Co., 1956.

Allport, G. *The Nature of Prejudice.* Boston; The Beacon Press, 1954.

Argyle, M. *The Scientific Study of Social Behavior.* London; Methuen Co., 1957.

Ausubel, D. P. *Theory and Problems of Adolescent Development.* N. Y.; Grune-Stratton, 1954.

Basowitz, H. et al. *Anxiety and Stress.* N. Y.; McGraw-Hill, 1955.

Bender, L. *Aggression, Hostility and Anxiety in Children.* Springfield, Ill.; C. C. Thomas, 1953.

—————— *Dynamic Psychopathology of Childhood.* Springfield, Ill.; C. C. Thomas, 1954.

Bernard, H. W. *Adolescent Development in American Culture.* N. Y.; World Book, 1957.

—————— *Psychology of Learning and Teaching.* N. Y.; McGraw-Hill, 1954.

Bertine, E. *Human Relationships: in the Family, in Friendship, in Love.* N. Y.; Longmans, Green & Co., 1957.

Blum, M. L. *Industrial Psychology: and Its Social Foundations,* rev. ed. N. Y.; Harper & Bros., 1956.

Bonner, H. *Social Psychology: An Interdisciplinary Approach.* N. Y.; American Book Co., 1953.

Bordin, E. S. *Psychological Counseling.* N. Y.; Appleton-Century-Crofts, 1955.

Cameron, N. and A. Magaret. *Behavior Pathology.* Boston; Houghton-Mifflin, 1951.

Cantor, N. *The Teaching-Learning Process.* N. Y.; Dryden Press, 1953.

Chant, S. N. F. and E. I. Signori. *Interpretive Psychology: The Nature of Human Activity.* Toronto; McGraw-Hill, 1957.

Cleckley, H. M. *The Mask of Sanity,* 3rd ed. St. Louis; Mosby Co., 1955.

Clinard, M. B. *Sociology of Deviant Behavior.* N. Y.; Rinehart Co., 1957.

Cole, L. *Psychology of Adolescence,* 4th ed. N. Y.; Rinehart Co., 1954.

Coleman, J. C. *Abnormal Psychology and Modern Life,* rev. ed. Chicago; Scott, Foresman, 1957.

Corsini, R. J. "Freud, Rogers, and Moreno: an inquiry into the possible relationship between manifest personality, theory and methods of some eminent psychotherapists", *Group Psychotherapy,* 1956 (3), 274-281.

—————— "Toward a definition of group psychotherapy", *Mental Hygiene,* 1955 (6), 647-656.

Dreikurs, R. "The contribution of group psychotherapy to psychiatry", *Group Psychotherapy,* 1956 (2), 115-124.

Dresher, R. H. "Seeds of delinquency", *Pers. Guid. J.,* 1957 (9), 595-598.

Duvall, E. M. *Family Development.* Philadelphia; J. B. Lippincott Co., 1957.

Ellis, A. and R. Brancale. *The Psychology of Sex Offenders.* Springfield, Ill.; C. C. Thomas, 1956.

English, O. S. and G. H. J. Pearson. *Emotional Problems of Living: Avoiding the Neurotic Pattern,* rev. ed. N. Y.; W. W. Norton, 1955.

Estes, W. K. et al. *Modern Learning Theory: A Critical Analysis of Five Examples.* N. Y.; Appleton-Century-Crofts, 1954.

Eysenck, H. J. *Dimensions of Personality.* N. Y.; Basic Books, Inc., 1950.

———— *The Scientific Study of Personality.* N. Y.; MacMillan Co., 1952.

———— *The Structure of Human Personality.* N. Y.; Wiley & Sons, 1953.

Foulkes, S. H. *Introduction to Group Analytic Psychotherapy: Studies in the Social Integration of Individuals and Groups.* N. Y.; Grune & Stratton Co., 1949.

Fraser, J. M. *Psychology: General, Industrial, Social.* N. Y.; Philosophical Library, 1956.

Fromm, E. *The Art of Loving.* N. Y.; Harper & Bros., 1956.

———— *The Sane Society.* N. Y.; Rinehart & Co., 1955.

Garrison, K. C. *Psychology of Adolescence,* 5th ed. Englewood Cliffs, N. J.; Prentice-Hall, 1956.

Giles, H. H. *Education and Human Motivation.* N. Y.; Philosophical Library, 1957.

Guntrip, H. *Psychotherapy and Religion.* N. Y.; Harper & Bros., 1957.

Hahn, M. E. & M. S. MacLean. *Counseling Psychology,* 2nd ed. N. Y.; McGraw-Hill Co., 1955.

Hall, C. S. & G. Lindzey. *Theories of Personality.* N. Y.; Wiley & Sons, 1957.

Havighurst, R. J. & B. E. Orr. "Aging and Personality Development", *Rev. educ. Res.,* 1955, Vol. 25, 477-486.

Hawthorn, H. B. *Sociology of Personality Functioning.* Sioux City, Iowa; Morningside Coll. Press, 1955.

Heintz, L. & R. R. Ausbacker. *The Individual Psychology of Alfred Adler.* N. Y.; Basic Books, 1957.

Hilgard, E. R. *Theories of Learning,* 2nd ed. N. Y.; Appleton-Century-Crofts, 1956.

Hollenbeck, H. E. "The group dynamic concept of the 'group' ", *Group,* 1955 (1), 13-16.

Honigmann, J. J. *Culture and Personality.* N. Y.; Harper & Bros., 1954.

Horney, K. *Neurosis and Human Growth: the Struggle toward Self-Realization.* N. Y.; W. W. Norton Co., 1950.

Hovland, C. I., Janis & Kelley. *Communication and Persuasion.* New Haven; Yale Univ. Press, 1953.

Hunt, W. A. *The Clinical Psychologist.* Springfield, Ill.; C. C. Thomas Co., 1956.

Hurlock, E. B. *Adolescent Development,* 2nd ed. N. Y.; McGraw-Hill Co., 1955.

Hutt, M. L. & R. G. Gibby. *Patterns of Abnormal Behavior.* Boston; Allyn & Bacon Co., 1957.

Illing, H. A. "C. G. Jung on the present trends in group psychotherapy", *J. Human Relations,* 1957 (1), 77-83.

Jersild, A. T. *Child Psychology,* 4th ed. Englewood Cliffs, N. J.; Prentice-Hall, 1957.

———— *The Psychology of Adolescence.* N. Y.; MacMillan Co., 1957.

———— *When Teachers Face Themselves.* N. Y.; Teachers College, Columbia Univ. Press, 1955.

Johnson, P. E. *Personality and Religion.* Nashville, Tenn.; Abingdon Press, 1957.

Jones, M. "The concept of a therapeutic community", *Am. J. Psychiatry*, 1956, Vol. 112, 647-650.

Kanner, L. *Child Psychiatry*, 2nd ed. Springfield, Ill.; C. C. Thomas Co., 1955.

Kantor, J. R. *Interbehavioral Psychology*. Bloomington, Ind.; Principia Press, 1957.

Karpf, F. B. *The Psychology and Psychotherapy of Otto Rank: An Historical and Comparative Introduction*. N. Y.; Philosophical Library, 1953.

Katz, B. & L. P. Thorpe. *Understanding People in Distress*. N. Y.; Ronald Press, 1955.

Kelly, G. A. *The Psychology of Personal Constructs*. N. Y.; W. W. Norton Co., 1955.

Kew, C. E. & C. J. Kew. "Principles and values of group psychotherapy under church auspices", *Pastoral Psychol.*, 1955 (1), 37-48.

Kingsley, H. L. (revised by R. Garry). *Nature and Conditions of Learning*, 2nd ed. Englewood Cliffs, N. J.; Prentice-Hall, 1956.

Laird, D. A. & E. C. Laird. *The New Psychology of Leadership*. N. Y.; McGraw-Hill Co., 1956.

Leary, T. *Interpersonal Diagnosis of Personality: A Functional Theory and Methodology for Personality Evaluation*. N. Y.; Ronald Press, 1957.

Lehner, G. F. J. & E. A. Kubie. *Dynamics of Personal Adjustment*. Englewood Cliffs, N. J.; Prentice-Hall, 1955.

Lewin, Kurt. *Field Theory in Social Science*. N. Y.; Harper & Bros., 1951.

―――― *Resolving Social Conflicts*. N. Y.; Harper & Bros., 1948.

Linden, M. E. "The older person in the family", *Soc. Casework*, 1956 (1), 75-81.

Lindesmith, A. R. & A. L. Strauss. *Social Psychology*, rev. ed. N. Y.; Dryden Press, 1956.

Lindgren, H. C. *Psychology of Personal and Social Adjustment*. N. Y.; American Book Co., 1953.

Linton, R. (G. Devereaux, ed.). *Culture and Mental Disorders*. Springfield, Ill.; C. C. Thomas Co., 1956.

Lloyd-Jones, E. & M. R. Smith (eds.). *Student Personnel Work as Deeper Teaching*. N. Y.; Harper & Bros., 1954.

Lorge, I. "Groupness of the Group", *J. Educ. Psychol.*, 1955 (4), 449-456.

McBurney, J. H. & E. J. Wrage. *The Art of Good Speech*. Englewood Cliffs, N. J.; Prentice-Hall, 1953.

McClelland, D. C., Atkinson, Clark. *The Achievement Motive*. N. Y.; Appleton-Century-Crofts, 1953.

McDaniel, H. B. & G. A. Shaftel. *Guidance in the Modern School*. N. Y.; Dryden Press, 1956.

Maier, N. R. F. *Principles of Human Relations*. N. Y.; Wiley & Sons, 1952.

Maslow, A. H. *Motivation and Personality*. N. Y.; Harper & Bros., 1954.

Masserman, J. H. *The Practice of Dynamic Psychiatry*. Philadelphia; W. B. Saunders Co., 1955.

Mathewson, R. H. *Guidance Policy and Practice*, rev. ed. N. Y.; Harper & Bros., 1955.

Menninger, K. A. *The Human Mind*, 3rd ed. N. Y.; A. A. Knopf Co., 1956.

Michaels, J. J. *Disorders of Character: Persistent Enuresis, Juvenile Delinquency, and Psychopathic Personality*. Springfield, Ill.; C. C. Thomas Co., 1955.

Miller, D. R. & G. E. Swanson. *Inner Conflict and Defense.* N. Y.; Henry Holt, 1957.

Montagu, M. F. A. *Anthropology and Human Nature.* Boston; Porter Sargent, 1957.

Mowrer, O. H. *Learning Theory and Personality Dynamics.* N. Y.; Ronald Press, 1950.

Munn, N. L. *Evolution and Growth of Human Behavior.* Boston; Houghton-Mifflin Co., 1956.

—— *Psychology: Fundamentals of Human Adjustment,* 3rd ed. Boston; Houghton-Mifflin Co., 1956.

Munroe, R. L. *Schools of Psychoanalytic Thought.* N. Y.; Dryden Press, 1955.

Mussen, P. H. and J. J. Conger. *Child Development and Personality.* N. Y.; Harper & Bros., 1956.

Nuttin, J. *Psychoanalysis and Personality* (Catholic viewpoint). N. Y.; Sheed & Ward, 1957.

Opler, M. K. *Culture, Psychiatry and Human Values: The Methods and Values of a Social Psychiatry.* Springfield, Ill.; C. C. Thomas Co., 1956.

Overstreet, H. and B. *The Mind Goes Forth.* N. Y.; W. W. Norton Co., 1956.

Phillips, E. L. *Psychotherapy: A Modern Theory and Practice.* Englewood Cliffs, N. J.; Prentice-Hall, 1956.

Powell, J. W. *Learning Comes of Age.* N. Y.; Association Press, 1957.

Pressy, S. L. & R. G. Kuhlen. *Psychological Development through the Life Span.* N. Y.; Harper & Bros., 1957.

Progoff, I. *Depth Psychology and Modern Man.* N. Y.; Julian Press, 1958.

Redl, F. & D. Wineman. *The Aggressive Child.* Glencoe, Ill.; Free Press, 1957.

Riesman, D. *The Lonely Crowd.* New Haven; Yale Univ. Press, 1950.

Roe, A. *The Psychology of Occupations.* N. Y.; Wiley & Sons, 1956.

Rose, A. M. *Sociology: The Study of Human Relationships.* N. Y.; A. A. Knopf, 1956.

Rotter, J. B. *Social Learning and Clinical Psychology.* Englewood Cliffs, N. J.; Prentice-Hall, 1955.

Selye, H. *The Stress of Life.* N. Y.; McGraw-Hill Co., 1956.

Schreier, F. T. *Human Motivation: Probability and Meaning.* Glencoe, Ill.; Free Press, 1957.

Shaffer, L. F. & E. J. Shoben, Jr. *The Psychology of Adjustment,* 2nd ed. Boston; Houghton-Mifflin Co., 1957.

Seward, G. *Psychotherapy and Culture Conflict.* N. Y.; Ronald Press, 1956.

Sherif, M. & C. W. *Outline of Social Psychology,* rev. ed. N. Y.; Harper & Bros., 1956.

Shoben, E. J., Jr. "Toward a concept of the normal personality", *Am. Psychologist,* 1957 (4), 183-189.

—— "Work, love, and maturity", *Pers. & Guid. J.,* 1956, Feb. pp. 326-332.

Smith, E. S. *Dynamics of Aging* (guide to the psychology of growing old). N. Y.; W. W. Norton Co., 1956.

Solomon, J. C. *Synthesis of Human Behavior.* N. Y.; Grune & Stratton Co., 1954.

Sorokin, P. *Social and Cultural Dynamics.* Boston; Porter Sargent Co., 1957.

Spence, K. W. *Behavior Theory and Conditioning.* New Haven; Yale Univ. Press, 1956.

Stein, H. D. & R. A. Cloward. *Social Perspectives on Behavior.* Glencoe, Ill.; Free Press, 1957.

Stern, E. M. *Mental Illness,* rev. ed. N. Y.; Harper & Bros., 1957.

Stewart, S. S. & A. D. Workman. *Children and Other People: Achieving Maturity through Learning.* N. Y.; Dryden Press, 1956.

Stock, D. & H. A. Thelen. *Emotional Dynamics and Group Culture.* N. Y.; New York Univ. Press, 1957.

Stone, L. J. & J. Church. *Childhood and Adolescence: A Psychology of the Growing Person.* N. Y.; Random House, 1957.

Strecker, E. A. & V. A. Lathbury. *Their Mothers' Daughters.* Philadelphia; J. B. Lippincott Co., 1956.

Sullivan, H. S. *Conceptions of Modern Psychiatry,* 2nd ed. N. Y.; W. W. Norton, 1956.

——— *Interpersonal Theory of Psychiatry.* N. Y.; W. W. Norton Co., 1953.

——— *The Psychiatric Interview.* N. Y.; W. W. Norton Co., 1954.

Super, D. *The Psychology of Careers.* N. Y.; Harper & Bros., 1957.

Symonds, P. M. *Dynamics of Psychotherapy: the Psychology of Personality Change. Vol. I: Principles.* N. Y.; Grune & Stratton Co., 1956.

Taylor, G. A. *The Sober Faith: Religion and A. A.* N. Y.; MacMillan Co., 1954.

Thomas, M. J. et al. *Climate for Learning.* Pittsburgh; Univ. of Pittsburgh Press, 1953.

Thompson, C. "The different schools of psychoanalysis", *Am. J. of Nursing,* 1957 (10), 1304-1307.

——— *Psychoanalysis — Evolution and Development.* N. Y.; Grove Press, 1957.

Thorpe, L. P. and A. M. Schmuller. *Contemporary Theories of Learning.* N. Y.; Ronald Press, 1956.

Traxler, A. E. *Techniques of Guidance,* rev. ed. N. Y.; Harper & Bros., 1957.

Tyler, L. E. *The Psychology of Human Differences,* 2nd ed. N. Y.; Appleton-Century-Crofts, 1956.

Viteles, M. *Motivation and Morale in Industry.* N. Y.; W. W. Norton Co., 1953.

Washington University: Committee on Publications. *Theory and Treatment of the Psychoses: Some Newer Aspects.* St. Louis; Washington Univ. Studies, 1956.

White, R. W. *The Abnormal Personality,* 2nd ed. N. Y.; Ronald Press, 1956.

Winnicott, D. W. *The Child and the Outside World.* N. Y.; Basic Books, 1957.

Witmer, H. L. & R. Kotinsky. *Personality in the Making.* N. Y.; Harper & Bros., 1952.

Woodworth, R. S. *Dynamics of Behavior.* N. Y.; Henry Holt Co., 1957.

PART II — GENERAL: SYMPOSIA, READING-COLLECTIONS, ETC.

Albee, G. W. & M. Dickey. "Manpower trends in three mental health professions", *Am. Psychologist*, 1957 (2), 57-69.

Alcoholic Anonymous Publishing, Inc. *Alcoholic Anonymous*, rev. ed. P. O. Box 459, Grand Central Annex, N. Y. 17, N. Y., 1955.

American Psychiatric Assn.: Committee on Public Information. *A Psychiatric Glossary* (distributed by Mental Health Materials Center, 1790 Broadway, N. Y. 19, N. Y.).

American Assn. Advancement of Science. *Symposium: Alcoholism: Basic Aspects and Treatment.* Washington, D. C.; Am. Assn. Adv. Science, 1957.

American Society of Group Psychotherapy and Psychodrama. "Bibliography in Group Psychotherapy", *Group Psychother.*, Vol. I, No. 3, Nov. 1956.

Anderson, J. E. (ed.). *Psychological Aspects of Aging.* Washington, D. C.; American Psychol. Assn., 1956.

Andrew, D. C. & L. N. Downing (eds.). *120 Readings in Guidance*, 2nd ed. Lincoln, Nebr.; Univ. of Nebraska Press, 1955.

Ansbacher, H. & R. (eds.). *The Individual Psychology of Alfred Adler.* N. Y.; Baics Books, 1956.

Bach, G. R. "Pathological aspects of therapeutic groups", *Group Psychother.*, 1956 (2), 133-147.

Balser, B. H. (ed.). *Psychotherapy of the Adolescent.* N. Y.; Intern. Univ. Press, 1957.

Benne, K. D. & B. Muntyan. *Human Relations in Curriculum Change; Selected Readings with Special Emphasis on Group Development.* N. Y.; Dryden Press, 1951.

Berdie, R. F. (ed.). *Roles and Relationships in Counseling.* Minneapolis; Univ. of Minnesota Press, 1953.

Blake, R. R. & J. S. Mouton. "Human relations problem areas in work", *Group Psychotherapy*, 1956 (4), 253-264.

Blake, R. R. & R. V. Ramsey, et al. *Perception, An Approach to Personality.* N. Y.; Ronald Press, 1951.

Block, H. A. & F. T. Flynn. *Delinquency: the Juvenile Offender in America Today.* N. Y.; Random House, 1956.

Borgatta, E. F. & H. J. Meyer (eds.). *Sociological Theory: Present-Day Sociology from the Past.* N. Y.; A. A. Knopf Co., 1956.

Bowman, P. H., et al. *Mobilizing Community Resources for Youth.* (Supplementary Educ. Monographs No. 85) Chicago; Univ. of Chicago Press, 1956.

Brower, D. & L. E. Abt. *Progress in Clinical Psychology, Vol. II.* N. Y.; Grune & Stratton, 1957.

Burton, A. & R. E. Harris. *Clinical Studies of Personality.* N. Y.; Harper & Bros., 1955.

California, Univ. *Personal Assessment and Research.* Berkeley; Univ. of Calif. Press, 1954.

Caplan, G. (ed.). *Emotional Problems of Early Childhood.* N. Y.; Basic Books, 1955.

Cartwright, D. & A. Zander (eds.). *Group Dynamics: Research and Theory.* Evanston, Ill.; Row, Peterson & Co., 1953.

Casteel, J. L. (ed.). *Spiritual Renewal through Personal Groups.* N. Y.; Association Press, 1957.

Co-Founder of A. A. *Alcoholic Anonymous Comes of Age.* N. Y.; Harper & Bros., 1957.

Cohen, F. J. (ed.). *Youth and Crime.* (Proceedings of the Law Enforcement Institute on Youth and Crime, N.Y.C., 1955.) N. Y.; Intern. Univ. Press, 1957.

Cruickshank, W. M. (ed.). *Psychology of Exceptional Children.* Englewood Cliffs, N. J.; Prentice-Hall, 1955.

Cumming, E. & J. *Closed Ranks: An Experiment in Mental Health Education.* Cambridge; Harvard Univ. Press, for The Commonwealth Fund, 1957.

David, H. P. & H. von Bracken (eds.). *Perspective in Personality Theory.* N. Y.; Basic Books, 1957.

Doniger, S. (ed.). *Healing: Human and Divine.* N. Y.; Association Press, 1957.

Donohue, J. K. *Baffling Eyes of Youth.* N. Y.; Association Press, 1957.

Dooher, M. J. (ed.). *The Development of Executive Talent.* N. Y.; Amer. Management Assn., 1952.

Dreikurs, R. & R. J. Corsini. "Twenty years of group psychotherapy", *Am. J. Psychiatry,* 1954 (6), 567-575.

English, H. B. & A. C. *Comprehensive Dictionary of Psychological and Psychoanalytical Terms.* N. Y.; Longmans, Green & Co., 1957.

Eysenck, H. J. *Sense and Nonsense in Psychology.* Baltimore; Penguin Books, 1957.

———— *Uses and Abuses of Psychology.* Baltimore; Penguin Books, 1955.

Festingen, L. & D. Katz (eds.). *Research Methods in the Behavioral Sciences.* N. Y.; Dryden Press, 1953.

———— et al. *Social Pressures in Informal Groups.* N. Y.; Harper & Bros., 1950.

Fromm-Reichmann, F. & J. L. Moreno (eds.). *Progress in Psychotherapy.* N. Y.; Grune & Stratton, 1956.

Funkenstein, D. H. et al. *Mastery of Stress.* Cambridge; Harvard Univ. Press, 1957.

Gardner, E. F. & G. C. Thompson. *Social Relations and Morale in Small Groups.* N. Y.; Appleton-Century-Crofts, 1956.

Garfield, S. L. *Introductory Clinical Psychology: An Overview of the Functions, Methods, and Problems of Contemporary Clinical Psychology.* N. Y.; MacMillan Co., 1957.

Gesell, A., et al. *Youth: The Years from Ten to Sixteen.* N. Y.; Harper & Bros., 1956.

Glueck, S. & E. *Delinquents in the Making.* N. Y.; Harper & Bros., 1952.

Grinker, R. R. (ed.). *Toward a Unified Theory of Human Behavior.* N. Y.; Basic Books, 1956.

Group for Advancement of Psychiatry: Committee on Social Issues. *Psychiatric Aspects of School De-Segregation.* (Report No. 37.) N. Y.; 1957.

Guetzhow, H. (ed.). *Groups, Leadership and Men.* Pittsburgh; Carnegie Inst. of Tech. Press, 1951.

Hare, A. P., E. E. Borgatta, R. F. Bales (eds.). *Small Groups: Studies in Social Interaction.* N. Y.; A. A. Knopf Co., 1955.

Haring, D. G. (ed.). *Personal Character and Cultural Milieu,* 3rd ed. Syracuse, N. Y.; Syracuse Univ. Press, 1956.

Hendrickson, R. C. & F. J. Cook. *Youth in Danger.* N. Y.; Harcourt, Brace Co., 1956.

Hewer, V. H. (ed.). *New Perspectives in Counseling.* Minneapolis: Univ. of Minnesota Press, 1955.

438

Hoch, P. H. & J. Zubin (eds.). *Psychopathology of Childhood*. N.Y.; Grune & Stratton Co., 1955.

Hsu, F. L. K. (ed.). *Aspects of Culture and Personality: a Symposium*. N. Y.; Abelard-Schuman, 1954.

Jahoda, M., M. Deutsch & S. Cook (eds.). *Research Methods in Social Relations*. N.Y.; Dryden Press, 1951.

Kentucky, Univ.: Dept. of Psychol. *Learning Theory, Personality Theory, and Clinical Research: The Kentucky Symposium*. N. Y.; Wiley & Sons, 1954.

Kluckhohn, C. et al (eds.). *Personality in Nature, Society, and Culture*. N. Y.; A. A. Knopf, 1953.

Krout, M. K. *Psychology, Psychiatry and the Public Interest*. Minneapolis; Univ. of Minnesota Press, 1957.

Kutner, B. "The problem of mental health among the aged", *Amer. J. Publ. Health*, 1956, Vol. 46, pp. 204-208.

Leighton, A. H. & J. A. Clausen (eds.). *Explorations in Social Psychiatry*. N. Y.; Basic Books, 1957.

Levy, A. V. *Other People's Children*. N. Y.; Ronald Press, 1956.

Lignon, E. M. *Dimensions of Character*. N. Y.; MacMillan Co., 1956.

Lindzey, G. (ed.). *Handbook of Social Psychology*. Cambridge, Mass.; Addison-Wesley Press, 1954.

Masserman, J. H. & J. L. Moreno (eds.). *Progress in Psychotherapy*. Vols. I, II, III. N. Y.; Grune & Stratton Co., 1957.

McCary, J. L. & D. E. Sheer (eds.). *Six Approaches to Psychotherapy*. N. Y.; Dryden Press, 1955.

McClelland, D. C. (ed.). *Motivation, Effort, and Performance*. N. Y.; Appleton-Century-Crofts, 1955.

Miner, R. W. (ed.). *Psychotherapy and Counseling*. N. Y.; New York Academy of Science, 1956.

Milbank Memorial Fund. *Interrelations between the Social Environment and Psychiatric Disorders*, N. Y.; 1953.

Moreno, J. L. (ed.). *Sociometry and the Science of Man*. Beacon, N. Y.; Beacon House, 1956.

———— *Who Shall Survive*. Beacon, N. Y.; Beacon House, 1953.

Moustakas, C. E. (ed.). *Explorations in Personal Growth*. N. Y.; Harper & Bros., 1956.

Mowrer, O. H. (ed.). *Psychotherapy: Theory and Research*. N. Y.; Ronald Press, 1953.

Mullahy, P. (ed.). *A Study of Interpersonal Relations*. N. Y.; Grove Press, 1957.

Murphy, L., E. Raushenbush, et al. *Personality and Education*. N. Y.; New York Univ. Press, 1957.

Nat'l Society for the Study of Educ. *Mental Health in Modern Education*, 54th Yearbook. Chicago; Univ. of Chicago Press, 1955.

Nat'l Train. Lab. in Gp. Development. *Exploration in Human Relations Training: An Assessment of Experiences*, 1947-1953. Washington, D. C.; 1953.

Progoff, I. *The Death and Rebirth of Psychology*. N. Y.; Julian Press, 1956.

Remmers, H. H. & D. H. Radler. *The American Teenager*. Indianapolis; Bobbs-Merrill Co., 1957.

Roback, A. A. (ed.). *Present Day Psychology.* N. Y.; Philosophical Library, 1955.

Rogers, C. R. & R. F. Dymond (eds.). *Psychotherapy and Personality Change.* Chicago; Univ. of Chicago Press, 1954.

Ross, M. G. & C. E. Hendry. *New Understandings of Leadership.* N. Y.; Association Press, 1957.

Schaffner, B. (ed.). *Group Processes.* N. Y.; Josiah Macey Found., 1956.

Seidman, J. M. (ed.). *The Adolescent: A Book of Readings.* N. Y.; Dryden Press, 1953.

––––– (ed.). *Readings in Educational Psychology.* Boston; Houghton-Mifflin, 1957.

Shock, N. W. *Trends in Gerontology,* 2nd ed. Stanford, Calif.; Stanford Univ. Press, 1957.

Skinner, B. F. et al. *Theory and Treatment of the Psychoses: Some Newer Aspects.* St. Louis; Washington Univ. Studies, 1956.

Skinner, C. S. (ed.). *Educational Psychology.* Englewood Cliffs, N. J.; Prentice-Hall, 1951.

Slavson, S. R. (ed.). *The Fields of Group Psychotherapy.* N. Y.; Intern. Univ. Press, 1956.

Stacey, C. L. & M. F. DeMartino (eds.). *Counseling and Psychotherapy with the Mentally Retarded.* Glencoe, Ill.; Free Press, 1957.

Stewart, M. S. (ed.). *Problems of Family Life and How to Meet Them.* N. Y.; Harper & Bros., 1956.

Stock, D. & H. A. Thelen. *Emotional Dynamics and Group Culture: Experimental Studies of Individual and Group Behavior.* Washington, D. C.; Nat'l Training Laboratories in Group Development, 1957.

Stogdill, R. M. *Leadership and Structures of Personal Interaction.* Ohio Studies in Personnel; Bureau of Bus. Research, Monograph No. 84. Columbus, Ohio; 1957.

Swanson, G. E., Newcomb and Hartley (eds.). *Readings in Social Psychology.* N. Y.; Henry Holt Co., 1952.

Taba, H. et al. *Diagnosing Human Relations Needs.* Washington, D. C.; Am. Council on Educ., 1951.

Taba, H. & D. Elkins. *With Focus on Human Relations.* Washington, D. C.; Am. Council on Educ., 1950.

Thelen, H. A. *Dynamics of Groups at Work.* Chicago; Univ. of Chicago Press, 1954.

––––– et al. *Methods for Research on Interactions in Groups.* Chicago; Univ. of Chicago Press, 1952.

Traxler, A. E. (ed.). *Vital Issues in Education.* Washington, D. C.; Am. Council on Educ., 1957.

Trecker, H. B. (ed.). *Group Work in the Psychiatric Setting.* N. Y.; Whiteside, 1956.

Ulett, G. A. & D. W. Goodrich. *A Synopsis of Contemporary Psychiatry.* St. Louis; Mosby Co., 1956.

Wallerstein, R. S. and associates. *Hospital Treatment of Alcoholism.* N. Y.; Basic Books, 1957.

Wilson, J. et al. *Trends in Psychology and the Behavioral Sciences.* Pittsburgh; Univ. of Pittsburgh Press, 1954.

Wolff, W. *Contemporary Psychotherapists Examine Themselves.* Springfield, Ill.; C. C. Thomas Co., 1956.

PART III — PROGRAM DESCRIPTIONS

Academy of Religion and Mental Health. *Manual of Procedures, Topics and Materials for Discussion in Mental Health.* Acad. Rel. & Ment. Health, 2 E. 103 St., N. Y. 29, N. Y.; 1956.

Anderson, C. *Beyond Freud: A Creative Approach to Mental Health.* N. Y.; Harper & Bros., 1957.

Aptekar, H. H. *The Dynamics of Casework and Counseling.* Boston; Houghton-Mifflin Co., 1956.

Arbuckle, D. S. *Guidance and Counseling in the Classroom.* Boston; Allyn & Bacon Co., 1957.

Assn. for Superv. and Curr. Development. *Fostering Mental Health in Our Schools.* Washington, D. C.; Nat'l Educ. Assn., 1950.

———— *Guidance in the Curriculum.* Washington, D. C.; Nat'l Educ. Assn., 1955.

Beckhard, R. *How to Plan and Conduct Workshops and Conferences.* N. Y.; Association Press, 1957.

Belson, D. *The Chairman and Speaker's Role Made Easy.* N. Y.; Bee Publishers, 1957.

Bender, L. *Child Psychiatric Techniques.* Springfield, Ill.; C. C. Thomas Co., 1952.

Benne, K. D. & B. Muntyan (eds.). *Human Relations in Curriculum Change.* N. Y.; Dryden Press, 1951.

Bennett, M. E. *Guidance in Groups.* N. Y.; McGraw-Hill Co., 1955.

Berdie, R. F. (ed.). *Roles and Relationships in Counseling.* Minneapolis; Univ. of Minnesota Press, 1953.

Bernard, H. W. *Toward Better Personal Adjustment,* 2nd ed. N. Y.; McGraw-Hill, 1957.

Beutner, K. R. & N. Hale, Jr. *Emotional Illness and What Families Can Do to Help.* N. Y.; G. P. Putnams' Sons, 1956.

Blake, R. R. & J. S. Mouton. *Theory and Practice of Human Relations Training.* Austin, Texas; The Hogg Foundation for Mental Hygiene, Univ. of Texas, 1955.

Blanton, S. *Love or Perish.* N. Y.; Simon & Shuster Co., 1956.

Boothe, W. *From Isolation to Acceptance.* Durham, N. C.; The Religion and Health Press, 1956.

Bordin, E. S. *Psychological Counseling.* N. Y.; Appleton-Century-Crofts, 1956.

Bradford, L. P., J. R. Gibb & G. Lippitt. "Human Relations training in three days", *Adult Leadership,* 1956 (10).

Brant, H. "Group therapy with large groups of psychotic patients", *Group Psychother.,* 1957 (2), 129-132.

Canter, A. H. "Observations on group psychotherapy with hospitalized patients", *Am. J. of Psychother.,* 1955 (1), 66-73.

Clinebell, H. J. *Understanding and Counseling the Alcoholic.* N. Y.; Abingdon Press, 1956.

Cockefair, E. A. & A. M. *The Story of You.* (Sex education for young children) Madison, Wis.; Milam Publ., 1955.

Combs, A. W. "Counseling as a Learning Process", *J. Counsel. Psychol.* 1954 (1), 31-36.

Cook, L. & E. *School Problems in Human Relations.* N. Y.; McGraw-Hill Co., 1957.

Coyle, G. L. "Proposed areas for concentration and study", *Group,* 1955 (1), 7-10.

Crow, L. D. & A. *Adolescent Development and Adjustment.* N. Y.; McGraw-Hill, 1957.

———— *Human Development and Learning.* (Teachers Manual.) N. Y.; American Book Co., 1956.

Davis, K. *Human Relations in Business*. N. Y.; McGraw-Hill, 1957.

Devereaux, G. *Therapeutic Education: Its Theoretical Basis and Practices*. N. Y.; Harper & Bros., 1956.

Dickens, M. "A statistical formula to quantify the spread of participation in group discussion", *Speech Monogr*. No. 22, 28-30.

Douglass, P. F. *The Group Workshop Way in the Church*. N. Y.; Association Press, 1956.

Dreikurs, R. *Psychology in the Classroom*. N. Y.; Harper & Bros., 1957.

Duvall, E. M. *Facts of Life and Love for Teen-Agers*, rev. ed. N. Y.; Association Press, 1956.

Eckert, R. D. *Sex Attitudes in the Home*. N. Y.; Association Press, 1956.

Edeston, H. *Problems of Adolescence*. (Sex Guidance.) N. Y.; Philosophical Library, 1956.

Eilbert, L. R. "A tentative definition of emotional immaturity utilizing the critical incident technique", *Pers. & Guid. J.*, 1957 (9), 554-563.

Frank, M. & L. K. *Your Adolescent at Home and in School*. N. Y.; Viking Press, 1956.

Franklin, R., J. Aiken & F. Schnert. "Training community development leaders", *Adult Leadership*, 1957 (3), 81 fol.

Froehlich, C. P. & J. G. Darley. *Studying Students: Guidance Methods of Individual Analysis*. Chicago; Science Research Associates, 1952.

Gibb, J. R. & L. M. *Applied Group Dynamics*. Newark, Del.; Fels Group Dynamics Center, 1956.

Gibb, J. R., G. N. Platts & L. Miller. *Dynamics of Participating Groups*. St. Louis; Swift & Co., 1951.

Glanz, E. C. & E. B. Walston. *Psychology and Critical Thinking, A New Approach to Guidance*. Boston; Allyn & Bacon Co., 1957.

Gleason, G. *Horizons for Older People*. N. Y.; MacMillan Co., 1956.

Gordon, I. J. *The Teacher as a Guidance Worker*. N. Y.; Harper & Bros., 1956.

Greenblatt, M., R. H. York & E. L. Brown. *From Custodial to Therapeutic Patient Care in Mental Hospitals*. N. Y.; Russell Sage Foundation, 1955.

Grinster, A. & E. Sterba. *Understanding Your Family*. N. Y.; Random House, 1957.

Hahn, M. E. & M. S. MacLean. *Counseling Psychology*. N. Y.; McGraw-Hill, 1955.

Healy, W. & A. F. Bronner. *New Light on Delinquency and its Treatment*. New Haven; Yale Univ. Press, 1956.

Hepner, H. W. *Psychology Applied to Life and Work*, 3rd ed. Englewood Cliffs, N. J.; Prentice-Hall, 1957.

Hoyt, D. P. "An evaluation of group and individual programs in vocational guidance", *J. Applied Psychol.*, 1955 (1), 26-30.

Jersild, A. T. and associates. *Education for Self Understanding*. N. Y.; Bureau of Publs., Teachers Coll., Columbia Univ., 1953.

Jones, A. J. *Principles of Guidance and Pupil Personnel Work*, 5th ed. N. Y.; McGraw-Hill, 1957.

Kanner, L. *A Word to Parents about Mental Health*. Madison, Wis.; Univ. of Wisconsin Press, 1957.

Klapman, J. W. "Common-sense group psychotherapy for mental hospitals", *J. Dis. Nerv. Syst.*, 1955 (1), 24-29.

Klein, D. B. *Mental Hygiene*, rev. ed. N. Y.; Henry Holt Co., 1956.

Klopf, G. J. "Leadership education in American colleges", *Adult Leadership*, 1957 (5), pp. 123 fol.

Knapp, R. H. *Practical Guidance Methods for Counselors, Teachers, and Administrators.* N. Y.; McGraw-Hill, 1953.

Konopka, G. *Group Work in the Institution: a Modern Challenge.* N. Y.; Whiteside Co., 1954.

Kotinsky, R. & H. Witmer (eds.). *Community Programs for Mental Health.* Cambridge; Harvard Univ. Press, 1955.

Kubie, S. H. & G. Landau. *Group Work with the Aged.* N. Y.; Intern. Univ. Press, 1953.

Lemkau, P. V. *Mental Hygiene in Public Health,* 2nd ed. N. Y.; McGraw-Hill, 1955.

Lerner, A. "Dynamics of help in teaching and counseling", *Peabody J. Educ.,* 1955 (3), 178-182.

Linden, M. E. "Growing up or growing down: the challenge of the geriactric patient", *Danville St. Hosp. Ment. Health Bull.* Vol. 30 (3).

Lindgren, H. C. *Effective Leadership in Human Relations.* N. Y.; Hermitage House, 1956.

———— *Mental Health in Education.* N. Y.; Henry Holt Co., 1954.

Lippman, H. S. *Treatment of the Child in Emotional Conflicts.* N. Y.; McGraw-Hill, 1956.

Lundy, R. M. & L. Berkowitz. "Cognitive complexity and assimulative projection in attitude change", *J. abnorm. soc. Psychol.,* 1957 (1), 34-37.

Luszski, M. B. *Interdisciplinary Team Research-Methods and Problems.* Washington, D. C.; Nat'l Train. Lab. in Gp. Develop., 1957.

Lykken, D. T. "A study of anxiety in the sociopathic personality", *J. abnorm. soc. Psychol.,* 1957 (1), 6-10.

Maier, N. R. F. *Principles of Human Relations: Application to Management.* N. Y.; Wiley & Sons, 1952.

———— *Psychology in Industry,* 2nd ed. Boston; Houghton-Mifflin, 1955.

Marzolf, S. S. *Psychological Diagnosis and Counseling in the Schools.* N. Y.; Henry Holt Co., 1956.

McCarthy, R. G. *Teen-agers and Alcohol: a Handbook for Educators.* New Haven; Yale Center of Alcoh. Studies, 1956.

McCaslin, N. "A critical look at group dynamics", *Sch. and Society,* 1955 (2), 168-169.

McDaniel, H. B. & G. A. Shaffel. *Guidance in the Modern School.* N. Y.; Dryden Press, 1956.

McGinnies, E. & W. Vaughan. "Some biographical determiners of participation in group discussion", *J. applied Psychol.,* 1957 (3), 179-185.

Mial, D., H. C. Mial & L. P. Bradford. "Learn by doing — provided . . .", *Adult Leadership,* 1957 (1), 4-9, fol.

Moreno, J. L. "Evolution of Groups" in *Who Shall Survive,* Book II, pp. 127-215. Beacon, N. Y.; Beacon House, 1953.

Moustakas, C. E. *The Teacher and the Child: Personal Interactions in the Classroom.* N. Y.; McGraw-Hill Co., 1956.

Murphy, L. et al. *Personality in Young Children.* N. Y.; Basic Books, 1956.

Newton, M. E. "Developing leadership potential", *Nurs. Outlook,* 1957 (7), 400-403.

Oliver, W. R. "Pre-retirement education", *Adult Leadership,* 1957 (1), 21-23.

Patty, W. L. & L. S. Johnson. *Personality and Adjustment.* N. Y.; McGraw-Hill, 1953.

Pepinsky, H. B. & P. N. *Counseling: Theory and Practice.* N. Y.; Ronald Press, 1954.

Rees, T. P. & M. M. Glatt. "The organization of a mental hospital on the basis of group participation", *Int. J. gp. Psychother.,* 1955 (2), 157-161.

Rogers, C. R. *Client-Centered Therapy*. Boston; Houghton-Mifflin Co., 1951.
——— "Personality changes in psychotherapy", *Int. J. soc. Psychiat.*, 1955 (1), 31-41.
Rogers, C. R. & R. F. Dymond. *Psychotherapy and Personality Change*. Chicago; Univ. of Chicago Press, 1954.
Rogers, D. *Mental Hygiene in Elementary School*. Boston; Houghton-Mifflin Co., 1957.
Rohde, A. R. *The Sentence Completion Method: Its Diagnostic and Clinical Application to Mental Disorders*. N. Y.; Ronald Press, 1957.
Rohrbough, J. & J. W. Getsinger. "Chain reaction forum", *Adult Leadership*, 1957 (5), pp. 131 fol.
Schutz, W. C. "What makes groups productive?", *Hum. Relat.*, 1955 (8), 429-465.
Schneiders, A. A. *Personal Adjustment and Mental Health*. N. Y.; Rinehart & Co., 1955.
Scott, W. A. "Attitude change through reward of verbal behavior", *J. abnorm. soc. Psychol.*, 1957 (1), 72-75.
Seagoe, M. V. *A Teacher's Guide to the Learning Process*. Dubuque, Iowa; Brown, 1956.
Sears, R. R., E. E. Maccoby & H. Levin. *Patterns of Child Rearing*. Evanston, Ill.; Row, Peterson Co., 1957.
Shephard, E. L. "A three-level in-service training program for advisors", *Pers. & Guid. J.*, 1957 (1), 48-50.
Sherwood, C. C. "Some recommendations for research in the field of group psychotherapy", *Gp. Psychother.*, 1956 (2), 126-132.
Skinner, B. F. *Verbal Behavior*. N. Y.; Appleton-Century-Crofts, 1957.
Smith, G. E. *Counseling in the Secondary School*. N. Y.; MacMillan Co., 1955.
Sonne, T. R. & L. Goldman. "Preferences of authoritarian and equalitarian personalities for client-centered and eclectic counseling", *J. consult. Psychol.*, 1957 (2), 129-135.
Steckle, L. G. *Problems of Human Adjustment*, rev. ed. N. Y.; Harper & Bros., 1957.
Stern, E. M. *Mental Illness: a Guide for the Family*, rev. ed. N. Y.; Harper & Bros., 1957.
Stevenson, G. S. *Mental Health Planning for Social Action*. N. Y.; McGraw-Hill, 1956.
Sullivan, H. S. *Clinical Studies in Psychiatry*. N. Y.; W. W. Norton Co., 1956.
Symonds, P. M. "Implications for the counselor", *Education*, 1955 (4), 246-248.
This, L. "Is the lecture obsolete?", *Adult Leadership*, 1957 (4), 106 fol.
Thorne, F. C. "Critique of recent developments in personality counseling theory", *J. clin. Psychol.*, 1957 (3), 234-244.
Turner, A. N. "Foreman, job and company", *J. Hum. Relations*, 1957 (2), 99-112.
Tyler, L. E. *The Work of the Counselor*. N. Y.; Appleton-Century-Crofts, 1956.
U. S. Public Health Service: Subcommittee on Evaluation of Mental Health Activities. *Evaluation in Mental Health*. Bethesda, Md.; Pub. Health Serv., 1955.
Wescher, I. R., R. Tannenbaum & J. Zenger. *Yardsticks for Human Relations Training*. Chicago; Adult Educ. Assn. of America, 1957.
White, R. W. *Lives in Progress*. N. Y.; Dryden Press, 1954.
Whiting, J. W. M. & I. L. Child. *Child Training and Personality*. New Haven; Yale Univ. Press, 1953.
Willey, R. D. & W. M. Strong. *Group Procedures in Guidance*. N. Y.; Harper & Bros., 1957.
Wolberg, L. R. *Technique of Psychotherapy*. N. Y.; Grune & Stratton Co., 1954.
Zander, A., A. R. Cohen & E. Stolland. *Role Relations in the Mental Health Professions*. Ann Arbor, Mich.; Institute of Social Research, Univ. of Michigan, 1957.

PART IV — SMALL-GROUP DISCUSSION: METHODS AND RESEARCH

Ackerman, N. W. "Group psychotherapy with mixed groups of adolescents", *Int. J. Gp. Psychother.*, 1955 (5), 249-260.

Ames, R. "Leaderless group discussion and experience in group leadership", *Calif. J. educ. Res.*, 1955 (6), 166-169.

Anon. "Multiple counseling: eight over-age boys, ninth grade", (*This book*, pp. 301-303).

Axelrod, J. "Group dynamics, nondirective therapy, and college teaching", *J. Higher Educ.*, 1955, 26:200-207.

Axline, V. "Group therapy as a means of self discovery for parents and children", *Gp. Psychotherapy*, 1955 (2), 152-160.

Bach, G. R. *Intensive Group Psychotherapy.* N. Y.; Ronald Press, 1954.

Balint, E. & M. "Dynamics of training in groups for psychotherapy", *Brit. J. of Med. Psychol.*, 1955, 28:135-143.

Barnlund, D. C. "Experiments in leadership training for decision-making discussion groups", *Speech Monogr.*, 1955, No. 22, 1-14.

Benne, K. D. & P. Sheats. "Functioning roles of group members", *J. soc. Issues*, 4 (2), 41-49.

Bennett, E. B. "Discussion, decision, commitment and consensus in 'group decision' ", *Hum. Relat.*, 1955, 8:251-273.

Bell, J. L. & C. J. Barnett. "Intensive insulin sub-coma treatments combined with group therapy in a mental hygiene clinic", *Dis. nerv. System*, 1955, 16:80-85.

Bergevin, P. & D. Morris. *A Manual for Discussion Leaders and Participants*, rev. ed. Greenwich, Conn.; The Seabury Press, 1955.

Berkowitz, L. & R. M. Lundy. "Personality characteristics related to susceptibility to influence by peers or authority figures", *J. Pers.*, 1957 (4), 306-316.

Blair, D. "The therapeutic social club: an important measure of social rehabilitation in the treatment of psychiatric cases", *Ment. Hyg.*, 1955 (1), 54-62.

Blake, R. R. & J. V. McConnell. "A methodological study of tape-recorded synthetic group atmospheres", *Amer. Psychologist*, 1953 (8), 395.

Blake, R. R. "The treatment of relational conflict by individual, group and inter-personal methods", *Gp. Psychother.*, 1955 (2), 182-185.

Blake, R. R. & J. W. Brehn. "The use of tape-recording to simulate a group atmosphere", *J. abnorm. soc. Psychol.*, 1954 (3), 311-313.

Blatt, A. "Group therapy with parents of severely retarded children: a preliminary report", *Gp. Psychother.*, 1957 (2), 133-140.

Bois, J. S. *Explorations in Awareness: How to Improve Your Skills in Observing, Thinking, Communicating.* N. Y.; Harper & Bros., 1957.

Brach, A. M. "Reaching young teens through group counseling", (*This book*, pp. 297-300).

Brashear, E. L. et al. "A community program of mental health education using group discussion methods led by volunteer workshop-trained discussion leaders", *Am. J. Orthopsych.*, July, 1954.

Bristow, W. B. "A group discussion approach in training courses for nurses and religious counselors", (*This book*, pp. 355-357).

Brody, E. B. "Modification of family interaction patterns by a group interview technique", *Int. J. Gp. Psychother.*, 1956 (1), 38-47.

Bromberg, W. "Sex deviation and therapy", *J. Soc. Therapy*, 1955, 1:203-210.

Bryan, Q. R. & E. M. Younker. "A multiple counseling project for pre-delinquent eighth-grade girls", (*This book*, pp. 293-297).

Buchmuller, A. D. & M. Gildea. "Group therapy for parents of behavior problems children in public schools", *Int. J. Soc. Psychiat.*, 1955 (1), 51-56.

Burke, H. R. "A training course for leaders in the Mental Health Association", (*This book*, pp. 372-375).

——— "Training program on conference leadership in industry", (*This book*, pp. 368-370).

Calia, V. F. "A group guidance program in action", *Junior Coll. J.*, April, 1957.

——— "A junior college guidance program with a team approach", (*This book*, pp. 318-321).

Cantor, N. *Learning through Discussion.* Buffalo, N. Y.; Foster and Stewart Co., 1951.

Caplan, S. W. "The effects of group counseling on junior high school boys' concept of themselves in school", *J. Counsel. Psychol.*, 1957 (2), 124 fol.

Clemmons, R. S. "When the Pastor leads the group", *The New Christian Advocate*, 1957, Dec. issue, pp. 73-76.

Corsini, R. "Group psychotherapy with a hostile group", *Gp. Psychother.*, 1954 (2), 168-173.

——— *Methods of Group Psychotherapy.* N. Y.; McGraw-Hill Co., 1957.

Crawford, P. "A disciplinary group guidance project", (*This book*, pp. 312-316).

Crowell, L., A. Katcher & S. Miyamoto. "Self-concepts of communication skill and performance in small-group discussions", *Speech Monogr.*, 1955, No. 22:20-27.

Crum, E. "A training project for lay leaders of children's play groups", (*This book*, pp. 376-379).

de Schill, S. *Introduction to Psychoanalytic Group Therapy* (for patient orientation). N. Y.; Am. Mental Health Found., Distributed by Robert Brunner, Inc., N. Y. C.

De Macedo, G. "Group psychotherapy in juvenile criminology", *Int. J. Gp. Psychother.*, 1955 (1), 54-59.

Driver, H. I. "Gripe sessions lead to better understanding", *Wis. J. Educ.*, Oct. 1952, pp. 7, 8.

——— "Learning self and social adjustments through small-group discussion", *Ment. Hyg.*, 1952 (4), 600-606.

——— *Multiple Counseling: A Small-Group Discussion Method for Personal Growth.* Madison, Wis.; Monona Publ., 1954.

——— "Organizing a large meeting for individual participation", (*This book*, pp. 387-390).

——— "A small-group counseling program for pupils, parents, teachers", (*This book*, pp. 306-308).

——— "The T-group: a learning laboratory for leadership skills", (*This book*, pp. 342-345).

Durkin, H. E. "Acting out in group psychotherapy", *Amer. J. Orthopsychiat.*, 1955, 25:644-652.

——— "Group dynamics and group psychotherapy", *Int. J. Gp. Psychother.*, 1954 (1), 56-64.

Dutcher, R. W. "A group psychotherapy project: Learning to live together", (*This book*, pp. 416-419).

Fabian, A. A. "Group treatment of chronic patients in a child guidance clinic", *Int. J. Gp. Psychother.*, 1954 (3), 243-252.

446

Farmer, R. A. "A group discussion approach in freshman orientation", (*This book*, pp. 321-325).

Farrell, M. L. & E. Forsley. "Enhancing patient adjustment by means of group sessions with attendants", *Amer. J. ment. Defic.*, 1956, 60:603-607.

Flecker, R. "The discussion-group approach in supervisory training", *Austin J. Psychol.*, 1954, 6:164-177.

Forizs, L. "Brief intensive group psychotherapy for the treatment of alcoholics", *Psychiat. Quart. Suppl.*, 1955, 29:43-70.

Foulkes, R. G. "Resolving the resistance of intellectualization in seminary students", (*This book*, pp. 350-352).

Foulkes, S. H. & E. J. Anthony. *Group Psychotherapy*. London; Penquin Books, 1957.

Fox, V. "Group therapy for alcoholics", (*This book*, pp. 414-416).

Fox, W. M. "Group reaction to two types of conference leadership", *Quart. J. Hum. Relations*, 1957 (3), 279-289.

Frank, J. "Some values of conflict in therapeutic groups", *Gp. Psychother.*, 1955 (2), 142-151.

Freedman, M. "A Mental Health Association lay discussion program", (*This book*, pp. 384-387).

Fried, E. "Combined group and individual therapy with passive-narcissistic patients", *Int. J. Gp. Psychother.*, 1955 (2), 194-203.

Geller, J. J. "An experiment in group psychotherapy as a teaching device", *Gp. Psychother.*, 1954 (2), 130-138.

———— "Group psychotherapy in a community psychiatric clinic", *Int. J. Gp. Psychother.*, 1954 (2), 103-108.

General Assembly's Training School. "Informal discussion groups for graduate students in Christian Education", (*This book*, pp. 358-360).

Glenn, J. "Values of group discussion with psychiatric aides in a mental hospital", *Int. J. Psychother.*, 1951 (3), 254-263.

Goldberg, M. et al. "Comparative effectiveness of analytic and psychodramatic group therapy with psychotics", *Int. J. Psychother.*, 1955 (4), 367-379.

Graeber, M. C. et al. "Group therapy on an acute service", *Am. J. Psychiatry*, 1954 (7), 677-680.

Grant, M. "The group approach for weight control", *Gp. Psychother.*, 1951 (2), 156-165.

Grunwald, H. "Group counseling in a casework agency", *Int. J. Gp. Psychother.*, 1954 (2), 183-192.

Hare, A. P. "Situational differences in leader behavior" (children), *J. abnorm. soc. Psychol.*, 1957 (1), 132-135.

———— "Small-group discussions with participatory and supervisory leadership", *J. abnorm. soc. Psychol.*, 1953 (2), 273-275.

Hargreaves, A. G. & A. M. Robinson. "The nurse-leader in group therapy", *Am. J. Nursing*, Vol. 50, pp. 713-716.

Haythorn, W. "The influence of individual members on the characteristics of small groups", *J. abnorm. soc. Psychol.*, 1953 (2), 276-284.

Herrold, K. F. "Applications of group principles to education", *Int. J. Gp. Psychother.*, 1954 (2), 177-182.

Higginson, G. K. "Multiple counseling with delinquent adolescents", (*This book*, pp. 402-405).

Hill, G. & S. Armitage. "An analysis of combined therapy-individual and group-in patients with schizoid, obsessive, compulsive or aggressive defenses", *J. nerv. & ment. Diseases*, 1957 (1), 113-134.

Horowitz, M. W. & H. Permutter. "The discussion group and democratic behavior", *J. soc. Psychol.*, 1955 (2), 231-246.

Hulse, W. "Transference, catharsis, insight and reality testing during concomitant individual and group psychotherapy", *Int. J. Gp. Psychother.*, 1955 (1), 45-53.

―――― "Dynamics and techniques of group psychotherapy in private practice", *Int. J. Psychother.*, 1954 (1), 65-73.

Janney, H. M. & C. E. Bemis. "Efficient use of the prison psychiatrist", *Prison World*, 1954, Jan.-Feb. p. 4, fol.

Jensen, G. E. "Small group counseling for under-achieving primary school children", (*This book*, pp. 286-290).

Johnson, P. E. "A training course in pastoral counseling", (*This book*, pp. 352-355).

Jones, Maxwell et al. *The Therapeutic Community*. N. Y.; Basic Books, 1953.

Jordan, P. H., M. Campbell & E. J. Hodge. "A therapeutically oriented group technique for the diagnostic evaluation of parents of disturbed children", *Gp. Psychother.*, 1957 (2), 114-128.

Katzenstein, A. "An evaluation of three types of group psychotherapy with psychiatric patients", *Int. J. Gp. Psychother.*, 1954 (4), 409-418.

Kawin, E. *A Guide for Child-Study Groups*. (The Parent Education Project, Univ. of Chicago), Chicago; Science Research Associates, 1952.

Kelly, J. N., Jr. "A semantic approach in group counseling", (*This book*, pp. 303-306).

Keltner, J. W. *Group Discussion Processes*. N. Y.; Longmans, Green Co., 1957.

Keppers, G. L. "A graduate course in group techniques in Guidance", (*This book*, pp. 338-342).

Klapman, J. W. "Group psychotherapy as catalyst in mental hospital treatment", *Int. J. Gp. Psychother.*, 1956 (1), 80-85.

―――― "Psychoanalytic or didactic group psychotherapy?", *Gp. Psychother.*, 1954 (4), 279-286.

Klein, A. F. "Study your group", *Adult Leadership*, 1956 (1), 18-20, fol.

Kramish, A. A. "Letter reading in group psychotherapy", *Gp. Psychother.*, 1956 (1), 40-43.

Leary, T. & H. S. Coffey. "The prediction of interpersonal behavior in group psychotherapy", *Gp. Psychotherapy*, 1954 (1), 7-51.

LeBovici, S. "Psychoanalytical group psychotherapy", *Gp. Psychother.*, 1956 (4), 282-289.

LeFevre, C. "A laboratory course in group discussion", *J. higher Educ.*, 1955, Vol. 26, pp. 489-492.

Lerner, A. "Considerations of content material of group counseling sessions with jailed alcoholics", *Quart. J. Stud. Alc.*, 1954 (2), 432-452.

―――― "Self-evaluation in group counseling with male alcoholic inmates", *Int. J. Gp. Psychother.*, 1955 (4), 286-298.

Leslie, R. C. "Group therapy: a new approach for the church", *Past. Psychol.*, 1955 (1), 9-14.

―――― "The therapeutic group experience as a course in the theological school curriculum", (*This book*, pp. 346-350).

Linden, M. E. "Group psychotherapy for the aging", (*This book*, pp. 423-429).

——— "The significance of dual leadership in gerontologic group psychotherapy", *Int. J. Gp. Psychotherapy*, 1954 (3), 262-273.

Lindsay, D. G. "Group therapy at an army mental hygiene center", *U. S. Armed Forces Med. J.*, 1955 (6), 633-644.

Logie, I. "An experiment in group guidance for later maturity", (*This book*, pp. 420-423).

Lovell, R. "Group counseling in family living", (*This book*, pp. 390-395).

Lowrey, L. "Group treatment of mothers", *Am. J. Orthopsych.*, 1954 (5), 589.

Luchins, A. S. "A social-experimental approach to group psychotherapy", *J. Soc. Psychol.*, 1955 (1), 121-127.

Mabee, F. C., Jr. "Solving a de-segregation problem through small-group activity", (*This book*, pp. 363-365).

Maizlish, I. L. "Group psychotherapy of husband-wife couples in a child guidance clinic", *Gp. Psychother.*, 1957 (3), 169-180.

Marcus, I. M. "Psychoanalytic group therapy with fathers of emotionally disturbed preschool children", *Int. J. Gp. Psychother.*, 1956 (1), 61-79.

Martensen-Larsen, O. "Group psychotherapy with alcoholics in private practice", *Int. J. Gp. Psychotherapy*, 1956 (1), 28-37.

McBurney, J. H. & H. G. Hance. *Discussion in Human Affairs*. N. Y.; Harper & Bros., 1950.

McCorkle, L. W. "Guided group interaction in a correctional setting", *Int. J. Gp. Psychother.*, 1954 (2), 199-203.

Medalia, N. Z. "Authoritarianism, leader acceptance, and group cohesion", *J. abnorm. soc. Psychol.*, 1955 (2), 207-213.

Menge, C. P. "A multiple counseling approach in an educational psychology course", (*This book*, pp. 331-335).

Missumi, J. "Research into buzz-group method with in-service classes for teachers", (*This book*, pp. 365-367).

——— "Theory and practice of group dynamics", *Educ. Statistics*, Vol. 22, pp. 21-23.

Moreno, J. L. *Group Psychotherapy: A Symposium.* Beacon, N. Y.; Beacon House, Inc., 1945.

Morse, P. W., L. H. Gessay & R. Karpe. "The effect of group psychotherapy in reducing resistance to individual psychotherapy: a case study", *Int. J. Gp. Psychother.*, 1955 (4), 261-269.

Morton, M. "A training program for junior student counselors", (*This book*, pp. 326-328).

Nat'l Congress of Parents & Teachers. *Study-Discussion Group Techniques for Parent Education Leaders*, rev. ed. Chicago, Ill.; 1951.

Ney, L. "A multiple counseling project for under-achieving sixth graders", (*This book*, pp. 291-293).

Noble, J. L. & R. H. Mathewson. "Evaluating a program of counselor training through group conferences", *Personn. Guid. J.*, 1956, Vol. 34, pp. 285-288.

Patty, W. L. "A combination psychology class and multiple counseling project", (*This book*, pp. 328-330).

Peck, H. B. "The group in education, group work and psychotherapy", *Am. J. Orthopsych.*, 1954 (2), 128-152.

Peck, H. B. & V. Bellsmith. *Treatment of the Delinquent Adolescent: Group and Individual Therapy with Parent and Child.* N. Y.; Family Service Assn. of America, 1954.

Peltz, W. et al. "A group method of teaching psychiatry to medical students", *Int. J. of Gp. Psychother.*, 1955 (3), 270-279.

Perry, E. "The treatment of aggressive juvenile delinquents in 'family group therapy' ", *Int. J. Gp. Psychother.*, 1955 (2), 131-149.

Peyman, D. A. R. "An investigation of the effects of group psychotherapy on chronic schizophrenic patients", *Gp. Psychother.*, 1956 (1), 35-39.

Phillips, H. U. *Essentials of Social Group Work Skill.* N. Y.; Association Press, 1957.

Pollak, O. *Integrating Sociological and Psychoanalytic Concepts: An Exploration in Child Psychotherapy.* N. Y.; Russell Sage Foundation, 1956.

Pratt, J. H. & P. E. Johnson. *A Twenty Year Experiment in Group Therapy.* Boston; New England Medical Center, 1950.

Rosenbery, P. P. & M. L. Fuller. "Human Relations Seminar", *Ment. Hyg.*, 1955 (1), 53-57.

Salzberg, T. H. "Rehabilitative therapy for convalescent mental patients", (*This book*, pp. 409-412).

Sandison, R. A. "Group therapy in a provincial out-patient department", *Int. J. Soc. Psychiat.*, 1955 (1), 28-32.

Schneider, L. I. "A proposed conceptual integration of group dynamics and group therapy", *J. soc. Psychol.*, 1955 (2), 173-181.

Schultz, I. M. & D. Ross. "Group psychotherapy with psychotics in partial remission", *Psychiat. Quart.*, 1955, 29:273-279.

Semrad, E. V. et al. "Experiences with small groups in teaching group psychotherapy", *Gp. Psychotherapy*, 1957 (3), 191-197.

Slavson, S. R. *Analytic Group Psychotherapy with Children, Adolescents and Adults.* N. Y.; Columbia Univ. Press, 1950.

——— "The nature and treatment of acting out in group psychotherapy", *Int. J. Gp. Psychother.*, 1956 (1), 3-27.

——— *Re-educating the Delinquent.* N. Y.; Harper & Bros., 1954.

Smith, W. L. & D. D. Glad. "Client reactions to therapist operating in controlled group situations", *Gp. Psychother.*, 1956 (1), 18-34.

Speroff, B. J. "Group psychotherapy in industry: a case of intragroup conflict", *Gp. Psychother.*, 1957 (1), 3-9.

Stone, P. & J. Kamiya. "Judgments of consensus during group discussion", *J. abnorm. soc. Psychol.*, 1957 (2), 171-175.

Talland, G. A. "Do therapists and patients share norms on the content of group discussion?", *Gp. Psychother.*, 1957 (1), 10-21.

Talland, G. A. & D. H. Clark. "Evaluation of topics in therapy group discussion", *J. Clin. Psychol.*, 1954 (2), 131-137.

——— "Task and interaction process: some characteristics of therapeutic group discussion", *J. abnorm. social Psychol.*, 1955 (1), 105-109.

Teirich, H. R. "Sociometry and group psychotherapy", *Gp. Psychother.*, 1957 (2), 85-94.

450

Torrance, P. "Getting mental hygiene practices into action through a college class", *Ment. Hyg.*, 1951 (1), 88-95.

Thompson, C. E. & W. P. Kolb. "Group psychotherapy and after care for alcoholic patients", (*This book*, pp. 406-409).

Verplanck, W. S. "The control of the content of conversation: reinforcement of statements of opinion", *J. abnorm. soc. Psychol.*, 1955 (5), 668-676.

Ward, M. "Group therapy for eleven pre-school cerebral palsied children", *Except. Child.*, 1955 (2), 207-214.

Warkentin, J. "An experience in teaching psychotherapy by means of group therapy", *Progr. Educ.*, 1955 (1), 79-82.

Warriner, C. K. "Leadership in the small group", *Am. J. Sociol.*, 1955, Vol. 60, pp. 361-369.

Wendland, L. V. "A therapeutic group with husbands and wives of poliomyetic patients", *Gp. Psychother.*, 1955 (1), 25-32.

Wickham, F. H. "The Navy character education program: use of discussion groups", (*This book*, pp. 360-362).

Williams, I. S. "Group discussion in industrial rehabilitation: a pilot study", *Occup. Psychol.*, Vol. 29, pp. 104-116.

Wilson, D. C. "Group psychotherapy and manic-depressive psychosis", *Am. J. Psychiatry*, 1954, Vol. 110:911-915.

Wishchmeier, R. R. "Group-centered and leader-centered leadership: an experimental study", *Speech Monogr.*, 1955 (1), 43-48.

Wolf, A. & E. K. Schwartz. "The psychoanalysis of groups: implications for education", *Int. J. soc. Psychiat.*, 1955 (1), 9-17.

Wolff, W. M. "Group counseling in a neuropsychiatric hospital", *Personn. Guid. J.*, 1956 (9), 504-507.

Wool, M. L., S. S. Kanter & W. Gray. "Group psychotherapy in preventive psychiatry: a preliminary report", *Int. J. Gp. Psychother.*, 1955 (4), 404-414.

Zimet, C. N. & H. J. Fine. "Personality changes with a group therapeutic experience in a human relations seminar", *J. abnorm. soc. Psychol.*, 1955 (1), 68-73.

PART V — ROLE-PLAYING AND PSYCHODRAMA METHODS

Baker, A. A. "The misfit family: a psychodramatic technique used in a therapeutic community", *Brit. J. Med. Psychol.*, 1952, Vol. 25:235-243.

Bard, J. A. & M. B. Creelman. "Parent education in a group therapy setting", *Int. J. Gp. Psychother.*, 1954 (4), 49-436.

Bikales, V. W. "Drama therapy at Winters V.A. hospital", *Bull. Menninger Clinic* (13), 127-133.

Bodwin, R. F. "The use of psychodrama in the psychiatric clinic", *Gp. Psychother.*, 1954 (2), 222-226.

Borgatta, E. F. "Analysis of social interaction: actual, role-playing, and projective", *J. abnorm. soc. Psychol.*, 1955 (3), 394-405.

Boring, R. O. & H. L. Deabler. "A simplified psychodramatic approach in group therapy", *J. Clin. Psychol.*, 1951 (3), 371-375.

Bowman, C. "The psychodramatic method in collegiate instruction", *Sociatry*, Vol. 2 (4), 421-430.

Bradford, L. P. "The use of psychodrama for group consultants", *Sociatry*, Vol. 1 (2), 192-197.

Bram, J. "The application of psychodrama to research in social anthropology", *Am. Psychol.*, 1954 (3), 139-145.

Bromberg, W. & G. Franklin. "The treatment of sexual deviates with group psychodrama", *Gp. Psychother.*, 1952 (2), 274-289.

Bruch, M. "An example of the use of psychodrama in the relieving of an acute symptom in a psychiatric children's clinic", *Gp. Psychother.*, 1954 (2), 216-221.

Brunelle, P. "Exploring skills of family life at school — sociodrama with a fourth-grade group", *Gp. Psychother.*, 1954 (3), 227-255.

Buck, B. "Psychodrama of drug addiction", *Gp. Psychother.*, 1952 (2), 301-321.

Cole, N. R. "Exploring psychodrama at the fifth grade level", *Sociatry*, Vol. 2:243-245.

Coleman, W. "Role playing as an instructional aid", *J. educ. Psychol.*, Vol. 39:429-435.

Corsini, R. J. "The method of psychodrama in prison", *Gp. Psychother.*, 1951 (2), 321-326.

Dreikurs, R. "Family group therapy in the Chicago community child guidance centers", *Ment. Hyg.*, 1951 (2), 291-301.

Eliasoph, E. "A group therapy and psychodrama approach with adolescent drug addicts", *Gp. Psychother.*, 1955 (2), 161-167.

Factory Management Journal. "Role-playing in training supervisors", Jan. 1954, pp. 102-105.

———— "Sixty-four hints to help you make role-playing work", Jan. 1954, p. 282.

Fantel, E. "Psychodrama in the counseling of industrial personnel", *Sociatry*, Vol. 2:384-398.

———— "Psychodrama in an army general hospital", *Gp. Psychother.*, 1952 (3), 190-300.

———— "Report on psychodramatic therapy", *Gp. Psychother.*, 1950 (1), 55-58.

Franks, T. W. "Role-playing in an industrial setting", *Gp. Psychother.*, 1952 (1), 59-63.

French, J. R. P. "Role-playing as a method for training foremen", *Sociatry*, Vol. 1: 410-425.

Gillies, E. "Therapy dramatics for the public schoolroom", *Nerv. Child*, Vol. 7: 328-336.

Goodspeed, E. J. "The use of psychodrama in the vocational guidance of eighth grade boys", *Sociatry*, Vol. 2:268-280.

Grambs, J. D. "Dynamics of psychodrama in the teaching situation", *Sociatry*, Vol. 1: 383-399.

Haas, R. B. (ed.). *Psychodrama and Sociodrama in American Education.* Beacon, N. Y.; Beacon House, 1949.

Hagan, M. "Psychodrama as a medium for mental hygiene education", *Dis. Nerv. System*, Vol. 10:74-80.

Hagan, M. & M. Kenworthy. "The use of psychodrama as a training device for professional groups working in the field of human relations", *Gp. Psychother.*, 1951 (1), 23-37.

Hamilton, J. L. "Psychodrama and its implications in speech adjustment", *Quart. J. Speech*, Vol. 29:61-67.

Harrow, G. S. "Effects of psychodrama group psychotherapy on role behavior of schizophrenic patients", *Gp. Psychother.*, 1951 (2), 316-320.

Harrow, G. S. & R. B. Haas. "Psychodrama in the guidance clinic", *Sociatry*, Vol. 1: 70-81.

Harshfield, H. W. & J. P. Schmidt. "Playing out our problems in sociodrama", *Sociatry*, Vol. 2:363-367.

Haskell, M. R. "Psychodramatic role training in preparation for release on parole", *Gp. Psychother.*, 1957 (1), 51-59.

Herriott, F. & M. Hagan. "The theatre for psychodrama at St. Elizabeth's Hospital", *Sociatry*, Vol. 5:168-176.

Hollister, W. G. & G. W. Husband. "Two role-playing methods of using mental health films and plays", *Ment. Hyg.*, 1955 (2), 277-283.

Hubbell, A. "Two-person role playing for guidance in social readjustment", *Gp. Psychother.*, 1954 (3), 249-254.

Janis, I. L. & B. T. King. "The influence of role-playing on opinion change", *J. abnorm. soc. Psychol.*, 1954 (2), 211-218.

Jones, M. "Acting as an aid to therapy in a neurosis center", *Brit. Med. J.*, 1949, pp. 756-758.

Kaull, J. L. "Combining role playing, case study and incident method for human relations training", *J. Am. Soc. Train. Directors*, 1954 (1), 16-19.

Kean, C. D. "Some role-playing experiments with high school students", *Gp. Psychother.*, 1954 (3), 256-265.

Kelly, J. G., R. R. Blake & C. E. Stromberg. "The effect of role training on role reversal", *Gp. Psychother.*, 1957 (2), 95-104.

Klein, A. F. *Role Playing in Leadership Training and Group Problem Solving.* N. Y.; Association Press, 1956.

Kline, N. S. "Psychodrama for mental hospitals", *J. Clin. Psychopath.*, Vol. 2:817-825.

Konopka, G. *Therapeutic Group Work with Children.* Minneapolis; Univ. of Minnesota Press, 1949.

Lassner, R. "Psychodrama in prison", *Gp. Psychother.*, 1950 (1), 77-91.

Lippit, R. & C. Clancy. "Psychodrama in the kindergarten and nursery school", *Gp. Psychother.*, 1954 (4), 262-290.

Lippit, R. & A. Hubbell. "Role playing for personnel and guidance workers: review of the literature with suggestions for application", *Gp. Psychotherapy*, 1956 (2), 89-114.

Liveright, A. A. "Role-playing in leadership training", *Personnel J.*, 1951 (5), 412-416.

Lonergan, W. G. "Role playing in an industrial conflict", *Gp. Psychother.*, 1957 (2), 105-110.

Maier, N. R. F. et al. *Supervisory and Executive Development: a Manual for Role Playing.* N. Y.; Wiley & Sons, 1957.

Mann, J. "Didactic use of sociometry and psychodrama: an introductory workshop on group dynamics", *Gp. Psychother.*, 1954 (3), 242-243.

Merchant, F. C. "The place of psychodrama in training the clinician", *Psych. Bull.*, Vol. 38:748.

Mifflin, A. B. & Z. E. Baum. "A settlement house uses role-playing", *Gp. Psychother.*, 1954 (3), 227-237.

Miller, M. M. "Psychodrama as a treatment method in a correctional institution", (*This book*, pp. 398-401).

Moody, K. A. "Role playing can be effective", *J. Industrial Train.*, 1950, Sept.-Oct., pp. 7, 8.

———— "Role-playing as a training technique", *J. Indust. Train.*, 1953 (1), 3-5.

Moreno, F. B. "Sociodrama in the Sociology classroom", *Sociatry*, Vol. 2:404-413.

Moreno, J. L. *First Book on Group Psychotherapy*, 3rd ed. Beacon, N. Y.; Beacon House, 1957.

———— *Psychodrama: Volume II.* Beacon, N. Y.; Beacon House, 1957.

———— "The significance of the therapeutic format and the place of acting out in psychotherapy", *Gp. Psychother.*, 1955 (1), 7-19.

Moreno, J. L. & Z. Toeman. "The group approach in psychodrama", *Sociatry*, Vol. 5: 191-196.

Moustakas, C. E. *Children in Play Therapy: A Key to Understanding Normal and Disturbed Emotions.* N. Y.; McGraw-Hill Co., 1953.

Mouton, J. S., Bell & Blake. "Role playing skill and sociometric peer status", *Gp. Psychotherap.*, 1956 (1), 7-17.

Parrish, M. M. "The development of a psychodrama program", *J. Psychiat. Soc. Work*, 1954 (3), 156-158.

———— "Psychodrama: description of application and review of techniques", *Gp. Psychother.*, 1953 (1), 63-89.

Parrish, M. M. & J. Mitchell. "Psychodrama in Pontiac State Hospital", *Gp. Psychother.*, 1951 (1), 80-84.

Rudhyar, E. F. & B. Branham. "The development of a psychodrama department in a mental hospital", *Gp. Psychother.*, 1953 (2), 110-114.

Schauer, G. "The function of an audience analyst in psychodrama", *Gp. Psychother.*, 1951 (2), 197-215.

Schwebel, M. "Role-playing in counselor training", *Personn. & Guid. J.*, 1953 (2), 196-201.

Shaw, M. E. "Training executives in action", *Gp. Psychother.*, 1956 (1), 63-68.

Sheats, P. H. "Sociodrama as an aid to large group communication", *Sociatry*, Vol. 1: 414-420.

454

Shor, J. "A modified psychodrama technique for rehabilitation of military psychoneurotics", *Sociatry*, Vol. 1:414-420.

Shugart, G. & E. A. Loomis. "Psychodrama with parents of hospitalized schizophrenic children", *Gp. Psychother.*, 1954 (2), 118-124.

Simos, J. *Social Growth through Play Production.* N. Y.; Association Press, 1957.

Slossen, R. *Child Guidance: A Mental Health Skit for Amateur Production; Discussion Leader Guide.* Buffalo, N. Y.; Erie County Health Dept., 1957.

Solby, B. "The psychodrama approach to marriage problems", *Amer. Sociol. Rev.*, Vol. 6:523-530.

Speroff, B. J. "Empathy and role-reversal as factors in industrial harmony", *J. soc. Psychol.*, 1953 (2), 117-120.

———— "Role-playing versus acting with script", *Nurs. Outlook*, 1955 (3), 377-379.

———— "Scripts versus role-playing", *Personnel J.*, 1954, Jan., pp. 304-306.

Stahl, G. R. "Role-playing is ideal for training", *Sales Management*, 1953 (1), 40.

———— "Survey: training directors' evaluation of role-playing", *J. Indust. Train.*, 1953, Jan. issue.

Standing, T. "Personal counseling through a creative drama club", (*This book*, pp. 308-311).

———— "A school mental health project", (*This book*, pp. 379-383).

Starr, A. "Psychodrama with a child's social atom", *Gp. Psychother.*, 1953 (3), 222-225.

Starr, A. & I. Chelnek. "Psychodrama at VA Hospital, Downey, Illinois", *Gp. Psychother.*, 1955 (1), 20-24.

Stevens, E. "Psychodrama in a speech clinic", *Sociatry*, Vol. 1:56-58.

Symonds, P. M. "Role-playing as a diagnostic procedure in the selection of leaders", *Sociatry*, Vol. 1:43-50.

Tawadros, S. M. "Spontaneity training at the Dorra Institute, Alexandria, Egypt", *Gp. Psychother.*, 1956 (2), 164-167.

Toeman, Z. *Role Analysis and Audience Structure.* Psychodrama Monograph, No. 12, Beacon, N. Y.; Beacon House.

———— "Synthesis between a group therapy, a psychodrama, and a sociodrama session", *Sociatry*, Vol. 2:417-418.

Torrance, P. "Psychodramatic methods in the college", *Sociatry*, Vol. 2:368-375.

Twitchell-Allen, D. "Psychodrama in the family", *Gp. Psychother.*, 1954 (2), 167-177.

Wilder, J. "The psychodrama as compared with other methods of psychotherapy", *Sociatry*, Vol. 5:185-190.

Wolozin, H. "Teaching personnel administration by role-playing", *Personnel J.*, 1948, July-Aug., pp. 107-109.

Yablonsky, L. "Preparing parolees for essential social roles", *Gp. Psychother.*, 1955 (1), pp. 38, 39.

Young, B. F. & M. Rosenberg. "Role-playing as a participation technique", *J. Soc. Issues*, Vol. 2, pp. 42-45.

AUTHOR INDEX

Asterisk (*) indicates the Authors who have contributed to this book